The Life and Achievements of
Sir John Popham
1531–1607

**Frontispiece. Sir John Popham (Littlecote Portrait). Courtesy of
Warner Holidays Ltd. Photo: Lis Elwell.**

The Life and Achievements of
Sir John Popham
1531–1607

Leading to the Establishment of the First English Colony in New England

Douglas Walthew Rice

Madison • Teaneck
Fairleigh Dickinson University Press

© 2005 by Rosemont Publishing & Printing Corp.

Associated University Presses
2010 Eastpark Boulevard
Cranbury, NJ 08512

The paper used in this publication meets the requirements of the American National Standard for Permanence of Paper for Printed Library Materials Z39.48-1984.

PRINTED IN THE UNITED STATES OF AMERICA

Library of Congress Cataloging-in-Publication Data

Rice, Douglas Walthew, 1942–
    The life and achievements of Sir John Popham, 1531–1607 : leading to the establishment of the first English colony in New England / Douglas Walthew Rice.
        p. cm.
    Includes bibliographical references (p.) and index.
    ISBN 0-8386-4060-5 (alk. paper)
    1. Popham, John, Sir, 1531?–1607. 2. Great Britain—History—Elizabeth, 1558–1603—Biography. 3. Great Britain—History—James I, 1603–1625—Biography. 4. New England—History—Colonial period, ca. 1600–1775. 5. Attorneys general—Great Britain—Biography. 6. Judges—Great Britain—Biography. I. Title.
    DA358.P67R53 2005
    942. 05′5′092—dc22

                                                                                        2005000688

SECOND PRINTING 2006

To my parents
in gratitude

Contents

List of Illustrations   9
Preface   11

  1. Gypsy   17
  2. Highwayman   21
  3. Homebuilder   34
  4. The Queen's Servant   40
  5. Attorney-General   55
  6. Undertaker in Ireland   71
  7. Lord of Littlecote   83
  8. Lord Chief Justice   93
  9. George's Guiana   105
10. Privy Councillor   114
11. Kimbolton's Killer   132
12. Prisoner of Essex   138
13. Friend of Blundell   152
14. Cecil's Correspondent   159
15. Ralegh's Opposite   174
16. Drainer of the Fens   193
17. Judge of Plotters   203
18. Acting Lord Chancellor   221
19. Virginia Planter   231
20. Ghost   261

Appendix 1. The Family of Sir John Popham   271
Appendix 2. Offices Held by Sir John Popham   273
Notes   275
Bibliography   305
Index   313

Illustrations

Color

Littlecote   133
Blundell's School   133
Sir John Popham   134
Popham's Coat of Arms   189
Popham's Eau   190
Popham's Tomb   190

Black-and-White

 1. Sir John Popham   frontispiece
 2. The British Isles   18
 3. London and Westminster   23
 4. The West of England   36
 5. Letter reporting the Armada   69
 6. Ireland   72
 7. Dudley's Map of Guiana   111
 8. *The Black Dog of Newgate*   117
 9. Essex   139
10. Robert Cecil   160
11. Ralegh   175
12. The Fens   196
13. Signatures of Guy Fawkes and Popham   212
14. Virginia   238
15. The Hunt Map   259

Preface

SIR JOHN POPHAM WAS THE DEVOTED SERVANT OF QUEEN ELIZA-
beth I and a terrifying man.

Working at the very center of government for more than twenty-
five years, he served his country, the Queen and King James
as Member of Parliament, Speaker of the Commons, Attorney-
General, Lord Chief Justice, and Privy Councillor. He played a
leading part in the most famous treason trials of the time, including those of Elizabeth's glamorous favorites. Energetic and
thorough, Sir John was consulted on all aspects of the law, commerce, and trade. His diligence made him a pillar of support for
the sovereign.

Across his desk came every manner of case, giving a vivid insight into an England of colorful, dangerous, troubled, eccentric,
and litigious people. Popham knew everyone's business; he sort-
ed out their affairs, resolved their differences, tried them, and
sentenced them to death. Much feared by religious extremists, he
acquired a reputation for "wholesome severity" that made him
the bogeyman of the English criminal; his notoriety lives on to
this day in legend and ghost story. It is this side of his personality that has attracted most comment hitherto.

My study draws attention to the more creative aspects of his
character. Like so many Elizabethans, Popham was extremely
acquisitive and anxious to proclaim his status through great
buildings. He was also willing to use his wealth in the service of
the sovereign, promoting several of the great dreams of the period: the settlement of Ireland, the draining of the Fens, and the
colonization of America. These remarkable enterprises provide
the visionary episodes in his story.

The many documents that have been preserved give a fascinating record of one man's work. I have tried to preserve a bal-
ance between the great issues of the time and the intriguing little oddities that so illuminate the study of a pre-industrial age.
My aim has been to present Sir John Popham as an eminence in
Elizabethan England from which one can both gain a panoram-
ic view and also perceive the details of the era. The flavor of a period is given by its language, so in quotations I have often re-

tained the original spellings and punctuations, only occasionally making very slight modifications.

This is the first full-length biography of a remarkably vigorous contributor to England's statutes and landscape, and to the history of both England and America. There have been several brief accounts of Sir John's life. The earliest, by the seventeenth-century writers Thomas Fuller, David Lloyd, John Aubrey, and Anthony à Wood, are based on hearsay. Thereafter chapters using written sources appear in: Campbell, *Lives of the Lord Chief Justices,* 1849; Manning, *Lives of the Speakers,* 1850; Hall, *Society in the Elizabethan Age,* 1886; Banks, *Blundell's Worthies,* 1904; and Caraman, *Henry Garnet,* 1964. The most detailed treatment is given by F. W. Popham in *A West Country Family,* 1976, which was my starting point.

Primary source material is widely scattered. Manuscripts are in the National Archives, the British Library, Hatfield House, the Bodleian, and the libraries of the Guildhall, the Middle Temple, the Inner Temple, the House of Lords, Lambeth Palace, and Cambridge University. There are documents in the USA in the Huntington Library and the New York Public Library. The County Archives or Record Offices of Bristol, Devon, Gloucester, Somerset, and Wiltshire have provided further primary material. There may well be more to be unearthed, and information leading to further documents, objects or pictures relating to Popham would be much appreciated.

I am extremely grateful to the authors of the many secondary sources I have used, all of whom I have tried to acknowledge in their place. The Cecil papers have been invaluable, and their general availability is due to the Marquess of Salisbury. Many people have been most helpful and encouraging in all kinds of ways, particularly Anthony Arlidge, John Bradford, Philip Brooke-Popham, Lis Elwell, Richard Giles, John Greenshields, John Jones, Elizabeth Lloyd, Colin Meays, Christopher Ondaatje, Mike Popham, Jenny Syred, Ann Thomas, Bud Warren, Lesley Whitelaw, and Katharine Wyndham.

I have particularly valued the expertise of Steve Goodwin and Nick Markell in the production of the illustrations. Color printing was made possible by the generous support of the Headmaster and Governors of Blundell's School, and the Masters of the Bench of the Honourable Society of the Middle Temple. Brian Jenkins made an essential and much-appreciated contribution in reading, commenting on, and refining the script. I am grateful too to my wife and family for their support during the years this book has been in the making.

Every effort has been made to trace the owners of copyright material, but if any remain unacknowledged, the author and publisher will be glad to know of them.

Finally, all errors and omissions in this book are entirely mine, though like one of Sir John's copyists I plead some excuse: "The hand of the Chief Justice is so very difficult to be read, that there may be some mistakes in the Transcriber."

NOTES ON THE TEXT

1. The currency of the time was £sd, and the mark (two-thirds of a pound, or 13s 4d) was also used. For a very approximate modern equivalent, multiply by 1,000. Thus, the Master of Blundell's school had a salary of £50, corresponding to £50,000 ($90,000) nowadays; an MP was paid 4s, or £200 ($360) a day; and children at Popham's almshouse were given 8d a week, or £33 ($60).

2. In this book italics are used in extracts to indicate Popham's own words, taken directly and as exactly as possible from manuscripts in his own handwriting. Other manuscript sources are given in roman type, sometimes with slightly modified spellings and punctuation. I have also often quoted from the various Calendars, which print modernized and usually summarized versions of the documents.

3. I have Americanized all spellings except in quotations, which I have left unchanged. The exceptions are the two terms "gaoler" and "councillor," which I have kept in the original spellings to preserve the ambience of sixteenth-century England.

The Life and Achievements of
Sir John Popham
1531–1607

1

Gypsy

THE POPHAM CHILDREN WERE OF ANCIENT, WELL-CONNECTED, and enterprising stock; but they lived in a backwater.

There were six of them, born in the 1530s and 1540s: Edward, John, Robert, Elizabeth, Katherine, and Frances.[1] Their home was Huntworth, a tiny hamlet near Bridgwater in the West Country, close to the Bristol Channel.

Their father, Alexander, though not aristocratic, was a substantial gentleman of ancient and worthy lineage.[2] He took on minor roles in the county administration[3] and served as a Commissioner of Sewers for the rhines or drainage channels of the wide marshy expanse near their home.[4] Their mother, Jane or Joan, was from a cultivated family in southern Wales: she was the daughter of Sir Edward Stradling of St Donat's Castle, Glamorgan.[5] To his children Alexander passed on two very Elizabethan qualities: an instinct for public service and a love of private profit.

John was probably born in 1531.[6] At this time Henry VIII's break with Rome was producing alarming changes throughout England as the dissolution of the monasteries came into effect. When former monastic lands came up for grabs, the local gentry were well placed to take advantage of the opportunities. Alexander Popham had already become involved with Buckland Priory, about four miles to the south of Bridgwater. He was appointed Steward in 1536, and when the priory was dissolved in 1539, he bought it. Other acquisitions followed, and before long Alexander was notorious. A saying at the time ran:

> "Popham, Wyndham, Horner and Thynne,
> When the monks went out they went in."

Hitherto the family had lived in the Manor of Huntworth that Pophams had held since 1285. Now with his new wealth Alexander built the Court House, situated on a modest piece of rising

The British Isles.

ground three miles to the south of the Bridgwater.[7] This was a tiny place, its port hardly more than a quay on the very tidal muddy banks of the River Parrett, its main business the export of wool and cloth produced in the country nearby. Four features of the area are significant in the life of John Popham: Huntworth was on the edge of an area very like the Fens of East Anglia; the port of Bridgwater faced out toward the Bristol Channel and the West; behind Huntworth lay the great estates of Somerset and Devon; and life in that flat and melancholy backwater must have been incredibly dull.

So it comes as a surprise to hear the first extraordinary story about John Popham. It is said that as a child he was captured by gypsies. These wandering folk, perhaps originally from north India, were recent arrivals in England who acquired their name because when they first traveled into Europe they carried forged papal briefs that declared them to be "Egyptians" on pilgrimage.[8] They were disapproved of by the authorities because they would not settle down in one place as wage laborers, and there was already an increase in vagabondage in England. Gypsies told fortunes and were thieves, with a reputation for stealing babies from their cradles, presumably in order to demand money for their return. Strict laws were passed to curb them, such as the statute of 1531 that ordered gypsies to leave the realm within sixteen days on pain of imprisonment, but like all such legislation it depended on local watchfulness and energy to be effective, and in North Somerset was evidently not implemented.

Where does this strange tale come from? It is not mentioned by Thomas Fuller, the earliest brief biographer in 1662, by David Lloyd in 1665, or by the gossipy John Aubrey and Anthony à Wood, who collected their information between about 1640 and 1680. The tale appears full-blown in 1849, Lord Campbell in his *Lives of the Lord Chief Justices* elaborating in confident and surprising detail. After his abduction by the gypsies, John remained with them for some months. His captors branded him, burning on his left arm "a cabalistic mark which he carried with him to the grave." Apart from this, the experience is supposed to have been a positive one: "his health, which had been sickly before, was strengthened by the wandering life he led with these lawless associates, and he grew up to be a man of extraordinary stature and activity of body." Campbell also suggests that the incident may account for "the irregular habits and little respect for the rules of property which afterwards marked one period of his life."[9]

How much attention should the biographer give to such imaginings? Throughout his life John Popham was the subject of rumors and myth making. Few of the tales can be supported by evidence, and, like the account of his abduction by gypsies, they have obviously been embellished in the retelling. However, stories are part of life, and particularly of the life of John Popham. In this book I have therefore recorded the stories told about him, and have done my best to suggest how they came into being.

The gypsy incident provides an emblematic focus for this biography. In it several of the themes in John Popham's life may be glimpsed: his fascination with the criminal and severity toward it; his concern for the poor and determination not to suffer poverty himself; and his love of movement and simultaneous desire to set down roots. Even if not branded, he was certainly marked with a strange quality that fascinated people at the same time as it frightened them. John Popham's personality stimulated people's imaginations: to them he was larger than life.

2

Highwayman

In 1547, THE YEAR OF THE DEATH OF HENRY VIII, POPHAM WAS SIX-teen and at about this time entered Balliol College, Oxford.

Among the fourteen colleges founded by that time, Balliol was small and undistinguished. There were ten fellows, to each of whom was assigned a scholar, the junior men probably having domestic as well as academic obligations toward their seniors. About forty undergraduates were in residence, taking an arts course. The fellows had recently been tainted with papistry, whereas the Pophams were inclined to the Protestant. Why then was Balliol chosen? It may be that a family connection had led to this choice, or that by now the atmosphere was changing. Certainly two years later the trappings of the old religion were being swept away: it is recorded in the Bursar's accounts that 8d was paid to a painter for obliterating Catholic images beside the altar.[1] John Popham would have been glad to see them go.

He was of an age to enjoy female company, but the college did not approve of such pleasures. At that time nobody was allowed to take a woman into the college on pain of expulsion, though a lady of noble birth, or the mother of a member, might dine at the Master's table if at least two Fellows were present. Clearly no chances were being taken. Even laundresses were kept out; washing had to be exchanged in the porch beneath the gate tower, beyond which they were forbidden to venture.[2] Popham did not have to suffer such constraints for long. Immediately after he completed his studies at Oxford, before 1550 when he was eighteen or nineteen, Popham was married. His wife, Amy Games, was the daughter of Hugh Games of Castleton, Glamorganshire.[3] On her father's early death in 1532 Amy had become a ward of John Popham's father, presumably through the families' Welsh connection.

In the following year John was admitted to the Middle Temple, one of London's four Inns of Court. The Inns were colleges of law, but as well as being technical training grounds for the legal profession were places where young gentlemen could complete their education. Here Popham would have had to take part in boltings, conversational arguments on cases put to to the student by a teacher—a Reader or a Bencher. Then he proceeded to mootings, being admitted to public disputations of the Fellows as an Inner Barrister. His earliest appearance in the Middle Temple Minute Book tells us that Popham was one of those chosen to deputize if necessary for the Steward at the Christmas feast in 1551.[4]

Popham was not a model student. Once, when asked to accompany a friend to hear an important case argued by great lawyers in Westminster Hall, he declared that "he was going where he would see disputants whom he honoured more—to a bear-baiting in Alsatia."[5] A lawless area between Fleet Street and the river, immediately to the east of the Temple, Alsatia had formerly belonged to an order of monks who made it a haven for debtors and other criminals. After the dissolution the inhabitants seem to have determined to keep free from the City's control, so the district was compared with Alsace on the borders of France and Germany, even then a well-known disputed area. It has been suggested that after his gypsy experience Popham felt at home among the criminal classes; perhaps he really was happier in Alsatia. Wood says he was "given at leisure hours to manly Sports and Encounters"[6] and Fuller that he was "as stout and skilful a Man at Sword and Buckler, as any in that age, and wild enough in his recreations."[7] It is true that he was at one stage put out of commons by the Inn, but this was the usual punishment for minor infringements of the rules. He was restored in November 1556 on paying a fine of 40s, his uncle, Mr Humphrey Waldron, standing as his pledge.[8]

The most remarkable story of Popham's dissolute youth is that he was an amateur highwayman. The diarist John Aubrey, born in 1626, wrote in *Brief Lives* that he "for severall [years] addicted himselfe but little to the studie of the lawes, but profligate company, and was wont to tak a purse with them."[9] Campbell expands, as usual, in colorful detail: "at this period of his life, besides being given to drinking and gaming—either to supply his profligate expenditure, or to show his spirit, he frequently sallied forth at night from a hostel in Southwark, with a band of desperate characters, and . . . planting themselves in ambush on Shooters Hill, or taking other positions favourable for attack and escape, they stopped travellers, and took from them not only their money, but any valuable commodities which they carried with them,—boasting that they were always civil and generous,

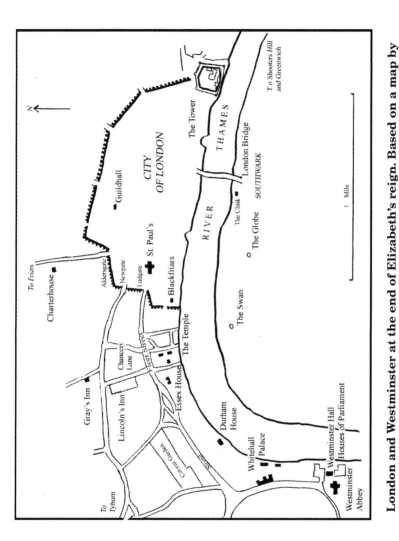

London and Westminster at the end of Elizabeth's reign. Based on a map by C. Walter Hodges.

and that, to avoid serious consequences, they went in such numbers as to render resistance impossible."[10]

There is an obvious parallel with Prince Hal, whose antics with Falstaff are supposed to have taken place in 1402–03 and were recreated by Shakespeare around 1596. It seems such mischief was not altogether unusual, though by Aubrey's account—should we believe it?—Popham's addiction was unusually severe, lasting for ten years or so throughout his twenties.

John Popham may have had some fun avoiding study and harassing travelers, but generally the reign of Queen Mary must have been an unhappy time for a Protestant family. In addition John lost his father in January of 1556. Alexander left Huntworth to Edward, his oldest son, but John and Amy received several properties in Somerset, "all my lands in Bridgwater, Bawdrype, Wembdon and Chylton"—apparently sixty houses in Bridgwater were Popham's[11]—and John alone "all my interest in the Vicarage of North Petherton and in the Parsonages of Bridgwater and Durleigh" as well as the Parsonage and Vicarage of Donington in Lincolnshire. John's progress to great wealth was thus given a vigorous start when he was only twenty-five. Then in about 1557 John Popham was called to the bar, and could now begin to practice.

Elizabeth's accession in November 1558 must have been a reason for deep-felt celebration in the family. Two years younger than Popham, the Queen was to be a major influence in his life. It is possible that his long service to his sovereign and country began in this year, for a John Popham was Member of Parliament for Lyme in Dorset. Whether this was our subject is not certain, but family connections could have made the seat available to him.[12] He was not exceptionally young for the job, and had he behaved sensibly at twenty-seven, membership of the Commons would have been perfectly appropriate. Incredibly enough, however, Popham is said to have still been an occasional highwayman, even after he had been called to the bar and was married to a respectable woman.[13]

In due course, let us say in 1560 or so, he was forced to knuckle down and accept his responsibilities. Aubrey maintains it happened like this: "His wife considered her and his condition," perhaps suggesting that she was with child, "and at last prevailed with him to lead another life, and to stick to the Studie of the Lawe; which upon her importunity he did, being then about thirtie yeares old. He spake to his wife to provide a very good Entertainment for his Camerades, to take his Leave of them, and after that day fell extremely hard to his Studie, and profited exceedingly. He was a strong, stout man, and could endure to sit at it day and night." A marginal note in Aubrey's manuscript sketches the common lawyer thus: "He must have an iron head, a brazen face, and a leaden breech."[14]

At the same time Popham embarked on what was to become one of his consuming passions, acquiring property. Of course he was not alone. In the absence of a Stock Exchange the three avenues for investment were property, venturing, and the Crown. Property was unquestionably the safest. Everyone was in it, and Popham's investments reveal to us who were his partners and friends. They included the violent Hugh Smyth.

As early as 18 May 1560 a Royal License of Proclamation was issued, in Latin, under the Great Seal, to Hugh Smyth and Matilda his wife to alienate [sell] to Thomas Phillipps, esq., Richard Michell esq., Francis Stradling, gent., and John Popham, gent., the Manors of Aisheton Lyons, Aishton Meryattes, and Durleigh with messuages, lands, and rectory of Longaisheton, and advowson of the vicarage of Longaisheton in Somerset, and seven messuages, five gardens, and 10s. rent in Bristol.[15]

The Smyths were in this instance selling property to Popham, presumably in lieu of payment for legal work, though on other occasions they are partners with him in acquiring property. Hugh had been at the Inner and his brother Matthew at the Middle Temple. At nineteen, Matthew had gotten into debt to one Master Lawton, who, tired of waiting for his money, tried to have him arrested. Hugh played the elder brother, landed Lawton a blow on the ear, and was fined and suspended from his Inn for three months. Hugh had an aggressive personality: when he married and settled at Ashton Court, near Bristol, he became a JP, but he soon reverted to his aggressive ways. In 1563 both Hugh and Matthew were accused of "Misbehaviour towards Mr Gorge, the Queen Majesty's servant, having been sent into these parts for the Queen Majesty's service," and were summoned to appear before the Privy Council.[16] They were not really desirable friends.

John Popham himself now seems to have led a respectable, diligent life, practicing as a barrister and producing children—six girls, Penelope, Elinor, Jane, Elizabeth, Katherine, and Marie, followed at last by a boy, Francis, born in about 1570. Although in the early years of their marriage the couple may have lived in London, by now the young family had their own house in Somerset. Edward having inherited the old home at Huntworth, John Popham established himself at Old Court on the main street in the small town of Wellington, about twenty miles to the southwest.

Popham's London base was the Middle Temple, where he had chambers, and here he worked during the Law Terms, the periods known as Hilary, Easter, Trinity, and Michaelmas, during which all legal business was conducted. We know that in 1562 he shared with Messrs Calvert and Washington, and that later Popham took over the chamber of Mr Baron Pyne, deceased.[17] About a month before he was called to the bar, Popham had taken into his service James Clarke, an eighteen-year-old Somerset man, placing him in New Inn and making him his clerk; the partnership lasted until Popham's death.[18]

In 1568 Popham became Reader at the Middle Temple. Readers were senior barristers who gave lectures to students at the Inns in the vacations in autumn and Lent when the courts were not in session. The subject would be a statute or particular branch of the law, often land law, and there is evidence that substantial lectures were delivered. Readers were expected to put on a grand feast at their own expense, a custom which continues, present-day Readers still contributing to their celebrations. Leave was given to him "to bring in thirty bucks" during his reading,[19] so by this time Popham was already considered well off and intended to make quite a show. Evidently students tended to skip lectures, and the Minutes of the Parliament of the Middle Temple frequently give the names of the offenders: Messrs Sparry and Hartopp[20] were fined 40s for non-attendance at the Cupboard during Mr Popham's reading, though Mr Hartopp got away with it "because Mr Fenner attended for him."[21] Another entry records that Robert Ayscough and twelve others were fined 20s. for missing Popham's reading. He must have performed well enough, however, for he was chosen five years later as Lent Reader—and from the most successful Readers were selected the Queen's Solicitor and Attorney-General.

The center of the legal profession was the Great Hall at Westminster, where the Court of the King's Bench at the far end of the hall on the left decided disputes between the King and his subjects.[22] Here young lawyers practiced as attorneys, representing the parties involved in the suits, or as pleaders at the Bar—the wooden bar that separated the Lord Chief Justice and his fellows from the crowds of litigants. Utter (outer) barristers could plead at the Bar after only eight years of training. A second court, the Court of Common Pleas, was situated on the right side, near the entrance doors at the northern end of the hall, and dealt with disputes between subjects themselves, rather than with the Crown. To plead here it was necessary to be a Sergeant-at-Law, which was the aim of the most skillful and ambitious men. Each of these courts had its own Lord Chief Justice and three judges. A third court, the Court of Chancery, at the far end opposite the King's Bench, was presided over with greater splendor by the Lord Chancellor, in whose keeping was the Great Seal, by which the authorizing stamp could be given to documents issuing from the crown offices. When no Lord Chancellor was appointed, a Lord Keeper of the Great Seal performed his functions. The three courts sat every morning from 8 to 11.[23] At such times Westminster Hall must have been a noisy place, full of business and bustle, and it is hard to imagine how Popham and his young colleagues could have made their complex arguments understood, or how the judges managed to concentrate in such circumstances. No wonder cases took a long time.[24]

It must have been a relief to get away from the Hall, take a boat back to the Inns of Court, walk up to the Strand and spend an hour browsing in the bookshops. At one of them, the "The Head and Star," between the gates of the Temple in Fleet Street, the printer Richard Tottel dealt in and printed legal books, for which he had the government license. Also on his shelves, no doubt, were copies of the famous first modern anthology of English poetry, Tottel's *Miscellany*. At this shop in about 1568 Popham made a poignant friendship, meeting frequently a young Catholic named Henry Garnet who worked there as a "corrector of the press."[25] Garnet wrote later: "There I dined often with him and told him that I was beginning the law."[26] It has been noted that the two men could not have been more contrasted in temperament, for Garnet was "a slender, gentle and delicate young scholar," whereas Popham was a "huge, heavie, ugly man"—that, at any rate, is how Aubrey described him later on the slight basis of having seen his portrait.[27] "Only in the keenness of their intellect was there any resemblance, and in their industry."[28] Thirty-five years later Popham and Garnet were to meet again, in appalling circumstances.

We still have several books that Popham must have bought at Tottel's.[29] They are essentially legal textbooks, a typical title being *A Table to al the statutes made from the beginning of the raigne of Kyng Edwarde the vi. unto this present xii. yeare of the reigne of oure moste gratious and soueraigne Ladye Queene Eliz-*

abeth. Tottel printed the book in 1570; a massive volume bound in calf, like the others it is heavily annotated in Popham's own hand, strong evidence of his diligent approach to study.[30]

The earliest surviving example of a letter in Popham's handwriting dates from this time. He wrote from Wellington to Hugh Smyth at Long Ashton concerning a lease:

To the worshippfull my assured ffrend Hugh Smyth esquier

I have sent yow herwith enclosed Mr Shepards wrytynges lett the rent charge beare the fyrst date and be sealyd and delyvered fyrst also and then lett the leas beare date the very day that the rent charge ys sealed and delyvered / yow may make the leas to any of hys ffreinds yow shall thynke good but lett ther be thre of them at the least and so fare ye well Wellyngton the iijrd of October 1570

your assured ffrend
John Popham

I pray yow as ye shall hyer of Mr Wynters and your Brother lett me understand how they doe and yf welle yow may retorne your letters by the fysshers that use Brystoll who dwell at Wellyngton[31]

The note illustrates that Popham was not simply an efficient lawyer; he had the personal touch, liked to be well-informed, and was thoughtful about practical matters.

The year 1571 marks John Popham's certain entry into public service. First he obtained the position of Recorder of both Bridgwater and Bristol. The latter must have been a prestigious appointment, as Bristol was at this time England's third largest city, with a population of around ten thousand. Only Norwich (twelve thousand) and London (about sixty thousand) paid more to the Crown in subsidy,[32] the accepted tax, raised—very inefficiently—whenever the sovereign's needs or a national emergency required it.[33] The Recorder was appointed by the Lord Chancellor and visited the town four times a year, when he acted as sole judge at the Court of Quarter Sessions.

It was usual practice at Bristol for the Recorder to be one of the city's two representatives in Parliament, but the election of 1571 was not so straightforward. Bristol's commercial, social, and political life was dominated at this time by the monopoly that had been granted by Edward VI to the Merchant Venturers of the city. In 1566 the Venturers had succeeded in restricting trading overseas entirely to their own members. Opposition had arisen immediately, with a determination to have the new statute quashed in the next Parliament. For this the city needed representatives of the right color: the two MPs from 1566, both Merchant Venturers, were opposed in the elections for the new Parliament by John Popham and Philip Langley, a grocer. There was "great variance"[34] during the campaigns, but eventually Popham and Langley were returned; it was a triumph for the anti-monopolists. Popham worked to oppose restrictions on free trade, particularly those imposed by the Merchant Venturers, for the rest of his life.

In Parliament Popham joined "a remarkable body of Englishmen. In quality, character and experience they were a tribute to a great age."[35] At the opening, as the Queen's procession in all its finery—horses covered with crimson velvet, forty-seven ladies and women of honor in attendance, the guard in their rich coats, trumpeters, and heralds—made for Westminster Abbey,[36] John Popham and his brother Edward, who represented Bridgwater, were sworn in. For the first time ever, each member had to take the Oath of Supremacy acknowledging the Queen as Head of the Church. Thus the Commons contained no Catholics. Popham sat as MP for Bristol in Elizabeth's third and fourth Parliaments. He was paid 4s a day plus a lump sum to cover expenses, including the hire of horses.[37]

Popham's attendance as a Member would have been required for only seven weeks or so in the spring or early summer of 1571, 1572, and 1576. It seems remarkable that so few sittings were necessary, but the main purpose of Parliament then was to authorize taxation for the Crown, and to recommend bills public and private for the monarch's approval. The actual government of the country—almost entirely rural and with a population in 1571 of only 3.27 million[38]—was carried out by the Privy Council, which issued the requirements of the Queen direct to a county-level network of justices and lords lieutenant.

In his opening address to the session of 1571 Sir Nicholas Bacon, the Lord Keeper, made it clear that the principal issues facing Parliament were money, of course, and the reform of the church. Sir Christopher Wray was elected Speaker, and on the Queen's leaving the Chamber she said she hoped that they would be "more quiet than they were at the last time,"[39] for in 1566 she had been much aggravated by Parliament's wish for her to marry and to settle the succession to the throne. Now she was again to be irritated on several occasions with the Commons for interfering in what did not concern them. One such subject was the Crown's financial dealings, and on this delicate matter Popham became involved in contentious debate. Robert Bell, a lawyer from Norfolk with a reputation as a radical, drew attention in a debate on the subsidy bill to two abuses in the way the Crown obtained its funds: licenses and promoters. The granting of licenses to her courtiers was one of the ways the Queen could give perquisites; promoters provided the government with information and were paid for their services. The management of the Exchequer was the Queen's business, and not to be touched by the Commons, so Bell's was not a diplomatic speech.[40]

But Popham (there is room for confusion between the brothers, but following Hasler[41] we take it that it was John) jumped to his feet in support of Bell and drew attention to another abuse: the way collection was practiced by treasurers of the Crown, "as manie havinge in their handes great masses of money, with which either they themselves or some others their ffrends doe purchase landes to their owne use and after become bankruptes, and soe cause or practise an enstallment of their debtes."[42] He was referring to a recent scandal involving £30,000, but it was a common problem, "a chronic evil of the times," and one that could not be eradicated.[43] Officials who held Crown money delayed their accounting and used the money for their private purposes, so that the Crown was in effect loaning money, interest-free, to its officers. Popham's speech was a bitter attack on the Crown, but justified.

After Popham, others drew attention to more abuses, including purveyance, by which the Crown's agents could buy, and indeed demand, supplies and produce at low prices, and "the fleecing of tenants-in-chief of the Crown by the charges for respite of homage."[44] Direct tenants of Crown lands, who in theory owed the Queen some service as their feudal lord, could postpone their duty by paying a sum at intervals to the Exchequer. The Privy Council saw it as their duty to defend the Queen's private income, so the instigator of this debate, Robert Bell, was summoned before them. He was "so hardly dealt with, that it daunted all the house in such sort that for several days there was not one that durst deal in any matter of importance."[45] Nevertheless the issues raised here were a constant source of friction for the next twenty years.

Much of Parliament's work was carried out, then as now, in committees. Popham was appointed to one which discussed financial grievances, and to two concerned with the security of the Queen. An Act was proposed to confirm the attainders [prosecutions for treason] of the men involved in the Northern Rising of 1569, and another to prevent the introduction of Papal Bulls like the one which had recently excommunicated Elizabeth.[46]

Popham was appointed to the committees on these, and to another discussing the new Treason Act, which proposed to make it high treason to say the Queen was not lawful, or to declare in any sort "that shee is an heretique, infidell, schismaticke, tyrant, or usurper."[47]

His other committees in this Parliament were on Navigation, and on the important Bristol Act. The feeling in the western city that had given Popham his seat in the House had led to action. On 11 April Popham spoke in favor of repealing the Act of 1566 restricting Bristol's trade to the Merchant Venturers. Thinking of "the common commodity of the city," he described the deceit used in the last Parliament in penning the Act, for the statute omitted a vital proviso "that the guild should not have continuance except it were to the commodity of the city." The monopoly had raised prices, consumed the wealth of the city, reduced customs and caused the navy to be decayed.[48] This debate must have established Popham on the Commons scene, for he soon became one of the hard core of a dozen or so speakers who did most of the talking there.[49]

The Queen summoned Parliament only when she had to, but in 1572 there was very great pressure on her to take action to defend herself from traitors. Mary Queen of Scots had become a powerful focus for Catholic activists opposed to Elizabeth's reign. After Elizabeth, she had the strongest claim to the throne. She was Catholic and at present imprisoned in England. Now a plot had been discovered that linked her with the Duke of Norfolk, the Pope, Philip II of Spain, and a Florentine banker called Roberto Ridolfi in a plan to land six thousand Spaniards at Harwich in order to depose Elizabeth and replace her with Mary. The Queen needed to do something: to sign the Duke of Norfolk's death warrant and take action against the Queen of Scots. The threat of Mary, and Elizabeth's recent critical illness, perhaps from food poisoning, made it particularly urgent that the succession to the throne should be decided.[50] Accordingly, both Popham brothers were back in the House in the Fourth Parliament, where John Popham took part in the most important debates on Mary Queen of Scots. These resulted in two bills, one to exclude her from the succession, and the other to execute her. Popham was noted as one of the "ripest wits" within the House who were appointed to sort out the complexities of the bills, but both were deferred.[51]

There was always concern in the Commons over the state of the church. The Calvinists in England had a strong leader now in Thomas Cartwright, "the most dangerous man in the church."[52] He considered neither Catholic nor Anglican churches to be organized according to New Testament principles, and recommended church government not by bishops but by ministers themselves and elected lay elders. Discussions along these lines in the House were doomed, as Elizabeth would not consider any bill on religion unless it had first been discussed by the convocation of the clergy, and was anyway determined to maintain a middle way in religion. So the reforming puritan bills "touching rites and ceremonies" on whose committee Popham served on 20 May, were impounded by the Queen.[53] When Parliament closed on 30 June only seventeen bills had been passed, for so much time had been spent on the main issue. The problem of the Queen of Scots was to exercise Popham and his friends for the next fifteen years.

Throughout his busy public career and like so many of his contemporaries, Popham constantly acquired more properties. This meant more partners, more friends. On 2 January 1572 a license was issued for John Popham, Matthew Smyth and George Fetyplace, a Middle Temple contemporary, to buy the Manor and lands of Snowshill in Gloucestershire "For £3 13s. 4d. in the Hanaper."[54] The Hanaper (low Latin *hanaperium,* a hamper) Office was so called because writs relating to the business of a subject, and their returns, were formerly kept in a hamper, *in hanaperio,* while those relating to the Crown were kept in a small bag, *in parva baga.*[55]

Two weeks later a particularly interesting acquisition was made "For £3 in the Hanaper." A license was issued for Robert Bell and Dorothy his wife to alienate the Manor of Upwell [on the border of Cambridgeshire and Norfolk] to John Popham, Francis Wyndham, Edward Flowerdewe—a Norfolk lawyer "of grasping temper"[56]—and Matthew Smyth.[57] This marks the beginning of Popham's long and intimate association with East Anglia. It seems very unlikely that a Somerset man should become seriously committed to anywhere so far away; his interest was probably a consequence of friendship with two of the men named here, Robert Bell and Francis Wyndham.

Popham had allied himself in the 1571 Parliament with Bell, who might have seemed a dangerous man to support as he had already gained a reputation for outspokenness in connection with the Queen's marriage. This suggests that Popham was not afraid of disfavor, though in the event Elizabeth turned out to be remarkably forgiving of critical speechmakers. Indeed in 1572 she appointed Bell Speaker of the Commons.[58] Wyndham too was a lawyer, from a family based at Felbrigg in Norfolk but with strong family links in Somerset. Through the fraternity of the law at London and perhaps on visits to his West Country cousins, Wyndham came to establish a close friendship with Popham. After Cambridge he had studied at Lincoln's Inn, where he had been Master of the Revels. In 1570 he made a brilliant marriage, with Elizabeth, daughter of Sir Nicholas Bacon, the Lord Keeper, and lived in Norwich. It must have been with Francis Wyndham's encouragement that John Popham acquired Bell's property in Norfolk and began to interest himself in East Anglian affairs. It was later to provide him with one of his greatest challenges.

Popham's public and private lives were becoming extremely full, varied, and absorbing. His main employment was in London, and his interests already spread far afield. Yet throughout his long life and in all his enterprises his heart remained at home in Somerset.

3

Homebuilder

EVEN AFTER FOUR HUNDRED YEARS THE SMALL SOMERSET TOWN of Wellington remembers John Popham as its most distinguished resident. Here he lived as a family man, with his wife Amy bringing up six daughters and a son. This is the town where he built himself a great mansion, performed charitable works, and acquired an uneven reputation. The supposed circumstances of his death will always be remembered in local legend.

By October 1570, the Popham family were established at Old Court House, standing on the site of the present 1–3 Mantle Street.[1] This house had been part of Wellington Manor, formerly church property and now leased from the Crown.[2] A passage is supposed to run eastward from Old Court to the parish church, so it is said that Popham went to church underground.[3] In the legends he is always a dark and fearsome figure.

Then a town of perhaps one thousand people, Wellington was centrally placed in Popham territory. John's elder brother Edward now lived at Huntworth.[4] A substantial gentleman in the family mold, he had been an MP since his twenties, sitting for Bridgwater. He was Recorder of the town, maintaining the Popham domination of Bridgwater politics.[5] Edward's wife came from Bristol; five of their children reached adulthood, and two of the couple's three sons, George and Ferdinando, we shall meet again in a piratical guise. John Popham's younger brother, Robert, was a merchant in Bristol. His life is not recorded except that in 1596 he was involved in a court action for the recovery of a debt from a hosier. It is likely that Robert was engaged in haberdashery, like one of his uncles, or in wool or textiles. John Popham also had three sisters: Elizabeth married first Sir Richard Michell of Cannington, near Bridgwater, and second a Dorset gentleman, Henry Uvedale.[6] Katherine married William Pole of Shute, near Colyton, Devon, where there is an effigy of her in the parish church. One of her children became the distinguished antiquarian Sir William Pole.[7] Of Frances Popham nothing is known.

John and Amy Popham's own family flourished at Old Court in Wellington, and it must have seemed a short time before the girls were ready for marriage. They offered fine prospects for profitable alliances: during the 1570s and 1580s, as the events of the following chapters took place, the family extended its roots vigorously in the West Country soil. It has been often remarked how skillfully John Popham arranged the marriages of his daughters, all of whom became mistresses of substantial estates.

The first to go was Penelope, married probably in 1572 or 1573, presumably at Wellington parish church, to a man exactly in the image of her father—Thomas Hanham of Dean's Court, Winterborne Zelston, Dorset. Admitted to the Middle Temple in 1562, he was destined to follow a very similar pattern in his professional and public offices, becoming Reader, Serjeant, and MP for Bristol, taking over as Recorder from Popham in 1584.[8] There were three sons, the second, Thomas, born in 1576, being an adventurous man who became associated with his grandfather's enterprises and will reappear in this book. There were also three daughters, one of whom, Anne, born in 1578, married Robert Wyngate of Harlington, Bedfordshire, and is remembered by an effigy in All Saints' Church, Leighton Buzzard.[9]

Elinor married Roger Warre, heir to Hestercombe, near Taunton, Somerset. Roger did not inherit the house until 1602, so the couple found a home at Old Court, John and Amy's home. It was here, on 28 May 1574 at about 3 A.M., that Popham's grandson Richard, perhaps his first, was born.[10] More remarkably, eleven more sons and two daughters were born at this house—it was a period of unusual fertility nationally[11]—but only three sons survived. Roger joined in Popham's Irish undertaking, and we shall meet both Richard and another son, Thomas Warre, in due course.

John Popham's daughter Jane became the second wife of Thomas Horner of Cloford, near Frome. Her husband sat as MP for Somerset, and the couple had eight children before Jane died in 1591. Thomas Horner inherited in 1587 huge estates acquired particularly by his father John, the Little Jack Horner of the familiar nursery rhyme. The Horner family had become enriched by investing in confiscated monastic estates at Glastonbury, Bruton, Bath, and Keynsham. In the well-known words:

> Little Jack Horner
> Sat in a corner,
> Eating his Christmas pie,

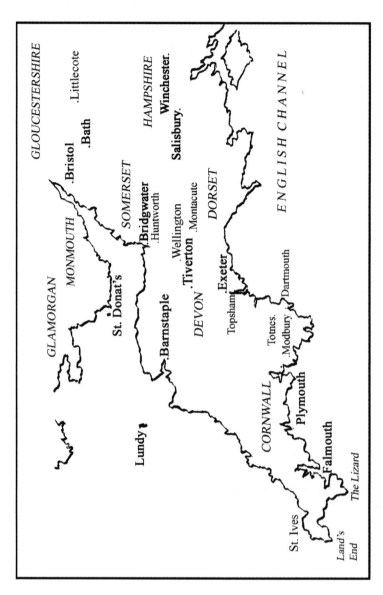

The West of England.

He put in his thumb,
And pulled out a plum,
And cried "What a good boy am I!"

The plum was an abbey estate, and the action was deserving because it was a blow against Catholicism.[12]

John Popham himself continued to acquire property. In 1577 he was bequeathed land in Wellington by the will of Richard Wykes. Although the bequest was disputed, Popham must have retained the land, for it was on this plot that he in due course built his mansion house.[13] In the same year Popham bought other lands in Wellington from Sir John Fortescue, the formidable scholar who had been tutor to the Queen; he was also appointed Keeper of the Great Wardrobe, so that the Queen could joke that Fortescue was "one whom she trusted with the Ornaments of her soul and her body."[14] The Wardrobe was in fact the depository in Blackfriars in which were kept "the ancient Cloaths of our English Kings" which they wore on great festivals; so that this wardrobe was in effect "a Library for Antiquaries, therein to read the Mode and Fashion of Garments of all ages."[15] Fortescue and Popham, who were exact contemporaries, worked together frequently throughout Elizabeth's reign, and it is noteworthy that in a drawing of her funeral procession they march side by side.

On 4 April 1581 the Queen knighted Francis Drake on board the *Golden Hind*. It was an important day too for the Pophams, for their daughter Elizabeth was married then, in London, to Richard Champernowne. He was quite a catch, for the Champernownes were one of the great families of Devon. The Modbury branch were descended from Sir Philip, whose daughter Katherine was the amazing mother of Sir John, Sir Adrian, and Sir Humphrey Gilbert, and by her second marriage of Sir Walter Ralegh. Interestingly, the Bishop of London's marriage license styles Elizabeth Popham Spinster, of St Dunstan's in the West, the church opposite the Middle Temple and very near Chancery Lane. This suggests that now that John Popham's family were growing up—Francis was eleven—they could be together in the City for at least part of the year. Popham bought a house in Chancery Lane and it was here that many of the letters that survive from the earlier part of his career were written. Elizabeth and her husband, whose marriage was long but childless, lived at Modbury, South Devon. Richard Champernowne pops up several times, in minor but interesting ways, in John Popham's story.

In about 1584 Popham's fifth daughter, Katherine, was married to Edward Rogers of Cannington, Somerset. Edward became associated with John Popham in his Irish interests. The couple had ten children, all daughters; it must have been a lively household. Marie or Mary must also have married at about this time, to John Malet of Enmore, near Bridgwater. They had seven children, and he was knighted at the Coronation of James I. The marriage of Francis, John Popham's only son, will be treated in its place; it occurred in 1590, and his bride was Anne Dudley.

Popham's house in Wellington becoming increasingly full of grandchildren, it is perhaps not surprising that he thought of moving out.[16] Probably by 1588 he had begun to build a new mansion some seventy-five yards from Old Court, on what is now the Wellington Playing Field. Though similar to Montacute, the magnificent house near Yeovil (now a National Trust property) begun at this time by the Phelips family, it was rather smaller and less grand. There were no large projecting wings, and the length of the building was only 142 feet compared with 166 feet at Montacute. Nevertheless it was a very substantial house.[17] Clearly Popham was extremely wealthy by this stage; indeed, the Phelipses and the Pophams were Somerset's premier families.[18]

Popham's great house at Wellington did not survive the Civil War, but its foundations were excavated after their chance rediscovery in 1952. Parts of the building were of Ham stone, quarried near Yeovil; several pieces of the original mansion turned up during the excavation of the site, including two pieces of window frame. A number of smaller finds were made, including from the Elizabethan period Devon slate roofing tiles and glazed earthenware ridge tiles, one of which at least was crested.[19] Such a grand place would have taken some years to build, so that in his will of 1604 Popham bequeathed "the Mansion House I have lately buylded" to his wife. No outward sign of the house remains, but a glance back is provided by the name "Popham House" on the Council nursing home nearby.

John Popham may have gained great wealth in Wellington, but he was also a public servant and a local benefactor. He acted as Justice of the Peace of the Quorum for Somerset from 1573 until his death. It was a coveted position, for there would have been only thirty or forty justices in the county; those with legal training formed an elite, one of whom (quorum) at least had to be present at each meeting. Justices acted as judges in minor cases, and four times a year dealt with more serious cases at quarter sessions. They also administered government legislation such as the

Poor Laws, and were sometimes required to raise men for the Crown when war threatened.[20] At times of emergency Somerset justices had to be on hand, for the beacon, placed where the Wellington Monument now stands, could not be lit without the "privitie" of the nearest member of the bench.[21]

John Popham is credited with having given the town a reliable water supply.[22] The Town Stream, or the Bolybrook, was brought from a weir Popham built at Woodlands across the Blackland brook to provide water for several of his farms, giving the surplus to the town. Three hundred years later, hardly surprisingly, the condition of the supply had deteriorated, for according to a letter to the local newspaper, "In 1894–5 the five farms for which Sir J. Popham had so well cared (one being the Charity Farm of Jurston, which he had bequeathed with other land for the support of the Almshouses and which had perpetual right to as much of the town water as will pass through a 1 inch pipe) were absolutely without water, and what had been a pretty stream in South Street, was only a dirty road-channel."[23] Repairs were made, and this watercourse still runs under the town's central road junction. An emergency tank filled from this stream was used during World War II.

The Almshouses referred to were given to Wellington by Popham. By the terms of his Will he established accommodation for "twelve poor and impotent or aged people whereof six to be men and six women." He specified exactly how the Almshouses were to be built and to operate, and his wishes were duly carried out. The Almshouse buildings are still to be seen at Wellington in much of their original form. Full details of this foundation, and of the trust he set up to help young people in the parish, will be found in chapter 20, with an account of his wonderful tomb in Wellington Parish Church and the extraordinary stories surrounding his death. John Popham certainly enriched his home town in an unusual variety of ways.

4

The Queen's Servant

DURING THE 1570S JOHN POPHAM BECAME A POWERFUL FIGURE
at the center of the nation's public life. The key to his promotion
was the Queen, and we can identify one moment that symbolizes
the beginning of his devotion to her Majesty's service.

On Saturday 14 August 1574, in his capacity as Recorder of
Bristol, Popham had the pleasant duty of welcoming the Queen
to the city. The details are very thoroughly recorded. The progress had begun in July, Elizabeth paying visits in Berkshire and
Gloucestershire. Bristol was the farthest point west in England
that Elizabeth ever visited, and in preparation the High Cross
and city gates had been painted and gilded, the streets pitched
and sanded: "Mr. Maior and the Common Counsell ridinge with
foote clothes, receaved her highnes within Laffardes gate. And
ther Mr Maior delyvered the gilt Mace vnto her Maiestie, and she
then presentelie delyvered it to him againe."[1] The exchange of
the mace was a symbolic act: the mayor relinquished the sign of
his authority as the Queen's lieutenant, and she returned it to
him, reinforcing by this action her authority over him and his dependence on her for favor.[2] The Mayor knelt "whiles Mr John
Popham esquier, Recorder of this citie, made an Oracon," which
being ended, the mayor stood up and "delyvered a faire purse
wrought with silke and golde vnto her Majesty, having an hundred poundes in gold in it."[3] The effects of this meeting seem to
have been profound. Thereafter John Popham was totally committed to the Queen and everything she stood for.

Elizabeth loved theatrical entertainments. At Bristol, however, even she must have been sated, for there she, and no doubt
Recorder John Popham too, had to endure three days of military
displays that seem to have suffered from the usual problems of
amateur productions: "A Fort was made beyond the water in a
ground fit for that purpose, and . . . a littell Bastillion, builded on
a hil, which was not strong by reason of the weak mayntenance
belonging thereunto." The show was an elaborate allegory, the

fort representing order, under attack from the forces of discord. On the second day "Now sarved the tied, and up the water from Kyng-road came three brave galleys, chasing a ship that cam with vitayls to the Fort. The Fort seying that their extremetie was great, sent a Gentilman to the Prince [the Queen] for aid . . . After he had swam over the water in som danger, cloes and all, he speak his part to the Prince. The gentleman was Mr John Robarts, of the Temple." After many further assaults and repulses, the Fort reminded the forces that its true defense lay in "the corrage of good peple . . . The force of a mighty Prince (who saet and beheld all these doyngs), was the thyng they trusted to, on which answer the Enemie retired, and so condicions of peace were drawn and agreed of; at which peace both the sides shot of their artillery, in sien of a triumph, and so crying 'God save the Queen,' these triumphes and warlik pastimes finished. The Prince, liking the handlyng of these causes verie well, sent ij hundreth [200] crowns to make the souldiors a banket." One hopes that the feast was a consolation to the performers for the Queen's slipping away early: "the Prince went into the gallees, and so down to Kyngroed, aer these things wear brought to an end."[4] The complete accounts for the visit are preserved in the Bristol Great Audit Book, so that we know that the purse presented by the mayor to the Queen on her arrival cost 1*l* 12*s,* and the "Summa totalis of all the charges of the Quenes Maiesties enterteignement was 1mliij*li.*xiiijs.xj*d.*"[5] or the enormous sum of £1053 14s 11d.

Popham would undoubtedly have been aware of another entertaining incident recorded in Adams's *Chronicle of Bristol* for 1577, and it may well have influenced his later thinking: "Captain Frobisher in a ship of our Queen's of the burden of 200 tons, came into Kingroad from Cathay; who brought certain ore from thence, which was esteemed to be very rich and full of gold; it was heavy, and so hard that it would strike fire like flint; some of it was tried in our castle, and the rest sent to London, where it was esteemed not worth the charges in refining. They brought likewise a man called Callicho, and a woman called Ignorth: they were savage people and fed only upon raw flesh. The 9th of October he rowed in a little boat made of skin in the water at the back: the like he did at the weir and other places where many beheld him. He would hit a duck a good distance off and not miss. They died here within a month."[6]

There was also a less romantic metal problem at Bristol in this year. The capacity of the royal Mint at this time was not enough to keep adequate supplies of official coinage in circulation, particularly the small denominations of copper and brass coins. Lack of small change made it impossible for shopkeepers to trade, so that "official" issues by a town or even by individuals were not uncommon. However, not all such new coinages were approved. The Privy Council wrote from Windsor "to Mr. Popham, Recorder of Bristowe, that where there is a certen smale coyne of copper latelie stamped at Bristoll, and there openly uttered and received from man to man," he is required "dilligentlie to examyn by whome the said coyne hathe ben stamped, and by what meanes it is become thus current both within and without the said cittie." In this case Popham's investigation seems to have found that the need justified the new coining, for from 1578 onward a warrant was procured from the Privy Council for Bristol to issue its own square farthings of copper or bronze.[7]

Bristol had welcomed the Queen with a display of its dependence on her Majesty's favor, but the Queen depended on Parliament when she needed funds for special purposes. Money was the main reason for the 1576 session, and Popham sat on the Commons committee discussing the subsidy, and on others discussing matters that he was to make his own: the poor, the coinage, cloth, and land reclamation. One of his committees debated the Queen's marriage, and another considered a bill that was intended to regulate dress, it being proposed not for the first time that the statutes should determine "what kynde of apparrell every degeree of persons within the realme should weare."[8] This idea is hardly in tune with the delight in show that seems so characteristic of the Elizabethan period. The famous images that stick in our minds, however, show the high fashions of her Majesty and courtiers like Ralegh, and it is easy to forget that Elizabethans felt it fundamentally important to preserve the outward signs of social order. The main drama of the session was provided by the brave attempt of the puritan Peter Wentworth to establish the right of the House of Commons to discuss all issues freely, without fearing their effect on the Queen; his words caused the House to send him briefly to the Tower.

Popham was working as a barrister in London at this time. Although no official court records were published, it became the practice for lawyers to compile their own notes of cases for wider circulation. A detailed study of Popham's legal work is beyond the scope of this book, but we catch glimpses of his bread-and-butter cases in several of the Reports produced by his contemporaries.[9] The actions concern leases and rents, disputes over the possession of land, the administration of wills, debt, trespass, and slander. It has been suggested that in the early phase of his career many of John Popham's briefs came not from Somerset but from Wiltshire. Hubert Hall argues that there was really little scope left in his home county for Popham's ambition and talents, for the local practice was almost monopolized by John Hippesley, perhaps the most successful country barrister of his time.[10] Wiltshire offered Popham openings through family connections, for his family had been related for years to the Darrells of Littlecote, near Hungerford.

One of John Popham's early cases is very revealing, if not to his credit, though as Hall observes, the account is no doubt one-sided. A complaint was made about his handling of the case of Thomas Pyke, a Wiltshire merchant who some years previously had made an agreement—a statute—to repay in due course a loan of £1000 used for a transaction in wool or some other staple. Being now unable to repay the loan, he called in Popham to help him out of his difficulty. At least one of the creditors was vulnerable because of his Catholic religious sympathies, so Popham took advantage of this, hinting to the creditors the advisability of coming to terms. Indeed, according to them, Popham "manaced them with terrible wordes and othes" that if they did not enter into a bond to himself for £600 to deliver up the statute in question to be canceled, they "sholde dye for it." Moreover, Popham was accused of having told the creditors that some of their own friends were in favor of the surrender, though they had never expressed this opinion. Through such deceitful practices Popham won the case and the statute was canceled, but not before the £600 bond had fallen due and been exacted in full. The poor creditors therefore begged for relief, as they were quite unable to cope with such "subtle and crafty" men as Popham and his client.[11]

Perhaps it is the subtle, crafty people who win promotion. On 28 January 1578 Popham was appointed a Serjeant-at-Law, or admitted to the "Brotherhood of the Coif,"[12] the coif being a white cap worn by barristers of this superior order, the highest degree in the Common Law. Again, it was a sign of Elizabeth's favor, for Serjeants-at-Law were appointed by the sovereign. As the Lord Keeper, Sir Nicholas Bacon, told Popham and Francis Rhodes, they had been chosen by her Highness "for the good opinion she hath of your learning and wisdom." The office was "the principal and greatest place in the law except the Judges. . . . Truly your places are of great worship and of mere [absolute, entire] high dignitie for all our goods and lands are guided and governed by the law which in deed of itself is but indeed a dead thing but it is the execution of the law that gives life to the law and that is now your office."[13] Serjeants wore distinguishing rings, and were required to present them to others on their induction.[14] They formed an Inn called Serjeants' Inn with buildings in Fleet Street, and it was from their ranks that the Common Law judges were always chosen. Some celebration of the appointment was called for: "His feast was on a scale of extraordinary magnificence, and he furnished some very fine old Gascony wine, which the wags reported he had intercepted one night as it was coming from Southampton, destined for the cellar of an alderman in London."[15]

In March 1578 Popham became an Assize judge, riding for the first time on the Oxford circuit, he and his colleague Francis Wyndham spending about four weeks in the towns of Berkshire, Gloucestershire, Herefordshire, Oxfordshire, Monmouth, Shropshire, Staffordshire, and Worcestershire.[16] His reputation was spreading; in September "Mr John Popham, learned in the law" was retained by the Chapter of Wells Cathedral, Somerset, for a fee of 40s.[17] In his private practice at the bar, Popham was becoming known for his skill in conducting real actions, which were tried in the Court of Common Pleas, and his business steadily increased. "He was likewise concerned in some cases in the Court of Wards and Liveries against the Crown; and Elizabeth, who had a regular report made to her of all suits in which her interests were concerned, expressed a wish that he might be taken in to her service."[18] In June 1579 this came into effect when Popham was appointed Solicitor-General, the second law officer of the Crown. Since the serjeants regarded the Solicitorship as beneath the dignity of their order, Popham was now "somewhat ashamed of the coif, of which he was once so proud," and, as was the custom at that time, he unserjeanted himself so that he was once more John Popham, Esquire.[19]

Even as Solicitor-General Popham could continue his private work, and at this time he was spending his fees in acquiring more property. Transactions in 1578 brought him together with his sons-in-law Thomas Hanham and Roger Warre in acquiring land in Somerset and Wiltshire. In 1580 Popham, Nicholas Wadham—later with his wife to found Wadham College, Oxford—and other friends bought a property in Huntbere, Woodbury, and Ottery St Mary, Devon. He was relentlessly extending his portfolio of investments.

Another source of income was a wardship like the one granted to Popham and John Horner in 1581. The system derived from feudal custom, when a knight holding land from the Crown owed service to his king. If the landholder died leaving an underage heir, how was the monarch to be compensated for the loss of service? The answer was monetary payment, made by the relative or friend to whom the guardianship of the young person was assigned. By Elizabeth's reign a substantial fee had to be paid each year until the young person came of age, more on that occasion, and again on his or her marriage. A guardian was obliged to provide for his ward's needs, but benefited from the income of his estate. The young people came under the jurisdiction of the Court of Wards and Liveries; incredible though it may seem, a ward would not necessarily be assigned to a relative or friend but might be made over to the highest bidder. By this means the Crown gained an income of several thousand pounds a year, and the Master of the Wards—at this time Burghley, and later his son Robert Cecil—profited too. Wardships could be valuable investments; the yearly value to Popham of the inheritance of Anne, Elizabeth and Eleanor, daughters of John Ashe, was £13 6s 8d.[20]

Popham worked hard at everything, and at this time the energetic pursuit of his career produced a stress-related illness, which we learn about in a letter concerning his friends the Smyth brothers. In September 1579 Hugh, the Justice of the Peace whose violent temperament we have noted, had a dispute with his Bristol neighbor Sir George Norton of Leigh Court. There had been a skirmish in which one of Hugh's men was killed by Sir George's gamekeeper Thomas Kenn, who was charged, with others, with felony—that is, an offense more serious than a misdemeanor.[21] Hugh's brother Matthew was brought in to help; he consulted John Popham, who wrote to him as follows:

To the worshyppful my very good ffreind Mr. Mathew esquier

Mr Smythe I have perused the whole Bookes consernyng your Brothers cause / and do fynd only Thomas Ken surely touched / for the rest ther be some fowle matter to touch them yet ys hyt eyther suche as ys pardoned or suche as they do coluerably excuse. . . . The perusing of the Books being very long with some other dysorder of dyet in myself, Brought me into my old greyff, which was very lyke to have cost me my lyffe / and are not yet very perfyttly amended but yet Resonably well agayn. I thank god for hyt / I have made my wyll which I carry with me in my capcase and do not doubt but whatever gods wyll shalbe to do with me yow wyll bothe advyse and help with your concell to the excusyon therof / I have a demerrer in law for the Bushoppe of london to be argued the second saterday thys next terme trewly I fynd my Body so in-

clynable to my Gryff of the wynd in my stomacke as I dare not as yet deal with hytt but I pray yow yf yow se my L Busshoppe lett hym know that I forgett hyt not, but wyll yf I fynd my selff apt for hyt go throughe with hyt / yf not I am sure he wyll rather holde me excused than I shold herte myselff / . . . and thus I do comytt yow to god trustyng that by hys help and the operacyon of the Brothers yow are made a perfytt man agayne / at sea thys sonday the iiij th of September 1580[22]

It seems that Popham suffered from Irritable Bowel Syndrome. It may be that death was particularly in his mind at this time, for the letter was written at Sea, the estate near Ilminster in Somerset at which his aunt Katherine had lived since her marriage to Humphrey Walrond. She died in 1580; Popham may well have been attending her sickbed or funeral at the time of this letter. As we have seen, Matthew Smyth was an old Middle Temple friend and a successful barrister, so it is appropriate that Popham should ask him to be his executor. Popham was evidently highly organized about his arrangements, though no copy of this will has survived. What we know as his final testament was made in 1604.

Popham needed to be in good health for his next challenge. Parliament was called again in January of 1581, its main purposes being to counteract the Catholic threat to the realm, and as usual to grant a subsidy. Sir Robert Bell having died, the Commons had no Speaker. The holder of this office was nominated by the Queen, although of course he had to be elected by the Commons, which had no formal existence until they had chosen him. Since he had conducted her business very satisfactorily as Solicitor-General, the Queen chose John Popham.

However, there was a technical difficulty, for as Solicitor-General Popham was expected to attend on the House of Lords as legal adviser to the peers, so he was not in the Commons. Nevertheless the Treasurer, Sir Francis Knollys, proposed Popham, and accordingly he and others "were sent up to demand the restitution of the said Mr. Popham and brought Answer again that their Lordships had resolved he should be sent down, the rather because he was a Member of this House, and this House possessed of him before he was Sollicitor or had any place of Attendance in the Upper House."[23]

He was brought from the Lords and after a special prayer had been offered—a nudge here perhaps from the puritan activists in the House—that it might please God "to direct them with His Holy Spirit" in this unusual situation (it had only ever occurred once before), the House proceeded to the election of a Speaker. "Mr Treasurer first speaking did for his own part name and commend the said Mr Popham, alledging many good reasons and causes moving him thereunto, but still leaving nevertheless liberty without prejudice to the residue of the House to name whom they would or thought good. And thereupon the whole House with full consent of Voices agreed upon the chusing of the said Mr Popham; who standing up and much disabling himself in dutiful and reverend wise, and alledging for himself many reasonable causes and excuses, besought them humbly to proceed to a new Election, whereof the House did not allow; and so then was he forthwith by the said Mr Treasurer and Mr Comptroller brought up and placed in the Chair."

This disabling was a normal part of the ritual—and it even had to happen again the next day, 20 January, when it seems that a substantial amount of business was discussed before it was remembered that "the House of Commons have no power to determine or resolve of any thing after the Election of the Speaker, till he be presented and allowed." Fortunately this was quickly arranged for the following afternoon, when "the House Assembled together, and about two of the Clock in the Afternoon they had notice that the Queen with the Lords Spiritual and Temporal were all set in the Upper House. Whereupon the Knights, Citizens and Burgesses hasted thither with Mr Popham their Speaker, and being let in as many as conveniently could, and the said Speaker brought up to the Bar at the lower end of the said House by two of the most eminent personages of the House of Commons, he there made his humble excuse, and alledged his insufficience for discharge of his place in such manner and form as in like case is usually accustomed.

"But notwithstanding his said excuse her Majesty by the Lord Chancellor signified her Allowance of him, for which the said Speaker rendred his humble thanks, and Petitioning in the name of the House of Commons for Liberty of Speech, for free access to her Majesty, and for freedom from Arrests, according to the usual form, the Lord Chancellor by the Queens Commandment made him a gracious Answer." As we have seen, Elizabeth did not want any trouble from the Commons, who had a way of nagging on about the old irritating topics—reform of the church, the Queen's marriage, the succession, the royal prerogative—so it is hardly surprising that on this occasion she gave the Speaker an admonition "to see to it that they did not deal or intermeddle with any matters touching her person or estate, or church or government."

Nevertheless, the next day they did, and Popham was in serious trouble. The Speaker was, and still is, both servant and ruler of the House of Commons. But he not only protected the interests of the Commons; at that time he also had a primary obligation to the Crown, and was seen by the Privy Councillors, the Crown's advisers, as a useful ally.[24] He could arrange the order of business and to some extent control debates, "while those privy councillors who were of the house sat around his chair and fed him with whispered advice and instructions."[25] On this occasion Popham seems not to have listened to them.

Popham began the session of 21 January, like so many new chairmen, by intending to keep meetings brief and to the point: "the Litany being read by the Clerk, and the Old Prayer, that was used in former Sessions, read also by the Speaker, Mr Speaker made a short Oration to the House, partly touching himself and partly touching them. For his own part acknowledging his infirmities and praying both their patience and assistance; and for them he advised them to use reverend and discreet Speeches, to leave curiosities of form, to speak to the matter: and for that the Parliament was likely to be very short, willed them further to forbear speaking to Bills at the first reading, and not to spend too much time in unnecessary Motions or superfluous Arguments. And further desired that they would see their Servants, Pages, and Lackies attending on them kept in good order." So far so good.

Then Mr Paul Wentworth, brother of the Peter whose offense to the House in 1576 had put him in the Tower, made a motion for a public fast and daily preaching, "the Fast to be appointed upon some one certain day, but the Preaching to be every Morning at seven of the Clock before the House did sit; that so they beginning their proceeding with the Service and Worship of God, he might the better bless them in all their Consultations and Actions." This might look like simple piety,[26] but there was more to it than that. The gatherings called prophesyings, which puritans so much valued for the discussion and propagation of their ideas, were banned, but fasts enabled them to circumvent the prohibition. Wentworth's motion was both subtly subversive and also directly controverted the Queen's admonition. In spite of this, Popham seems to have permitted the matter to be debated, either through inexperience or because he sympathized with the puritan proposal. The motion was carried by 115 to 100, the fast being settled for the following Sunday week in the Temple Church.

When the Queen heard about it, she was incensed. She summoned Popham for a thorough carpeting. On the Monday morning, "the House being assembled did sit till eleven of the clock without the Speaker, for that he was all that time at the Court." When he arrived it sounds as though he was flustered: he "declared unto the House that the time was then so far spent as leisure could not then well serve them to proceed unto the reading of any Bill" and adjourned the sitting.

The next day, "Mr. Speaker declared himself for his own part to be very sorry for the error that happened here in this House upon Saturday last in resolving to have a public Fast, and sheweth her Majesties great misliking of the proceeding of this House therein, declaring it to fall out in such sort as he before did fear it would do; and advising the House to a Submission in that behalf, further moved them to bestow their time and endeavour hereafter during this Session in matters proper and pertinent to this House to deal in." Popham suggested that as "of old time," all bills be submitted first to the scrutiny of a standing committee of four, and no motions be made except for privilege or good order. He had received a severe chastisement, to quote his own words, "such as himself could not bear."[27]

It was the Vice-Chamberlain's duty to convey to the House the text of the Queen's message. Sir Christopher Hatton, Elizabeth's handsome intimate friend, showed them "her great admiration of the rashness of this House in committing such an apparent contempt against her Majesties express Commandment . . . to attempt and put in Execution such an innovation as the said Fast without her Majesties Privity and Pleasure first known; blaming first the whole House and then Mr Speaker." She recognized, however, "the Zeal, Duty and Fidelity" of the whole House, and was prepared to construe the offense as "rash, unadvised and an inconsiderate Error of this House," proceeding from zeal and not from malicious intent. After four more speeches Mr Carleton, a supporter of Wentworth, "stood up and offered to have spoken," but now everyone could see the danger and he was interrupted by Mr Speaker and the House. A few minutes later Mr Carleton tried to speak again, but the Speaker did "rise and would not tary."[28] In the end it was agreed that Hatton should carry the Submission of the House to the Queen.

She responded gently: the answer from her Majesty spoke of "her most gracious acceptation of the Submission, and of her Majesties Admonition and Confidence of their discreet proceeding; with one special note, that they do not misreport the cause of her misliking, which was not, for that they desired Fasting and

Prayer, but for the manner in presuming to indict a form of public Fast without Order and without her Privity, which was to intrude upon her Authority Ecclesiastical."

During the course of the next weeks the House, "that independent, wayward body of men,"[29] discussed Bills both public and private on a wide range of matters:[30] "for punishing of unlawful having of two Wives at once, that Children of Aliens not being Denizens and born in England should not be reputed English, against unlawful Hunting of Conies, for Cloths called Tauntons, Bridgewaters and Charde, for the re-edifying of Cardiff-Bridge, for the repair of Dover-Haven, for the Inning [enclosure] of Erith and Plumstead, against the multitude of common Inns and Ale-Houses, against the Family of Love,[31] touching Glas-Houses, against sowing of Lineseed or Hempseed within the County of Hertford, for the true folding and winding of Woolls, for the true melting and working of Wax, against certain deceitful stuff used in the dying of Cloths, for the better fortifying of the Borders and Frontiers towards Scotland."

More important to the State were a "Bill for Obedience to the Queens Majesty against the See of Rome," which stiffened the sinews of the laws against Catholics, and another "for maintenance of the Navy and Mariners, and also for a supply of Souldiers, and setting idle persons on work, and by Fishing to procure increase of Gain and Wealth to the whole State of this Realm." The nation needed to be defended too against propaganda, or "slanderous practices words and rumors against the Queens Majesty." This was a domestic problem too: on 14 February 1581 a Member of the House, Mr Arthur Hall, was summoned for having published a scurrilous book insulting "some particular good Members of this House"—including Popham's friend the late Sir Robert Bell—and "charging this House with Drunkenness . . . and then also with Choler." After much time had been expended on the case, Popham in the name of the whole House pronounced judgment: Hall was expelled from the Commons and sent to the Tower for six months.

On Friday, 17 February, "Francis Drake Esquire was Licensed this day by Mr Speaker to depart for certain his necessary business in the service of her Majesty." It is not quite clear what this business was. Since his return in September 1580 from the circumnavigation of the globe, Drake had been one of the richest men in the country.[32] The obvious financial success of the venture stimulated plans for more, so that in early 1581 there were proposals to send Drake to "the Equynoctiall lyne," to the Moluccas in the Pacific, to the Indies, and to the Azores.[33] The Queen, however, contrived to deflect these efforts in order to further her plans to help Dom Antonio claim the throne of Portugal, recently annexed by Spain. It may have been in this connection that she required Drake's assistance.

In addition to being Solicitor-General and Speaker of the Commons, John Popham was now Treasurer of the Middle Temple. It is not surprising, therefore, to find a Committee of the House of Commons meeting for the first time at the splendid new Middle Temple Hall on 17 February 1581.[34] The subject of their deliberations was a bill framed "against the Excessive Multitude of Attornies in the Court of Common Pleas." After this, the Hall was often used for such meetings: among subjects discussed there were the true making of Hats, the preservation of the game of Pheasants, Trinity College, Cambridge, and Witchcraft and dealing with Evil Spirits.

The Treasurer is the Middle Temple's most important officer, the principal rather than the finance officer, and Popham held the post for eight years. It was common practice for senior members of the Inn—Benchers—to build chambers within the Inn at their own expense, and in the Minute Book for February 1583 we read that "All gentlemen admitted into chambers built this last summer by the Attorney-General shall choose a chamber-fellow on any vacancy, to be admitted for a fine [fee] fixed by the Treasurer." Popham at that time held both posts. From the recorded names of admissions to chambers, we can discern that Popham's building had two or three chambers on each of three floors, and at least two garret chambers in addition. Fifteen admittances were granted. It was one of the perks that men who built chambers could place in them whomever they wished: "The Masters and Benchers authorise the Attorney-General to place such gentlemen as he pleases in the chambers which he has built, and to assess such fines and to grant such terms as he thinks meet."[35]

So we can read that Messrs Thomas Ford and James Clarke were admitted "to the chamber on the north side of the third floor of the building erected by Mr Popham" for a fine of 40s. Ford, of Ilsington in Devon, was a relative of Popham's mother, and his son John Ford, born in 1586, was to become a well-known playwright. James Clarke, Popham's devoted personal assistant, had transferred to the Middle Temple to study the Common Law. He later wrote that he had been "admitted and putt in trust" by Popham "in his greatest affairs during his lyf" and his name reappears frequently in these chapters.[36] A Mr Champernoune—

presumably son-in-law Richard—was also accommodated there. Popham himself moved chambers in February 1585 into rooms "formerly occupied by Mr Plowden." This is particularly striking in view of Hubert Hall's remark in *Society in the Elizabethan Age* that Popham was "the greatest lawyer of the day, after Plowden and before Coke."[37]

No one, however great, was at this time free from attack in the House of Commons if he seemed to be exercising power in an arbitrary manner. In the last days of the session, on 16 March, the fervent puritan Anthony Cope charged Popham with partiality: "Mr Speaker in some such matters as he hath favoured, hath without Licence of this House spoken to the Bill; and in some other Cases which he did not favour and like of, he would prejudice the Speeches of the Members of this House with the Question." This undoubtedly refers to Popham's silencing of Carleton during the debate on fasting at the start of the session.[38] Cope was a supporter of Peter Wentworth's insistence on the House's independence from control by the sovereign, and here he is demonstrating that a Speaker too might exceed his brief. No response to this attack is recorded. On the whole, Hasler comments, Popham did quite well for an Elizabethan Speaker, especially in view of the drubbing he had received at the Queen's hands over the public fast incident.[39]

In spite of the Queen's having prohibited discussion of such matters, the House was still very determined to bring about reforms in the church, for its failings were nagging sores: inadequate ministers were permitted to hold several posts, excommunication was used for minor offenses, and penances even for serious faults could be paid off in money. The Queen thought that any action by the House was unnecessary as the bishops were already considering these grievances. The House felt that the bishops were procrastinating, and knew very well that Elizabeth was doing the same, but were anxious to avoid another confrontation. They therefore cleverly resolved "that Mr Speaker, in the name of this whole House, do, in his oration to her Majesty upon the last day of this present session of Parliament . . . put her Majesty in remembrance for the execution and accomplishment thereof at her highness' good pleasure, in such sort as to Mr. Speaker, without receiving instructions or direction of any of this House, shall seem most meet and convenient."[40] They were evidently quite confident that Popham would be able to strike the right note with Elizabeth.

On 18 March 1581 therefore, the Queen enthroned in the Upper House and the Lords and Commons attending, Mr Speaker began:

"In makinge of lawes he said three thinges were specyally to be considered: 1. First, that they shoold be to the honor of God and to the'advauncement of his true religion. 2. Next, to the safetye of hir Majestie's person and state. 3. And last, to the publicke benefitte of the subiects of the realme. Everye of which partes he handled severallye, notinge in the first two thinges requisite: one, the diligent and sinceare preaching of the woorde by the bishopps and ministers of the same, whiche he tearmed to be the wateringe and refreshinge of the soules and consciences of men as gardens were refreshed with sweete showres to make them bringe foorthe plenty of good fruites; and the other by discypline, for th'exterpacyon of heresies and reformacyon of mannors as in gardens weedes are rooted out, least the good plantes be choked upp or hindred.

"In the second he remembred the great benefitts and blessings that we receyve of almightye God thorowe the ministerye of our most gracyous Queene, that so manye yeares together hath maynteyned us in so great pease and wealthe, together with hir singular vertues, justice and mercye, seene and deeply felt of all her people, being causes sufficient to make us carefull to provide by all meanes the honor and safetye of hir, by whom we all live and enioye that we have. And in the third parte he noted how necessary it was to provide lawes tendinge not onely to the maintenance and encrease of the wealthe of the subiects of the lande, beinge the strength and glorye of the Queene, but also the refreshinge and correctinge of those ill members which, by indirect meanes and of private respect to them selves, woold any wise procure the detriment of the common weathe. Uppon which occasion he made peticyon to the Queene that seinge all such lawes as had passed booth Howses to th'ends aforesaid remayned yet unperfect, without hir Majestie gave life unto them: that therfore it might please hir to geve hir royall assent so as therby they might take the force of lawes."

And now came the crunch, the sensitive issue. No one could tell whether Elizabeth would flare up as the forbidden topic was raised yet again.

"This doone he remembered a peticyon made by the Common Howse the last session of Parliament to the Queene's Majestie for redresse to be hadd of certaine enormities in the Chirche which he noted to be theise: the admittinge of unlearned and insufficient ministers; next, th' abbuse of excommunicatyon used in things of small momente;

thirdlye the commutacyon of pennance into monye even in the greatest offences; and lastlye, the great inconveniences growen by reason of pluralyties and dispensatyons."[41]

"Wherunto hir Majesty made them a most gracyous awnswere, that she had and woold geve ordre therein, ffor the which he rendred to hir most humble and dutyfull thanckes. He remembered lickewise that bycause those thinges for lack of time were not fullye refoormed the House had eftsoones this session presumed to put hir Majestie in mynde therof agayne, wherunto also as to the former they received a graycous answere, that those matters belonginge to hir as incydente to that supreame authorytie which she hathe over the cleargie and state ecclesiasticall, she woold geve such directyon therin as all the disorders shoold be reformed so farr as shoold be necessarye. For the which answere also he rendred the like most humble thancks, besechinge hir Majestie in the name of the whole commons that it might please hir to commaunde that to be doone without delaye which the necessitye of the thinges did require.

"Finallye he presented unto hir a subsidie and two fiveteenes graunted by bothe the Houses towardes the maytenance of hir great charges: moste humbly besechinge hir not to wey the smalnes of the guifte, being farr lesse then was nedefull, but the good wills and mindes of the gevers, who beside this woold be ever redye accordinge to their most bounden dutyes to employe all the rest which theye have and their lives also for the service of hir Majestie and the realme."[42]

The Lord Chancellor, Sir Thomas Bromley, replied by her Majesty's command. She thanked the House for their care for her safety; but within those general thanks she did not include some members of the Commons who in this session "forgot themselves," dealing more rashly in some things than was proper. Concerning Popham's petition about the reform of the church, "it needed not any such reiteration. The Howse might have beene satisfied with her answer before made."[43] She thanked the House for the subsidy, and gave her consent to thirty Acts, fifteen public and fifteen private, an unprecedented number. It had been a very busy time, and Popham may have been happy not to remember some of it. There is a kind of wishful thinking in his joke with Elizabeth related by Francis Bacon: when the Queen asked, "Well, Mr. Speaker, what hath passed in the Lower House?" he replied, "If it please your Majesty, seven weeks."[44]

5

Attorney-General

ON 1 JUNE 1581 POPHAM WAS APPOINTED ATTORNEY-GENERAL. HE was approaching fifty, and must have felt on the crest of a wave. The Queen valued his services, he had recently won rapid promotion, and his new office was demanding but essential. He was now the Crown's principal legal adviser and chief public prosecutor, responsible for combating in the courts the enemies of the state.

In the 1580s England was under attack from within and without. Her "most pernicious and dangerous Enemies," as Popham himself described them, were Spain under Philip II and the widespread forces of Catholicism under Pope Gregory XIII.[1] During the next decade these came to be mobilized in four main ways: English priests, trained abroad, were to subvert the country from within; Ireland was to be a base for attack; Mary Queen of Scots would become a focus for uprisings; and there was to be a direct attack from Spain by sea. The aim of all these efforts was the death of the Queen.

That there was a concerted plan to overthrow the Queen and re-establish Catholicism there is no doubt. Pope Pius V had excommunicated Elizabeth in February 1570 and in 1580 the Jesuits—the missionary arm of the Catholic Church—were instructed to undertake an undercover campaign in England. The murder of the Queen was officially approved, as is clearly stated in a letter from one of the Pope's officials to a colleague in Spain: "whosoever sends her out of the world with the pious intention of doing God service, not only does not sin but gains merit."[2]

The new energy of the campaign by Jesuits and seminary priests—those trained abroad—caused Elizabeth's government much concern. Two aspects of the official response were to engage John Popham's energies for the next twenty-five years. First, because it was a fundamental Tudor belief that a united England was an invincible England, backsliding in religious matters had to be discouraged. Absence from church, now called recusancy, had hitherto been punished by a small fine, only 1s per Sunday. In 1581 a new Act raised the fine to the huge amount of £20 per month. Saying or singing Mass cost a fine of 200 marks (£166) and a year's imprisonment. Secondly, legislation against priests was strengthened: in 1581 it became treason to practice to withdraw subjects from obedience to their Queen or from the established religion. Thus although one could be a Catholic, to become one was treason. Later, by an Act of 1585 it became treasonable merely to be a Jesuit or seminary priest and enter or remain in the Queen's realm, or to assist or shelter such a priest.

There was of course at this time no police force, so information about suspects had to be gathered from paid informers—at least, they were promised pay. The most famous of these men was Richard Topcliffe, the only man in England known to have kept a private rack so that he could conveniently torture suspects at his own home. Agents like him were the lowest rung of the prosecution ladder, their masters being the officers of state. Chief of these was the Lord Treasurer, Elizabeth's beloved father figure William Cecil, Lord Burghley (1520–98). The Secretary, Francis Walsingham, maintained a powerful intelligence network; Popham too had his own group of spies. Using the information these agents brought him, the Attorney-General himself examined the accused and witnesses, or provided interrogatories, the questions intended to be asked by others. When the accused were brought to court, Popham often conducted the prosecution, in all aspects of the process working closely with the Solicitor-General, Thomas Egerton. Popham was thus a key member of the small group of strong, hard-working, intelligent men who under the Queen herself and Robert Dudley, Earl of Leicester, her chief courtier, took responsibility for the safety of the state. With absolute confidence in the rightness of the Protestant cause and unbounded energy, Popham was a formidable opponent of the forces aiming to destroy England.[3]

The penalties for treason were horrific. Peers were simply beheaded, but commoners were hanged up to be exposed to public vilification, cut down quickly while still alive, and disemboweled. Their hearts were plucked out and exposed and their entrails burnt. Their limbs were quartered and the parts placed on gateways and bridges as a warning to others. But faith produces extraordinary self-sacrifice; although the priests knew the terrible death that awaited them, there was a steady supply of potential martyrs in training at Douai, the Jesuit college near Lille in northern France. The English Jesuits Edmund Campion and Robert Parsons were the vanguard, arriving in Britain in 1580.

Campion was a brilliant man. Born in London and educated at Christ's Hospital and St John's College Oxford, where he was a Fellow at seventeen, he had been Orator of Oxford University before his conversion to Catholicism, welcoming the Queen with a noteworthy speech in Latin. A recipient of Leicester's patronage, historian of Ireland, Professor of Rhetoric and later of Philosophy at Prague, he was recognized in England as a great loss to the Anglican cause. His part in the English Mission lasted only a year, spent ministering and preaching in the shires. On 14 July 1581 he was captured and sent to the Tower.

On 29 October the Privy Council wrote to the Attorney and Solicitor-General, the Lieutenant of the Tower, and others "for thexamining of Edmund Campion, Thomas Fourd and others, prisoners in the Tower, uppon certen maters, and to put them unto the Rack."[4] Several rackings producing no confession, Campion was tried along with seven others. Sir Christopher Wray, the Lord Chief Justice of the Queen's Bench, presided, and the prosecution was conducted by Edmund Anderson, Popham, and Egerton.[5] Treason proceedings happened like this: first, investigations by prosecution lawyers led to the compilation of a dossier on the suspect, on the basis of which his guilt or innocence was decided. If guilty, the traitor was put on trial; even though there was a jury, the public performance was a show trial, designed to demonstrate to others the dangers of trying to overthrow the state. Thus at his trial Campion was certain to be convicted. It seems, however, that no one really wanted him to die. The Queen herself attempted to win him back to the Anglican Church, but Campion was not to be bought or to admit to any wrongdoing: "If our religion do make traitors, we are worthy to be condemned; but otherwise we are, and have been, true subjects as ever the Queen had."[6] Having taken the prosecution so far, the government had no choice but to carry it through. Campion was executed in the sight of a devoted audience for whom he was a truly heroic figure, saintly, sincere, devout, and impassioned.

Several letters referring to Campion have survived and are in The National Archives in London. Their contents, as summarized in the *Calendar of State Papers Domestic* and in *Acts of the Privy Council,* show how the reverberations of the Campion affair continued to occupy John Popham in the following months: "Nov 12 1581 John Popham, Att. General, to Walsyngham. Examinations of Jane, wife of William Gryffyth, and of Ambrose and John Gryffyth, touching the resort of Campion and Parsons[7] to their house. Wm. Gryffyth was in the house when it was beset by Mr. Blount, yet was not discovered. Desires instructions how to proceed."[8] Many Catholic families provided shelter to priests, who would stay a few days, conduct Masses, and hear confessions before moving on to another safe haven. Popham was in this case searching out those who might have been tainted by treasonable hospitality to the visitors.

It is reassuring to discover that not everyone suspected in such cases was harshly treated: "15 Dec 1581 Phillipe Pollard of Litle Haddon in the countie of Oxford, detected by the confession of Edmunde Campion the Jesuite . . . she being examined by her Majesties Attorney and Sollicitour Generall confessed the receiving and harbouring of Campion and acknowledged her faulte and offence . . . . the said Phillipe promised to be conformable in Relligion and repaire to the churche and heare Devine Service and sermones as sholde become a ductifull subjecte . . . their Lordships did dismisse her and remitted her said offence."[9]

Not even the most noble families were exempt from suspicion. The Wriothesley family, Earls of Southampton, were known Catholic sympathizers, and in the following letter the household of the second Earl, father of Shakespeare's patron, is under investigation: "20 Dec 1581 A letter unto Mr Recorder of London by the which he is required to resorte unto the Earle of Southampton's howse in Holborne, and there to make searche for the apprehending of one William Spencer, noated unto their Lordships to be a very badd fellowe and practiser against the State . . . according to suche instructyons as he shall receyve fro Mr. Attorney Generall; and, furder, he is required to searche the said howse for bookes, letters and ornaments for Massinge, and the same, together with the parties whome he shall apprehend, to delyver to Mr. Attorney to be examined and further delt withall as shall appertaine."[10]

Campion's was one of the first treason trials in which Popham was involved. There were to be many more; almost exactly the same number of Catholics were martyred under Elizabeth's government as Protestants had been during Mary's much shorter reign—282. At least four sectarians, members of independent reformist groups, were also executed for treason. In Mary's reign Protestantism had been a religious offense, the martyrs being tried for heresy by ecclesiastical courts. But under Elizabeth, Catholic priests were tried for treason in secular courts, so the

Queen could maintain that no subjects of hers suffered for their religious beliefs. The quiet pursuit of observances of any kind she was happy to allow, but religious fanaticism, then as now, could present a threat to national security. It was easy for all Catholics to be tarred with the same brush, to be regarded as subversive, and to be persecuted. There is no doubt that Popham was zealous in the pursuit of any suspects.

The catching of priests was in one instance a family affair. Popham's son-in-law Thomas Hanham, married to Penelope, was a Serjeant-at-Law living in Dorset. In February 1583 he must have been very surprised while riding across Hounslow Heath to see the familiar face of John Munden, whom he would have remembered from his home county as a schoolmaster at Netherbury. The local children had certainly needed instruction in the 1560s when Munden started teaching, for there was at that time an active witch in the village. His name was John Walsh, and he had for seven years been servant to a popish priest who had taught him medicine, surgery, and witchcraft. After the priest's death Walsh had reappeared in Netherbury, armed with his master's book "which had great circles in it, wherein he would set two wax candles and a cross of virgin wax to raise the familiar spirit," which came to him in the form of a grey calf, a brindled dog, or a man with cloven feet.[11]

This was the kind of influence with which Munden had to contend. After many years of striving for genuine religious principles, both in the schoolroom and within himself, Munden went to Rome, where he was ordained. In August 1582 he was sent on the English Mission, although as a middle-aged man well-known in the country his papist activities were bound to be discovered. When he was caught, Munden objected that Hanham had no authority as a Justice outside Dorset, but to no avail. Munden soon found himself being questioned; he was sent to the Tower, and lay for twenty days on the floor in chains. Then he was examined by John Popham, who accused him of having "led a lewd life" as a schoolmaster in Dorset. After spending a year in the Tower, Munden was tried and executed in February 1584.

The second thrust of the Catholic campaign was a direct attack from Ireland. In order to repel invasions and put down any rebellious tendencies in the local population, a stronger English military presence was needed. Walter Ralegh was already there, and in October 1580 a George Popham went to Ireland, like him as a Captain.[12] It is unlikely that George's men were any more disciplined than those who occasioned a letter in June 1581 from the Privy Council to the Attorney-General. He was to understand that there had been a "mutynous disorder and disobedience of certen souldyers at Chester and Liverpoole, who were sent thither to be embarqued and transported for her Majesties servise into the Realme of Ireland. This indiscipline should be mett withall by some sharpe and exemplary punishement to be inflicted uppon them."[13] It was John Popham's job to consider their offenses and to advise how they might be proceeded with.

Mary Queen of Scots was the other major focus of Catholic interest, for if Elizabeth died, she would succeed to the throne.[14] At this time a prisoner in England, the Queen of Scots still contrived to communicate with her supporters; in the summer of 1583 a messenger of the Spanish Ambassador in London, disguised as a dentist, had been stopped crossing the Scottish frontier. Among his possessions was a mirror, containing hidden in its back a letter that revealed a conspiracy in which Mary herself, the Ambassador, King Philip, and the Pope were all involved. There was to be a joint Catholic rising and Spanish invasion, designated by the code name "Enterprise of England."

As the first stage Elizabeth was to be struck down by Francis Throckmorton, a devoted former servant of the Queen of Scots. In October 1583 this young Catholic of good family was suddenly arrested in the act of penning a letter in cipher to Mary. In his house were found lists of people, plans of harbors, treatises in defense of Mary's claim to the English throne, and "six or seven infamous libels against Her Majesty printed beyond sea."[15] Popham was responsible for examining several of the plotters, recording "Notes touching an intended invasion of the realm by Spain, collected from the depositions of John Hart, Ralph Nicholson, and Francis Throckmorton."[16] On the rack Throckmorton confessed his part in the plot.

A year later the eighth Earl of Northumberland, a Catholic who had been associated with the Throckmorton conspiracy, was found dead in his bed in the Tower. He had been shot through the head by three slugs on the night after his guard had been changed by the orders of Sir Christopher Hatton, the Vice-Chamberlain. Hatton was a favorite; it was said that he had danced his way into office, first attracting the Queen's favor at a masque. He was one of her closest counselors, and this must have been a nasty moment for him. Although the coroner's jury returned a verdict of suicide, the rumor spread that Northumberland had been assassinated as a danger to the state, and Hatton's involvement was suspected.

In order to cope with such rumors the state had its own forum for spin-doctoring. Since Parliament seldom met, and there were no newspapers, radio, or television through which officials could seek to justify their actions, an assembly was held in the Star Chamber, to which the great and good of the political world were invited. The members of the government concerned in the issue then spoke in their own defense.

On this occasion, when the audience was "very great of knights, esquires, and men of other quality," it was Popham's task to demonstrate the Earl's history of treasonable actions. He recounted how Northumberland had been involved in an attempt to free "the Scotish queen" from imprisonment. Elizabeth's mercy to him then had been rewarded by a second attempt to deliver Mary, this time out of the custody of the Earl of Shrewsbury. "Notwithstanding these traiterous practices," Popham continued, "the queen's majesty was contented to remit all within a short time, and then accepted most graciously of him both in honour and favour, though unworthily bestowed upon him; for that he utterly forgetting those graces and favours received at her majesty's merciful hands, with a graceless resolution was contented to enter into a new Plot, now lately contrived, not only for delivering the Scotish queen, but for the invading of the whole realm, the overthrow of the government . . . and advancing of the said Scotish queen to the regal crown and scepter of this realm."[17]

Popham outlined Northumberland's involvement in the Throckmorton plot, after which the Solicitor-General and other lords made their contributions. The case was summed up by Hatton himself, the chief suspect. He declared it was suicide, that "God by his just judgment had for his sins and ingratitude" taken from Northumberland his spirit of grace, and "delivered him over to the enemy of his soul, who brought him to that most dreadful and horrible end, whereunto he is come; from which, God of his mercy defend all christian people."[18] In spite of these fine words, it seems to have remained the common opinion that the Earl of Northumberland was murdered by the contrivance of Hatton. He nevertheless retained the Queen's favor, becoming Chancellor two years later.

Since Elizabeth was so obviously in danger, the succession problem continued to be a source of intense concern. Mary Queen of Scots was first in line, but it was essential that the throne should be secured to a Protestant. There were several other candidates, among them Lady Arbella Stuart, but it was not clear which of them had the best claim.[19] In January 1585 Popham and Burghley worked on the draft of a scheme whereby if Elizabeth should die, a council of regency, whose members would be named by the Queen in her will, would govern until Parliament resolved the matter. Elizabeth rejected the scheme.[20]

In August 1586 it was revealed that the Queen of Scots had herself been directly involved in another plot to kill Elizabeth. Walsingham had masterminded a skillful spying operation. Encrypted correspondence had passed between the Queen of Scots and her sympathizers, letters in a waterproof case being popped into the bunghole of Mary's household beer barrels, which were carried out by the draymen under the very eyes of her guards. Walsingham had employed code breakers and read every word. The plot again aimed to assassinate Elizabeth, provoke a Catholic rising, and support an invasion and conquest by Spain. Anthony Babington of Dethick, Derbyshire, formerly a page in Mary's household, was twenty-five and a rich landowner as well as a seminary priest. He and several companions had offered to attempt the murder of the Queen and the release of Mary. Anticipating heroic martyrdom, the young men "grew to that height of vanity" that they had their pictures painted together like a team photograph.[21]

Popham conducted the trials of all those implicated in the Babington conspiracy. One of them was Charles Tilney, "of a remarkable and famous race; who was the onely hope of that house";[22] in a short extract from his case we see in action both Popham and Chief Justice of the Common Pleas Edmund Anderson, his close colleague for many years. The charge against Tilney was that he had planned the murder of Queen Elizabeth in her coach. The chief evidence consisted of a confession of Abington, an avowed accomplice, in which he said that "Tilney was disposed to kill the Queen," and that Babington, in his own trial, had said the day before that "Tilney would have had her Majesty set upon in her coach."

"Tilney.	No! I said not so; only at the Three Tuns, in Newgate Market, I said 'it might be her Majesty might be set upon in her coach,' and I said no more. But that proves not I did consent.
Popham AG.	You have said enough, if we had no other evidence against you.
Tilney.	How so?
Popham AG.	Because you have confessed high treason; your words

	prove that you were devising on the manner of her death.
Tilney.	I tell you there is no such matter intended in my words. If a servant which is faithful, knowing where his master's money is, do say, "If I would be a thief I could rob my master, for in such a place his money is," this proves not that he would rob his master albeit he used such words. And so, though I said "she might be set on in her coach," it proveth not that I assented to the same; for I protest before God I never intended any treason in my life.
Anderson CJ.	But if a servant, knowing where his master's money is, among thieves which are devising to take away the master's money, do say, "this way my master's money may be taken," and be in view when it is taken, I say that he is an accessory. And you, Tilney, being amongst traitors that were devising how to kill her Majesty showed by what means her Majesty might be killed. This manifestly proves your assent. Therefore let the jury consider of the evidence."[23]

On 18 September the Privy Council at Windsor wrote "to Her Majesties Attorney Generall for the order of the execucion of the traytors latelie condemned,"[24] and two days later, amid general rejoicing, the would-be assassins were dragged across London on hurdles to St Giles's fields, to be executed with hideous barbarity.

And what happened to the property of traitors? On 22 December 1587 Popham wrote to John Manners of Haddon Hall, a leading Derbyshireman: "The Queen has granted to Sir Walter Raleigh the manors of Lee and Litchurch, in the county of Derby, and divers lands in Creech, Wirksworth, Hever and Tannesley, in the same county, being part of the lands of Anthony Babington, lately attainted of high treason. I understand that the evidences are in your hands, and so I pray you to send them up under your seal by the bearer, Henry Butler."[25] Ralegh was enjoying a period of royal favor; the course of his association with Popham is the subject of chapter 15.

Feeling against Mary was now overwhelming. In spite of her reluctance, Elizabeth was forced into agreeing to bring the Queen of Scots to trial for treason. The Attorney-General acted as adviser to Burghley on how the Commission was to be drawn up; Popham wrote that "there must be good Consideration had by what Name she was to be named in the Commission," which "should be written in a set Hand; in respect it was of great Importance, and to continue in After-ages." Popham recommended that "beside her Christian Name, she might also have either the Surname of her last Husband, or the Name of her Father, as was set down," for "no Name of Dignity, is taken Notice of by our Law, but that which is grown, or created within her Majesties Dominions." However, "in the Alias dictus any Thing may be said that shall please her Majesty, being once surely named." Being anxious "to set off the Blame that hereafter might grow" to the Lawyers thereby, he stated that the name "might be this without Peril, Maria filia & haeres Jacobi Quinti, nuper Regis Scotorum, alias dict. Maria Regina Scot. Dotar. Franc.[Mary daughter and heir of James the Fifth, lately King of Scotland, also called Mary Queen of Scots, Dowager of France] For it is not regarded what the alias dict. is."[26] We can sense a cunning, careful mind at work, anxious to safeguard Elizabeth and the legal profession, fully aware of the profound implications of the forthcoming drama.

In October the Commission assembled at Fotheringhay in Northamptonshire. Mary at first declined to recognize the authority of the court. However, on "Oct 14 1586 Friday morning she determined to appear, and so about 9 of the clock came forth into the Presence Chamber, prepared and hanged with cloth of state; in the upper part, and down along both sides, formes were covered with greene for the Earles and Lordes on the right side, and Barons on the left; somewhat belowe the middest of the Chamber was a barre set, within which barr a form for the Knights of the Privy Counsell to sit, and before the formes a chayer with a cushion and foote carpet for the Queene of Scotts; directly against the state, below the middle of the Chamber, was a table, wherat sate the Queene's Attorney and Sollicitor, and Sergeant, the Clerkes of the Crowne, and the two Notaries."[27] The part of public prosecutor was acted in turn by Lord Chancellor Bromley, Lord Treasurer Burghley, and Vice-Chamberlain Hatton, who were sitting as her judges.[28] Popham was not required to speak in these proceedings, but in recognition of his work on the case he was paid £100, a huge fee.[29]

The execution of Mary Queen of Scots was carried out on 8 February 1587. When Elizabeth heard about it, she was furious. For diplomatic reasons William Davison, the unfortunate official who had sent off the letter authorizing the execution, was made the scapegoat and found himself arraigned in the Star Chamber:

"*Mr Popham*. My Lords, I am to inform your lordships in her majesty's behalf, of a certain great and grievous Contempt and Misprision against Mr Davison, there prisoner at the bar, late one of her majesty's secretaries." Following so many threats to her own safety, Elizabeth had reluctantly at last signed a warrant for the Queen of Scots' execution, to be kept in readiness "if any attempt should be begun, and yet not in haste to execute the same: this so signed, she left with Mr Davison to carry the great seal, to have it in readiness as aforesaid. And he, after the sealing, and without her majesty's commandment, presented it unto the lords without her privity . . . wherein Mr Davison did break the secrecy her majesty reposed in him . . . and dealt very contemptuously in not making her privy, knowing her mind to be to the contrary . . . her majesty doth take it a matter of high indignity and abuse of her counsellors, and a thing of the greatest moment that ever happened since her reign, since which time never any counsellor in matters of far less importance proceeded without her resolution or privity: which thing she leaves to your honours consideration for punishment thereof." Davison replied "with a comely countenance, replenished with gravity, a fine deliverance of speech, but a voice somewhat low (which he excused by late sickness)," but was nevertheless unable to avert two years in the Tower.[30]

While these historic high dramas were being enacted, the Attorney-General's office was constantly dealing with the lesser issues affecting English life. To Popham instructions were sent on all manner of affairs; from him advice was constantly requested. In London the Tallow Chandlers have been committing abuses; a preacher at Paul's Cross has delivered a sermon libeling the Lord Mayor; the butler of the Inner Temple has been involved in "undutifull misdemeanors and slaunderous speches concerning the State."[31] At Norwich a man has been "buyeng of wolles" contrary to the proclamation affecting the poor. There too because of a scarcity of food the city fathers need to dispense with the statute "prohybytinge the killinge of calves." At Chichester the Dean and Chapter want to refound the Hospital of St. Mary's for the use of the indigent people.[32] A gang in Wiltshire have been "coyning of mony" and in Dorset there is a dispute between two nobles "touching the right of a house and certain alume works" called Okemans House.[33]

In Exeter Popham was consulted in a case where a suit by Mrs. Levermore had gone against her as a result of partiality by the jurors. He wrote to the Mayor suggesting a compromise, ending with a stern warning: "Yf you shall see and suffer the jurors of your Cyty thus to pass agaynst all treuth and agaynst your and their own consciences and trwthes you can but hepe Godes wrath upon your cyty."[34] On another occasion, the Earl of Bath complained bitterly about the "insolencie and extreame delaings of common attornys and unfitt sollicitours," particularly two "men of bad behaviour, breeding, contencion and debate amongest manie poore inhabitauntes of the countie of Devon"; one wonders whether Popham managed to pacify him.

Another concern was the uniformity of weights and measures, an issue on which Popham became an authority. The *Calendar of State Papers* summarizes a letter of 16 February 1583 from John Popham to the Earl of Pembroke, Lord Lieutenant of Wiltshire, thus: "Dispute between the Mayor and Burgesses of the city of Sarum relative to the measures for ale and wine. His opinion of the statutes on this head. There ought to be but one kind of measure in all England, according to the standard in the Exchequer." When Pembroke sent this letter on to Walsingham, he thought it best to send a copy, Popham's hand being "not well to be read"[35]—how right he was. Popham himself sent to Walsingham notes from various statutes concerning the uniformity of weights and measures: "The English penny, sterling, must weigh 32 grains of wheat in the midst of the ear, and 20 pence make an ounce, and 12 ounces maketh the pound weight."[36] This revision introduced standards that remained unaltered until 1824.[37]

Matters of the sea also concerned the Attorney-General, and are particularly fascinating at this time. Piracy was a continual problem for commerce, so that we find in 1582, for instance, a Commission by the Queen to John Popham and others, directing them "to search and make enquiry for the apprehension and punishment of pirates, dealers or aiders of pirates."[38] Ironically, John Popham's own nephew Ferdinando had been involved in an incident of this kind: "Petition of Edmund Tyrry, of Cork, merchant, to the Privy Council. Spoiled of 500*l* at Mount's Bay in Cornwall by Thomas Walshe, Fernando Popham, William Waghan, and others, the 12th Sept 1581. Prays for a warrant to take F. Popham."[39]

The Attorney-General was often involved in the drafting of Patents, the Crown licenses granted to individuals for various commercial undertakings. One of the many draft patents now in The National Archives consists of twenty-two pages in a clerk's hand, every sheet being signed by Popham. It dates from March

1584 and grants to Walter Ralegh Esquire "free libertye and ly-
cence . . . to dyscover serche finde owt and viewe such remote
and hethen and barberouse lands countrys and terrotorryes not
actuallie possessed of any Christian Prynce."[40] It was this
Patent, originally Sir Humphrey Gilbert's, that provided the basis for the expedition sent by Ralegh which discovered Virginia
in the same year. When in December the House of Commons was
presented with a Bill to confirm these Letters Patent it was
added that Ralegh had discovered "Wyngandocoia." Ralegh himself noted this as an example of a problem common to travelers,
for on arrival at the American coast his men had asked the local
Indians what their country was called. They replied, "Wyngandocoia," which actually meant "You weare good clothes, or gay
clothes."[41]

Meanwhile, the Spanish prepared their great Armada. Plans
to invade England by sea had existed for more than thirty years,
so it was no surprise when in 1584 the fitting of a large Spanish
fleet was rumored. Orders were issued to put men in readiness
for defense of the sea coast. Not only did England have no police
force; it also had no standing army. When attack seemed imminent, farmers and gentlemen as well as rogues and vagabonds
had to take up arms. The gentry were required to fund the soldiers, every justice of the quorum, like John Popham, having to
provide two petronels on horseback. Popham's were named Henry Warde and Morgan Griffythes, and the weapon each carried
was a kind of large pistol or small musket, which when not in use
rested against the chest.[42]

The following October an Instrument of Association was drawn
up and adopted by the Lords of the Council. Two copies were sent
to every county, one to be signed and returned to the Council. It
is a magnificent piece of writing, conveying the intensity of feeling Elizabeth's security aroused: "wee and every of us . . . doe
hereby vowe and promis before the majestie of almightie God
that with oure whole powers bodies lyves landes and goodes and
with oure children and servantes wee and every of us will faith-
fullie serve and humblie obbaye oure saide soveraigne ladye
Quene Elizabethe against all estates dignities and earthlie powers whatsoever. And will as well with our jointe and particuler
forces duringe our lyves withstande offende and pursue as well
by force of armes as by all other meanes of Revenge all manner
of parsons of what estate soever they shalbe and ther abetters
that shall attempt by anye arte consaile or consente to anye
thinge that shall tende to the Harme of her Majesties Royall par-

son. And wee shall never desiste from almanner of forcyble pursuite againste such parsons to the uttermost exterminacion of them their Consellours Ayders and abetters." Signed and sealed by John Popham, John Horner, and many others. Dated at Hampton Court the 19th of October 1584.

Drake singed the King of Spain's beard at Cadiz in April 1587. An unusual occurrence connected with this famous event is recorded in the State Papers on 29 July 1587: "Note of certain examinations taken before the Judge of the Admiralty, the Attorney and Solicitor General, and Dr. Hammond . . . concerning the running away of the Golden Lion under the command of Captain Borough."[43] The defection was caused by Sir Francis Drake's autocratic management style. After the daring attack on the Spanish Navy, Drake was at the height of his popularity—with everyone except his Vice-Admiral, William Borough, who found him "always so wedded to your own opinion and will, that you rather disliked and showed as that it were offensive unto you that any should give you advice in anything."[44] Drake sacked him, and on 27 May the ship's company of the *Lion* ran away with the vessel and took her back to England, presumably at Borough's instigation.

Open war with Spain, in English waters, was a real prospect at last. By the middle of June 1588 it was known that the Armada was on its way, but a month later it had still not been seen. The western counties were on edge. Popham was at home at Wellington, where no doubt he authorized the lighting of the beacon on Friday, 19 July to pass on the message of the sighting of the Spaniards. Very soon Popham received further top-level information, and it must have been with excitement as well as anxiety that on Monday, 22 July he sent off to Walsingham the first detailed information to reach London about the opening engagement with the Armada:

My dewties unto your honour most humbly remembered. It may please you to understand that upon ffriday last the spanyshe flete was discovered towards the west partes and upon saturday they were all to the number of 160 and two sail over against fawmouth. And yesterday being more esterly towards dartmouth. I am advertised ffrom my L Cheyff Justice Anderson that my L admyrall [Lord Charles Howard of Effingham] *contynewed in fight with them ffrom 9 off the clocke in the forenone untyll thre in the afternoon.*[45]

How Edmund Anderson came to have this information we do

The opening of Popham's letter reporting the first engagement with the Spanish Armada. Photo: The National Archives.

not know; perhaps he was himself at Plymouth. However, it is not surprising that he wrote to the Attorney-General immediately, for the arrival of the Armada had particular significance for both men. Popham's letter continues: *My L Chieff Justice hathe wryten unto me to understand my opynyon what were ffyt to be done touchyng our jorney towards Ireland whyther we resolved to take our voyage upon monday next in the mornyng.* The

English attempts at settlement in Ireland were proving extremely problematic, and it had been planned that Popham and Anderson should go to Munster in person to try to sort out the business there. If they are to sail, the letter continues, since the sea near Ireland is *very full of pyratts* they will have to *passe somewhat strongly*—that is, they will need an armed guard.

The two lawyers must have been told to carry on. It is remarkable that at a time of national emergency both the Attorney-General and one of the two Lord Chief Justices should be sent out of the country, even if the visit was intended to be a short one. Ireland was evidently thought to be of the first importance. Popham's letter to Walsingham prays that *her majestie in thys so dangerous a tyme may . . . have a specyall care off her selff, which beying hadd we have such an unyted strengthe as her enemyes can never prevayl agaynst so gracyous a Queene.* His faith proved justified. A two-pronged attack by the English trapped the Spanish fleet in Calais Roads. Confused by fireships, the Armada dispersed. In the main battle fought off Gravelines on Monday 29 July the English used their guns to powerful effect, and the Armada took advantage of a sudden change of wind to escape the fray into the North Sea.

On 13 August the Spanish fleet lay off the Firth of Forth, watching the English ships withdraw to the south. The Armada was about to head for home, taking a course around the north of Scotland and west of Ireland. On 22 August John Popham landed at Waterford. This was his first visit, but he already knew rather too much about Ireland.

6

Undertaker in Ireland

For John Popham, as for many other Elizabethan English-men, Ireland had already proved an expensive failure.

When he set foot on Irish soil he must have felt disappointment and frustration. Two years previously he had enthusiastically joined in a government project to colonize Munster. He had acquired a substantial tract of land there, and had encouraged his family to do the same. Nothing had worked out. Now he had an opportunity to see the country for himself, and a challenge—to help sort out the problems the settlement had created.

They were nothing new. The English had been settling in Ireland for centuries. Soon after the Conquest some Anglo-Norman barons had made their own way to Ireland, adopted Irish ways and become powerful overlords. As time went on, such men tended to oppose the government in Dublin, established on an English pattern with a Parliament and English laws in 1210 by King John. Within the Pale—the area of English control around the capital—English farmers and administrators made their homes. Beyond the Pale, Gaelic habits and traditions prevailed.

Rebellions by the Anglo-Irish lords frequently made an English military presence necessary, and when they were defeated their lands were sometimes taken over by the Crown. In Elizabeth's reign there had been two major rebellions, the first by Shane O'Neill in 1559; when he was murdered and his lands declared forfeit, the question arose as to what should be done with them. The Queen's Lord Deputy in Ireland, Sir Henry Sidney, father of the poet Philip Sidney, recommended in 1566 that the lands should be parceled out to enterprising English colonists.[1] It was largely a West Country enterprise, at least forty adventurers, including Sir Humphrey Gilbert, attempting to settle in the south of Ireland. Hardly surprisingly, the native people resented the invaders who treated them brutally and helped themselves to their lands. They made the colonists' lives as uncomfortable as they could, with the expected miserable conclusion.

Ireland.

After two more unsuccessful attempts in northern areas, interest in Irish colonization lapsed for ten years. Then came the second major rebellion. In Munster, the southern province, the Fitzgeralds of Desmond posed the most dangerous threat yet, for at a time of extreme national tension they made the war into a religious issue. Support by the Fitzgeralds for Catholicism led to their active engagement in war against Protestant England, and James Fitzgerald, called Fitzmaurice, even went to Italy in 1580 to obtain papal approval for a Catholic crusade against Elizabeth. To counteract the threat there were about two thousand

English soldiers in Ireland, among them George Popham,[2] chosen by the Somerset Justices to be captain of a body of two hundred men. The Justices described him to the Privy Council as "a gentleman of good parentage, forward in service and of honest behaviour"; he would be "acceptable to the Souldiers" and they doubt not that his doings would be "answerable to your lordships' expectations."[3] Although George did not get himself mentioned in any actions, his familiarity with Ireland must have contributed to the Popham family's interest in the country. The rebellion dragged on, now in the hands of the 14th Earl of Desmond, Gerald Fitzgerald, but at last the leader was captured. In 1583, his head arrived in Bristol on its way to prominent display in London. The huge and fertile Desmond estates, estimated at first to be five hundred thousand acres of the best land in Ireland, were appropriated by the Crown.[4]

The project to settle the lands with Englishmen may have owed something to Ralegh, who while on military duty there had picked out some desirable property for himself. Burghley was probably the main force behind the settlement, and Popham soon became officially involved. He was already familiar with the issues in Ireland through his legal work, having drawn up the charter for the Corporation of Dublin in 1581, for instance, and examined the rebels William Nugent and the Earl of Kildare the following year. No doubt John Popham had heard about the country from George, and perhaps his new family connection with Ralegh aroused his interest. To Burghley, Popham looked like a dependable link between the Westcountrymen who, it was intended, should settle on the Desmond estates, and the government in London. Skilled in legal affairs, hard-working, and an efficient adminstrator, he was a sensible choice for the new undertaking. Popham took on a focal coordinating role in the processes leading to the settlement of Munster.

This time the whole affair was more thoroughgoing and on a much larger scale. It was not just a private initiative, like the colonizing attempts of Ralegh in Virginia. The government was committed to organizing and promoting the whole scheme. A draft advertisement of December 1585 bore the title "A Note of the Benefit that may grow in short time to the younger Houses of Gentlemen by this course, in perpetuity, taking the greatest Portion in the Plot." It represented the attractions of being "chief lord of so great a seignory or parish" and made it seem easy to farm the land profitably, "considering the smallness of the charge which groweth, even in the first year, which is the greatest year of burden."[5] How small was the charge? The costs were estimated for gentlemen, farmers, copyholders, and cottagers. Copyholders, for instance, would need: One hind (laborer), 40s.; one maidservant, 26s 8d.; 4 qrs. wheat and rye for diet, 4 qrs. of oats for drink; weekly victuals 20d.; 5 kine; 2 yearling steers, 25s. the two; 10 ewes, at 3s 4d each. Adding in the cost of seed made the total 28l. 16s. 8d—an outlay in today's terms of something like £25,000. The undertakers would pay rent to the Queen, and bear the initial cost of transportation and stocking of the holdings; they might expect to spend £278 in the first year.[6] They would then charge a rent from their tenants. It was the first determined effort by the English to colonize anywhere involving settlers not just as landlords but as cultivators too.[7]

So the Privy Council wrote to a number of Somersetshire gentlemen:

> "Her Majesty has entered into consideration of some plot for the repeopling of such parts of Munster in Ireland as are now in her possession. The plot offers many advantages to the younger children, brethren, and kinsfolk of gentlemen of good families, and to those of inferior callings and degrees. We therefore have made choice of you to treat with such of the county of Somerset as you find able and willing to accept of and undertake the same; and have given order to John Popham, Esq., Attorney-General, to confer with you therein."[8]

A similar arrangement was promoted in Cheshire, Lancashire, and Dorset, but it must have been due to Popham's own personal influence that by far the greatest response was from Somerset, thirty-one applicants putting in for 306,000 acres.[9] Popham indeed became so personally excited by the prospects that he himself took on a substantial financial interest and encouraged several members of his family to do so too. Probably the prospect of gain was the main motivating force. John Popham was himself a second son and did not possess a large estate; it must have been very tempting to acquire one at a cheap rate, and to be seen as patriotic at the same time. No doubt he shared the view that bringing civilization to Ireland would be good for its people and for the peace of the realm. He may also have felt he was doing a good turn to Somerset men, offering them an opportunity to make a better living. Of course the undertakers were risking their own money—Elizabeth was too cautious to spend a great deal on Ireland[10]—but Popham was so confident of the investment that three sons-in-law and two cousins were carried along on the wave.

On June 17 1586 Burghley himself inscribed the undertakers'

names on a map now in The National Archives.[11] In the county of Cork nineteen seignories were allocated to "Mr. Attorney, Sir John Popham,[12] and Somersetshiremen, Sir John Stowell, Sir John Clifton, Edward Sentbarb, John Popham, Rogers, and Coles." The area around Youghall and Inchequin was given to "Sir Walter Rawley, Carew Rawley, Richard Champernown, and Chydley."[13]

The men responsible for preparing the articles were Burghley, Popham, Egerton, and Sir Valentine Browne, who was link man between the Privy Council and Dublin.[14] Egerton, the Solicitor-General, was to prepare the "books," and draw the patent; Burghley was particularly anxious that it should protect the Queen's interest as much as the undertakers', realizing that among them were several influential officers of state including the Attorney-General himself.[15] According to Francis Bacon, Popham "laboured greatly" in the Munster plantation project.[16]

Four days later, on 21 June 1586, details were set out.[17] The land was to be divided into seignories of 12,000, 8,000, 6,000, and 4,000 acres. Tenants were to hold their land rent free until Michaelmas 1590, half rent until 1593 and at the full rent of 2d. or 3d. an acre thereafter. The undertakers were to be planted together as near as possible. The heads of every family were to be English; daughters eligible to inherit their lands might not marry Irishmen. The intention was to establish a solid block of "uncontaminated" English; no Irish were to be allowed into the settlement except as laborers. It is strange that Elizabeth's government should have produced a policy of complete segregation, for although hardline Protestant policies were authoritarian and insisted on conformity, such ideas were contrary to the moderate principles of the Queen, Burghley, and Ralegh.[18]

How was the land allotted? Not all applicants were successful—those tainted with Catholicism, such as the Wingfields of Kimbolton, were not granted holdings. Presumably some of the undertakers applied for land in specific areas, using knowledge gathered from military service in Ireland, their own or that of their family and friends. The West Country ports had been shipping men and supplies there for years, so there must have been plenty of information, and misinformation, to be had. Favorites could get what they wanted by a word with the Queen—Ralegh's courtly skills won him more than three times the normal allocation as well as exclusion from the procedures governing the others. For the ordinary knights, esquires, and gentlemen of the West Country, it was mostly first come, first served.

The lands were parceled out, sight unseen, in London on the

basis of an inadequate survey. In the best of circumstances, people do not find it easy to agree about land boundaries. It is hardly surprising that before long the undertakers asked to be allowed to sort out the allotments later, when they had got to Ireland. They would "seat themselves as may serve fittest for their society and defence" rather than tying themselves to "an uncertain course here in England." A list of the undertakers at his point includes John Popham, Esq., and George Popham, Gent.[19]

The basic allotment was not entirely satisfactory, and John Popham was unhappy with his portion. It was an oblong patch about six miles by three, centered on the small town of Mallow at a crossing place of the River Blackwater, twenty-two miles north of Cork. Its ruined castle had been home to Desmond's brother, recently executed for his part in the rebellion. There is no evidence that Popham had seen the land, though his sons-in-law or cousins may well have visited the area by this time. Nevertheless he took against it. However, Thomas Norreys, the Vice-President of Munster, was much attached to the property. He wrote to Burghley, "for that I understand that Mallow (a place which I have hitherto had the keeping of) is assigned to her Majesty's Attorney General, who as I understand doth little esteem of it; I am humbly to crave that by your honour's favour I may be admitted for an associate in the county of Cork, and that I may still keep that place, which by your honour's good means I doubt not but Mr. Attorney will easily yield unto."[20]

In spite of this request, on 14 March 1587 Popham's portion was officially allotted to him. The Certificate lists his lands in the county of Cork as: "the castle, town, and lands of Mallo, and all the cantred of Moallo; and all the lands, tenements, and hereditaments in Ballinferrykerry, otherwise the Old Town; Ballingerald, otherwise Geraldstown; Ballinhogh, otherwise Loaghneston; the Old Town within the Earl's Wood; Farrenkorohenesondry, otherwise the Shopemakers' town; the Short Castle, otherwise Castle Agar; Dornigere, otherwise the Shepes Butter; the land of Corrobagg and Cloghlacas with the fishing in the river called Awmore; 12,000 acres."[21] Later Popham seems to have agreed to let Norreys have this property and himself to have applied for part of the Barony of Imokilly, south east of Cork and nearer to the coast.[22] This would have been much more accessible by sea, and much nearer Ralegh's plantation too—certainly a more desirable prospect. But that plan did not work out either.

Popham's own personal stake was only part of his involvement.

As well as being an undertaker himself, as a principal administrator of the scheme he had to sign the certificates of others. His name appears very often in these documents, along with those of three of his sons-in-law and Ralegh. A certificate signed by Popham and others was issued to Sir Christopher Hatton for lands in Co. Waterford. Popham and Ralegh signed the certificate for Andrew Reade to the property subsequently owned by the poet Edmund Spenser. On the same day certificates were issued to Hugh Worthe[23] of Somerton in Somerset, signed by Popham, Ro. Warre, Edward Rogers, Tho. Hanam; and another to Sir Walter Rawley signed by Popham, Thomas Hanam, and others.[24]

The certificates were their official authority, but men and their families had already begun to sail for a new life in Ireland. Edward Rogers and Roger Warre were among those licensed to transport £1000 "for the inhabiting, storing, and manuring" of their lands.[25] The intention was that on each 12,000-acre seignory the undertaker should settle 90 households—six freeholders with 300 acres each, six farmers (400 acres), 42 copyholders (100 acres) and 36 cottagers, (10, 25, or 50 acres).[26] Although the undertakers were easily found, it was harder for them to persuade tenants to uproot themselves from England. Nevertheless a good number did risk the uncertain prospects in a notoriously difficult land.

The Englishmen may have been issued with certificates, but what did that mean? Most of the Desmond land had been held by tenants who had legal rights to it quite independently of Desmond's treachery. They very strongly opposed the English claims and it soon became clear that the prospect of huge areas of land completely free of native Irish was an illusion. In fact the ownership of most of the land was disputed. Sorting out the claims was a job for that unusual person, a hero with a legal mind. Popham wrote on 8 April 1587 that "the action for Ireland is so discouraged, that if he does not take a journey westward he fears it will be much quailed."[27] Clearly he saw himself as the only man who could resolve the many problems. But he did not make the desired expedition, and as a result of protracted legal wranglings the Munster settlement became smaller and more vulnerable. Although originally it had been estimated that 500,000 acres were available, the final figure was 202,000.

Popham yielded the Mallow plot to Norreys, sending his own men farther west to Bantry, where his son-in-law Edward Rogers was to have settled. In that distant place they found only 4,000 acres, and those were surrounded by Irish; it was an uninviting prospect.[28] Not surprisingly, by December 1587 Popham had decided to back out. "It hath cost Her Majesty's said attorney and his said two sons-in-law, whereof he can show the particulars, above twelve hundred pounds; his humble suit therefore that where they have, at their own charge, furnished and sent over 30 horsemen that the pay for these may be answered for the time, and since there is no hope left of their placing that they may be permitted presently to call back their people to avoid their further charge."[29] By the spring of 1588 many of the first to undertake the enterprise had withdrawn, including all the Popham family except Roger Warre. George's portion went to settlers from Cheshire.

It must have been a difficult decision, though in the event a swift withdrawal was probably wise. Popham must have seen that a profitable return on his investment was a very long way off.[30] In spite of everything, some other families did manage to hold on. Grants had been issued to thirty-five undertakers, and by 1589 there were at least one thousand New English settlers in Munster and several hundred women and children as well. The Grenville estate had on it 108 men. Ralegh's much larger portion held 144 men, half of whom had their families with them. These numbers, although impressive, were much less than the full quotas.[31]

The settlers who remained continued to be subject to disputes over land claims, which could not be ignored. If the colony was to succeed, it was essential that enough land should be freely available to form a solid presence. The Queen resolved to sort things out at top level, and wrote in March 1588 that she intended to send out Chief Justice of the Common Pleas Sir Edmund Anderson with other commissioners. She proposed that they should go to Ireland in August—presumably they could not go earlier because of their obligations during the Law terms. For their better instructions "she has caused search to be made in the records here, as well in the Tower as elsewhere, upon certain points set down by the Attorney-general, tending to the strengthening of her title."[32] Dublin was similarly to be searched, and the records sent to Munster for the use of the commissioners. Popham met with Sir Valentine Browne in London to draw up their instructions.[33] He was not a member of the commission, but nevertheless attached himself to the expedition. Perhaps he wanted to see whether anything could be salvaged from what he had invested in Ireland; or it may be that some of his family were still there.

At last he was all set to see the country to which he had been so committed. Then came the Spanish Armada, and Popham had to ask Walsingham for advice as to whether the trip should continue. As we have seen, he thought it should.

So at last, more than two years after the Munster plantation had been set in train, Popham sailed to Ireland. With the commissioners he landed at Waterford, a busy port with a strong European trade, and then would have had two days of riding to get to Cork. The party may well have broken the journey at the small port of Youghal, where the mayor, Sir Walter Ralegh—he had been knighted in 1585—had a house nestling by the side of the parish church. At length they arrived at Cork, rather too late to do much, Lord Deputy Fitzwilliam complained.[34]

The proceedings eventually got under way, no doubt at the Court House. The intention was that the commission's decisions should be final. Anderson had a reputation for conducting court business swiftly and harshly,[35] and no doubt Popham's powerful, if disillusioned, presence gave the hearings a certain edge. Nevertheless he reported home: "For the business here, it hath gone very slowly on, for we were 10 days here before there was anything to effect done, sithence which many bills have been exhibited to the number of 80, but most of them of no great moment or frivolous. We hope to make an end so far forth as may be, the next week; and then to return if our bark which we have sent away with this messenger may return again so soon. The Commissioners in their proceedings with the people do use the matter in such good and temperate sort as the time requireth, hear all that is exhibited, and give such answer as in reason may pacify them."[36]

Not everyone felt the proceedings were so equable. Of the many claims heard in the sessions held at Cork in 29 August 1588, resulting in the Book of the proceedings in Munster,[37] almost all were claims by the Irish to the land which the English had seized for the Queen. Only one was successful. There were one or two claims by Englishmen: Roger Warre, for instance, "claims the barony of Imokilly, county Cork, by grant from Her Majesty, and complains that one James White has disturbed him in the following lands being parcels of Imokilly:, viz.: Kylrashe, Campane, Cronewalley, Ballyvoickwellie, Mugelly, Garry Ightragh, Killinmuckie, Bane-ni-Voyrd, and Hrandsheagh." Apart from the poetry of the names, the interesting feature of this entry is that here, as in a similar claim by Sir Warham St. Leger, no indication is given that the claim was rejected. The implication is that if an Englishman makes a claim, he wins; if an Irishman does, he loses.

That was the Irish Lord Roche's complaint to Walsingham: "howbeit myself with many other suitors of this province had great expectations of justice, with favour and expedition, at the hands of the Commissioners, whom Her Majesty for the ease of suitors hath appointed to repair hither, yet when they came we found the success of our suits to proceed and fall out quite contrary, for in all their proceedings only one petition for half a ploughland, to one of the traitors, the late archrebel, the Earl of Desmond's servant was allowed, in respect of some service . . . neither any other suitor besides, obtained one foot of land, or any redress or remedy, in anything he complained of . . . so as we are left entangled and subject to the suppressions and heavy hand of the undertakers without redress as before, and every one discontented."[38] Roche made such a fuss that he was imprisoned in Cork until the commission was over, but there is no doubt that the policy was to sweep aside objections in the interest of the undertakers and that injustices were done. There were many dissatisfied suitors, and a further commission in 1592 was needed to resolve the claims more impartially.

It is not an excuse, but no one's mind can have been on the subject. Completely dominating every thought was the Spanish Armada. The ships had been swept up the North Sea, and were forced to return to Spain by the northern route—round Scotland and down the west coast of Ireland. There fierce southwesterly gales drove the ships onto rocky shores. So John Popham, having transmitted from Wellington to London the first information about the arrival of the Armada, now also sent news of the Armada's end. On 10 September he wrote from Cork to Burghley: "My duty unto your Lordship most humbly remembered. For that it is taken to be of importance here to certify unto your Lordship and the rest of the Lords what hath happened here by the arrival of sundry of the ships of the Spanish fleet on the north west coast of this realm with all expedition, the Lord Chief Justice Anderson and others here thought it best to despatch away a servant of mine this bearer with the same in one of the barks stayed here for the Chief Justice's return into England. The advertisements are that on Thursday last and sithence that time, there arrived first a bark which wrecked at the Bay of Tralee another great ship being also now near that place. After that two great ships and one frigate at the Blasquets in the Sound there, seven other sail in the Shannon by Karryg-ni-Cowly, whereof two are taken to be a thousand tons apiece, two more of 400 tons the piece, and three small barks. At the Lupus Head four great ships and toward the Bay of Galway four great ships more. It is thought that the rest of that fleet wherein the Duke of Medina Sidonia was, which were severed by a late tempest, are also about some other parts of this land. Before they were last severed it seemeth by the Spaniards taken, there were not passing 70 sail left. The people in these parts are for the most part dangerously affected towards the Spaniards, but thanks be to God, that their power, by Her Majesty's good means, is shorter than it hath been, and that the Spaniards' forces are so much weakened as they are, whereby there is no great doubt had here of any hurt that may grow thereby, although they use all the diligence and provision they may to provide for and prevent the worst of it."[39]

Popham proved right. A few shipwrecked Spaniards could hardly provoke a sympathetic uprising, though in some parts they were executed just in case. Another contemporary account estimated that eighteen ships were lost in Ireland, 6,194 men being "drowned, killed and taken."[40]

Meanwhile the underlying tensions intrinsic to the colonial enterprise came out into the open. Popham met Hugh Cuffe, another undertaker who had twelve thousand acres in the great wood at Newtown.[41] We do not know what Popham thought of his skills in land management; he may have been one of the good landlords who had a humane attitude toward the local people, giving them employment and treating them fairly. Not all were like this. Roger Wilbraham, Solicitor-General in Dublin, was so dissatisfied with the attitude of the undertakers that in October 1588 he wrote to Burghley: "I find all things wax faint in the enterprise; undertakers seek nothing but money, and Irish lands yield nothing but meat, and sure I hope never to see any two undertakers people their seignories with English families near to the limitation in Her Majesty's articles, so difficult it is to draw honest English families to dwell in this tickle and unstable country, and so many causeless contentions happen between the undertakers, striving who shall have most, when much less were sufficient."[42]

Another critical observer was Sir William Herbert, a high-minded and fervently Protestant undertaker in Castleisland, Kerry: "Our pretence in the enterprise of plantation was to establish in these parts piety, justice, 'inhabitation,' and civility, with comfort and good example to the parts adjacent. Our drift now is, being here possessed of land, to extort, make the state of things turbulent, and live by prey and by pay."[43] One cannot help feeling that the Pophams were well out of it.[44]

John Popham had been disappointed in what Robert Cecil called "the land of Ire,"[45] but the experience does not seem to have dimmed his enthusiasm for colonization, and indeed in this he was typical. For Popham, as it had been for Humphrey Gilbert,[46] Ireland was a preparation for America. Two important lessons were there for the learning: it was essential to have good relations with the local people, and the leaders had to be motivated by something other than greed. Whether that knowledge was carried into the Popham colony in Maine remains to be seen. For John Popham there were to be sixteen years of action-filled public and private life before he could turn again to the idea of planting. Now, in 1589, a new vista was opening out for him: it involved a different kind of settling, not in Ireland but in Wiltshire.

7

Lord of Littlecote

IN 1589 JOHN POPHAM ACQUIRED LITTLECOTE.

Behind this simple statement lies a story of passion, murder, and confusion.

> "Sir . . . Dayrell, of Littlecote, in co. Wilts, having gott his ladie's waiting woman with child, when her travell came, sent a servant with a horse for a midwife, whom he was to bring hood-winked. She was brought, and layd the woman, but as soon as the child was borne, she sawe the knight take the child and murther it, and burnt it in the fire in the chamber. She having donne her businesse was extraordinarily rewarded for her paines and sent blinfold away. This horrid action did much run in her mind, and she had a desire to discover it, but knew not where 'twas. She considerd with herselfe the time that she was riding, and how many miles might be rode at that rate in that time, and that it must be some great person's house, for the roome was 12 foot high; and she could knowe the chamber if she sawe it. She went to a Justice of Peace, and search was made. The very chamber found. The knight was brought to his tryall; and to be short, this judge [Popham] had this noble howse, parke, and mannor, and (I thinke) more, for a bribe to save his life. *Note.*—Sir John Popham gave sentence according to lawe; but being a great person, and a favourite, he procured a *noli prosequi.*"[1]

That is the account of John Aubrey, who was born in 1625, over forty years after the events he describes. It is not accurate, and though it is impossible now to establish the truth of the affair beyond all doubt, we will try to clarify it a little.

Littlecote was a magnificent estate, the medieval house beautifully placed in 6,500 acres of farmland and water meadow on the banks of the Kennet, between Hungerford and Ramsbury in Wiltshire.[2] The estate had come into the Darrell family in about 1415, and it was here that Henry VIII courted Jane Seymour, a Darrell relation. In 1549 Littlecote should have passed to the heir, a boy of ten named William. However, his father had bequeathed much of the property to his mistress, and it was not until William was twenty-one that he regained his proper inheritance of Littlecote. The family of Darrell's mother, the Essexes of Lambourn, were offended by the outcome, so Darrell inherited not only a house but a whole pack of enemies as well.

They were not the only people hostile to him, for he had two major faults of character. He lived beyond his means, and he was extremely litigious. William Darrell managed his large estate quite successfully and farmed scientifically, but his tendency to go to law with almost all his neighbors made him hated by them, and his owing money both to them and to tradesmen and usurers caused further bad feeling.[3] As far as we know he had no legal training and in the sea of suits that he was involved in all his life he needed a life raft. There had for some years been a distant connection between the Darrells and the Pophams,[4] and perhaps that was why he went to John Popham for legal advice. Darrell does not seem to have been the sort of man for whom John Popham would have had any natural sympathy. A "proud, reserved, and scrupulous man," as Hall describes him, he took little part in public service, sitting for only one session of Parliament. Nevertheless Popham assisted him, providing expertise and supporting him in his troubles. Darrell made himself very knowledgeable about the law of real property, and "he ordinarily employed several first-rate counsel, besides some admirable attorneys, notaries, and agents who were with good reason devoted to his interests." But Popham was "the master-mind that directed and revised everything. The draft of a bill, interrogatories, or answer, carefully prepared by the joint wisdom of Darrell and his ordinary advisers, was another document when returned from Popham's perusal."[5]

Darrell aroused yet more hostility by having a scandalous love affair with the wife of a neighbor. Anne, the second wife of Sir Walter Hungerford of Farleigh, was a highly cultivated woman who bore her husband four children, but her love for William Darrell was intense, sincere, and lasting. In 1570 Sir Walter charged his wife with attempting to poison him, and with committing adultery with Darrell between 1560 and 1568.

The Abstract of Sir Walter Hungerford's case for a divorce includes surprisingly intimate details. It was stated that "William Darrell was wont to enter the bed chamber of Dame Anne in the absence of Sir Walter Hungerford and lie down with her 'solus cum sola familiariter jocando, ridendo, osculando, palpando, et amplectando' [alone together, familiarly talking, laughing, kissing, touching and embracing]." On one occasion Darrell had broken a bone, which was set in plaster; "the said plaster was found in Dame Anne's bed 'inter litheamina' [between the sheets]."[6] Domestic spies had been employed, and they produced juicy evidence too: "John Golif . . . wente to my ladies chambre dore and there harkening hard Mr Darrell and my Lady in bedd together. Wheruppon he called Alice Check, in the nurcery chamber going to bedd, who came forth unto him and they two went togetheres to my Ladies chamber and secretlie conveyed themselves into the chamber behind the portal and the hangings of the chamber when they hard and sawe the saide Darrell and Lady in bedd together"; they were able to see the lovers, there being "a fier in the chamber the mone shining bright and the windowes open."[7]

In what appears to be a complete miscarriage of justice, Anne was acquitted and Hungerford committed to prison. It might be supposed that the puritanically inclined Popham would have been unwilling to support an adulterer like Darrell. Why did he do so? He was an intensely loyal and practical man; his kinsman and friend needed legal help, so Popham continued to give it. No doubt he was also well paid, or had at least the prospect of considerable benefit in due course. Indeed, this was the issue in the horrifying incident that has given William Darrell and John Popham their greatest notoriety.

For at about this time a hideous crime was perpetrated in Wiltshire. A midwife named Mother Barnes was there, and twelve years later, in 1578 or so, she told everything she remembered:

"there came unto her house at Shefforde, two men in maner leeke servinge men in blacke fryse cotes, rydinge upon very good geldinges or horses wch declared unto her that theyre mystres (as they then called her) nameing Mrs Knevett, wch is nowe the wyfe of Sr Henry Knevett, Knighte of Wiltesh, had sente by them comendacions unto her prayenge her of all loves to come unto her forthwt accordinge to her promise; shee beinge as they said, at that time neare her tyme of traveyle of childe whoe presently prepared her selfe redy to ryde, and beinge somwhat late in the eveninge, shee departed from her said house in the company of the two before recited persons, whoe rode wth her the most parte of alle that nighte. And towardes daye, they brought her unto a fayre house and alighted her neere a doore of the said house at the wch doore one of those that broughte her made some little noyse, eyther by knockinge or rynginge of some belle, wheruppon there came to the said doore a tall slender gentleman, having uppon hym a longe goune of blacke velvett, and bringinge a lighte wth him, whoe so soone as shee was entred into the said doore, made faste

the same, and shutt out those that broughte her, and presently
broughte her upp a stayres into a fayre and a large greate chambre,
beinge hanged all about wth arras in the wch chambre there was a
chymney, and therein was a great fyre and from thence through the
said chambre shee was conveyed unto an other chambre [of] leeke
proporcion, and hanged in leeke sorte as the fyrste was, in the wch
chambre was also a chymney and a great fyre, and passinge through
the said seconde chambre, shee was broughte into a thyrde chambre,
hanged also rychlye wth arras, in the wich chambre there was a bed
rychlye and gorgeouslye furnished the curteynes of the said bed
beinge alle close drawen about the said bed.

"And so soone as shee was entered in at the doore of the laste re-
sited chambre, the said partye in the longe velvet goune ronned
[whispered] softly in her eare sayinge; loe, in yonder bed lyethe the
gentle woman that you are sente for to come unto, go unto her and
see that yow doe youre uttermost endevoyre towardes her, and yf
shee be safely delivered, you shall not fayle of great rewarde, but if
shee myscarry in her traveyle, yow shall dye. Wheruppon, as one
amased, she departed from the said gentleman to the beddes side,
fyndinge there a gentelwoman in traveyle, lyenge in grate estate, as
by the furniture uppon her and aboute her it dyd appeare, this gentlewoman's face beinge covered eyther wth a viser or a cell, but wth
wch I doe not remembre.

"And shortly after her cominge she was delivered of a man childe,
whoe for lacke of other clothes was fayne to be wrayped in the myd-
wyfes apron, and so was carried by the said midwyfe into one of the
two fyrste chambres that shee passed throughe at the first wth the
gentleman, fynding the said gentleman there at her coming thither,
whoe demaunded of her whether the partye that shee came from was
delivered of a childe or no, whoe aunswered that shee was safely delivered of a man childe wch shee there presently shewed him, re-
quiringe him that some provision of clothes might be had to wrapp it
wth alle, who incontinently broughte her to the fyre syde, into the
wch fyre he commaunded her to caste the childe, whereuppon shee
kneeled doune unto him, desyringe him that he would not seek to destroy it, but rather geve it unto her, promisinge him to keep it as her
owne, and to be sworne never to disclose it, the wch thinge the gentleman would not yelde unto, but forthwth the childe was caste into
the fyre, but whether by the mydwyfe her selfe, or by him, or by them
both I doe not perfectly remembre.

"And so soon as this horrible facte was done, shee was commaunded to goe backe agayne to the gentlewoman, where shee remayned
all that day and by nighte was broughte backe agayne by those two
men that broughte her thither, whoe sett her some myles distante
from her house, but whether two myles or more I doe not remembre.
And I demaundinge of her wch way shee wente in rydinge thither,
shee aunswered that as shee supposed shee wente faste by Duning-

ton Parke, leavinge the said parke on her righte hande, and demaundinge of her by what houses shee traveyled by, shee aunswered
that shee traveyled by dyuers houses wch shee knewe not, and demaundinge ouner [over] or throughe what waters shee passed, shee
aunswered shee passed over a greate and a longe bridge wch as shee
truly supposed was a bridge over the Thames, as by the water wch
passed through the said bridge beinge very greate shee dyd imagine."[8]

Now there seems little doubt that Mother Barnes had been involved in a child murder about twelve years before these words
were spoken. But the midwife made no reference whatever to Littlecote or Darrell. Nevertheless Darrell's enemies worked on the
matter with great zeal. It was a means by which they could ruin
him, and they did. The calumny prevailed, so that John Aubrey,
the first to print the story in 1670, was in no doubt at all about
who was responsible. He is not reliable, however. Darrell was not
a knight; he never married, so he had no lady. Popham was not
in a position to give sentence, for he was Attorney-General, not a
judge on the Wiltshire circuit.[9] Of course it could be that Popham's influence prevented the case ever coming to court. However, the same could be said with equal justification of at least
two other great statesmen, Sir Thomas Bromley and Sir Francis
Walsingham, both very powerful officers of state and also Darrell's allies.

It is certainly true that Popham was Darrell's legal mainstay,
and it is worth illustrating their relationship more fully. The two
men were very different in character, Darrell being "fidgety,
querulous, and self-willed to the last degree, faults almost re-
deemed, however, by the gentle constancy and pathetic melancholy of all his expressions touching himself and his friends.
Popham was the opposite of this. He was confident and peremptory, but ever courteous in tone towards his unfortunate client."[10]
These characteristics are fully seen in Darrell's correspondence
with Popham relating to the dispute over the manor of Axford, a
case considered "one of the most weighty causes of those times"
and lasting from 1560 to 1589.[11]

Darrell liked to fell trees.[12] The ownership of the Axford estate
was disputed between Darrell and the Essex family. Darrell was
confident that he was the life tenant, and so considered he had a
right to the wood on the Axford grounds. Without otherwise disturbing the Essexes' tenant, Mr Stukely, he began to fell timber
on the manor. On 3 March 1583 Popham wrote from Cloford to
Darrell at Littlecote: "Wheras the matter between Mr. Stukeley

& you is by the consent of bothe referred to Order, I pray you to forbeare to cutt downe any more woode or trees in Axford during suche tyme as the matter dependeth in comprymys. I was moved herein by Mr. Stewkeley after your departure from me and as the case standeth, I think hit verie resonable you yeld unto yt. I mene if God please to be at Salisburie the wekes daie at night before Easterdaie; where for divers respectes I would gladlie speake wth you."[13]

Darrell replied that he had received Popham's letter "by the handes of a Shepherde cominge from the downes by some distaunce from me the vjth [6th] day after." He understood, he wrote, that Popham thought it reasonable Darrell should yield to the request not to cut down more timber: "Wherat I have and do marvell me much, and am in the same sorely perplexed, sithence I was not easily drawen to have speach in it, no not althoughe I love you and doo reste upon you before any other. . . . But what be men, and what minds be in them in thes dayes. Wher is become the integrete, clearnes of consciens and vertu that sometyme have bin. I have learned one rule in books from the auncyent fathers, and have found it in experience among'st men; that that day that a man would have another's landes or his goodes, that day he would have his life also if he could. I pray you pray for me, for I am at this present in sory case. . . . Amyddest the wilfullnes of other men's speaches I have bynn alwayes beholding to you. I am indebted to you, and as I do acknowledge it so am ready to acquitt my selfe in the other."[14]

Popham replied immediately: "Mr. Darrell, wheras you wryte to me that (as I tak hyt) you marveled I shold be off opinion hyt were convenyent you shold forbeare the fellyng of woodes dependynge the comprymyse; trewly I was and am of that opynyon and so wold you be also yf the case were tried that the possessyon were off the othersyd. And the rather I am so induced, for that yf hys counsell hadd well loked unto hyt, I thynke they myght have restreyned you therof by the lawe. And wheras I gather by yor letter you wryte that you dydd not thus conceave of me, when you comytted hit unto me I assure you that neyther yor selff nor any man else shall justly charg me wth any abuse of any thyng comytted to me . . . I never yet deserted any and I wyl not now begyn wth you. I thinke you have hadd better proff [of] me. And so wth my herty comendacyons do comytt you to God. At Sarum, the xxviijth of marche 1583."[15]

Very soon after these letters were written Darrell saw that his financial and legal problems were becoming overwhelming. He would have to mortgage his estates in exchange for ready cash, protection from his enemies, and friendly support. William Darrell had no heir, and the legitimacy of the next in line was in doubt. He and John Popham may have been close, but it was not to Popham that Darrell turned first when he needed help. Littlecote was offered in 1583 to his kinsman Sir Thomas Bromley, the Lord Chancellor,[16] and his son Harry.[17] To them he would assure, on his own death, a manor "standing in as good a sort in every condition" as any in the land, the clear rental of which alone amounted to £300 by the year of the money at the time— perhaps £300,000 p.a. now. The second estate Darrell wished to trade was rather smaller, producing rents of £51—only three thousand acres of land, eight hundred acres of meadow, two thousand acres of pasture, and two thousand acres of wood, and the offer was made to Sir Francis Walsingham.

Bromley never owned Littlecote, for he died before he could benefit from the arrangement. His son did not acquire the estate either. Darrell managed to hang on for another four years, until in 1587 his affairs were again at breaking point. Through the machinations of his enemies he was thrown into gaol and had to promise a huge bribe in order to obtain his release. There were threats: "strange courses" were intended against him, and he was told to "look to it." He answered impatiently, "Is there nothing always but strange courses in hand?"[18] Then he abandoned his life as a country squire, and fled to the Court for protection. Littlecote was made over to Popham, to be his on Darrell's death.

Popham and other influential lawyers exercised themselves vigorously on his behalf. Darrell had at least a dozen lawsuits on hand, but they "pushed his matters through, and curbed his impatient rashness with calm and often stern advice." The Armada threatened, and Walsingham managed to enthuse Darrell, "his very loving friend"[19] in the national cause, gaining the Queen's appproval for his employment in Walsingham's own military obligations. So Darrell lived during his last London season near Ludgate Hill in some comfort. Existing documents record his expenses for travel by boat, and show that he ate extremely well, smoked heavily, and employed at least half a dozen liveried servants.[20]

Darrell returned to Littlecote on a visit in July 1589, sickened, and died on 1 October. The legend is that his end came in a riding incident on the estate, at a place known as "Darrell's Leap." He was apparently riding hell for leather in true character when his horse failed a jump and he fell, breaking his neck; hence the other name for this place, Darrell's Style.[21] Some say that his horse shied at the apparition of the murdered child, and that Darrell's own ghost still walks the spot.[22]

The child murder scandal has given "Wild" or "Black" Darrell a permanent place in literature. In his long poem "Rokeby" Sir Walter Scott includes a brief ballad combining the Littlecote legend with details from a story of strikingly similar horrors in Edinburgh. After the event, according to Scott,

> Wild Darrell is an alter'd man,
> The village crones can tell;
> He looks pale as clay, and strives to pray,
> If he hears the convent bell.
>
> If prince or peer cross Darrell's way,
> He'll beard him in his pride—
> If he meet a friar of orders grey,
> He droops and turns aside.[23]

Littlecote also has a poignant ghost. Whoever the mother of the murdered child was, she is supposed to haunt the bedroom and the landing at Littlecote House beyond where the murder was committed. Accounts I have heard consider that the room has a chill sense of evil rather than an identifiable apparition.[24] Darrell himself is said to haunt Ramsbury, two miles from Littlecote. If at midnight you go to the door on the north side of the thirteenth-century Church of the Holy Cross and count the iron nails which stud it (there are said to be one hundred), the door will open and "Wild" William Darrell of Littlecote Manor will emerge from it.[25] It is said too that on surrendering Littlecote, Darrell laid a curse on John Popham, that his family should perish in the male line—and that has occurred.[26]

No one will ever know who the lady was, but Darrell is stuck with the murder, although he was never charged with it, let alone found guilty. Popham's name is also tarnished by Aubrey's gossip, although he seems to have acquired Littlecote as a proper repayment for many years of legal assistance. It looks as though Darrell's enemies seized on the story, worked the suspicion on to him, and later involved Popham too because he was Darrell's friend and adviser.

On Darrell's death, Popham was characteristically quick to act. He had an agent in Wiltshire who seized Darrell's papers and sent them to London to substantiate his claim to the estate. So John Popham, Her Majesty's Attorney-General, became master of the Littlecote estate, consisting of 136 messuages, 110 tofts, 46 cottages, 10 gardens, 100 orchards, 6500 acres of land, 2320 acres of meadow, 500 acres of pasture, and 1550 acres of wood and underwood.[27] He took up residence in the medieval manor house that the Darrells had begun to expand. It is another sign of Popham's extraordinary energy that he found time to remodel the house on an even grander scale, though he was also at this time building the huge manor house at Wellington. No doubt he saw himself as providing for his children and grandchildren, and Littlecote was obviously a house at which one could entertain even the very greatest visitors.

William Darrell and his father had probably extended the house, constructing the handsome Long Gallery on the north front; its elaborate frieze incorporates the Darrell lion rampant. But it was Popham who "finally brought order to it and realised the quadrangular plan."[28] Popham added the symmetrical south front—his coat of arms is over the South Porch—giving "a semblance of unity to the straggling medieval complex behind it."[29] He gave the house the Great Hall, entrance, and parlors it had been lacking for sixty years. His Great Hall, with its simplified fan-vaulting, twin-arched screen, English and Flemish stained glass, and grey and white marble floor, is "one of the most complete examples of its kind in the country." The parts attributed to Popham are built entirely in two-inch brick, now beautifully mellowed. The house is a striking illustration of Popham's character, well founded and impressive without any excessive grandeur or sophistication.

A curious note by Aubrey states that "Lord Chief Justice Popham first brought in (i.e. revived) brick building in London (scil. after Lincolne's Inne and St James's)."[30] This has never been adequately explained. Popham's only contribution to London housing was the set of chambers he built at the Middle Temple in 1582, but "Bricke Buyldings" had been erected at the Temple before 1568.[31] Aubrey may have thought that the success of the alterations to Littlecote, the only major brick mansion in Wiltshire, promoted a fashionable increase in brick buildings, but there is no evidence that this occurred. Another interpretation is that Popham's contribution to the legislation of the time was designed to reduce shanty dwellings and promote substantial housing in London.

Littlecote proved a lasting benefit to Popham's descendants, remaining in the family until 1929. In 1996 the house was bought by Warner Holidays and sensitively converted into a hotel. The

Elizabethan rooms remain open to the public, and the visitor can enjoy the Long Gallery and Hall, and risk the Haunted Landing with its notorious Fireplace. In one of the bedrooms may be seen the arms of Queen Elizabeth, added in anticipation of her proposed visit to the house in 1601.

But that is another story. In the meantime Popham seems to have divided such leisure as he enjoyed between Littlecote and Wellington. The law terms were spent in London, to which we now return.

8

Lord Chief Justice

At this point, in 1590, we can think of John Popham as having achieved a kind of tranquility. He was fifty-eight or so; his daughters were all married and the production of grandchildren was proceeding apace. Francis was at the Middle Temple. Popham was building a very substantial house in Somerset and had acquired a splendid estate in Wiltshire; Ireland was behind him, he was established in his work, and all seemed calm.

There must have been one particular source of interest at this time: finding a suitable wife for Francis, who was now nineteen. Popham probably already knew Thomas Sutton; his stepdaughter would be an excellent match. She was Anne Dudley, fifteen-year-old daughter of the brewer John Dudley of Stoke Newington, Middlesex, and related to the Earl of Leicester. Anne's father had been a great favorite of the Queen; on paying him a visit, her Majesty took "a jewel of great value" from her hair and gave it to his daughter, afterward Lady Popham.[1] John Dudley died in 1580, and her mother remarried two years later. Elizabeth Dudley's new husband, Thomas Sutton, was a very wealthy man, having made extremely profitable use of his appointment in 1569–70 as Master and Surveyor of the Ordnance in the northern parts of England. During his time there Sutton noted the abundance of coal in Durham, and secured leases of lands from the bishop and the crown. These proved the foundation of an immense fortune, and Sutton became known as one of the richest Englishmen of the day. It is said that he was the model for Volpone in Jonson's play of 1607. Popham must have been delighted by the connection. On the marriage in 1590 Popham settled his old home, Old Court House at Wellington, on Francis.[2]

The excitements of the wedding over, there came sadness in the following year with Popham's first loss. His daughter Jane, married to Sir Thomas Horner, died in 1591, the year in which Sir Richard Grenville came to his famous end on the deck of the valiant *Revenge*.

The threat from Spain continued. After the Armada the political atmosphere changed, but Popham's last three years as Attorney-General were as busy as ever. National security continued to be high on the agenda. In a letter of 10 March 1590 to Mr Attorney and Mr Solicitor-General, the Privy Council at Greenwich remarked "how necessary yt was that a watche shud be kept by th'inhabitauntes of the seaven hundrethes uppon the sea coaste at a place called Dengeness."[3] It was a sound watch upon the coast that had caught the unhappy Philip Howard, First Earl of Arundel of the Howard family, in the spring of 1585. Heir to two of the greatest families in England, "a very tall man, somewhat swarth-coloured," gifted with extraordinary power of memory and noted for his quickness of wit, Arundel had led a dissipated life at Cambridge.[4] Turning gradually through the influence of his wife to Catholicism, he came under suspicion and in due course attempted to flee from England. In April 1585 he embarked on a ship at Littlehampton in Sussex, but his movements were watched, and no sooner was his ship in the Channel than it was brought back. Arundel was committed to the Tower, where he devoted himself to religious studies. Eventually he was accused of organizing a twenty-four-hour pray-in for the success of the Spanish Armada, and tried for high treason, Popham being responsible for providing evidence against him.[5] Arundel was condemned to death in April 1592, but the sentence was not immediately carried out. Taken ill after dinner in August 1595, Arundel begged to be allowed to see his wife and children before he died. He was told that if he would once go to church he would be liberated and restored to his estates. He refused, and died without having seen his family.

Not only Catholics suffered at the hands of the law at this time. It may be true that the threat from the puritans too receded after the Armada, but John Whitgift, Archbishop of Canterbury, and Richard Bancroft, later to become his successor, campaigned relentlessly against them nevertheless. Dissident clergymen were summoned to the Ecclesiastical Commission, which could bypass the normal processes of trial but nevertheless had behind it the whole authority of the state. It followed, in fact, the example of the Romish Inquisition.[6] Suspects and witnesses were required to give an oath, the oath *ex-officio* as it was known, which obliged them to answer all questions. If they gave it, they became subject to punishment without right of appeal; if they refused, they were sent to the court of Star Chamber for punishment. There was no open trial or jury.

Not surprisingly, some Presbyterian leaders refused to take the *ex-officio* oath, among them Whitgift's old enemy Thomas Cartwright, whom he had expelled from his fellowship at Trinity College, Cambridge twenty years previously. In May 1591 Cartwright was brought before the Ecclesiastical Commissioners, the Bishop of London, the Attorney-General, and four doctors. The Bishop began in a long speech by demanding that Cartwright should take the oath. "Mr Cartwright opening his mouth to speak, Mr Attorney took the speech from him and also showed at length how dangerous a thing it was that men should upon the conceits of their own heads and yet under colour of conscience refuse the things that had been received for laws of a long time. This oath that was tendered was according to the laws of the land, which he commended above the laws of all other lands, yet because they were the laws of men, they carried always some stain of imperfection." In spite of such reasonableness, Mr Cartwright still refused to take the oath. He was sent to prison, where he stayed until 1592 when Popham decided to take no further action in the matter since no overt breach of the law could be proved against the objectors.[7]

It was never a question of two clearly defined groups, Catholics and puritans, subverting uniform adherence to the Church of England, but there were some extreme eccentrics, one of whom caused a riot in London in July 1591. William Hacket had been a servingman in several Northamptonshire households before becoming a maltster. Riotous living gave him the reputation of an atheist, and he is supposed to have quarreled with a schoolmaster in an alehouse in Oundle, bitten off his nose, and eaten it. Suddenly he abandoned his dissolute courses and gave out that he was "converted to religion and knowledge of the trueth."[8] After attempting to prepare the way for the Messiah in York, Leicester, and Northamptonshire, and being well whipped for it, Hacket went to London where, supported by a small group of hangers-on, he said that he had been moved by God to warn the Queen to reform herself, her family, commonwealth, and church. Hacket and his friends paraded to Cheapside, shouting out that Hacket was Christ, and warned the people to repent. Crowds collected, and the scene became so tumultuous that the fanatics had to seek refuge in the Mermaid tavern.

William Hacket and his friends were arrested. Popham and Egerton provided the interrogatories that led to his being adjudged a "most sedytios and pernytyos person," and sent to Bridewell. At his trial in July 1591 both lawyers spoke at length.

Hacket seems to have been quite mad by this time, but he was nevertheless condemned to death. The Privy Council instructed Popham and Egerton "that Hacquet . . . be exequted on Wednesday next . . . in Cheapsyde . . . betwixt x and xj of the clock when the market time is, in soch good sort as to the quallety and heynousness of th'offence apperteineth, wherin praieng you there may be no defalt, we bid you hartely well to fare."[9] The sentence was carried out, Hacket "rayling and cursing" the Queen and uttering execrable blasphemy to the last.[10] Writing *A Briefe View of the State of the Church of England,* published in 1653, Sir John Harington remembered Popham's trenchant views on such people as Hacket; he had called them "seditious sectaries" and "would not have them call'd Puritanes."[11]

It is hard to believe, but in 1592 the Privy Council was concerned that the laws for dealing with recusancy, which laid down stated penalties, did not always have the teeth to deal adequately with offenders. Popham was consulted and agreed, reluctantly, that the law did indeed limit the pressure that could be applied. But there were ways round the problem; he suggested a stratagem by which a few recusants might be hanged "and by ye ensample executed towardes some, others happelie may reforme them selves."[12] The approach is typical of Popham, but the device was not practicable because the Queen was known to dislike it.

Although the persecution of religious nonconformists continued, the main impression given by the documents at this period is that other domestic matters were the core of the Attorney-General's work. An unusual controversy arose, for instance, between St. John's College, Oxford and the officers of the Queen's Household. By one Act of Parliament purveyors for Her Majesty were allowed to find provisions for her, and pay below market prices, anywhere in the land. Another Act designed to protect the supplies of the universities had given St John's the right to exclude the Queen's purveyors from their lands. Popham and others held for the College. In a further clarification, the lawyers stated that "for the better furnishing of the marketts of Oxon and Cambridg with victualls for the relief of the schollers there," no purveyors should be allowed within five miles of the cities. They even specified that in their opinion a mile "ought to be accompted according to the measure of eight furlongs to a myle, forty luggs or pole to a furlong, and every lugg or pole to containe sixtine foote *dimidium* [a half], the measure to be taken *circuita ex recta linea* [round from a straight line]";[13] presumably that made it perfectly clear.

Popham was often consulted on matters of trade, and given a remarkable degree of personal responsibility in sorting out disputes. The Privy Council wrote to him, for instance, about restrictions on the leather business, involving curriers who were "restrained to sel leather redie dressed by them" and "the abuse of the shomakers, to the great prejudyce of the comon welth. We have thought good to let you understand that we can not but like wel of your proceedings therein." Popham had taken an "orderlie course" in the examination of the allegations on both sides "by calling unto you sundrie Aldermen of the best sort in the presence of the shomakers and others interested therein, and therfore we knowe noe cause whie you maie not proceed as you shall thincke best."[14] A little later he was asked to ensure no action was taken against immigrant craftsmen in Kent. These refugees from religious intolerance—asylum seekers—had settled in Canterbury and used the "traide of making baies [baize] and other stuffes, whereby the realme dothe reap great benefitt and comoditie." Local people resented their presence; they were "dalie troubled and molested with informers" and Popham was asked to stay such information against them.[15]

Criminal activity continued unabated. The Attorney-General was asked by the Council to examine "Pepper and Ellys, two lewde persons," who had "by counterfaicting our handes to certaine warrauntes gone up and downe the countrie in the Northe partes abusinge and vexing of her Majesty's subjectes in the moste dysorderlie maner." These "badd fellowes" had been examined by the Archbishop of York; if Popham and Egerton too found them culpable, they should consider the fittest course "for the due and exemplar punyshment of those offendors, as for the terryfyinge of others that goe about or shall put in use soche or the lyke lewde and unlawfull practizes."[16] The Attorney-General also had to act in a cause by the Earl of Essex against Henry Skidmore, gentleman, "concerning an outrage and riott committed at Rosse in the county of Hereford uppon Anthonie Pembridg of the Inner Temple, gentleman, late Undersheriffe of the said county."[17]

Local government was evidently a dangerous business. It is small wonder that John Harington, the Queen's gossipy godson, did not relish becoming Sheriff of Somerset. "I will not gibe at the judge, as my neighbour did, when he was appointede to that charge, and with more wit than good heed, told the judge, who complained of stonie roades, and fearede muche the dangers of our western travellinge; 'In good soothe, Sir, it is but faire playe, that you, who so ofte make others feare for theire neckes, shoud in some sorte beginne to thinke of savinge your owne.' Herewith Judge Minos was not well pleasede, but saide, 'Goode maister Sherife, leave alone my necke, and looke to youre owne heeles, for you may one daye be laide by them.' Nor did his anger here reste, for on very slighte offence in cowrte, he fined my wittie neighboure five poundes: felix quem faciunt aliena pericula cautum [*happy is he who learns caution from the misfortunes of others*]—so shall I (when in such companie) make no accounte of the countie wayes, but looke well to my owne."[18] How like Popham this judge sounds.

London had its dangers too. Popham prosecuted Arnold Cosby on 25 January 1591 for the murder of Lord Burke, who had allegedly pulled his nose the previous night. A duel had been arranged at Wandsworth, but Cosby "most cowardly" wounded Burke while he was unbuckling his spurs before the fight had begun.[19] He had to examine another murder, "of the wyfe of Richard Webb, whoe had ben wickdly made awaie by Lodovicke Grevile and by one Wickham"—the names alone are enough to convict them.[20] Prison management was troublesome then as now: William Devies, "Keeper of the goale" [*sic*] of Newgate, was charged by one Gunston with "many foule matters"; at the same time Devies was bringing "divers accions of slaunder" against Gunston; both actions were to be heard by Popham.[21] At the Tower there was a controversy between Michael Blunt, Lieutenant, and Mr Thomas Shelton, gentleman Porter there, concerning "certaine thinges which either of them pretendes to be incident to their offices, which they booth clayme in right of her Majestie." Since "discord is not fit to be contineud there (especially betwen them two)," Popham and his colleagues were asked to examine the case "that some good order myght be taken therin agreable to equity."[22]

Fair treatment was by no means the norm. In December 1590 the Privy Council expressed concern to the Attorney-General and others about the administration of justice: "We understand by the pitifull complaint of Jone Hussie, widow, that her late husbande, John Hussey, was wilfully and cruellie murdred by one Edward Phillippes, a citizen of London, about Shrovetyd last uppon certein greivous woundes, whereof he languished untill Easter following and then died, to the utter undoing of her self and of her vij [7] fatherles children, and that by reason of the welth and coutenance of the offendour no triall of the fact according to justice could hitherto be had with expedicion."[23]

All was indeed not well, for four days earlier the law's notorious delays had caused Popham to receive a sharp letter from the Privy Council at Richmond. Christopher Whitson had complained that he had been restrained in the Fleet prison "without any lawfull cause," the only reason being Popham's "often and earnest mocions against him." Popham was therefore required "presently to certefy their Lordships what can be alleaged against him, and what can be aunswered to his severall objections and demaunds, and whether his offence is or hath been so hainous and notorious that imprisonment for two yeres space will not suffice for the punishment of the same." In a postscript the Lords added: "This peticion alleageth unto us that there hath been no proofe made of the matters wherewith he is charged, and therefore his imprisonment seemeth to us so much the more greivous. You shall therefore certefy us of your proofes and of your aunswere to the severall pointes of his peticion."[24] The Privy Council would have been quite used to the idea that a man could be held in the Fleet for a while. At that time imprisonment was not in itself considered a punishment. It was only a stage on the way to a trial that would result in acquittal, or a fine, or a physical punishment.[25] Nevertheless, and however lax the regime at the Fleet, it sounds as though a serious injustice had been done.

There may have been lapses in Popham's performance, but reservations of this kind should not blind us to the fact that he remained much respected by his colleagues. On 8 May 1592 the Lord Chief Justice, Sir Christopher Wray, died. Burghley invited John Popham to succeed him in the office, and his careful reply has been preserved:

I do humbly acknowledge my selff very muche Bownden to your Lordship for the favorable regard you have of my ease now that my years are growen to be suche, as I shall not be so well able to endure the Toyle of the place I serve in as I have ben in respect whereof I shold wryte otherwyse to your Lordship then the trewth, yf I shold not advertyse your Lordship that I were very wyllyng to be in a place of more ease thoughe Inferyor to the place your Lordship now wryteth off and trewly my Lord I am the more bownden unto your Lordship herein in that it hath pleased you to vouchsaff me this favour, without any mocyon from my selff, and as both her majestie in her own wisdom and your Lordship in the experience you have hadd off me more than others could best dyserne of my worth any way to have supplyed the place your Lordship hadd speche with me off in the way towards Osterley;[26] and therefor move no excuse off myne owne so for this yor Lordship now wrytes to me off (beying now agreable to my profession, and the corse of lyff I have taken) I humbly submytt my selff to her majestie's good pleasure and your Lordship's recommendacyon therof, as you shall have occasyon and therupon to dyspose of me therin as it shall please yow and yet nevertheless I have thys respect therin that I would be very loth to become an opposyt to any, who in respect of their place or desertyngs myght herein account themselves any wayes injured or prevented of their expectatyons by me who in Respect of my owne particular would not wyllyngly geve occasyon of offense or dyscontentment to any and so submyttyng this cause and my selff to your Lordship's grave consydracyon I humbly take my leave of your Lordship at my house at ffreerne the 14 May 1592[27]

This is the first letter we have that was written from Friars, or Friern House. Although it has been said that "Friern Barnet has no history," this residence, about seven miles north of London, was an old preceptory, and Popham probably rented it.[28] The house stood on Friern Park, in what is now North Finchley, London N12. In a time of plague—fifteen thousand people died from the disease in London in 1592–93—it was a very wise health precaution to live in the country. Popham would still have been near his colleagues, Sir John Fortescue, for instance, having a house at Hendon.

On 25 May 1592 Popham became Lord Chief Justice of England.[29] The position carried a knighthood, and the Queen performed the ceremony at Greenwich. Mr Thomas Egerton became Attorney-General, and Sir Edward Coke Solicitor-General. Egerton was universally respected, and Popham evidently had much personal admiration for him. Some years later it was noticed by the diarist John Manningham that a portrait of Egerton hung in Popham's chambers at Serjeants' Inn. On it were the words:

In vita gravitas, vultu constantia, fronte
Consilium, os purum, mens pia, munda manus.[30]
[In life, gravity; in expression, constancy; in brow, wisdom;
a pure mouth, a holy mind, a clean hand.]

Coke was at this stage not an appealing character, but he was later to achieve real distinction as defender of the subject's rights. The Chief Justice of the Common Pleas was Sir Edmund Anderson, and the Keeper of the Great Seal Sir John Puckering, a Yorkshireman who had worked with Popham in the prosecutions of the Queen of Scots and Arundel.

Hitherto at treason trials Popham's role had been to prosecute on behalf of the Crown. Now, as Lord Chief Justice of England, his duty was to preside and give judgment. The promotion did not endear him to the Jesuits. In October, when he must have been still flushed with success, malice gave tongue and rumor spread. Henry Garnet, whom Popham had known as a law student at Tottel's bookshop, had for six years been the lynchpin of covert Catholic activities in England. He was utterly opposed to Popham, "the chief prosecutor of our brethren," the man who had tried Campion and his companions and more recently passed sentence on two priests and on a Catholic schoolmaster, Swithun Wells. Garnet heard that Popham was dead. He interpreted the incident as a sign of God's intervention in the Catholic interest, seeing "the finger of God in his unexpected death, at the very time when he was threatening dire measures against the Catholic people." The report was false. Popham was alive. It is cruelly ironic that fourteen years later he was instrumental in securing Garnet's own execution.[31]

Many people of conscience dislike uniformity, and the attempt to achieve it in religious matters continued to create intense difficulty for many worthy men and women. Henry Barrow of London, John Greenwood, Robert Bowle, Robert Stokes, Daniel Studley, and James Forester were tried in March 1593 for writing and publishing books tending "to cry down the Church of England and to lessen the Queen's prerogative in matters spiritual." These men were separatists or independents, who believed that each congregation should elect its own ministers, members pursuing their own way to salvation without the authority of any superior body. The movement had started in the 1560s, and was reinvigorated by Robert Browne in 1581. Brownists had been rivaled by Barrowists; Barrow had already spent several years in prison, and while there actively organized separatist groups. When Barrow came up for examination in March 1593 the questions were asked by Popham, and he evidently had no clerk on hand, for the records of the depositions are in his own almost illegible script. Seeking to find out just how radical Barrow's views were, he asked him, for instance, "Whether all sett and stinted [authorized] prayers are mere bablinge in the sight of the Lord, and whether it be lawfull to use any such." Barrow replied, "I hould it not lawfull for any man to ympose any forme of Lyturgie, or stinted praiers in the Churche."[32] Barrow and Greenwood were executed at Tyburn, two more deeply religious men who were unable to accept any middle way. Three other puritan ministers, including John Penry and John Udall, who were suspected of being authors of the scurrilous attacks on the bishops known as the Marprelate letters, were also sentenced to death. Popham's signature is on Penry's death warrant, and Thornton points out that it was to escape this wave of persecution that those men and women escaped to Holland who later became the Pilgrim Fathers.[33]

Policy toward Catholics had been steadily hardening. The last legislation against them, the statute of 1593 (35 Eliz. Cap 2), struck heavily at popish recusants who "wander and shift" about the country and "seduce and corrupt" the Queen's subjects. All such, being above the age of sixteen years, were ordered to repair to their normal place of abode, and not henceforth remove above five miles from it, under pain of forfeiture of goods, chattels, and land: if too poor to have confiscable goods and lands, their only option was to abjure the realm. By the same enactment, suspected Jesuit or seminarist priests who refused to answer when questioned, were to be imprisoned without bail until they made true answer.[34]

But what, exactly, was a true answer for a priest under oath? This issue was first brought to the public eye during the trial of Robert Southwell before Popham in 1595. Southwell had advised his mistress, Anne Bellamy, that if necessary she should deny that she had seen a priest when she had in fact seen one; he was prepared to defend this stratagem as "agreeable to the word of God" and essential to the government of all states. Popham responded civilly, a welcome contrast to the extreme unpleasantness of Coke and Topcliffe, acting for the prosecution. "Mr Southwell," he said, "if this doctrine were allowed, it would supplant all justice, for we are men and not gods, and can judge but according to men's outward actions and speeches, and not according to their secret and inward intentions." The practice of equivocation did not stop with Southwell's death but became a notorious feature of Jesuit policy in the aftermath of the Gunpowder Plot.[35]

If recusants traveled about the country, so did the Lord Chief Justice. It was while he was at Fulford near Exeter, as a guest of Sir William Periam, the Lord Chief Baron, that he was called on to deal with the case of John Levermore, a trader and "a man of extraordinarily high and irritable temper." A constant troublemaker, Levermore had twice been disenfranchised by the Exeter Chamber but nevertheless continued trading. When his goods were seized, he appealed to Popham; "in the informal style so typical of Elizabethan government, the Lord Chief Justice heard the case not in his official capacity, but as a private arbitrator."[36] A lasting reconciliation was achieved. Popham must have given effective service to the City of Bath too, for the Bath Chamberlain's Accounts for 1594 record: "paid for banquitinge dishes given unto the Lord Chiefe Justice 5s 6d, and for wine and sugar bestowed upon him 5s 8d."[37]

Feasting and gifts were no doubt welcome, and perhaps we can see them as happy prologues to the swelling act of royal favor that was to come. They were certainly deserved, for Popham worked extremely hard. Records of some of his official work at this time were kept by Popham himself, and published in his Reports (1656). A vivid example is Bayne's Case: "At the sessions holden at Newgate presently after this term the Case was this; one Baynes with another came in the night time to a Tavern in London to drink, and after they had drank, the said Baynes stole a Cup in which they drank in a Chamber of the same House, the owner of the said House, his Wife and servants being then also in the House, and the Cup being the owner's of the said Tavern, whereupon he was indicted and committed, and the matter appeared in the Indictment, and agreed by Popham, Anderson, and Periam with the Recorder and Serjeants at Law then being there, that this was not Burglary, and yet was such a Robbery, whereby he was ousted of the benefit of his Clergy by the Statute of 5 Eliz 6, Cap 9 and was hanged."[38]

Meanwhile, treason was in the air again. On 28 February 1594 her Majesty's physician Dr. Lopez was arraigned at the Guildhall, tried, and convicted of plotting to poison the Queen. Popham was on the commission when this "perjured, murdering traitor and Jewish doctor, worse than Judas himself: to poison the Queen in exchange for a reward of 50,000 crowns" as Coke said, was found guilty in the highest degree and judgment passed on him with universal applause.

Lopez was taken back to the Tower. So long as he remained there, the sentence could not be executed without a royal warrant. Elizabeth had been close to her personal doctor, and as before in Mary's case, she could not bring herself to sign. It was Essex who, seeing how it was, resorted to a legal subterfuge. With Popham's connivance Lopez was removed from the Tower to the King's Bench Prison at Southwark. This brought him under the ordinary jurisdiction of the Courts, and the royal signature to a death warrant was no longer required. Lopez was executed at Tyburn.[39]

It is hardly surprising that Popham retained the Queen's favor when his methods, however devious, were so effective. He gained his reward. On 27 May 1594 William Hamond noted: "I heard it yesterday the Lord Cheefe Justice was admitted to her M's presence & that her highness proposes to visitt him this progresse which begins to morrow or Wednesday at his house clept Friar by High gate about vij [7] miles of London."[40] Records suggest that after visits to Sir William Cornwallis at Highgate on 7 June and Sir John Fortescue at Hendon, the Court was indeed at Popham's house on about 10 June 1594. Although we have no details at all, we can be sure that Sir John and Lady Amy did their very best to provide the lavish entertainment the Queen still loved. Afterward Elizabeth probably stayed with Lord Burghley at Theobalds from 13 June to 23 June. The progress finished about 5 July.[41]

Like so many great men of this reign, Popham also felt a sense of duty toward the poor. At the very same time as the Queen's visit to Friern he must have been discussing with his new kinsman Sir Thomas Sutton the idea of founding a benevolent institution. On 20 June 1594 Sutton conveyed to Popham, Egerton, and others "all his manors and lands in Essex, in trust, to found a hospital at Hallingbury Bouchers in that county." Perhaps it was the influence of Sutton that spread to Popham, for in the same year Sir John petitioned for leave to erect two hospitals, one for men, the other for women, at Wellington, Somersetshire.[42] The plan was to house "fyve poore decrepitt or maymed men" in the one house and five poor women in the other. Popham would also provide a stock [fund] "to set poor children of that towne on worke whereby their ydelnes maye be avoyded," and every year two of them would be delivered to be "prentices to a fytt trade," with £5 stock to each of them "that the more thereby may be encouraged to drawe themselves to honest labours." The intention was most worthy, but it was another thirteen years before the plan came to fruition.[43]

9

George's Guiana

WHILE SIR JOHN POPHAM WAS THINKING ABOUT ESTABLISHING almshouses at Wellington, his kinsman George was dreaming of El Dorado.

George Pophams recur throughout Sir John's story, but it is impossible to be certain which actions were performed by whom, or to establish definitely how they were related to him. In fact a totally convincing George Popham remains as unattainable as the mythical golden city. However, this man was probably Sir John's nephew, son of Edward. At nineteen or so—he was born about 1559[1]—George had been involved in a privateering incident in 1578. To seafaring merchants at this time, a little piracy on the side was the norm, so it is no surprise to find that "A letter of assistance" was issued "to all officers, as well within Liberties as without, for the apprehencion of the bodies of Roger Sidnam, John Gallingham and George Popham, at the suite of the Ambassadours for the King of Portingall residing here in England."[2] Presumably George's crew had been lucky in capturing a Portuguese prize—Portuguese ships, like Spanish and French vessels, were fair game as all were regarded as enemy nations. It is certain that Ferdinando Popham,[3] George's brother, was also involved in a privateering incident in September 1581, when a merchant of Cork was "spoiled of £500 at Mounts Bay in Cornwall." They were quite a family gang.

In 1589 privateering suddenly became not only acceptable, but all the rage. For many years and by all nations privately owned ships armed with guns had been put into action in time of war against an enemy's trade. Such vessels were commissioned by letters of marque, which licensed them to take prizes, and which served as official letters of reprisal and bonds of good behavior. Although this system had operated in England since 1293, it was only now that the law was changed to provide for the value of prizes to be divided—usually 10 percent to the Crown and 90 percent to the owner. With the change in the law, gentlemen, noble-

men, syndicates, and the City itself put their money into privateering, which had become more formally profitable.[4] John
Popham, then Attorney-General, was not one to miss a chance of
profit. However, he needed a captain for his vessel, and typically he looked to his family to provide one. On 8 May 1589 he wrote
from Chancery Lane to Dr Julius Caesar,[5] judge of the Admiralty Court:

*I am very earnestly to entreat that according to my mocion
made unto you touching a Barke of myne being allreddi, uppon
some occasion as I have made knowne unto you, victualled and
prepared to go to sea which I desire may go by lawful warrant,
that you will procure a letter of Mark to George Popham and his
company and a commission to be directed to Richard Warre and
Gabbriell halley esquiers or to either of them for the takynge bond
of the said George for his good demeanour in and during the said
service as in such cases is accustomed.*

And in a note Popham adds: *The young gentleman is honest
and I do assure myself he wyll doe well in it otherwise I woud [not]
wryte for him.*[6]

George would now have been thirty, and Sir John fifty-eight.
The enterprise was at least partially successful, for in 1589 an
unnamed caravel of Bridgwater, promoted by Sir John and cap-
tained by George, "took part in spoil of a French vessel."[7] Popham
calls his vessel a bark, which usually meant a three-masted ship
of fifty tons burden or more;[8] the word caravel suggests a light
square-rigged vessel. Such craft must have been common, for no
fewer than 236 English ships are known to have been involved
in privateering in the three years from 1589 to 1591, 29 of these
being from Bristol and Bridgwater.[9]

The most celebrated of all privateering incidents occurred
three years later, and John Popham would have heard all about
it. His son-in-law Richard Champernowne was appointed a commissioner to investigate the looting of the fabulous Portuguese
carrack *Madre de Dios,* captured at the Azores coming from the
East Indies in 1592 by ships financed by a syndicate that included both Ralegh and the Queen. They had won the jackpot. In
an orgy of plunder, both the sailors and their officers grabbed the
amazing riches. On docking at Dartmouth they sold off as much
as they could to anyone: 537 tons of pepper, cloves, cinnamon,
mace, and nutmeg; and jewels, pearls, amber and musk "to the
value of 400,000 crusados." Champernowne wrote to Robert Cecil giving an account of his work: "1. We finde an emerod made in
the form of a cross 3 inches in length at least of great breadth

who of the Company sold hytt hys name set down. 2. We finde that won Mr Chychester who went in thys fleete sold 41 diamonds. 3. We finde of an other that sold 21 dyamonds some very fayr whose name also ys set down in the xamynatyons. 4. We finde of 1400 very great Pearles who sold them."[10]

It was enough to make anyone itch with acquisitiveness. Who would not have taken ship immediately in the hope of more such profit? George Popham followed the fashion, and he may well have been still captaining the Attorney-General's ship when in 1594 he had a most amazing piece of luck. He managed to capture from a Spanish vessel a packet of letters from some citizens of the Canary Islands to their relations and friends in Spain. They carried extraordinary promise.

"*Allonso his Letters from the Gran Canaria to his brother being commaunder of S. Lucas. . . .* There haue beene certain letters receved here of late, of a land newly discovered called Nuevo Dorado . . . they write of wondefull riches to be found in the said Dorado, and that golde there is in great abundance, the course to fall with it is 50 leagues to the windwarde of the Marguarita.

"*The report of Domingo Martines of Iamica concerning the Dorado. . . .* there came a Frigot fom the saide Dorado, bringing in it the portraiture of a Giant all of Gold, of weight 47 kintals, which the Indians there helde for their Idol. But now admitting of Christianitie and obedience to the Kinge of Spaine, sent their saide Idoll unto him in token they were become Christians, and held him for their King. The company comming in the saide Frigot reportes Golde to be there in most greate abundance, Diamondes of inestimable value, with greate store of pearle." And certain merchants reported that "lately was discovered a certain province so rich in Gold as the report thereof may seeme incredible, it is there in such abundance, and is called the Nuevo Dorado."

The idea of El Dorado had existed since the late 1530s, a realm of untold riches, a kind of archetypal dreamland, always desired but always unattainable. It had its origin in reports of the rituals of an Andean tribe at the sacred lake of Guatavita. The central figure in the ritual was known as el dorado, the golden man, and the place El Dorado was his empire, kingdom, or city. By the end of the century El Dorado was believed to be located in the Guiana Highlands south of the Orinoco River. The explorer of this area, and officially its Governor, was the elderly Spanish soldier Antonio de Berrio.[11] Although Berrio had reported to the King of Spain his "certain knowledge" of El Dorado, "the object of so many years' search, which by the grace of God I have found," this was not actually the case, and two further expeditions had failed to locate the mythical city. A third was organized, and another of the letters captured by George Popham reports on the attempt.

Berrio's men under Domingo de Vera had headed for the mainland opposite his headquarters named San Jose at Trinidad. Twelve leagues [a league was three miles] inland they met a chief called Renato who "brought us to a very large house where he entertained us well, and gave us much gold, and the interpreter asking him from whence that gold was, he answered from a province not passing a day's journey off, where there are so many Indians as would shadow the sun, and so much gold as all yonder plain will not containe it. In which Country (when they enter into the *Borachera*) they take of the said gold in dust and anoint themselves all over therewith to make the braver show, and to the end the gold may cover them, they anoint their bodies with stamped herbs of a gluenous substance. . . . And being asked how they got that same gold, they told us they went to a certaine downe or plain and pulled or digged up the grass by the root, which done, they took of the earth, putting it in great buckets which they carried to wash at the river, and that which came in powder they kept for their *Boracheras* and that which was in pieces, they wrought into Eagles. . . . We asked him how they made their *Borachera,* he said they had many Eagles of Gold hanging on their breasts and pearls in their eares, and that they danced being all covered with Gold."[12]

George Popham must have heard these words—could he read Spanish himself?—with his eyes popping out of his head. The Spaniards were already within reach of El Dorado. Something needed to be done by the English, and quickly. George had the letters copied; the originals somehow were forwarded to Spain, where they still survive.[13]

When he returned to England with the enticing information in the autumn of 1594, what did George Popham do with it? The obvious, patriotic, unexciting course would have been to give the letters to Ralegh, who was well known to be determined to establish the rule of Queen Elizabeth in Guiana and by September had an expedition at Plymouth already prepared for that very purpose.[14] George did not do so. Perhaps he took the letters to Sir John, the promoter of his privateering career, and Popham diverted him from an approach to Ralegh. Probably he just thought it would be more exciting to hold on to the letters and wait for a suitable occasion to show them off. By sheer chance the occasion very soon arrived, when Robert Dudley sailed in to Plymouth.

Dudley was a brilliant fellow of twenty-one, already obsessed with maritime exploration. He was the son of Elizabeth's principal courtier, the Earl of Leicester, though whether the birth was legitimate was a matter of lengthy dispute.[15] Robert had studied at Christ Church, Oxford, where he had been in the care of Thomas Chaloner, and was handsome, an admirable horseman, and a skillful mathematician. Before he reached nineteen he had married a sister of Thomas Cavendish, the second English circumnavigator of the globe, whose achievements he longed to emulate.[16] Inheriting two ships from Cavendish in 1593, he proposed an expedition to the South Seas, but the government frustrated his intentions.[17] In 1594, therefore, he was a fertile bed for the seed of Popham's letters.

Did George Popham already know Dudley? Did Sir John bring the two young men together? Or was it simply that Dudley's ships were in port, en route to the West Indies, when George Popham with his letters happened to be there too? We cannot tell. However it was, Popham recognized that this was what he had been waiting for, a young man like himself bent on adventure, and with ships set for a voyage of discovery. The two men even had a family connection.[18] Dudley seems not to have had definite aims for his expedition; he himself said it was "rather to see some practise and experience then any wonders or profite," though no doubt he wanted to capture as many Spanish prizes as possible. George Popham showed Robert Dudley the letters. The fantastic accounts Dudley read there gave his expedition a brilliant focus.

Robert Dudley must have met Sir Walter Ralegh while their ships were in Plymouth, but the two expeditions do not seem to have been working together. During the course of conversation, however, Dudley let slip to Ralegh that the letters captured by George Popham existed, and tantalized him with an indication of their contents.[19] Ralegh was already intent on establishing an English base to counteract Spanish mining and shipping activity in the area, and did not want rivals to his own dominance of the campaign. Understandably, he was rather cool to Dudley, both at this stage and later. He pretended no great interest, but must have been intrigued.

Dudley's four vessels gathered at Plymouth on 19 November 1594, George Popham not yet being ready to join them. After losing some of his ships in a catastrophic false start, Dudley eventually set sail in the *Bear* of two hundred tons: "all alone I went wandering on my voyage." He had a crew of nearly 140 men in very cramped conditions, but at Tenerife the capture of a pair of Spanish caravels "amended my company, and made me a fleete of 3 sailes. . . . Thus cheared as a desolate traveller, with the company of my small and newe-erected fleet, I continued my purpose for the West Indies."[20] He was two months ahead of Ralegh, whose departure continued to be delayed.

In due course Dudley arrived at Trinidad and settled his men: "I had caused to be made for them a little skonce, like a halfe moone, for their defence."[21] He must have been keenly aware that Berrio, with three hundred soldiers, was very much the landlord there. The Englishmen were delighted with the island, which was "ful of fruits, strange beasts and foules, whereof munkies, babions and parats were in great abundance." Dudley meant to stay there some time and explore the mainland opposite Trinidad. This was the entrance into the empire of Guiana; Dudley had been "shewed the discovery thereof by Captaine Popham, who received the discovery of the saide empire from one Captaine Harper, which, being a prisoner, [he] learned of the Spaniards at the Canaries." It must have been when they were planning the expedition in England that Popham showed Harper's discovery to Dudley; unfortunately no traces of this document have come down to us.

Two caravels were sent into the interior, "not appointing any other place to meet but England." By water and land they traveled, the men thought, 150 miles to Orocoa, where they made contact with Armago, Captain of the town and responsible for the mine the expedition particularly sought. He refused to supply them with the ore, but told them that though they would achieve nothing by force, "if they would bring him hatchets, knives, and Jewes-harps, he bid them assure me he had a mine of gold, and could refine it, and would trade with me; for token whereof he sent me 3, or 4, Croissants or halfe moones of gold, weighing a noble apiece or more, and two bracelets of silver. Also he told them of another rich nation, that sprinkled their bodies with the poulder of golde and seemed to be guilt, and farre beyond them a great towne called El Dorado, with many other things."

Lacking food and numbers to pursue these claims, the ship's boat returned, the crew estimating that they had rowed 250 miles altogether in sixteen days. The men were almost dead from lack of food. Captain Wyatt records that they were taken aboard, "wheare they weare with great joye and tryumph receaved both

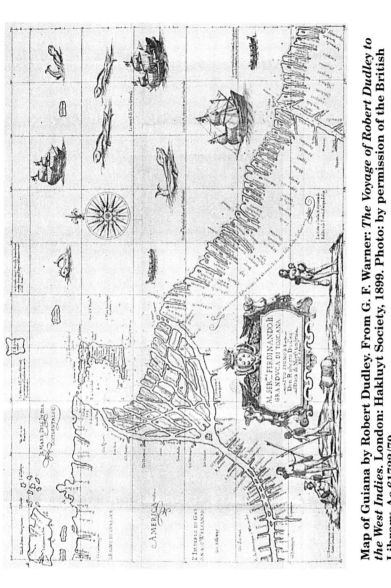

Map of Guiana by Robert Dudley. From G. F. Warner: *The Voyage of Robert Dudley to the West Indies*. London: Hakluyt Society, 1899. Photo: by permission of the British Library, Ac 61722/79.

by the Genereall and the whole companie, the which was signified by the shootinge of the great ordenance and small shott for
the space of a whole ower both owt of the admerall and alsoe Captain Pophames shipp." Dudley explains: "In this time of my
boates absence there came to me a pinnesse of Plimmouth, of
which Captaine Popham before named was chiefe, who gave us
great comfort. And if I had not lost my pinnesses, wherein I might
have carried victuals and some men, we had discovered further
the secrets of those places."

They had become the first Englishmen to penetrate the Orinoco. After some attempts to trace a mine in Trinidad, Dudley
and Popham recognized that they could do no more with their
present resources. Dudley wrote that "this Captaine and I stayed
some sixe or eight dayes longer for Sir Walter Ralegh (Who, as
wee surmized, had some purpose for this discouery) to the ende
that by our intelligence and his boates we might have done some
good; but it seemed he came not in sixe or eight weekes after. So
Captaine Popham and I helde it not convenient to stay any
longer; therefore . . . we set saile to see further of the Indies, leaving the yle of Trinidad the 12 day of March."

Could this have been youthful competitiveness at work? They
knew that Ralegh was heading for the same coast, and suspected him of aiming for El Dorado too. There is a kind of pragma-
tism about their plan: since they had failed to find El Dorado
themselves, they might as well be involved in Ralegh's attempt.
Since he did not arrive immediately, too bad. Let's go and find adventure somewhere else. They sailed off westward, but Dudley's
and Popham's ships became separated. Dudley arrived in St. Ives
at the end of May 1595.[22] Popham's return is not recorded.

Ten days after Dudley and Popham had left Trinidad, Ralegh
arrived. The English lost no time in attacking San Jose, capturing Berrio, slaughtering his men, and razing the town. They too
endured an adventurous journey up the Orinoco, not quite discovering the fabled El Dorado. Ralegh returned early in September 1595 after a "painful and happy" expedition. He had nothing to show for it, and met a hostile reception. On his return
George Popham sent "part of the copy" of the Spanish letters to
Robert Cecil, who forwarded it to Ralegh.[23] At last the letters
were in his hands. Ralegh printed them as an appendix to his account of his own travels.[24] They were just what he needed, for he
was desperate to return to Guiana and the information they provided justified further searches for El Dorado: "it is no dreame,"
Ralegh told Cecil.[25]

For George Popham the Guiana business was over, and we hear no more of him for eleven years. He had contributed to the dream of finding great wealth in the Americas, for without doubt those enticing glimpses of gold remained in the mind of his backer, the Lord Chief Justice. Sir John tucked the information away, and later, when the settlement of North America was in the air, recalled the Captain's experience. In 1606 he persuaded George to undertake another adventure of a more substantial kind, crossing the Atlantic to establish a colony there.

10

Privy Councillor

It is a small step from imagined wealth to actual poverty. The years 1594–97 found England in a state of starvation as a result of poor harvests caused by bad weather.[1] Coping with the immediate problem was one responsibility of government; dealing with the social problems consequent on it was another.

Edward Hext, a Justice of the Peace in Somerset, has given us a moving account of the problem. "I do not see howe yt ys possible for the poore Cuntryman to bear the burthens dewly layde uppon hym . . . there be (some) that styck not to say boldlye they must not starve, they wyll not starve. And this yere there assembled lxxx [80] in a Companye and tooke a whole Carte loade of Cheese from one dryvynge yt to a fayre and dispersed yt amongest them, for which some of them have indured longe imprisonment and fyne by the Iudgement of the good Lord Chief Iustice att owr last Crisman Sessions, which may grow dangerous by the ayde of suche numbers as are abroade, especyally in this tyme of dearthe. . . . (they say) that the ritche men have gotten all into ther handes and wyll starve the poore."[2]

Hext reports that "the Infynyte numbers of the Idle wandrynge people and robbers of the land are the chefest cause of the dearthe": they do no work, but lie in the ale-houses eating stolen meat and drinking excessively. In spite of the proclamations suppressing them, there are more "wandrynge souldiers" than ever before. These are the most dangerous people, for they consort together and evade justice with great skill; they are so forceful that even the Justices are terrified of convicting them.[3]

As a result of such concerns, new legislation came into effect in 1597. "Overseers for the poor" were to employ the able men and women and administer relief; everyone was to be obliged to contribute to poor-rates, dwellings were to be provided for the disabled, and financial provision made for the relief of prisoners and soldiers passing through. This seems sensible and humane legislation.

It must be admitted that another Act, also in 1597, seems to bear more of the stamp of Popham. By this, an Act for the Punishment of Rogues, Vagabonds, and Sturdy Beggars, all previous Acts dealing with these matters were repealed. Justices were to see that houses of correction were erected in all counties or cities. "All persons calling themselves scholars going about begging, all seafaring men pretending losses . . . shall be deemed rogues, vagabonds and sturdy beggars" and if caught were to be punished by being "stripped naked from the middle upwards . . . openly whipped until his or her body be bloody" and returned to the parish of birth or last residence.[4] Incorrigible rogues were to be "conveyed unto such parts beyond the seas as shall be at any time hereafter for that purpose assigned by the privy council" or sent to the galleys. Thus the idea of transportation was now enshrined in the statutes.

The catching and punishment of rogues needed vigilance and cunning, for the criminals were up to all the tricks. So were the authorities. The following September Robert Cecil wrote to commend one Richard Dyer, Esq., for apprehending John Seymor, a sailor, a "naughtie person" who had counterfeited the Privy Council's signatures. At the beginning of the next term Dyer is to "send him up unto the Lord Cheif Justice of England (at what tyme his Lordship wilbe retourned to the cittee), that he may take order for the punishing of him according to his desert. And for the avoyding of to[o] muche and needeles charge, we require you to send the sayde Seymour fast bounde with his legges under the horse bellye, so as some one man (whome you are to make choice of to sende with him) may suffice to guard and bring him up."[5]

Among the wandering threats to peace in this time of dreadful need were the gypsies, whom Popham was asked to help deal with in November 1596. The Privy Council wrote to the Recorder of London and others: "Whereas there were of late certaine lewd persons to the nomber of 80 gathered togeather calling themselves Egypcians and wanderers through divers countyes of the realme [who] were stayed in Northamptonshire, wheruppon we caused some of the ringleaders of them to be brought up hether and have committed them to prison, thes shalbe to require you by vertue hereof to examine the said lewd persons upon such artycles and informacions as you shall receive from the Lord Cheif Justice . . . and yf you shall not be able by faire meanes to bring them to reveale their lewd behavior, practyces and ringleaders, then wee thincke it meet they shalbe removed to Brydewell and there put to the manacles, wherby they may be constrained to utter the truthe in those matters concerning their lewd behaviour that shalbe fit to be demaunded of them."[6] In view of his own personal experience of gypsies, we can imagine Popham felt divided loyalties on this occasion.

His former acquaintance with rogues and highwaymen brought some lightness into the court. It is said that on one occasion, having to try one of his erstwhile profligate companions, he asked after old friends and was told, "You and I, my lord, are the only ones left."[7] Popham knew very well how to deal with such people, yet in 1596 a highwayman, prisoner, and writer called Luke Hutton thought he needed more advice. He paid Popham an unusual compliment, dedicating his book *The Black Dog of Newgate* to him:

"To the Honourable Sir John Popham, Knight, Lord Chief Justice of England: all increase of honour and happiness.

"Two reasons, my honourable good Lord, me especially moved to dedicate this book to your Honour. The first, for I held it my duty, to certify you of the notable abuses daily committed by a great number of very bad fellows, who under the colour of office and service, do mightily abuse both justice and Justices; which in this book is largely discovered. The next, for your Honour being thereof certified, such bad fellows shall be the sooner looked into, and their outrages qualified; so that the sooner by you the like mischiefs may be prevented. What I have done, is in love and zeal; both which I doubt not but they will excuse my boldness. And so the work be acceptable in your good opinion, I will not regard the malice of the threatening cony-catcher[s], [tricksters] who hath sworn, if I publish this book, they will do me what mischief they can. But how little I regard their windy words, they may well perceive by my proceedings. If this work had been worth a talent, it should have been your Honour's: and being a poor man's mite, I desire it may be acceptable. And if hereafter I shall be better able, your Honour shall not fail but find me ready to do your Honour service, even to the uttermost of my power. Thus, assuring myself safe shielded with your favour, to whom I present this book, desiring you to take the full view of this Black Dog of Newgate, I humbly and in all duty cease to be tedious; praying to the Almighty to lengthen long your days, with increase of all virtue and honour, and after this life, to send you to everlasting happiness, and joys endless. Amen

"To do your Honour service whilst he liveth,
Luke Hutton"[8]

Frontispiece of *The Black Dog of Newgate,* by Luke Hutton (1596).
Photo: by permission of the British Library, C.30.d.15.

Hutton probably wrote *The Black Dog* when himself in the prison. The verse introduction shows him in his nightmarish cell, asking his gaoler where he is:

> "This house is Newgate," gently he replied;
> "And this place, Limbo, wherein now thou art.

> Until thou pay a fine here must you bide,
>   With all these bolts which do aggrieve thy heart.
> No other place may here provided be,
>   Till thou content the keeper with a fee."

Hutton is outraged by the gaoler's corruption, but links it to the similar practices of the inmates. In the body of the piece, a prose dialogue between Hutton and his fellow prisoner Zawny, the two lags take it in turn to explain how thieves dupe their victims: in the hope of getting their money returned, they are induced to part with even more of it. *The Black Dog* is clearly dedicated to Popham in hope of favor or in gratitude for the Lord Chief Justice's intercession on Hutton's behalf in a capital charge.[9] For Hutton the Black Dog was itself the gaoler of Newgate, who for his cruelty was compared with a dog. Elsewhere it is described as a specter which appeared in the time of Henry III to prisoners at Newgate who had eaten a fellow prisoner; a great black stone standing in the condemned cell known as Limbo; and a black conscience, haunting black-conditioned people.[10]

The Lord Chief Justice was not one of the wandering poor, and did not experience privation. On All Hallows Day, 1 November 1595, Arthur Throckmorton, the diarist and brother of Ralegh's wife Bess, sent Lord Chief Justice Popham four partridges, six quails, six snipe, two woodcocks, four dozen larks—evidently for a feast.[11] And there was certainly cause for celebration the following year, when Francis Popham returned from the great adventure of his life, the sacking of Cadiz. This attempt to destroy some of Philip of Spain's renewed fleet was in many ways a successful expedition. Essex and Lord Admiral Charles Howard were in command, with Ralegh as principal lieutenant; 150 vessels and ten thousand men took part,[12] among them the poet John Donne.[13] A surprise attack on the city led to its capture and destruction, and two galleons were taken. In a state of elation Essex and Howard knighted sixty of their officers, among them Francis Popham and Robert Dudley of the Guiana expedition.[14] Unfortunately it was not Essex's privilege to dub knights, as he well knew; possibly he did so as a way of gaining a body of loyal supporters. The Queen was furious, and this was a significant milestone in the deepening rift between monarch and favorite. After this exhilarating episode, Sir Francis Popham began to settle into his long career of public service by sitting in the Parliament of 1597 as Member for Somerset.

By contrast with the high drama and celebration of Cadiz, the minor village jollifications involving drinking were an irritation to the puritan mind. In a letter to Sir Francis Hastings in January 1595, Popham had made an interesting distinction, suggesting that he understood the everyday necessity of alehouses. Although he was anxious to suppress disorderly ones, he also felt it important "to have the drynke convenyent and stronge for drunkards but moderate for sustenance expecially in this tyme of dearth of corn."[15] However, the special occasions known as ales were a different matter. They had originated in quite early times and often caused trouble to the authorities.[16] People who were in financial difficulty would hold a bod-ale, [from biddan, to beg] a gathering where ale was sold at a profit, and frequently a collection of money was made. Bride ales were favorite means of helping newly married couples. Church ales were similar boisterous events, the profits of the entertainment being devoted to some Church purpose.[17] Evidently they led to public disorder: the justices in Bridgwater decreed in 1596 that "no church-ale, clerks-ale, bid-ale, or tippling be suffered, and that such only be suffered to tipple as be or shall be lawfully licensed according to the orders made at those sessions."[18] The order was signed by, among others, John and Alexander Popham (George's elder brother, and thus another nephew of Sir John). Even now he was Lord Chief Justice, Popham continued to carry out the humble duties of a Justice of the Peace.

Popham himself was able to enjoy a modest tipple following his involvement in the problem at Bristol over ship money. In February 1596 the Queen revived this unpopular tax in order to defend the English Channel against Spanish warships and foreign privateers. Bristol was required to provide for three ships fully manned and provisioned, the outlay being estimated at £2,500, though of this sum Somerset was to contribute £600 and other towns £346. The city complained vigorously but eventually did pay up, and three ships duly joined the navy, taking part in the sack of Cadiz. The Somerset gentry had never paid their contribution, and after a year of further weak excuses the Council instructed the Lord Chief Justice to persuade the gentry to do their duty. It seems that he must have been successful as Popham was presented soon afterwards with a butt of sack by the Bristol city Corporation.[19]

During this period we have glimpses of other interesting family matters. We know, for instance, that Popham's son-in-law Richard Champernowne of Modbury stayed with him at Littlecote in September 1595.[20] Richard had been Sheriff of Devon the previous year and seems to have lived at Modbury considerably above his means, though he and Elizabeth Popham had no children. His passion was music. He maintained his own band of musicians, and seems to have been envied for this luxury. No doubt Richard discussed with Popham the remarkable castrato slander.

In March 1595 Champernowne had received a letter from Sir Francis Drake alleging that he had heard him accused of gelding boys in order to preserve their treble voices.[21] Champernowne immediately wrote to Sir Robert Cecil asking him to help in scotching the rumor, but Cecil did not oblige. Quite the reverse: apparently one boy in the consort had a particularly fine voice, and Cecil demanded the singer for himself. Understandably Champernowne refused and complained of ill usage. He received Cecil's response while he was staying at Littlecote, and in October Champernowne replied that "He is sorry if anything he has written has been misunderstood but what grieved him was that Sir Francis Drake wrote to him that it was told Cecil and in Court that, to satisfy his own humor, he used boys to continue their voices otherwise than it were fit for anyone professing Christianity, wherein he has been exceedingly wronged by the author of such a report. He confesses that being naturally and often oppressed with melancholy more than he would wish, he had (though to his own charge) bought such as he has found whose voices contented him.

"If he should lack this youth, he knows not where to get another, otherwise Cecil should not so readily require as he [does to] yield him, and yet he perceives the report as to the boy's voice is far beyond his deserts. As the case stands, losing this boy, his whole consort for music, which most delights him, were overthrown. . . . If for his private contentment Cecil would like to have the youth attend him sometimes for a month or two, and so to return again, that that comfort of music wherewith he is delighted be not utterly overthrown, the youth shall be at his command."[22] Although the calumny seems to have been public property, the castration of choirboys, though common in Italy at this time, was not practised in England. One cannot help wondering what old grudge should have led Drake, by then a grizzled pirate preparing for his last voyage, to concern himself at all with silly rumors about Champernowne.

Popham exerted his considerable influence for the benefit of his family. At this stage in their lives his grandchildren needed him. One, Anne or Amy, daughter of Penelope and Thomas Hanham, is to marry Mr Robert Wyngate in Bedfordshire; Popham helps with negotiations about the lease of the manor of Luton.[23] He pulls a string for Anne's brother John Hanham, who seems to be on a foreign travel year, writing to Sir Robert Cecil: "I thank you for the favour you are willing to shew my grandchild. I hope he may so employ himself upon his travels, as to be the better able to serve at home upon his return. I would only entreat that you would speak to Mr Nevill to know him where he now is, at Paris."[24] Another brother, Thomas, enters the Middle Temple in 1594, along with three other of Sir John's grandchildren, Richard Warre, Thomas Warre, and John Horner. The four young students seem to have been typically dreadful housekeepers, for two years later the chamber they shared is described as "ruinous," and henceforth is to be for two men only.[25]

Popham was careful of his family, and also of his colleagues. Sir Francis Hastings, a strong Emmanuel College puritan, author and MP for Somerset and Bridgwater, was a man very much in the same mold.[26] In December 1595 Hastings lost his brother, Henry, third Earl of Huntingdon. In his youth a companion of Edward VI, Henry Hastings had married Leicester's sister, Katherine Dudley, and had himself been a claimant to the throne after Elizabeth.[27] His zealous character elicited from Popham a most fulsome letter of condolence:

My good Sir Francis Hastings / I assure you I can hardly withold my self from teares to enter unto consydracion of the loss of so trew a servant of god, so loyall and faithfull a subject, and servant to our most gracious Queene / and so careful a man of the countryes good and his soverayns seale as your Brother hath ever showed him self to have ben / I would to god that god of his goodness would yet rayse unto her many such / though his worldly deth be a gain to hym self yet no doubt a great loss both to hys province and country / He yet is happy for no doubt god hath hym, but we unhappy for that we lacke him. while we lyve in this world lett it be our comfort and ankerhold that hope to be wher he now is and in the meane lett us not surcease to use all our endevour to serve god and her majesty sincerely carefully and effectually and now lett it suffyse concernyng your brother that he is a most happy man in the syght both of god and man. . . . I would be very glad if my happe myght be to se yow before I depart out of the cuntry; to confer with you of our countrys causes and so with my very harty comendacions both to your self and my good lady I betake you both to the proteccion of the almighty at Wellington the 24th december 1595.[28]

Less worth was evident among the people of Nottingham in the autumn of 1597. A boy called Somers, who fell into fits, had the evil spirit cast out of him by a preacher named John Darrell, a man with a reputation for dealing with such matters. When in April 1598 Somers again fell into fits, it was alleged that Darrell had taught the boy to counterfeit. Darrell maintained the boy was genuine, but when the Lord Chief Justice very sensibly directed that he be taken away from Darrell and his friends, Somers confessed to dissimulation. Nottingham was in tumult: "the town is extraordinarily divided." As was noted by the ecclesiastical commissioners when Darrell was summoned before them, "Few grow to be sick or evil at ease but straightway they are deemed to be possessed." The following year was published *A brief apology concerning the possession of William Somers,* by Darrell and dedicated to Egerton, Popham and other judges. Darrell, who had been imprisoned, defended himself, arguing that the boy's confession had been wrought by the threats of Satan and his instruments in the shape of a black dog, a mouse and an ass. The inquiry, he said, had not been properly heard, and "the matter dependeth undecided."[29]

The endless differences that came to Popham's desk take us to the center of Elizabethan England. The Mayor of Chichester had been required to provide the Lord Admiral with a great quantity of powder "to be speedyly sent to me, the Lord Admyrall, for her M's service when her Navy was uppon the coast of Sussex in the foresaid yere when the Spanyards intended to have invaded the realme," and is now sued for payment.[30] The church, bridge and stairs at Blackfriars are in an appalling condition, and Popham is asked to examine the man responsible and sort the matter out.[31] A case in April 1598 brought a bargeman and a miller before the Lord Chief Justice. They had "overthrown" 53 quarters of wheat that was provided for her Majesty's use at London Bridge in passing the Bridge; "since it happened cheeflie thorowe the default of the bardgman and the miller, and they have a whole yere and more kept both the corne and paied no parte of the money" they are to be sent for trial before the highest lawyer in the land.[32] In June 1598 Popham and others were busy sorting out a controversy over a new charter for Totnes in Devon, which "some few private persons" were said to have procured "for their owne benefitt and advantage."[33]

This was the issue too in the very serious matter of the enclosure of common grounds, which the Privy Council discussed on 25 December 1596, Christmas Day and a Sunday too. It concerned a petition of tenants of George Rodney, a Somerset landowner, who do "complain grievously against him both for taking away their commons and converting arable grounds to feed sheep, and he doth molest them with sundry actions in divers Courts." Two Justices were requested to confer with "our very loving friend the Lord Cheif Justice of her Majesty's Benche and the Masters of the Requests," to call Rodney and "take such final order . . . as you shall think to be agreeable to equity."[34] However, things are rarely simple. In March 1596 there is another complaint in the same case by twenty-three tenants who want the enclosures continued because some of the rich tenants have so many cattle on common ground that the poorer sort "can reap little or no benefit thereby."[35] Again Popham is requested to sort the matter out to the satisfaction of both parties. It cannot have been easy. Popham was evidently known to be very capable, for we have two requests by petitioners that he should be appointed to arbitrate their cases.[36]

The enclosing of common land by the corporation of Cambridge was one of several grievances in a long-standing conflict between the town and the University. The Vice-Chancellor, John Jegon,[37] was a fervent defender of the University's rights, but Popham had several times found it necessary to admonish him and his fellow officers for wrongful exercise of authority. On 4 July 1597 Popham arrived at Huntingdon to be met, he told Jegon, with petitions and complaints concerning improper imprisonment by the University of one Leonard Whallie, "& concerninge certaine sutes prosecuted in your Courts against two Constables of Cambridge, for taking an horse of a schollers servaunt to do her Majestie service, & touching the violent breakinge of an howse by som of your officers."[38] If they did not reform their ways, Popham threatened, "you will presse me & other my bretheren the Justices, to doe that for the reliefe of her Majesties subjectts as is requisite in suche like case." Jegon was unrepentant: "We are hartely sorie," he wrote, "that your Lordship hath conceyved so hard opinion of our proceedings in the universitie, made knowne unto us, not only by our good frends abroad, that love and tendre this place of learninge; but also by our Adversaries of the Towne of Cambr., who so greatly triumphe in that displeasure, which (they give out) they have wrought us with your Lordship."[39] The bad feeling intensified, so that by 1600 Jegon was writing to Popham in desperate tones: "I doe oftentimes with great greefe condemne myselfe, that in the former tymes of my office of vicechan. I did not more wholley putt myself uppon your most Honble. Favour, for matters of the universitie, especially allwaies findinge you most lovinglye and kindlye affected in any thing that concerned myne owne person or any schollers good."[40] He asked to be pardoned for anything Popham might have thought defective in his government, protesting that the God of Heaven knew "how unwilling and fearfull I was to incure your least displeasure." Now the Cambridge townsmen "adventure to break our chartres in all things, and proclayme themselves sole Governours in this place. Whereupon execucion of Justice, releefe of the poore, and all good Discipline is so much neglected, that I fearfully forethinke, what is likelye to followe." The conflict only seems to have been calmed when in 1601 Robert Cecil replaced the Earl of Essex as Chancellor of the University, and more stringent demands were made of its government.

Cambridge was of particular concern to Popham as since 1592 he had visited the town on circuit. In September 1598 Roger Wilbraham, who had pleaded cases before him, made a complimentary observation on his work as an assize judge. As Lord Chief Justice, he noted, it was Popham's custom "to give a short exhortation & charge, touching treasons and felonies and insisting upon idle roages & other enormities in the country." He was anxious to have "espials" everywhere, and a month before the assizes would give to the head constables of each county "12 articles to enquire & present in writing at the next assizes . . . wherby manie recusants, felones, conversion of tillage to pasturage &c. are discovered, much more than the graund Jurie do present."[41] Popham saw the need to improve the procedures of the courts, and found simple ways to make law enforcement more efficient.

On 21 November 1598 the Privy Council wrote to the Lord Chief Justice as a result of an unusual action being taken against the Mayor of Dartmouth. Two men, Richard Lumbard and William Yonge, had been thought deserving of punishment "in that they beinge appointed to warde [keep watch] at the place accustomed for dyscovery of the ennemy or any shippes that should aryve upon that coast, and to give notice to them by hoystinge of a flagg upon a longe mast there sett up for the same purpose, suddainlie at the same tyme there came into the mouth of that harbour some 18 or 20 shippes, of which 6 were fly botes, men of warre freighted with men and munycion, at whom the Castle made a shott and so staied them until they were knowne, of whose approchement (as they informe) the said Lumbard gave no notice unto that towne as he was appointed and comaunded to doe, and Yonge attemptinge to place a woman in the church contrary to the order of the wardens and the Deane of Exon [Exeter], promysinge to stabb any officer that should come to remove him or yf the Maiour him self should come to pluck his beard from his face, usinge other very disloyall and reprochefull wordes as the Maiour and the rest doe certyfie us, it was thought fyt by the Maiour for theire neglect of dutie that they should be comytted to prison in the pryson there, called the Guildhall of that towne, and now of late bothe of thes parties have commenced accion against Thomas Holland, then the Maiour, of faulse imprysonment, thereby to put him to chardge and trouble."[42] As the men were committed "for matter concerning her Majesty's service" Popham is asked to stay the suit until it is examined further.

Careful watching was still needed. Sir John's nephew William Pole wrote from Devon to the Lord Chief Justice concerning "one Hill, the corrupter and seducer of Sir Robt. Basset." Hill was "a blasphemous fellow" who had lately resorted to a Jesuit in Newgate. "I fear the sequel, for though Sir Robt. Basset stands not curious in any religion, yet lately he has practised popery, and has confessed that Sir Wm. Courtenay and himself have combined that way. I doubt some practice is in hand, as Sir Robt. Basset has prepared to travel with Hill, and confesses he has a matter of some moment to pursue, and has also resolved to have the Isle of Lundy, and to place there one Ansley, a malcontent, a Somersetshire man. I am bound, both in regard of my country and my love to Sir Robt. Basset, to acquaint you with this, that the beginning of these things may be prevented by the stopping of this travel, and imprisoning that most pernicious lewd man, Hill, who otherwise will be the overthrow of the gentle nature of Sir Robert; I hope, in the general cause that touches all those that fear God, you will put your assistance."[43]

Hill is thought to be the English atomist philosopher Nicholas Hill, a member of the Earl of Northumberland's circle.[44] Basset was Pole's brother-in-law; he was twenty-four, an Oxford man with a fine country estate near Barnstaple, and unsettled in religion. He owned a privateer, and because his home port served Ireland he became involved with Irish affairs, leading to an association with the Earl of Essex. Basset did later carry out the plan mentioned, pretending a right to the throne and raising his standard on Lundy Island. Unfortunately, nobody noticed.[45] Sir William Courtenay of Powderham Castle, near Exeter, came from a family well-known to be Catholic sympathizers.[46]

Less dangerous to the state was the case in Bath which caused the Privy Council to write to the Lord Chief Justice: "Upon a complainte exhibited unto us by Dr. Sherwood, Dr. of Phisick, of the ryotuous behaviour of somme of the inhabitants of the citty of Bathe that have of late digged and deverted away a springe that did feede a private bathe or water in his house, which alwayes tyme out of mynde (as wee ar informed) hath bin used as a private bathe and hathe bin now used fore noble men and ladyes of honor that repair hither to have the benefitt of those waters, wee hereupon have writen our letters unto the Maiour and Alldermen of Bathe to cause those persons that have defaced the same to restore and repair yt againe in soche sorte as yt was before they did spoyle yt. And because the supplyant doubteth how they will performe the same, and our very good Lady the Lady Marques of Northampton ys very shortly to repair thither to use that bathe for some occacion, wee have thought good to pray your Lordship . . . [to] send for the cheifest of the offendours . . . and not onely to cause them to repair and restore the same in soche sort as in equity they ought to do, but to l[a]y such punishment on the offendours as your Lordship shall thincke they have deserved by their disorderly and badd dealinges."[47]

The Bath Chamberlain's Accounts for 1597 give a fascinating insight into the vigorous theatrical life that flourished in the city at this time:

"Giftes and rewardes . . . gave to the Queenes players at two sundrie times 4s 10d, gave unto the Lord of Penbrookes players 20s, gave unto the Lord Chamberlins players 20s, gave unto Sir John Stawell a gallonde of wine and a pound of suger 4s 10d, gave to my Lord Bishopp a firkin of secke 24s 6d, and a loffe of suger 12s, gave unto Mr Thomas Hornor a quarte of secke 20d, and a pound of suger 18d, gave unto the Lord Ritch a pottle of Canara and a pottle of clarrett 3s 4d, gave to him also on loafe of suger of 6 pounde and a halfe at 18d the pounde 9s 9d, gave to my Lord Cheiffe Justice at Wells on runlett of Malager wine, seaven gallans at 4s the galland and the runlett, 29s, more to him on loafe of suger 16s 6d, [Lewes was paid 10d to carry these gifts to Wells] gave to Marie Tovie at Mr Maiors appoyntment to help her to London 5s, gave unto the Lord of Darbies players 14s 4d, paid unto the Lord Shandowes plaiers 10s."[48]

The theater in London now recognized Shakespeare as the greatest of the English dramatists, and in 1599 the Globe was built on the South Bank of the Thames. Two or three years previously Shakespeare had written the Gadshill incident in *1 Henry IV* (act 2, scene 2), so similar to Popham's own highwayman activities on Shooters Hill. It has even been suggested that Popham inspired not only the roguish young manhood in this play but also the Chief Justice, Gascoigne, in the sequel, *2 Henry IV:* "The rugged personality and upright character of Popham must often have been in Shakespeare's mind during the composition of his plays."[49]

In the theater of the courtroom, the central drama of the time continued to run, with some of the audience thinking rather differently of Popham's performance. The Jesuit Henry Garnet hated Popham, describing him as "detested by all classes . . . and prepared to inflict extremities of injustice on poor Catholics."[50] Garnet wrote very long letters to his friends abroad, and in one of them records a trial following the death of the Franciscan priest John Jones, executed at St Thomas Waterings in Southwark in the previous July. Christopher Blackall, a young law student from the Temple, "unknown to be a Catholic to his best acquaintances," while walking in Lambeth fields on a "moonshine night" took down from a pike one of Fr Jones's quarters. Blackall was overtaken by hue and cry for robbery, and appeared the following day in July 1598 before the Lord Chief Justice, accused of removing a traitor's quarter. Perhaps Garnet was present himself and heard the exchange in court. Blackall said that he did not know Jones was a traitor.

"Popham: 'What, was he not hanged and quartered?'

'Yes, for I was by and saw it.'

'Is he not then a traitor?'

'No, for I heard your lordship say that you condemned him not for any treason committed, but because he was a priest; and priesthood alone is no treason; and therefore I, knowing him in prison and hearing no evil of him, but loving him, was loth the crows should eat him."

When the Chief Justice threatened to torture Blackall, the young student replied that he had "forecast all difficulties." He was taken to prison, and maintained there on a fund Garnet raised from his friends.[51]

As head of the legal system Popham came in for more criticism as a result of the law's delays. A letter of 1596 about the Norfolk murderer Thomas Thirsbye urges haste in the proceedings and expresses fear of "the Chief Justice's and Mr. Attorney's slackness."[52] Popham justifies himself however, writing from Bedford that in this case "there be some matters to be further and better looked into before it proceed . . . which done I do assure myself the matter will be most like to be carried in a just and even course, which is the matter her Majesty desireth."[53] Evidently the Queen took a direct personal interest in such matters. On one occasion in 1598 the Lord Chief Justice and Attorney-General were requested by the Council to confer speedily and proceed to trial, "which wee wish to be with the more speede because her Majestie conceaveth alreadie somme dislike that the matter hath bin so longe delaied."[54]

There are other complaints. Edward Earl of Oxford writes in 1599 to Cecil that he has been employed by the Queen "for getting her money wherewith to supply a stock to buy the tin yearly in Cornwall and Devonshire." He objects strongly to Fortescue's and the Lord Chief Justice's treatment of him in the matter, reporting nothing of it to the Queen, but saying she has no money in her coffers for this purpose.[55] Oxford is still dissatisfied in January 1602. "Now, as I understand that it is meant to delay the report to the end to get a composition of her Majesty, whereby all my hopes will end in smoke, I must solicit her to call for the report, which I had not needed to do, had gospel been in the mouths of my Lord Chief Justice and the Attorney, who assured me that at the next hearing on the second of this term, it should have a full end."[56]

Popham is accused of siding with his relatives. One William Cicill writes to Sir Robert Cecil that being in prison, "compelled by dire misery" he has no one to turn to for help save Sir Robert. "Sir John Popham, the Chief Justice, favours his adversary John Arnold, his (the Chief Justice's) kinsman, to whom Cicill is not and never was indebted. A word from Sir Robert to the Chief Justice will be sufficient to secure his release."[57] It seems to be suggested, too, in a case involving Sir Robert Drury, that Popham was open to bribes. Drury advises his uncle to "bid Mr Danby fear no colours . . . and let him be sure my LCJ will be a buckler [shield] good enough for him . . . and let him be well dealt withal by you. . . . For my LCJ shall do all my Lord's will nor may appear in the case but underhand."[58]

Popham was thought very severe in his judgments even on petty criminals. On 20 October 1598 John Chamberlain wrote to Dudley Carleton that the Lord Chief Justice "hath plaide rex of late among whoores and bawdes, and persecutes poore pretty wenches out of all pittie and mercy."[59] Unfortunately he gives no details, so we can only guess what playing the king entailed. It may be that it was Popham's notorious character that led to his servant Henry Hill of Draycott, Somerset, being assaulted by a riotous assembly of five husbandmen of Wedmore and eleven others at Nyland on 25 June 1595.[60] No less than death was threatened him in Norfolk, where he was told afterward of Sir Bassingbourn Gawdy's care in "committing the man to Norwich Gaol for affirming and publishing to such as he took to be his servant Frame, that he and 20 others had determined to kill his Lordship, and that if he should not ride strongly he should be very sure never to ride circuit again." His Lordship took it very kindly of Gawdy but said "he cared not for them at all."[61]

A most undignified fate would have met Sir John if one Captain Elliot had had his way. This wild-speaking man was resolved to kill Elizabeth, and was heard to say that "when he had taken the Queen's life he would quarter the Lord Treasurer [Burghley] and the Lord Chief Justice, and throw them both into an old privy, and not suffer them to die openly, and to say that they died for their gospel."[62]

Popham could afford to ignore such hostile opinions. With the men—and woman—who really mattered, he was hand in glove. A little later Henry Garnet gave a fascinating view of the Queen's attitude to her Lord Chief Justice: "I well know that this Popham is a cruel man of low extraction. The felons he condemns to death tell him brazenly to his face that he deserves the halter far more than they do, since he has been a thief. The Queen, when out of temper, often calls him a 'bluecoat,' which is the term used for those ordinary servants who attend at their ease on their patrons, and many of whom are the greatest thieves." A blue coat was formerly the dress of servants and the lower orders, and hence came to be applied to almsmen and charity children. Garnet adds that the most influential Councillor with the Queen was always the man prepared to take on himself the odium for executing unpopular measures. Popham offered no objection to filling this role.[63]

Popham had also won the respect of Robert Cecil. In a note at the bottom of a letter he wrote to Cecil in 1599 Popham adds: *P.S. I thank your lordship for the good opinion I fynd (many wayes) you have conceaved and delyvered of me I hope I shall not lyve to wronge you, in so conceaving ffor (as I am most bounden) my endevours always have ben and styll shalbe to the uttermost off my power to do her majestie trew and ffaythfull servyse in all that myght or may stand within the compas off my knowledge or inablyng.*[64] Cecil's favor was a hint of greatness to come.

On 20 September 1598 the gossip Dudley Carleton wrote that "The Court is at Nonsuch, where on Sunday my Lord Chief Justice's expectation of being councillor was deceived, God be thanked."[65] He was soon proved wrong. On 3 May 1599 Sir John was sworn to the Privy Council, the elite central body of government.

It was truly elite, for the Council at this time was smaller than ever. Only eleven men effectively ran the country. They were, in the order recorded in the Privy Council's own book, Dr John Whitgift, Archbishop of Canterbury; Sir Thomas Egerton, Lord Keeper of the Great Seal; Robert, Earl of Essex, Earl Marshal; Charles Howard, Earl of Nottingham, Lord High Admiral; Sir George Cary, Lord Hunsdon, Lord Chamberlain; Sir Roger North, Lord North, Treasurer of Her Majesty's Household; Sir Thomas Sackville, Lord Buckhurst, Lord Treasurer; Sir William Knollys, Comptroller of Her Majesty's Household; Sir Robert Cecil, Principal Secretary; Sir [John] Fortescue, Chancellor.[66] Sir John Popham, Lord Chief Justice, was an unusual appointment as judges were not normally admitted to the Council. Probably Elizabeth chose Popham because she had known him for a long time.[67]

He was now more than ever the devoted servant of her Majesty. Camden calls him a Chief Justice of "unwearied diligence,"[68] but he was at times exhausted. On 28 July 1599, for instance, Sir John wrote to Cecil from Compton, near Littlecote: "I am very glad her Majesty has given so good allowance to the course devised for her ease in the signing of these grants, which otherwise would have been very troublesome to her. . . . I thank you heartily for the respect you have had for my ease now after my travel, which truly in respect of the great heat has almost tired me out, and must acknowledge myself, as always I have done, most bounden to her Majesty, as in that it has pleased her to admit unto me some time of stay in these parts, to recover my weariness and settle my own business, as for many favours that it has pleased her to extend towards me heretofore without any deserving of mine; but to my power and what is in me, it is wholly devoted to her service, and it is a great comfort unto me that it has rather pleased her ever to look upon my willingness to do her service than upon my insufficiency to perform the same."[69]

He gave the Queen a tangible token of his gratitude at New Year 1599–1600, which occurred in March. It was the custom at Elizabeth's court for New Year's Gifts to be presented to her Majesty, so the records tell us that "Sir John Popham, Lorde Cheif Justyce, gave in golde £10 0s 0d, delivered to Mr Sackforde."[70]

To Popham's many duties was now added attendance at Council meetings. They happened frequently—almost every day at this time, in both mornings and afternoons—at whichever royal palace the Queen was staying, most often Whitehall or Greenwich. Between six and nine councillors were present at most meetings, Sir John being among them increasingly regularly. During the twelve months from January 1600 he attended seventy-five sessions of the Council, and in the year from January 1601 no less than eighty-two. He was constantly in movement, the only respite being the summer months from July to September. The job must have been fascinating, for all matters of any import, private or public, came to the Council to resolve; everything that went on in England was its business. The Council's functions—advising the Queen on policy, administering the realm, and adjudicating disputes—made it responsible for the country's finance, dealing with religious dissent, and organizing national defense.

At this moment one of the councillors had caused a crisis. In Ireland with a large army, Robert Devereux, second Earl of Essex, had disobeyed the Queen's instructions by negotiating with the rebellious leader in Ulster, Hugh O'Neill, Earl of Tyrone, and making an ignoble truce. Essex returned at speed to England without command to do so and immediately presented himself to the Queen—before she had her makeup on. The nobles at the Star Chamber on 28 November 1599 were clearly outraged; serious trouble was in store for Essex.

They were also strangely agitated about "railing speeches and slanderous libels" made against the Queen by "traitorous monsters," as the Lord Keeper called them. Near the end of the proceedings the Lord Chief Justice contributed thus: "As my other offices prevent my being much in Council, I was not present when the affairs of Ireland were in question. . . . But as to the punishing of libel, this is properest to me; the fashion of it has been to scandalize the Queen, censure Councillors, and write against all authority; and the purpose is to disgrace those in authority, and cause disobedience and sedition, and bring all to confusion; for if a slander fall ever so carelessly on a man, he cannot clear himself of it. Therefore every well-wisher to his country should be diligent to find out these vipers. If men be not careful to honour their prince and discharge their duties, worse will fall out."[71]

It is appropriate that Sir John Popham saw libel and slander as particularly his concern, for he was and has remained a victim of them both.

11

Kimbolton's Killer

IN KIMBOLTON, A SMALL TOWN NEAR HUNTINGDON IN EAST ANGLIA, everyone knows that the Castle is haunted by the ghost of Sir John Popham.

The Lord Chief Justice is said to have thrown his newborn daughter through an upstairs window because she was not a boy. The child, perhaps the offspring of a maidservant, died, and every year at a certain time the stones in the courtyard below glow red with the child's blood.[1]

Another story is that "the Bad Judge" can be seen walking the hills around the Castle, sitting astride the wall that encloses the Castle's park, or on a stile at the corner of Warren Spinney, near the old priory, lying in wait for rogues and poachers under the great elms.[2]

Yet, as we could almost predict, Popham is not simply the subject of outrageous calumnies. He is also honored in Kimbolton. In the inner sanctum of the Castle, a magnificent portrait of Sir John glares down from the wall. How can this strange contradiction have arisen?

Popham was well known in Kimbolton. He had good reason to visit the town, for in 1600 he was appointed Justice of the Peace of the quorum for Huntingdon as well as Bedfordshire, Suffolk, the Isle of Ely, and Cambridgeshire. During his visits to the town for the quarter sessions, he may well have made the Castle his base. He would certainly have been the focus of much lively interest and tittle-tattle. Sir John had already been in the public eye at the top of the Queen's legal service for nearly twenty years. As the leader of the government's campaign against recusants, he would have been an obvious target of hostile opinion, and here there may well have been considerable local Catholic support. Kimbolton Castle was used as a prison for recusants,[3] and no doubt they aroused some sympathy. The rumors about Popham's acquisition of Littlecote were probably still good for a run by the tavern gossips.

Littlecote, Wiltshire. Photo: Lis Elwell.

Old Blundell's School, Tiverton, Devon.

Sir John Popham (Kimbolton portrait). Painting reproduced with the permission of the Governors of Kimbolton School.

The Castle had for many years been in the possession of the Wingfields, a large and widespread family with whom Popham had some significant connections. Sir Richard Wingfield, for instance, like his kinsmen Jaques and Edward Maria, had applied to be an undertaker in Ireland. None of the family were allotted land, probably because there was more than a hint of Catholicism about them; indeed, Edward Maria's father had been godson of Queen Mary and Cardinal Pole.[4] The estate had been wasted in the 1580s, which is perhaps why the Wingfield family seems not to have been considered responsible—Popham expressed the opinion that no member of the family should be a trustee of Kimbolton School.[5]

The owner of the Castle since 1592 had been Sir Edward, "the Great Warrior," a prominent jouster at Elizabeth's court. He had been at Cadiz and with Essex in Ireland, where he took part in the notorious parley with Tyrone. Following Essex's disgrace, Wingfield was exiled to Ireland, serving with the new Lord Deputy, Charles Blount, Lord Mountjoy. Although he often petitioned to be allowed home, the request was always refused. As a result, Kimbolton Castle was unoccupied, and it has been suggested that Popham took the use of it in return for saving Wingfield from the death penalty.[6] Sir John is supposed to have rented the castle in about 1600. He cannot have been in residence there for long; no letters written by him from Kimbolton have survived, and he was very heavily committed at this time both in London and at Littlecote.

How can the appalling legend have arisen that Sir John was a child-murderer? At the time he is supposed to have resided at the Castle he was sixty-nine, a little old for throwing illegitimate daughters through windows. It could be that a violent incident of some kind had occurred earlier, in the years before 1570, when after producing six daughters Popham might reasonably have been desperate for an heir. However, there is no evidence that Popham was ever in Kimbolton at that time, nor is there the slightest suggestion anywhere else in his life of a tendency to domestic violence. Is it possible that after 1589 the notoriety he acquired as a result of the alleged "Wild" Darrell child murder may have spread to East Anglia, so that by some strange distortion the story was transferred from Darrell at Littlecote to Popham at Kimbolton?

Sir John's appearance as a ghost perhaps derives from Kimbolton's earlier and more famous apparition. The Castle had been rebuilt as a Tudor manor house in the 1520s, and became home to Katherine of Aragon in 1534 after her divorce from King Henry VIII. Confining herself to the southwest corner of the building, she died there in 1536. Her body was buried at Peterborough Abbey,[7] but the ghost of Katherine of Aragon, in white robe and crown, is supposed to walk the west gallery, even though it was not built in her day. The unhappy Queen was last seen in 1939, when the army were billetted at the Castle.

It is likely that the ghostly ambience created by Katherine has been transferred over time to Popham, for in terms of place they are closely linked. The gallery along which the Queen's spirit walks is now called the Popham Gallery, because it contains the window from which Sir John is said to have thrown his infant. Beneath on the flagstones a reddish stain can definitely be seen, though skeptics might not be entirely convinced it was blood.

Katherine and Sir John share another location too, for in the very room in which she died there hangs a magnificent portrait of the Lord Chief Justice. Popham's physical presence emanates strongly from this picture; we do not know for whom it was painted, but it probably descended through the family to Alexander Popham (1669–1705). He married Elizabeth, daughter of the first Duke of Montagu; as they had no children, the picture probably went into the possession of the Montagu family, by then Dukes of Manchester, who had been the owners of Kimbolton Castle since 1606.[8] The Castle was redesigned in 1690–1720 by Vanbrugh, and is now the splendid home of Kimbolton School. Sir John Popham, grave and bristly, hangs in The Queen's Room behind the Headmaster's desk.

Another curiosity of Popham's Kimbolton connection is that in 1607, when he was seventy-six, he bought a windmill nearby. Several familiar names are included in the transaction by which the mill, described as in Kimbolton, Great Staughton, Overstowe, and Netherstowe, was sold to Popham by Sir Anthony Mildmay, Sir Richard Wingfield, Sir Francis Popham, Sir Robert Wingfield, Sir Thomas Wingfield, Robert Throckmorton, and John Pickering.[9] What could have led his son and partners to make over their interest to the very elderly father? Today we might think of tax evasion of some kind.

The connection between Popham and Kimbolton remains mysterious. We can only surmise that the legends exist because people were fascinated with Popham's official role, severe public image, and doubtful reputation. Disaffected men and women, or simply those with lively imaginations, had plenty to work on when Popham visited the town on circuit. Pre-existing ghost stories contributed, and later visitors to the Castle perhaps had an additional focus in the portrait.

Whatever their origin, these deplorable legends form a striking contrast with the eyewitness accounts of Sir John's exemplary conduct at the time of the Essex rebellion.

$$
\begin{array}{r}
1607 \\
76 \\
\hline
1531
\end{array}
$$

12

Prisoner of Essex

ROBERT DEVEREUX, SECOND EARL OF ESSEX, WAS A CONSUMMATE charmer. His personal magnetism had made him many friends, including the Queen, who had become infatuated with him in 1587 when he was twenty—and she fifty-four. He was a Cambridge man, a dashing military figure, handsome, rash, and given to prodigality. He was also extremely ambitious: "Not content with being made, within 11 years, from a boy of 19, master of the horse and ordnance, and Earl Marshal of England, and having 300,000*l*, he would be Lieutenant of Ireland, and wanted to be Secretary, Admiral, and what not."[1] Although not wealthy himself, the young Earl had wealthy friends, among them Henry Wriothesley, Earl of Southampton, Shakespeare's patron. Essex was a popular hero, and seems to have enjoyed the playwright's admiration too. When the Earl was sent to Ireland on 27 March 1599, Shakespeare referred to him as "the general of our gracious empress"; if he were to come back victorious, "How many would the peaceful city quit/ To welcome him!"[2]

It did not turn out like that. Essex easily made enemies too. The Queen herself was often put out of temper by his indifference to her commands, his volatility and excess, including the unauthorized knighting of his comrades in arms. Ralegh, her former favorite, was understandably hostile. But the main conflict was with Robert Cecil, son of Lord Burghley, the complete opposite of Essex in every respect except religion. Short, misshapen, uncharming, efficient, clever, trustworthy, and loyal, he became after his father's death in 1598 the man on whom the Queen relied. Popham must have felt very torn; he admired Essex, but was a close friend of Cecil too.

For ten years Essex had tried to establish himself in power, without success, for disputes over precedence and military policy led to increasing tension, arguments with Elizabeth, and personal insults. Finally he disobeyed the Queen's commands and made a failure of the Irish expedition. Essex returned impetu-

Robert Devereux, 2nd Earl of Essex, in 1590. Painting by William Segar. Photo: National Gallery of Ireland.

ously, as we have seen,[3] bursting unannounced into Elizabeth's bedchamber on 28 September 1599 at ten o'clock in the morning. By the afternoon, Elizabeth was furious, and sent him to answer before the Council, of which he was himself a member. He was kept standing and placed in the custody of Egerton. On 29 November 1599 Essex was charged in Star Chamber with maladministration and abandoning his command against the Queen's express orders. He was held under house arrest, where his mind seethed with wild purposes.

The Council had suspected for some time that Essex harbored extreme ambitions. He had been associated with the publication in 1599 by Dr John Hayward of *The First Part of the Life and Reign of Henry IV,* a prose history that seemed to support the overthrow of Richard II. Hayward appeared to have used stratagems to get the book past the censors, for after its approval a dedication to Essex had been inserted. Elizabeth thought that the book's great popularity with Londoners implied her own unpopularity, and Hayward was summoned before the Privy Council.[4] The questions to be put to the author were framed by Sir John Popham. Among them were: "What moved him to maintain, with arguments never mentioned in the history, that it might be lawful for the subject to depose the King, and to add many persuadings in allowance thereof? What moved him to allow that it is well for the common weal that the King was dead? Might he think that this history would not be very dangerous to come among the common people?"[5]

Following the latest evidence of his proud willfulness, Essex was brought before a private hearing by a special gathering of eighteen commissioners, nobles and judges of whom Popham was one, at York House on 5 June 1600. Essex was charged with "First, the makinge of knightes contrary to Her Majesty's instructions . . . Secondlye, the makinge the Erle of Southampton Generall of the Horse," which the Queen had required him not to do yet; thirdly, he had wasted his forces in Munster although he had express instructions to journey to Ulster; fourthly, he accepted "a base parly" with Tyrone; lastly, although he had express command not to return from Ireland until she had appointed a deputy and settled the forces there, he "did sodenly of his owne accord returne."[6]

The Earl was allowed to retain the Mastership of the Horse, but was to stay secluded at Essex House during the Queen's pleasure. The sentence was relaxed in August, but he was still banished from Court. The final blow to Essex's ambition was that in September the Queen refused to renew the patent which empowered him to levy customs charges on all sweet wines imported from the Mediterranean and the Levant.[7] Without this, his main source of income, he faced penury. It was then that he resolved on desperate action.

Exactly what Essex was hoping to achieve does not seem to have been clear even to him; broadly, he seems to have wanted to displace the Cecil faction in the Council and restore the nobility to their natural position as leaders. He was extraordinarily self-confident: he would easily surprise Whitehall palace, take the Tower and call a Parliament. The Earl thought he had friends in

Wales, in Ireland, in Scotland, and among his soldier comrades. Most importantly, he believed he could rely on huge popular support in the City of London.

By Christmas he had vague plans. By the beginning of February 1601 they were no more definite, but Essex learned that he was suspected and that the Queen's guard had been doubled. The source of this information was Sir Ferdinando Gorges, who was to become an important figure in Sir John Popham's story. Born in Somerset, he was the second son in a family of Norman origin. At Oxford briefly, he called himself "a plain soldier and one that is no scholar." Gorges had been knighted after an action before Rouen in 1591, and through Essex's influence became commander of the fortifications at Plymouth. His personality seems full of contradictions; at this point he was a conspirator, but a most unsatisfactory one. Summoned by Essex to a meeting on Tuesday, 3 February 1601, with his disaffected friends, he listened to their wild plans to "attempt the Court" and refused to go along with them: "As I would not condescend to that course, my Lord of Southampton said in a passion, 'Then we shall resolve upon nothing, and it is now three months or more since we first undertook this'"; as a result, "we broke up, resolved upon nothing, and referred all to the Earl of Essex himself."[8]

In fact no final plan was ever determined.[9] The action Essex took was virtually improvised, and has about it a feeling of desperation. Behind it all was the sense that overthrowing Elizabeth's government would be widely supported. Essex's followers seem to have felt that all they needed to do was give a nudge, and a wave of fervor for uprising would wash over England. Sir Charles Percy's idea was to use the theater as a stimulus, getting Shakespeare's own company at the Globe to put on a special performance of a play, usually taken to be his own, showing "the deposing and killing of Richard II."[10] The company disliked the proposal. According to a later examination before Popham of Augustine Phillipps,[11] servant to the Lord Chamberlain and one of his players, the company "were determyned to have played some other play, holdyng that play of Kyng Rychard to be so old and so long out of use as that they shold have small or no company at yt."[12] *Richard II* had probably been first performed in public in 1596, so it was five years old. The Queen had always regarded the play with suspicion and aversion. "I am Richard II," she cried on a later occasion, "know ye not that?"[13] and the abdication scene had hitherto been omitted in the printed texts. However, at the request of Essex's friends the company "were content to

play it." The extra 40s. they would receive for the special performance must have convinced them.[14]

The company could certainly relearn their parts quickly. Phillips may have got his dates wrong, but according to his testimony the negotiations happened only one or two days before the performance. On Saturday, 7 February, as Essex's steward Sir Gelly
Merrick told Popham later, he dined at Gunter's[15] in company
with Lord Monteagle, Sir Christopher Blount[16] and others, and
at the suggestion of Sir Charles Percy, "they all went together to
the Globe over the water . . . and were there somewhat before the
play began."[17]

It was not just entertainment. An armed uprising directed
against the Queen was clearly imminent. Men were gathering at
Essex House in the Strand, and they were in a kind of frenzy.
Blount later confessed that they should "(rather than have been
disappointed) even have drawn Blood from herself."[18] Elizabeth
summoned her advisers. A messenger was sent commanding Essex to attend the Council and explain his activities. With his
friends and supporters gathered about him, Essex was in an excited, paranoid state; he refused, claiming that he feared for his
life.[19] Action was now unavoidable.

The Captain of the Guard, Sir Walter Ralegh, was on the spot.
Bitterly opposed to Essex, he had nevertheless managed to maintain contact with the rebels through Sir Ferdinando Gorges, an
old Devon friend. So at dawn on Sunday, 8 February, Ralegh was
rowed down the Thames to a rendezvous on the water near Essex House. Gorges was evidently uneasy, but could tell Ralegh no
details of Essex's likely actions, for there was no agreed plan.[20]
He could only confirm that "you are like to have a bloody day of
it." From the bank, one of Essex's friends fired a number of shots
at Ralegh, who hurried back to Whitehall to rouse the Queen and
Court.

Elizabeth maintained cool control, selecting four men to go immediately on a peacekeeping mission directly to Essex House.
The Queen chose Essex's "best friends and nearest allies he had
in the court; the Lord-Keeper, the Lord-Chief-Justice, two that
loved him exceedingly well while he stood a good servant and a
true subject; the earl of Worcester and Sir William Knollys his
near kinsmen."[21]

The Lord Keeper, Sir Thomas Egerton, had since Essex's first
coming to court been a close friend of the younger man. He had
warned the Earl of Elizabeth's disfavor, and had been his custodian while Essex was detained at York House. The Lord Chief

Justice, Sir John Popham, would understandably have approved of Essex's knighting of his son. Egerton and Popham were both zealous Protestants, as was Essex.[22] Edward Somerset, 4th Earl of Worcester, had been considered in his youth the best horseman and tilter of his time and in spite of being a Catholic, became a favorite of Elizabeth, who said that he "reconciled what she believed to be impossible, a stiff papist and a good subject."[23] Deputy Master of the Horse to Essex, he was cleverly chosen for his similar skills and experience. Sir William Knollys was Essex's uncle, a man born to statesmanship and an experienced soldier and diplomat.

When the four Lords, with the purse-bearer carrying the Great Seal, arrived at Essex House in the Strand at 10 A.M. they found the gate manned by "six partisans"—men bearing long-handled spears with an axe-like cutting edge—under Sir William Constable.[24] They were let in through the side, or "wicket" entrance, but their followers were refused admittance: Owen Salisbury, who seems to have been an impetuous chief guard, shut the gate after the Lord Chief Justice, "whom he had like to have hurt thereby, if Constable had not helped him."[25] In the court there were about one hundred men, weaponed only with swords. Among them were the Earl of Southampton, Robert Catesby, Francis Tresham, and Sir Christopher Blount.

According to the declaration made later by Egerton,[26] the rebels "flocked together" about him, whereupon he "told the Earl of Essex that they were sent for from Her Majesty, to understand the cause of this their assemblage, and to let them know that if they had any particular cause of grief, it should be heard, and they should have justice." Hereupon "the Earl loudly declared that his life was sought [Ralegh and his friend Lord Cobham were accused];[27] that he should have been murdered in his bed; that he had been perfidiously dealt with; that his hand had been counterfeited, and letters written in his name; and that therefore they were assembling to defend their lives, &c. Hereupon the Lord Chief Justice said to the Earl that if any such matters were attempted, the Earl should declare it, and it should be truly related to Her Majesty, indifferently heard, and justice done, whomsoever it concerned.

"Upon this there was a great clamour raised amongst the multitude, crying [to Essex] 'Away, my Lord, they abuse you, they betray you, they undo you, you lose time.' Whereupon the Lord Keeper put on his hat, [the men had been bareheaded before as a sign of respect] and said with a loud voice, 'My Lord, let us speak with you privately, and understand your griefs; and I command you all, upon your allegiance, to lay down your weapons, and to depart, which you ought all to do, being thus commanded, if you be good subjects, and owe that duty to the Queen's Majesty which you profess.' Whereupon they all broke out into an exceeding loud shout and cry, crying 'All, all, all.'"

Popham himself persuaded the Earl to retire from the fray in the courtyard.[28] Egerton continues: "the Earl of Essex and most part of the company put on their hats, and so the earl went into the house, the Lord Keeper following him, thinking that his purpose had been to speak with them privately. As they were going in, some of that disordered company cried, 'Kill them;' others, 'Cast the great seal out of the window,' and others, 'Let us shop them up.' The Lord Keeper often called to the Earl of Essex to speak with them privately, thinking still that his meaning had been so, until the Earl brought them into his back-chamber, [it was upstairs, a closet off the great chamber] and there gave order to have the further door of that chamber shut fast."[29] The councillors had been tricked. They were hostages.

According to the Earl of Worcester, the Lord Keeper told Essex and his friends that if they would stay the Queen's messengers, they must keep them as prisoners, otherwise they would depart to Court; "to which the Earl replied, that if his Lordship and the rest would have patience until his return, both he and they would go together, and lay himself this cause at the feet of her Majesty; and so the rest cried out . . . 'Kill them, keep them as prisoners . . . Let them be pledges until their return.'" When Popham requested the Earl to dismiss his company, Essex replied, "He would not cause them to depart, that they should not think he would betray them."[30]

Essex said that he would "be here again within half an hour"; he evidently thought it would be a mere bagatelle to walk the few hundred yards to the City and inspire his waiting fans. Essex left the councillors in the reluctant charge of Sir John Davies, who would understandably much rather have gone to London with the Earl.[31] As Essex left through the lobby, other groups were coming up toward them, swearing they would stab and make an end of the Lord Keeper and Lord Chief Justice. One Henry Woodrington persuaded them that it was not a good course to be used toward such as were sent from Her Majesty, and told the Earl of Essex what violent courses were intended. "Others coming by and hearing, swore that it was no time then to make orations, but said 'Let us make an end of them, and then we have the fewer to deal with;' to which the Earl of Essex said nothing and went away. Going down amongst the company afterwards, Woodrington perceived that order was given that if any violence was offered to the house, or the Earl of Essex miscarried in London, the Lord Keeper and Lord Chief Justice should be killed."[32]

Popham looked through the keyhole. In the next room he could see men standing at the great chamber-door "with muskets charged and matches in their hands."[33] Then, Davies continues, "captain Salisbury having the guard of the muskets, was very violent and so disordered, as he doubted what he would attempt, and, contrary to the will of others, brought up the shot so near the door. And . . . that lest the fury of Salisbury should attempt beyond that was meant, [Davies] sometimes passed amongst the shot, and to satisfy the lords that no harm was meant them, he came in to them, whom when he perceived in some fear, he assured them that there should be no force offered them. But the Lord Chief Justice said: If they did take their lives, it was but the cutting off of a few years."[34]

Popham did his best to restore common sense to his gaolers. "The Lord Chief Justice said to Davies that seeing they were sent by her Majesty, and were of her Council, they should return to deliver what answer was made to them; [Davies] answered that the Earl would return within half an hour, being gone into the city; the Chief Justice said that the Earl would be deceived there, for the Queen had many good subjects in the city; answered that the Earl had great hopes of the city, or else he would never go thither. 'Then,' said the Chief Justice, 'if it were so, it will be an occasion of effusion of much English blood, and an occasion of spoiling of the city by desperate persons, and it will be the worst for the Earl and his company in the end.' Answered, that he assured himself the Earl would take care that no such thing should ensue."[35]

The councillors were lucky in their custodian. Sir John Davies had been intended to have a more public role in the rebellion; he was "meant to have carried the lord-keeper with the Great Seal into London; and to have had with [him] the lord-chief-justice, a man for his integrity, honored and well-beloved of the citizens."[36] Davies was a civilized man, though undistinguished except for a reputation as "a conjuror and Catholic, who in Oxford occupied himself in the idle art of figure casting [making horoscopes]."[37] He had been with the Countess when the councillors arrived, and "the better to assure the lords that no harm was meant them, he went up to the ladies, and intreated the countess of Essex to come down, and be amongst them; she making some pause at it, saying, With what comfort can I go amongst them?" Staying at the house too was Essex's sister, Penelope Lady Rich, the "Stella" of Sir Philip Sidney's sonnets and the most celebrated beauty of the time. According to Henry Garnet, as Lady Rich passed through the garden courtyard she called up to the guards, saying that "if they were true gentlemen, they would throw her down the head of that old fellow [Popham]." Such, wrote Garnet, "is the general detestation in which he is held by all classes."[38]

Davies persuaded the ladies "to go and be amongst them, the better to assure them that no barbarous usage should be offered unto them. . . . he behaved himself respectfully towards them, being uncovered before them, when others stood covered by them; and such provisions as the house had, he prepared for them, and set them a dinner." But the Lord Chief Justice and Lord Keeper told Davies that "they would eat none of my lord's meat."[39]

After six long hours in captivity, the councillors must have been surprised to hear steps, and find at the door a single person. It was Sir Ferdinando Gorges. He said to the councillors that Essex had authorized him to free one of them only—Sir John Popham. The Lord Chief Justice refused to go, "except they might all go; and said, as they came together, so they would go together, or die together."[40] Gorges bowed to the inevitable, and ordered them all in the Earl's name to be discharged. The councillors returned to the Court by water, Gorges accompanying them, rather uneasily, one imagines.

How much of what he had seen did Gorges tell the councillors as they were rowed up the Thames? On leaving Essex House, the Earl had marched his company into the Strand, walking in front accompanied by three earls and three barons, and followed by over a hundred gentlemen and their servants. As they passed along Fleet Street, the general multitude were entirely affected to the Earl, and "all the way he went, the people cryed, 'God save your Honour, God blesse your Honor.'"[41] The Earl rode on toward Fenchurch, and entered the house of the Sheriff of London, Thomas Smith, on whom he thought he could rely.[42] While the Earl drank, however, the Sheriff slipped out by the back door and informed the Lord Mayor, who took immediate action. By eleven o'clock the gates of the City were shut and strongly guarded. Essex went into an armorer's house, requiring munition, which was denied him, "and from thence the Earle went to and fro, and then came backe to Gracechurch-streete, by which time the Lord

Thomas Burghley [Cecil's step-brother] was come thither, having there, in the Queene's name, proclaymed the earle and all his company traytors, as he had done before in Cheapeside." Upon hearing this, "one of the Earle's followers shot a pistoll at Lord Burghley." It was at this point that Sir Ferdinando, "provident for himselfe," says Camden, at last did something decisive.[43] He advised Essex to return to the councillors, release them, and go with them to ask for the Queen's pardon, since so far no blood had been spilt.

While Gorges was rowing upriver with Popham and the other councillors, Essex's followers were in retreat, trying to force their way back to Essex House. Ludgate was shut against them, a fight broke out, and the Essex men were repulsed with casualties. They ran through Bow churchyard and Bow Lane to the river at Queenhithe, where as many as were able to find boats returned by water to Essex House. The Earl was "wonderfully discontent" at finding the councillors had gone, released a quarter of an hour before his return.[44] They must have been his last hope.

Now the rebels were themselves under attack. The siege of Essex House began at dusk, and when heavy artillery was fetched from the Tower, the rebels surrendered. The revolt had lasted twelve hours.

Dealing with the fallout from the Essex rebellion dominated Popham's life for several months. At the Tower, "and in my Lord Chief's chamber at Serjeants,"[45] examinations were held of all the participants and their associates. Every little bit of information helped. One Robert Berry, for instance, wrote to Popham: "Coming from Westminster by water to-day, I fell in with Harrison, a skinner from Fenchurch Street, and Emery of Distaff Lane; the former told us that a neighbour dwelling over against Sir Hen. Lindley, saw four or five persons on Sunday morning carrying muskets into his house; which, from the rebellion that followed I was of opinion were to supply men or others who came unarmed." Out of such observations the cases were compiled.

On 19 February 1601 the arraignment of Essex and Southampton took place at Westminster Hall. Twenty-four peers sat in judgment, with the Lord Treasurer and Lord Steward presiding. Popham was, remarkably, both assessor and witness. He was also consulted on a matter of law: when Essex asked if he might not except against any of the peers, the Lord Chief Justice said that he could not object to any peer, alleging a precedent to that effect in Henry VIII's time, "where no exception was to be taken against any Peere for that they spake uppon their honors, and that there was 24 of them, wherof 4 were enough to judge the treason yf they thought any of the rest not indifferent."[46] Essex pleaded Not Guilty, "for that he had don no thinge then by the law of nature and conscienc every man should doe."

The events of the day of the insurrection were summarized, and then the witnesses spoke. The second was Popham; Fuller notes "the rarity thereof, that a Lord Chief-Justice should be produced as witness in open Court."[47] Ralegh gave his account, Sir Ferdinando Gorges was "called to witness his going and coming from Sir Walter Raleigh," the Earl of Southampton "protested a long speech of his inocency and justification," and Essex asked pardon of Worcester and Popham for keeping them prisoners.[48] In due course judgment was given: "the Lord Steward made an exhortation and pronounced hanging and quartering &c. My Lord of Essex said presently 'Theise heades and quarters have donne Her Majestie good service, and if she had pleased might have donne her more.'"[49]

The Queen characteristically delayed the carrying out of the sentences. The very next day Popham received a letter "to signyfye her Majesty's pleasure that the executions shalbe stayed of those that have bene condemned for those late treasons and all proceedings also forborne against the rest untill he shall understand further of her Majesty's pleasure."[50] He was required by the Council for consultation. It has been suggested that Popham, grateful for having been spared at Essex House, appealed for the Earl to be pardoned.[51] If so, he did not succeed, and the sentence was reinstated. The Queen vacillated again on Shrove Tuesday, 24 February 1601, when the Lord Chamberlain's players, evidently forgiven for their role in the drama, performed before her.[52] Finally she steeled herself, and on the following day, Ash Wednesday, Essex was beheaded. The crowd attacked the executioner on his way out, for as Camden later wrote, "to this day there are but few that ever thought it a capital crime."[53]

The trial of Essex's friends makes absorbing reading, for at it was exhibited "the unbecoming spectacle of prisoners tried, and sentence pronounced, by a judge who had himself been a sufferer"—Sir John Popham.[54] His particular grief, he said before pronouncing judgment, was that "men of worth, service and learning" should be the actors in a conspiracy. There is no doubt Popham spoke personally here, for he put great faith in such qualities. "Shall it be said in the world abroad, that we Englishmen, now after forty-three years peace under so gracious and renowned a prince, are become weary of the government of such a queen, whom all the world else admires for her government? Consider it well, whoever had best hopes in this attempt of change, what would have followed upon it? Let me tell you of the smallest hurt, the blood of children, families and friends; for none of yourselves can otherwise think but this action would have cost much blood."[55]

Several others of the conspirators were executed too, but Popham must have interceded successfully on behalf of Sir Ferdinando Gorges. His situation was curious, for although he was arrested along with Essex, Gorges seems to have become at once a witness against him. It was an uncomfortable role. When Gorges spoke at Essex's trial against his former friend, Essex drew attention to his facial expression: "My lords, look upon Sir Ferdinando and see if he looks like himself. All the world shall see by my death and his life whose testimony is the truest."[56] Gorges was not even prosecuted: "the reason of forbearance was not that he had deserved better, or was otherwise conceited of to be an Arch-Traitor: but because he was the instrument of saving and letting go those that were sent from the queen to essex-house: and for this cause divers of her majesty's Privy-council had been suitors to her majesty for sparing his life for a time, though for their opinions of him, they held him an original and principal Traitor." On 26 November 1601 Her Majesty wrote to the Lord Chief Justice that she "is pleased out of her gracious inclinacion that he shalbe inlarged out of prison and commytted to the charge of his brother Edward Gorges, esquier, who is to enter into bond in the somme of 1,000*li* for his forthcomming."[57] The strange experience at Essex House was to be the basis of a close collaboration, for five years later Sir John Popham and Sir Ferdinando Gorges together directed their energies to a very different enterprise—the colonization of America.

The Queen's four councillors had behaved valiantly at Essex House, said Sir Edward Coke, "for so I will term it, and to their honours I will speak it, that it shall appear that in some gownmen there rests as valiant minds, where the cause requires it, as in them that wear swords."[58] After such stalwart service for her Majesty, it was only right that Popham should be rewarded. On 13 August the Queen was at Windsor, and was expected shortly at Mr Comptroller's [Sir William Knollys] at Caversham; "and so the progresse should hold on as far as Litlecot a house of the Lord Cheife Justice in Wiltshire: but there be so many incounters to hinder yt, that I will lay no great wager of the proceding."[59] We can easily imagine what a flutter this must have put the household into. Popham and Lady Amy would no doubt have been anxiously refurnishing, decorating, and ensuring the servants knew their roles perfectly. It is very likely that the royal crest in the Queen's Room at Littlecote was added in expectation of this visit. Incidentally, a letter in July from Sir John Gilbert to Cecil at this time recounts some news the writer had heard from "a Portuguese, who was once butler to my Lord Chief Justice six years, and wished himself again in his service."[60] Popham certainly needed a good butler now.

On 21 August 1601 Cecil wrote at length to Popham and the Archbishop of Canterbury to give them accurate information about affairs of state in Ireland and the Low Countries. He ended: "Of our Progress, I am sorry that I cannot write unto you that it were abridged, you being well able to judge how ill these growing troubles concur with her Majesty being so far removed from her Council: for which purpose because her Majesty sees you will not come to her, it is like that she will come to you."[61]

Popham replied to Cecil from Littlecote on 26 August: "I have received your kind and friendly letters, whereby you have made known unto me things that I was before utterly ignorant of, otherwise than as the bruit of the country carried them: and your letters do satisfy me of her Majesty's coming into these parts, which before I stood very doubtful of: and it is my greatest comfort to understand her Majesty has that strength of body as she is able to undergo such travail in hunting and otherwise as I hear she has done, since she set forth in this progress. God continue it still. I hope you will be pleased to take your lodging with me at her Majesty's being here. I trust the harbinger and your own servant shall find some place to content you, as the time and case stands, whereof I shall be very glad. And now I must entreat all my honourable friends to make the best of what they shall find here, and to take all in good part; otherwise I fear me I shall be utterly ashamed."[62]

The progress was altered and abridged. Entertaining foreign statesmen was the Queen's duty, and a party of three hundred Frenchmen were on the doorstep. Elizabeth did go to Sir Humfry Fosters [Sheriff of Berkshire], "and so meant to have gon on to the Lord Cheife Justices and to the earle of Hartfords [at Elvetham in Hampshire] yf these Frenchmen had not staide her: but now I thincke she be at the farthest for this yeare, and they say is drawing backe to Windsore." It must have been particularly galling to Sir John and his wife that at the Queen's last being at Windsor, she had "made a step to Master Atturneyes [Sir

Edward Coke, Popham's colleague and friend] at Stoke, where she was most sumptuously entertained, and presented with jewells and other guifts to the value of a thousand or twelvehundred pound."[63] What is more, the present progress was truncated because her Majesty had to entertain the Marshal of France, Charles Biron and his large retinue. When he was himself truncated for treason in the Bastille on 29 July 1602, it was said that "His death is generally lamented, yet his best friends do acknowledge that from his infancy he hath been a great blasphemer and that he was of a disposition so savage that he has with his own hands murdered five hundred persons in cold blood."[64] Such was the man who kept Queen Elizabeth from Littlecote.

The visit was not to be—at least this year.

13

Friend of Blundell

Aт this time Popham became very closely involved in the affairs of his wealthy and charitable friend, Peter Blundell.

Ten years or so older than Popham, Blundell was born in Tiverton, Devon, a leading town in the cloth trade. At first a poor boy, Blundell is supposed to have earned a few pennies by running errands for visiting kersey-traders. Saving enough to buy a single kersey—a kind of coarse narrow cloth woven from long wool, usually ribbed—he had a piece of luck: the kersey was taken to London by a friend without any charge and sold for Blundell's profit. The young merchant made rapid progress in the kersey trade, setting up a factory of his own, and eventually accumulated a huge fortune.[1]

Little is known about this man, and no correspondence remains to illuminate his friendship with Popham. All we can suggest is that Peter Blundell, who lived only fourteen miles from Wellington, must have been a leading figure among West Country clothiers. He would have been concerned with protecting the trade, and is likely to have met Popham in that connection.

The cloth industry had experienced problems during the time Blundell was building his fortune, an Act being passed in 1551, for instance, to restrict the trade and prevent it from expanding out of towns. But by 1571, when Popham first sat in Parliament, it was thought necessary to stimulate the trade, and new legislation required all citizens of England to wear caps of wool on the Sabbath and on holidays. In 1576 Popham sat on a House of Commons committee on cloth, and later he acted at least six times for the clothiers of Somersetshire and other counties against the Merchant Venturers, who tried for half a century to establish a monopoly on the export of cloth from England. In November 1591 the council wrote to Popham, then Attorney-General, Sir George Bonde, and Mr Milwarde, who had been given to understand "by divers of the Justices of the Peace and other gentlemen of creditte in the countie of Devon" that in spite of existing legislation concerning "the true and perfecte makinge of clothe called Devonshire kerseyes or doosens" that defined and prescribed the proper weight and measurements of such cloths, "certaine evill desposed persons usinge the trade of weavinge and sellinge of kerseies have invented and put in use divers slighte and badd devises" in making such kerseys.[2] The council requested the three lawyers to find out more from "some merchantes experienced in the trade of buyinge and sellinge of clothe" what inconveniences resulted from these abuses, and to recommend action to remedy the situation. It is more than possible that Peter Blundell was one of those consulted.

Peter Blundell must have been impressed by Popham and evidently got to know him well, for when he came to make his will on 9 June 1599—the only document we have from his long life—he appointed Sir John to carry out for him one specific task. Blundell wished to establish in Tiverton a free grammar school.

This would be the first such establishment in a town that certainly needed charity. On 3 April 1598 Tiverton had been devastated by fire, which began about one o'clock in the afternoon "at a poore cottage: a woman there frying pancakes with strawe (for lacke of other fewell) the same fiered the house and so the towne." According to Stow the rage of the fire consumed 409 houses, £150,000 in money, plate, merchandise, and household stuff. Fifty persons perished, but an almshouse was preserved "with poore men therein, in the midst of the flames." Nine thousand people had been maintained in Devonshire, Cornwall, and Somersetshire by the clothing industry in Tiverton, but the disaster was thought by many to be "a just punishment of God uppon that towne for the unmercifullnesse of the riche, and small regard of the poore, which were daily seene to perish in the streetes for lack of releife."[3]

Blundell needed a person of energy and practical experience who would be capable of bringing his vision into actuality. To carry out his wishes "I doe also most humbly desier and praie the Directions of my deare Frende Sir John Popham, Kt. Lord Chief Justice of England whome it hath already pleased to promise me his lawful help and furtherance for the better Execution of this my last Will. Item I give unto the same Lord Chief Justice in token of my dutifull Love and good Will to his Lordship one hundred Powndes."[4] Having already built chambers at the Middle Temple and a manor house in Wellington, as well as undertaking major reconstruction at Littlecote, Popham understood stone, bricks, and mortar; having himself contemplated setting up an almshouse, he knew the legal considerations. He was a wise choice, and it says much for Popham's probity and worth, in spite of all the allegations against him, that Peter Blundell trusted him with his regard.

Blundell died in London on 18 April 1601 and was interred in the church of St Michael Paternoster. A bachelor, he appears to have lived in the care of Ann Whitmore, a widow of Lombard Street; to her and her family, as well as to his own nephew and cousins, he left substantial legacies.[5] Having accumulated a fortune far beyond that of the richest merchant in Exeter at this time,[6] he was able to leave nearly £40,000 in benefactions: to the London hospitals and the city companies, to various institutions at Tiverton—£400 was left to be divided equally between twenty "maides, native of Tiverton" that they might be better able to find husbands—and to the city of Exeter for the encouragement of the city's craftsmen. But the chief work was the endowment of Blundell's School, for which £2,400 was earmarked.

The Will is very specific about details. The executors should "with all convenient Speede upon a fytt and convenient Platt and piece of Grounde in Tyverton . . . erecte and buyld a faier School house." The teaching place was to be one hundred feet long and forty-two feet broad, with "a Hawle Buttery and Kitchin all of convenient Space and Biggness" joined to it. All the windows were to be "well and strongly glassed and barred with Iron Barrs and well covered." The floor was to be "well plancked with Plancks of Oke supported and borne from the Ground with strong Ledges or Beames with soe many fitt and strong Settles and Formes as shall be convenient having regard to the Bigness of the same Schoole and number of Schollars to be taughte therein." The teaching space was to be divided into two and paneled— "strongly wainscotted rownde abowte and the same Wainscotte to extend abowte five or six foote above the Settles or Formes"— presumably to protect the walls. The domestic arrangements had been thought of too: in the kitchen was to be "one faier great Chimney with an Oven and a Chamber over the Kitchen with a Chimney therein." Adjoining the schoolhouse there should be "a convenient Garden and Woodyard with a fit House and Easements therein of and for the Ease of the Schollars uppon or as near the River of Ex there or Loman as may be," and the schoolhouse and toilet block were to be "rounde aboute well walled and inclosed with a strong Wall the goinge in and forthe to be at one only place with a fair strong Gate with a little Dore as is usual in the Schooles."

"My Will and Meaning is," continued Blundell, "that in and aboute theis severall Buildings Plott Frame and all the Partes thereof the Advise and Directions of my saide righte deare and honorable Friende Sir John Popham Knighte Lord Chief Justice of England shall be taken and followed and to him I give Power and Authority to alter and chaunge what parte or partes thereof for the Manner of building largeness and conveying the Premises he shall think good." His "Directions in every Thinge for the effectinge of my said Purpose herein" were "to be still followed and executed."

If the exact site had not yet been acquired, Blundell evidently knew where he wanted the building to be. He was also very careful to define exactly the sort of school he had in mind: 150 boys, born or brought up in Tiverton, were to be eligible. If these numbers were not filled up by local children, then "Forreyners" could be admitted, children of "such Forreyners as are of honest Reputation and feare God," selected by ten householders of Tiverton "without regarding the riche above or more than the poore." Blundell also insisted that "there shall bee noe Scholer bee or continue in the said Schoolle as a Scholer but Boyes and none above the Age of Eighteen Yeares and none under a Grammer scholler." The boys were to be taught by a Schoolmaster, paid £50 a year, and an Usher who would receive "twentie Markes" [£13 6s 8d]. They were not to take private fees, for Blundell's meaning was that "yt shall be forever a Free Scholl and not a Schole of Exaction."

Blundell then appointed the Feoffees [trustees]: Sir Francis Popham heads the list of twenty-seven local men, which includes Roger Warre, Sir John's son-in-law, John Waldron, also a Popham relation, and James Clarke Esquire, Sir John's faithful factotum. Blundell left "eight Powndes yearely to goe alwaies to the Repairations of the saide Schoole and other Things necessary concerning the same for ever."

Popham set about the task with his usual energy, and building must have started very soon on the four-acre site beside the river Lowman. A headmaster had to be found able to put Blundell's idea into practice. Popham asked the advice of Dr Chaderton, Master of the puritan Emmanuel College, Cambridge, founded as recently as 1584 by Sir Walter Mildmay. Joseph Hall, a brilliant man of only twenty-seven, later recalled that Chaderton recommended the position to him, "assuring me of no small advantages, and no great toil; since it was intended the main load of work should lie upon other shoulders." No doubt headmasters are still lured with promises like that. Hall thought it not wise or safe to refuse good offers, so "Mr. Dr. Chaderton carried me to London; and there presented me to the Lord Chief Justice, with much testimony of approbation. The Judge seemed well apaid with the choice. I promised acceptance; he, the strength of his favor."

But it was not to be. "No sooner had I parted from the Judge, than, in the street, a messenger presented me with a letter, from the right virtuous and worthy lady, of dear and happy memory, the Lady Drury of Suffolk, tendering the rectory of Halstead [Hawstead, near Bury St Edmunds], then newly void, and very earnestly desiring me to accept of it.[7] Dr. Chaderton, observing in me some change of countenance, asked me what the matter might me. I told him the errand, and delivered him the letter; beseeching his advice; which when he had read, 'Sir,' quoth I, 'methinks God pulls me by the sleeve; and tells me it is his will, I should rather go to the east than the west.' 'Nay,' he answered, 'I should rather think that God would have you go westward, for that he hath contrived your engagement before the tender of this letter; which therefore coming too late, may receive a fair and easy answer.' To this I besought him to pardon my dissent; adding, that I well knew, that divinity was the end whereto I was destined by my parents; which I had so constantly proposed to myself, that I never meant other, than to pass through this western school to it: but that I saw that God who found me ready to go the further way about, now called me the nearest and directest way to that sacred end. The good man could no further oppose; but only pleaded the distaste which would hereupon be justly taken by the Lord Chief Justice, whom I undertook fully to satisfy: which I did with no great difficulty; commending to his Lordship, in my room, my old friend and chamber-fellow Mr Cholmley: who finding an answerable acceptance, disposed himself to the place; so as we two, who came together to the university, must now leave it at once."[8]

It is possible that Cholmley taught at Tiverton, but it was the third appointment, Mr Samuel Butler, who is regarded as the first Headmaster of Blundell's. He had held a similar post elsewhere, "brought his scholars with him,"[9] and stayed for many years. The school was intended not simply to teach poor Tiverton boys the rudiments of Latin and Greek. Blundell had greater things in mind. He bestowed £2000 to establish "Six Schollers to be Students in Divinitie in the Universitie of Oxford or Cambridge or in both for ever," his purpose being "the Increase of good and Godly Preachers of the Gospel"—a typically puritan senti-ment.[10] These places were to be supplied "out of the saide Gram-mer Schoole of Tyverton and not elsewhere." It was left to Popham and the other executors to negotiate with the universi-ties and nominate the first six scholars.

At Oxford, Popham approached Balliol, where he himself had studied. Closed scholarships were not always thought desirable, as they limited the power of a college to select students as it wished.[11] However, Popham was persuasive, and Balliol, which had puritan leanings at this time, was sufficiently poor to make the endowment acceptable.[12] So Popham succeeded in carrying out Peter Blundell's wishes, though he did change the terms of the gift. By the time the college received the money—£700 to be invested in lands—it was to endow not just a scholarship but a fellowship as well, to be held automatically by a man who had completed his studies as a Blundell Scholar. Thus Popham se-cured a permanent residence at Balliol for at least two men from Blundell's School at Tiverton.[13]

At Cambridge too some colleges disapproved of closed scholar-ships. Emmanuel rejected the offer, so the places were estab-lished at Sidney Sussex, the newest college, founded only in 1594. Quick to act as ever, Popham had made the arrangements by 1602, well before Blundell's School was completed.[14] The young men who became the first scholars were either at the universi-ties already, or went as a result of some personal recommenda-tion. A Corpus Christi College student, John Berry, and Christo-pher West were the first scholars at Balliol, and William Durant and John Pokington at Sidney. The scholars were to study divin-ity, remain unmarried, and be of good conversation. They would receive £8 p.a. for their maintenance, and were to be "called by the names of Peter Blundell Scollers." Fellows had similar obli-gations, and received £15 p.a.[15] John Berry, said to have been the son of a Tiverton weaver, in due course became the first Blundell Fellow of Balliol.

The school eventually cost £3,400 to build,[16] and has always claimed a foundation of 1604. "This noble edifice, somewhat re-sembling the colleges of the Universities . . . is a strong stone building, having a durable roof of chestnut wood, built similar to that of Westminster-hall, and covered with blue slate."[17] The walls were, and indeed still are, about three feet thick, the north front being cased with Ham stone. It was a fine building to house an exceptionally large school for the time.[18] Recent commenta-tors have observed that Blundell's was among the first schools to be planned with its components architecturally differentiated,[19] and great care was taken to make the composition symmetrical.[20] William Morris thought the buildings very valuable "both for general completeness and for great beauty and fitness of design."[21]

Popham's buildings continued in use, with only minor modifications, until 1882, when a new school was built a mile out of town. The old building was sold to a local brewer, who divided up the fine schoolrooms to be let as private dwellings. Old Blundell's still has this form, although the school repurchased the building in 1939 and in 1946 presented it to the National Trust. The fellowships arranged by Popham continued into the nineteenth century, when they were melted down into scholarships. The last Blundell's Scholarship at Balliol was awarded in 1977, and the final Sidney Sussex Exhibition the following year. Soon afterward the whole system ceased to exist. However, like other colleges, Balliol still awards internal scholarships after first-year examinations, and former Blundell's students winning them are even now entitled to call themselves Blundell Scholars. Close links between the School and Balliol and Sidney Sussex Colleges remain to the present day.

In the course of time Blundell's School, like all such early foundations, has changed remarkably. Boys and girls can now be educated there from the age of three months to eighteen years. They have to pay, however. Peter Blundell's intention to create a free school is preserved only in the award of a number of full and part scholarships each year, and a reduction in fees for Tiverton children. If he and Sir John Popham could see the school now, they would be amazed and astonished that the original intention had been so distorted. They would also be proud of what their vision had produced.

14

Cecil's Correspondent

THE FAILURE OF THE ESSEX REBELLION LEFT ROBERT CECIL TRI-
umphant. The Queen's Principal Secretary, son of Lord Burghley,
was the most powerful man in England.

The Queen respected him greatly, relying on his administrative skill, hard work, and efficiency. She nicknamed him her "elf"
or "pygmy," which suggests that though he was physically far
from the perfect model of a courtier—he suffered from a physical
deformity—Cecil enjoyed a special place in the Queen's confidence. This was not likely to make him popular. Something similar is true of Popham. Powerful, large, peremptory, and intensely hard-working, he was respected by other royal servants
but a bogeyman to many ordinary folk. Both officers were entirely devoted to their Queen and country, but aroused much en-
mity among the people.

The documents of this period reveal that Sir John Popham was
more than Cecil's very close associate in the business of government. He was his friend. Few of Cecil's letters have survived, but
Popham's show him corresponding with the Secretary on a wide
variety of issues in a chatty, almost intimate way. He wrote at
length, in detail, and with an easy fluency; Popham must have
felt very comfortable with Robert Cecil. Perhaps it was the Secretary's particular skill to invite this unguarded response.

On 22 June 1601, for instance, Popham wrote from Serjeants'
Inn: "You know how late I came home yesternight so as I could
not meet with the party that makes the discovery until this
morning. [This party was a woman, informing on a man called
Arthur Bedle.] These speeches the woman said he used to her.
'He wished God to convert her Majesty or God to confound her,'
adding withal that he hoped 'ere it were long we should have a
merry world in England'; and, after meeting her in the Strand,
told her, asking whither he went, he said to dine with a company of gallants that were to pass over with him; for which purpose,
he said, he had a ship of his own ready at Portsmouth to pass

Robert Cecil, 1st Earl of Salisbury, in 1602. Painting by John de Critz the Elder. Photo: National Portrait Gallery.

thence the latter end of this month. This man . . . lieth not two nights in one place, which, with his speeches aforesaid, moved her to suspect he had some evil purpose in hand, and therefore discovered it. He is of good stature, very well complexioned, black hair, well made, very bold and of between 40 and 50 years old, and a very comely and handsome man. . . . the woman doth use all means she may to discover where he may be had; which I will have all the care I may of, but in my opinion it will not be amiss to send some trusty and secret person to Portsmouth to discover whether his speech for the ship be true. I had written sooner but

I heard you would be here this evening and so my letters might have missed you."[1]

Popham was able to share his anxieties with Cecil. In July 1601 he wrote from Aylesbury: "Having well observed the state of things as they stand in all these parts through which I have lately travelled, besides what I have heard from other parts, it makes me to fear what may follow if it be not foreseen in time. Through the great 'dryeth' [drought] that has been and is yet like to continue, I doubt me that which is the chiefest food of the common sort of people (which is butter and cheese) will (if God give not a more fruitful latter end of the year than the former part hitherunto has been) grow to such a scarcity and dearth as the common sort of people shall not be able to endure it this next winter: and withal there is so great a want and dearth like to be of hay and other fodder." Popham goes on to suggest that fish brought in from Newfoundland, and herring "both at Yarmouth and in Severn" should not be exported as they have been; keeping them at home "may give great relief and contentment to the people, and make them well able to undergo the other wants."[2]

Popham sounds more like a constructive friend than a Lord Chief Justice. Together he and Cecil took on anything. Both gained credit for resolving a curious quarrel at the Middle Temple. John Davies, lawyer and poet, had been expelled from the Inn for assaulting Richard Martin, a noted wit, to whom he had dedicated his poem *Orchestra,* a work now regarded as a central text in Elizabethan thought. John Chamberlain reported that "The Lord Cheife Justice and Master Secretarie have taken great paines to compound the quarrell twixt Martin and Davies which they have effected to the satisfaction of both parts."[3]

One wonders whether both men were present when *Twelfth Night* was performed in Middle Temple Hall, on 2 February 1602. Judges normally attended, so the likelihood is that Sir John was there to watch, and it is possible that Shakespeare himself was acting.[4] Evidently Popham needed to exert pressure on his senior colleagues to agree to expenditure on entertainment for the Queen—another performance of the play, perhaps. "I have so dealt with some of the Benchers of the Middle Temple," he wrote to Cecil on 8 February, "as I have brought that the House will be willing to bear 200 marks towards the charge of what is wished to be done, to her Majesty's good liking, and if the young gentlemen will be drawn in to perform what is of their part, I hope it will be effected. Some of the young men have their humors, but I hope that will be over-ruled."[5]

Popham took great pains too in all matters connected with trade and finance, on which he was routinely consulted. Cecil had asked him to investigate the affairs of the copper mine near Keswick in Cumberland. Opened at the beginning of Elizabeth's reign, it had become "the most famous at that time in England, perhaps in Europe."[6] However, by 1601 it had fallen into financial straits, producing only 92 cwt of copper in twelve months.[7] So in May 1602 Popham wrote to Cecil: "It pleased you some year now past, in respect of your so great employments other ways, to move me to look into the matter of the copper mines at Cheswicke, the estate whereof you then suspected, and we since have at sundry meetings found to be so desperate as there was in effect no hope left to continue them." Nevertheless Popham had encouraged the company to keep going; "seeing to how great a commodity the very use of this copper might be to the commonwealth, and how hard it is to be had good from foreign parts," he had "moved her Majesty in it, and for renewing the patent in respect of some defect in it, which it pleased her to refer to my Lord Treasurer and yourself. I beseech you some course may be taken for the despatch of it, whereby the book may be made ready for her Majesty, otherwise I do not see how these works can continue, unless it shall please her Majesty to be at the charge and hazard of it herself, and take them into her own hands, which I think you would not willingly advise."[8]

In the summer of 1602 a Report on the mines at Keswick was prepared for Popham and Cecil.[9] It is likely that it led to action that achieved an improvement in results, for both Sir John and Sir Francis Popham were shareholders in the company in 1605.[10] There were the usual family reasons for their interest; Sir Francis's wife's father, John Dudley, had been a shareholder, as had Cecil's father, Lord Burghley. In 1606 John Popham and Robert Cecil were to be given a substantial share of the profits of the Mines Royal by James I.

Another occasion which may have brought him reward was his election in April 1602 as High Steward of Dunwich.[11] This unfortunate town on the coast of Suffolk had formerly been a vigorous port, able in 1241 to send eighty ships to the help of the king, but in the fourteenth century storms and floods had caused its quays to be blocked with shingle.[12] By 1585 nearly half the medieval town had been swallowed up by the sea. It was still a busy little port, but only a shadow of its former self. The High Steward would normally have advised the corporation on legal matters, but the appointment may also have been made in the hope that the Lord Chief Justice would exercise his influence in favor of the town. Unfortunately no records remain to show whether the post brought Popham responsibility or remuneration.

On 20 December 1602 the subject of correspondence was the exchange rate for the new currency of Ireland, issued by the Queen in May. Popham wrote to Cecil: "I send you herein a project of that which was moved yesterday for 40*l* sterling to be delivered upon the exchange of each 100*l*. I am persuaded the substance of your project must be hearkened unto, and I pray you think well of that which was moved to be permitted current also here, for I fear me it will bring upon the state here an infinite many of discommodities and inconveniences, which I shall be ready to impart unto you. I make choice to write this much unto you, as to one that I do specially respect, and for that I hold these things are of a kind as you will better satisfy yourself upon a full digesting of it with yourself than upon any sudden speech or motion of others."[13]

Cecil evidently respected the Judge too, for in a letter to Richard Topcliffe he refers to a case with which he had been concerned: "For the matter, I was glad to find that my Lord Chief Justice had some understanding of the cause, for besides that I know him very wise, he is well acquainted with the condition of these knaves that will accuse one another."[14] Another remarkable knave must have been discussed by the two men in July 1602, when Popham received a letter from Rome written by the extraordinary Sir Anthony Sherley.

Sherley was a former soldier, an Essex man—he had secretly married Frances Vernon, a first cousin of the Earl—and a much-traveled adventurer of the boastful kind.[15] His missions as a semi-official ambassador and secret agent to several countries often had an improvised flavor, as a result of which he had been forbidden to return to England. These travels had taken him across the Atlantic as well as to Ferrara, Venice, Persia, Moscow, Prague, and Rome. A man of wild schemes, he was a vain spendthrift, always in debt; the English government distrusted him, and Robert Cecil, who had an affair with his wife, kept him under surveillance. An agent in the pay of both Scotland and Spain,[16] Sherley was in 1602 in Rome and very short of funds. He learned that "letters had been sent against me by Queen and Council," and was moved to write on 20 July to Popham: "I appeal to you, as in the highest seat of justice, to hear my extraordinary case and unjust sufferings." After outlining his military career and his attempts to influence the King of Persia to break with Spain, Sherley complained: "I think it strange to be now persecuted by those from whom I should have expected comfort. I hope not to be driven by violent courses to desperation. I beg you, as set in that seat to redress wrongs, to look upon me . . . . My innocence is proved by my being in want; I should never have been allowed to want had I been useful to the Spaniards . . . . Pardon the importunity of a heart full of bitter anguish."[17] Popham passed the letter on to Cecil, who remained unmoved. Sherley never returned to England, but after many further adventures died in poverty at Granada in Spain.

A prisoner called Geoffrey Gronno was another who received little sympathy. He complained to Cecil that he had written to the Deputy-Marshal of the Queen's Bench gaol "to pray him move my Lord Chief Justice touching my liberty. His Honour took bail of me half a year past and again at Michaelmas, intending, as I took it, to set me at liberty. One Farr, my adversary's attorney, had order of discharge for me, but because I sent to put his Honour in remembrance again, he would not discharge me . . . . I was very sick, for I had been in prison ten years, in a close house, doubly ironed. I prayed my Lord to give me one day respite to speak to the Queen, but he would not grant it, and committed me to the common gaol of the Bench. Here I have been three years. I sent many petitions, and my Lord Chief Justice did put my messenger in prison. Another time, one of his men threatened to set my messenger in the stocks. Then I sent to the council table, but the matter was committed from them to the Lord Chief Justice to end it. Michaelmas last, I made a prisoner here write to the Attorney General, wherein he enclosed my petition to her Majesty. Whereupon my Lord said he would set me in the pillory if I did speak any more. I pray, therefore, that some order may be taken that I be no longer driven by imprisonment to such clamorous and outrageous outcries."[18]

Popham was called upon to hear a case against Cecil himself, as well as Egerton, Sackville, the Lord Treasurer, and the Council in general against accusations made by Arthur Hale, one of a group of "bold fellows that lay high matters to the Lords' charge." The Council members were said to have shared 100,000*l* intended for Ireland among themselves, to have been disloyal to the Queen, whose state they considered so weak that "if she yielded not to the Council's will, they would (which is fearful for the heart of man to think) cut her off," and to have indulged in widespread profiteering. Hardly surprisingly, "they were heard in great secrecy, and sent to the Gatehouse"; as Dudley Carleton remarked, "their cause will thrive ill when their adverse party is *juge et partie;* the Lord Chief Justice and Attorney Coke have the hearing of the matter."[19]

Cecil and Popham, with the Lord High Admiral, were the councillors recusants most feared.[20] Father Anthony Rivers was Henry Garnet's secretary, and like him sent long and detailed reports abroad, in his case to Fr Robert Parsons, the controller of the Jesuit English campaign: "My Lord Chief Justice concurreth with all his industry to further Felton in his finding out the livings and goods of the recusants, and that course is with all extremity prosecuted without any commiseration, insomuch as many poor gentlemen that have wives and children are driven to great miseries, and more are like daily to succeed.[21] The said Lord Chief Justice hath promised her Majesty in a short time, by these means, to bring her in so much money and revenue as shall defray the greatest part of the charge of the wars of Ireland."[22] In March 1602 Felton has won a suit for 3s 4d in the pound of all the property of recusants he can win for the Queen; "The Chief Justice maintaineth his proceedings, *quo jure quamvis injuria* [by whatever right, however unjust]. This benefit to himself will make him even more eager in the pursuit."[23] There can be little doubt that Antony Bonneville, an informer working for Cecil, speaks for many others when he calls Popham simply "that wicked judge."[24]

The Queen herself was hard on the priests. In April Rivers reported a dramatic incident at the Clink prison on Low Sunday [the Sunday after Easter], when "the Chief Justice's men, with pursuivants and other officers, rushing in suddenly, with drawn swords, upon them, found their altars and massing stuff prepared, and three priests, Barneby, Clark, and Watson, with well near forty Catholics (most women and some poor folks of the city), all assembled in the same chamber and some others adjoining, all amazed at this sudden accident."[25] Referring to the execution of the three priests, Rivers wrote a few weeks later that "The Chief Justice, the day before their execution, going to the court to know the Queen's pleasure, she wished him to proceed, adding that she beshrewed [cursed] his heart if he spared them or any other of their coat."[26]

Elizabeth's friends were roused at this time against Popham, in rather belated defense of a staunch Catholic woman. When Father Francis Page came up before Popham in April it was remembered that the Chief Justice had the previous year condemned to death Anne Line, a devoted harborer of priests. "The ladies of the Court had, either in jest or earnest, stormed against the Lord Chief Justice and loaded him with maledictions because he had condemned a lady to be hung for receiving a priest into her house, yet had not apprehended and convicted the priest himself, but let him escape. When therefore his lordship learnt that this was the very same priest who had escaped from Mrs Line's house, after examining, he at once committed him to Newgate, where he was thrust down into 'Limbo,' a dark and damp underground dungeon; that he might there remain and, with a macerated human body, rot away alive."[27] It had been a woman who had informed against Page, "a wicked woman that had pretended a desire of Papistry, suborned to betray, and effecting her desire, and continuing long in her dissimulation, thereby coming to know some priests, revealed at length all, and more than all, to the Chief Justice."[28]

Popham was suffering from overwork. On 21 May 1602 he forwarded to Cecil a letter he had received from his nephew William Pole about a dangerous Scot with Spanish connections. "I send you a letter from the west parts. You know best what use may be made of it, and whether it be fit to deal with this Scot. . . . Excuse my absence for six or seven days, in which time I hope to recover the grief I have in my eyes through overmuch poring on papers, which I cannot avoid here from morning until night, unless I should have many exclaim of me."

He needed a boost, and in July it came. Excitement was in the air once more, for in spite of the continued Catholic threats against her life, the Queen again intended to travel westward. The progress would be "first to Sir John Fortescue's in Buckinghamshire, then to the Earl of Hertford's and the Lord Chief Justice's, where there were jewels and presents provided last year that should not be lost, and so to Bath and Bristol."[29] Even in her old age, the Queen had not lost her appetite for gifts. Sir John and Lady Amy must have been more than ready to part with theirs, but the elements were against them. The visit was postponed.

Sir John took it with his usual stoicism, writing on 22 August 1602 to Cecil: "I am very sorry that the unseasonableness of the weather hath been such as to hinder her Majesty's passage this way."[30] Immediately he turned to matters of state. In Ireland the military campaign by Lord Mountjoy had led to the defeat of Tyrone in December 1601.[31] Peace in Ireland was beginning to look a real possibility: "Touching that matter of Ireland . . . I doubt lest the end of the wars there will breed some interposition to our quiet at home; for many of these which cannot live but by the wars there will not content themselves to live according to their callings here. I find by your letters that the purpose of the Irish is not only against the religion professed by her Majesty's authority whereunto they have not been by any violent means constrained, but rather to shake off her Majesty's Government."[32] Popham felt that keeping a large peacekeeping force there was expensive and ineffective, because "though there were many of the ancient gentlemen of quality that kept their companies as full as they might, yet there were many others of the meaner sort, and especially of those last employed, that wanted more than half of their companies of those English that were assigned, whereby the enemy no doubt will be emboldened, or else they are reinforced by the Irish, who upon any accident are thereby made ready to become opposite to her Majesty, whereof we have already had too dangerous a precedent."

Popham had great faith in the natural leadership of the aristocracy—one can see why he had approved of Essex—arguing that "Now that these wars are grown towards an end, the new supplies might be of gentlemen of the best sort, to be accompanied with their friends, neighbours, and tenants, who would keep their companies full for their own safety, and expedite the service for their speedier return. By this course I think the enemy would be most terrified, who haply now conceive we have none to be employed in this service but such mean persons, when they shall soon find the contrary . . . . There is no better means to employ any man in than the service of his country and I hold it better that some few may fall into danger in the making of many to be good members of the commonwealth, than that in sparing of these few all should become unserviceable . . . . At Lytlecott, where I would be glad to know whether I shall yet see you."[33]

Eight days later Popham wrote to Cecil again, for trouble was brewing once more. A tailor from Dorset, John Ellys, had been sent to him, and he revealed that "there should be a plot or combination set down among the Papists of England, which is distributed or divided into eight parts of this realm, for a party to be made. . . . But I hope in God they shall never live to see the day they expect which are so wickedly disposed . . . . I have willed the party to be secret and learn farther what he can, and to be with me again some ten days hence, whereby I might in the mean season be directed what I should do further herein. It may haply be but a practice, but howsoever, I held it my duty to make it known." Popham added a note showing that the royal visit was still a possibility. "My very hearty thanks for the kind offer you made unto me by my servant this bearer, whereupon I shall depend her Majesty coming this way, as now I hope she will."[34]

The progress did happen in the summer of 1602, but the Queen went less far than originally planned: first to Chiswick to Sir William Russell's, then to Ambrose Coppinger's, "who, because he had ben a master of art intertained her himselfe with a Latin oration."[35] She then went on to Harefield in Middlesex, recently bought by Sir Thomas Egerton from Sir Edmund Anderson. Egerton knew what was expected in the way of entertainment. The Queen had been kept indoors by the weather, so when it was time to go, "one attyred in black mourninge aparell" made the farewell speech: "Sweet Majestie, be pleased to look upon a poor Widow mourning before your Grace. I am this Place, which at your comming, was full of joy; but now at your departure, am as full of sorrow." For the poor weather she blamed St Swithin, who "of late hath raysed soe many stormes, as I was faine provide this Anchor for you"—whereat she presented the Queen with an anchor jewel, hoping that "in all places where ever you shall arrive, you may anchor as safly, as you doe, and ever shall doe, in the harts of my Owners."[36]

The progress continued to Sir William Clark's at Burnham, "who so behaved himselfe that he pleased nobody, but gave occasion to have his miserie and vanitie spread far and wide"; then to Oatlands, and then Richmond. "The causes that withheld her from the Erle of Hartfords and the Lord Cheife Justices were the fowle weather, and a generall infection of the small pockes spred over all the countrie." So Popham's long and devoted service to her Majesty was never rewarded by a visit to his magnificent house. Elizabeth had stayed briefly at Friern, but it was left to her successor to appreciate the hospitality of Littlecote.

It is time for a cheerful dramatic interlude. On 19 November 1602 John Chamberlain reported "a cousening prancke of one Venner [Richard Vennar] of Lincolns Ynne that gave out bills of a famous play on Satterday was sevenight on the Banckeside [at the Swan]" to be performed by certain gentlemen and, interestingly, "gentlewomen of account." The entry charge was two shillings or eighteen pence, and "when he had gotten most part of the mony into his hands, he wold have shewed them a fayre payre of heeles, but he was not so nimble to get up on horsebacke, but that he was faine to forsake that course, and betake himselfe to the water." He was pursued, caught, and taken before the Lord Chief Justice, "who wold make nothing of yt but a jest and a merriment, and bounde him over in five pound to appeare at the sessions: yn the meane time the common people when they saw themselves deluded, revenged themselves upon the hangings, curtaines, chaires, stooles, walles and whatsoever came in theyre way very outragiously and made great spoyle: there was great store of goode companie and many noble men."[37]

Vennar was a Balliol man and something of a writer. The play he did not put on was called *England's Joy*.[38]

England's sorrow remained religious division. The Catholics had by this time become split, a group known as Appellants (because they appealed to Rome on certain matters) being willing to compromise somewhat, offering loyalty to the Crown in exchange for a measure of toleration. They were regarded by the traditional Catholics, among them Father Anthony Rivers, as informers; "It is already a common received position amongst them, that it is not only lawful but meritorious to discover a Jesuit to the State. My Lord Chief Justice saith he hath information from them of all the Jesuits in England, what disposition they are of, where they keep most, and where their starting holes are, not doubting but that shortly he shall meet with some of them, and for that purpose another great and general search is intended."[39] In September 1602 a proclamation against all priests was daily expected, "and for that purpose the Chief Justice is sent for to be in London ten days before the term."[40]

In November the proclamation was made, "that Jesuits, priests, and their adherents shall avoid the realm within 30 days upon their peril, and secular priests before the beginning of February, unless they submit to the Queen's mercy, and make profession of their loyalty." John Chamberlain thought "It comes late, yet better late than never."[41] The proclamation was read in all the parish churches of England.[42]

A trenchant unsigned note was delivered to Popham on 1 December, and passed on by him to Cecil: "Seeing the insolence of the seminaries has awakened your justice, and you think it full time to apprehend and punish both them and their relievers; our hope and trust is that you, being the greatest minister of justice, will no longer tolerate the intolerable and dangerous impieties of them that live in Court amongst you (who daily entertain, relieve and maintain seminaries and perverse papists). Many your Lords and Ladies are popishly affected, and use a common phrase ('We must learn to draw homeward'). Their attendants are papists, seminaries, and intelligencers for Spain. They plot against your counsels and study to destroy both the Queen, yourselves, and the whole land. Your remissness and neglect of justice has given them heart against you; and being grown strong, they care not to front you. They interpret the proclamation rather to be a reproof of the busy Protestants called pamphleteers than a denunciation of justice against their treacheries; for, (say they) the greatest are sound Catholics, meaning some of you councillors. The Bishop[s] of this land are idle and more than half blind, for the Indian earth [gold] has sealed up their eyelids. It is a common saying in this West country that the Court has infected the country with popery. If this be true (which God forbid) woe be to you that guide the stern, for your ship will sink to the pit of hell. Labour therefore to redeem the time, for the days are evil. And so, praying the Jehovah to direct you and the rest to seek his glory and to see yourselves, I commit you to his grace that guideth all aright."[43]

With such fanatical support, the persecution of Catholics continued. In February William Richardson, a priest of Seville College, was betrayed to Popham. "The evening of Richardson's apprehension, the Lord Chief Justice came to the Sessions house, and calling for him, caused his indictment of high treason to be read, for being a priest and coming to England contrary to the statute. He pleaded not guilty, and refused trial awhile because the jury was ignorant, and the Chief Justice made the law, and therefore on him would lie the guilt of his blood. The Chief Justice asked him who was head of the Church, he answered, 'The Pope'; 'Thou art a Jesuit!' 'No,' said the prisoner. 'What dost thou think of Jesuits!' 'That they are good and religious men.' 'Thou art a traitor!' 'As good a subject as your Lordship, or any assistant on the bench.' He at last consented to trial and was condemned. He desired, the little time he had to live, to be amongst his fellow Catholic prisoners, complaining of unchristian restraint, but the keeper was commanded to use him as before. Next morning he was executed at Tyburn. He prayed for the Queen, showed great courage, yet with mildness and discretion; many pitied him, and inveighed against the cruelty of the Chief Justice, for he had not a day's liberty to provide for his death, as common thieves have."[44] Richardson was the last martyr of Elizabeth's reign. "His behaviour," wrote Father Rivers, "moved many to compassion and to speak against the Chief Justice's cruelty, on whom alone be laid the guilt of his blood. Such spectacles do nothing increase the gospel."[45]

By January 1603 the senior judges were giving cause for concern. Cecil wrote that the two chief justices were both old, and Justice Walmsley had gout and palsy. "The Chief baron, baron Clerk, and Justice Clench are to be put to pension, and Justice Fenner will never run mad with learning. There remains only Justices Gawdy, Kingsmill, and Yelverton, the youngest of whom is 60 years old." He proposed that "All these places are to be supplied with serjeants, who will be judges hereafter."[46] Popham, now seventy-one, thanked Cecil for this recommendation: "It doth more content me to see such a call of serjeants to supply the places of the ordinary justices of this realm, when I shall be at my rest, than if I had a thousand pounds given me."[47] It had already been suggested that the elderly judges ought to give up going on circuit,[48] but they were made of sterner stuff, and on 26 February Popham reported to Cecil from Thetford in Cambridgeshire: "I have thoroughly heard the cause touching Burley for the killing of Kilby. It appeared that they had been together by the ears twice before that day, and were parted and gone clear asunder the one from the other; and that later . . . some brawl grew between them, offered by Burley, depending which Kilby came to them again, having not so much as a knife about him, and upon the sudden, the rest being going their way, Burley and Kilby were grappled together and Burley stabbed Kilby into the body, whereof he presently died before the rest could come to him." After Burley had been sentenced, he told Popham that a plot was afoot by some of his friends, but would not say who they were unless Popham would reprieve him for a month and remove him from London. The Lord Chief Justice refused, but stayed his execution pending Cecil's advice.[49]

Another murder in this year prompted one of the few letters to have survived from Robert Cecil to Sir John. It is reasonable, flattering, and beautifully phrased; to resist such an appeal would be impossible: "Your lordship has so much proof, I hope, of my religion to God and reverence to you, as the principal Justice of this kingdom, that I shall not need to use long prefaces to assure you that I favour no wilful crimes nor ever mean to make any proposition unworthy of your sincerity. One Thomas Lane is to receive his trial before [you for] the killing of a man, whose life I confess I should be very glad to save. I have many probabilities to suspect that much rancour is used in the prosecution and that the coroner has dealt but indirectly in it. You will be pleased to use some narrow circumspection into the circumstances of the carriage of the cause. I would be silent if I were persuaded that he had a murderous heart in the action, nor would I write to you if I were not secure that you free me at all times from having a thought that any mediation can carry you to the right hand or to the left in a matter of justice."[50] Although the verdict has not come down to us, we can have little doubt what it was.

On the other hand, Popham seems to have resisted an appeal by the Privy Council against what seemed to them his severe sentence on a servant of Sir Edward Dennys: "The fact was one of the foulest of that kind that I have heard, in so cruel and inhuman a manner to kill a silly woman, who did no manner of thing to grieve him any way offens[ive]. He not only hurt her in several parts of her body very grievously but also hurt another young woman very sore and was like to have killed two more, as the proof stood, if by very good hap they had not escaped from him. Had your lordships heard the matter at large as myself and others did I doubt not but you would have been satisfied that without great scandal to justice so foul a fact could not well be stayed from the due execution of justice. If drunkenness might excuse men in such a case I know not who can be in safety of his life and I have no manner of excuse for him but that, which nevertheless I found him not to utter."[51]

By now the Queen was very ill, "and every man's head is full of proclamations as to what shall become of us afterwards. She raves of Tyrone and Arabella, and is infinitely discontented: it is feared she will not long continue."[52] Popham was required to be in London, as he wrote to Cecil on 12 March 1603 from Littlecote: "I have received the Lords' letters and will not fail to do what they require me thereby, but matters for which I have already appointed certain days will occasion that I shall hardly get hence these 15 days without some suspicion unto these parts. After that I have so carried the matter as it will not be expected that I am to stay much longer in these parts, I doubt not but all will be well. Of all other places, the confines of London would be well looked unto, for the most dissolute and dangerous people of England are there, and upon the least occasion will repair thither."[53] Violent actions were expected in support of Lady Arbella's claim to the succession; her English birth endeared her to those prejudiced against the Scots.

The following day Popham explained more fully: "Bear with me if I become somewhat troublesome to you in this time of your disquiet. You may conceive how I have been perplexed since the receipt of my Lords' letters, and the rather that if I suddenly return hence I might add some impression to the rumours that might spread in these parts. Hence (having already put stay to some happenings since these letters) by [not] stirring from thence, howsoever the state of my body were, it might lay some imputation of lack of duty in me, which I had rather die than endure. I will still carry the matter as no suspicion shall be anyway conceived. I pray I may either receive two or three words of comfort from you, or if not, that I may be permitted to be a present partaker with yourself, and the rest, of the grief and in whatsoever my befall."[54]

The Queen was on her deathbed. The Council gathered at Whitehall. In the early hours of 24 March 1603 the reign of Elizabeth I was over.

15

Ralegh's Opposite

IN 1603 SIR JOHN POPHAM AND SIR WALTER RALEGH FOUND THEM-
selves facing each other in the most agonizing circumstances.
Popham was seventy-two and Ralegh forty-nine, and the careers
and interests of the two men had in the past had much in common. In personality, however, they were a complete contrast, and
it is fascinating to trace the different courses their lives took to
bring them to this appalling confrontation.

Both were Oxford men, Ralegh studying at Oriel from the ages
of fourteen to seventeen, and both were at the Middle Temple,
where Ralegh was admitted in 1575. He probably did not study
there, since he later protested, "If ever I read a word of the law
or statutes before I was Prisoner in the Tower, God confound
me."[1] There was no compulsion at the Inn to study anything; for
him, as for many other young gentlemen, the Inn was a social opportunity, not an academic one.[2] However, Ralegh was no idle,
rich young gentleman; though well connected, he was without
lands or income. Engaged in active military service in his teens,
he soon became a seafaring man whose main source of income
was privateering. In 1578–79, the very year in which George
Popham captured a Portuguese craft, Ralegh commanded the
Falcon in an unsuccessful expedition led by Sir Humphrey
Gilbert. Then in the spring of 1581 a formal link was forged between Walter Ralegh and John Popham when Richard Champernowne, a cousin of Gilbert and of Ralegh, married Elizabeth
Popham.[3]

Ralegh, like George Popham, had been a captain in Ireland in
1580. It was his return carrying dispatches to London in December 1581 that brought him to the notice of the Queen. "This Captain Raleigh coming out of Ireland to the English Court in good
habit (his Cloaths being then a considerable part of his estate),
found the Queen walking, till meeting with a Plashy place, she
seemed to scruple going thereon. Presently Raleigh cast and
spred his new Plush Cloak on the ground, whereon the Queen

Sir Walter Ralegh in 1598. Painting: English School. Photo: National Gallery of Ireland.

trod gently, rewarding him afterwards with many suits for his so free and seasonable tender of so fair a foot Cloath."[4]

Suits would have been welcome, for Ralegh was always a very snappy dresser, but the word also suggests grants or gifts in a more general sense. Soon the Queen gave him the lease of Durham House in the Strand, where he lived extravagantly with forty men and forty horses in attendance.[5] In 1584 he received the hugely valuable license to export woollen broadcloths, and also the farm of wines, which meant that he was entitled to collect from every vintner one pound annually for his license.[6] This was hardly likely to make him popular, and the patent aroused strong feelings among English drinkers. A request by Ralegh to Burghley for official support in administering the licenses was referred to Popham for his opinion. This letter, with Popham's sensible note and Burghley's instruction that the commission should be drawn up, is now in the New York Public Library.[7]

Ralegh's special place in the Queen's affection, as well as his independence of mind and pushy manner, made him hated everywhere except in Cornwall and most of Devon. By 1582 Hatton was complaining that there was "too much water [Walter]" at court. He was a personal enemy of Essex, with whom he later exchanged challenges to a duel. His friends were brilliant but odd: Edmund Spenser the poet; Dr John Dee, astrologer and physician; Thomas Hariot, mathematician; and the notoriously atheistic playwright Christopher Marlowe. Ralegh was not of high birth, so his promotion was resented; he was proud, variable, far too much of a free spirit for the government's comfort, and not always lucky in his adventures at sea.

Popham was unpopular too, but it was more of an institutional hatred, the product of his severe style in carrying out an inevitably disliked role. His physical presence may well have induced fear; it combined with the terrifying power he exercised in the courts to make him a bogeyman in the popular imagination. Aubrey says of Ralegh that "He was no slug,"[8] and the same is true of Popham; both men were unusually energetic and extremely hard workers. But whereas Ralegh was brilliant, independent-minded, easily deceived, and single, Popham was conventional, dependable, sound in judgment, and solidly married.

Popham's interest in foreign exploration must have been stimulated by his new kinship with the Gilberts. Sir Humphrey Gilbert's death at sea in 1583 led to Ralegh's taking over his rights of exploration in America. In his capacity as Attorney-General Popham checked every word of the Patent granted to Ralegh in the following year for the exploration of Virginia,[9] thus beginning a link that was to last the rest of his life. It is ironic that everyone associates Ralegh with Virginia, to which he never went. Similarly, though he too later had a major practical role in sending an expedition there, John Popham never himself went to America.

Popham would certainly have known about the attempts at settlement made by expeditions sent by Ralegh to Roanoke in 1585 and 1587. It may have been because he had been disappointed in Virginia that Ralegh determined to influence the plantation of the lands in Ireland forfeited by the Earl of Desmond.[10] As we have seen in chapter 6, both men became heavily involved in Munster during 1586–87, and Ralegh's interest continued until 1602.

Popham and Ralegh were both Members of Parliament and Justices of the Peace. These are not roles for which one remembers Ralegh, as they are not of the glamorous, chivalric, or poetic kind. He first became an MP for Devon in 1584, four years after Popham's Speakership, and served in the House until 1601. As a prominent local man—Ralegh was JP in Dorset and Somerset from about 1592 to 1603—he was trusted with, for instance, the examination of a suspected agent of Spain, which still planned further Armadas. Early in 1590 the Privy Council drafted a letter giving instructions "to sett Tristram Winslade at libertye, for that he hathe not only bene often examined by Sir George Carey, Sir Walter Rauleighe, Sir Richard Grenevile, knightes, Mr. Atturney Generall and Justice Younge and others, as by their handes appeareth, but hath bene also uppon the rack to drawe from him his knowledge of the intended invasyon."[11]

Ralegh also held more demanding offices: in 1585 he was made Lord Warden of the Stannaries, a post carrying responsibility for the country's sternly independent tin-mining communities in Cornwall. Some years later Popham and Sir William Periam, the Lord Chief Baron, were asked by the Privy Council to sort out a case in which they had worked with Ralegh over a controversy "concerning the tynne-worke of St. Margarettes within the Stannery of Blackmore in Cornewell." The plaintiffs had received a copy of an order "signed with the hande of the said Sir Walter which they pretend to be repugnant to that which was agreed on." Popham and his colleague were required "calling unto you Sir Walter Raleighe," to peruse the document, to establish the defect in it, and to "reforme the same" as appropriate.[12]

Ralegh was Steward of the Duchy of Cornwall, and Lord Lieutenant and Vice-Admiral of Cornwall and Devon. He held the office of Captain of the Guard from 1587. But he never achieved the highest office, failing much to his chagrin to became a Privy Councillor; in this Popham outdid him. Within two months of Popham's reaching the summit of his profession as Lord Chief Justice, Ralegh's fortunes suddenly plunged into an abyss. He had succumbed to the temptation of having an affair with one of the Queen's Maids of Honor. The marriage to Elizabeth Throckmorton was secret, but the Queen heard of it and took the couple's behavior as a personal affront. Both were sent to the Tower. Ralegh was released in September only because he was needed at Dartmouth to help Robert Cecil sort out the crisis resulting from the capture of the *Madre de Dios*.[13] Shortly before his disgrace he had been given the lease of Sherborne Castle. Now he was in effect rusticated there, and with typical energy set about building and replanting it. He still had Durham House in London too, but was not permitted at Court for five years, and his duties as Captain of the Guard were performed by deputy.[14]

Ralegh was determined to win his way back into Elizabeth's favor. Since she loved gold, he would find it for her. In spite of the severe restrictions he suffered, in 1595 he managed to organize an expedition to Guiana. As we have seen in chapter 9, he was beaten to the Orinoco by Robert Dudley and George Popham. Ralegh failed to meet up with them at Trinidad, and was no more successful than they had been in the quest for untold riches.

John Popham's feelings about Ralegh must have been complex. He would have admired him as an adventurous spirit and promoter of exploration, but certainly distrusted him because of his atheistical reputation. In earlier times he would have felt uneasy about Sir Walter's rivalry with Essex, but following the Earl's rebellion that probably changed. It was not Popham's attitude to him, however, but Robert Cecil's that mattered most for Ralegh's fortunes at present. At one time Ralegh and Cecil had been close, Lady Ralegh caring for Cecil's son after his mother's death in 1597. Cecil generally supported Ralegh, and after the death of Essex the common view was that little Cecil and Ralegh were triumphant.[15] But Cecil also found Ralegh threatening. He blocked further promotion for him, gave him harmless employment as a courier for visiting foreign deputations, and made him Governor of Jersey to get him out of London. Ralegh's views on foreign policy were out of date. Whereas he saw Spain as still the enemy, the feeling of the time was for peace; it was an aim very dear too to the heart of James VI, waiting in Edinburgh for his call to the English throne. Cecil was also for peace, and John Popham was a close friend of Cecil.

At the funeral procession of the Queen in April 1603, Popham walked in a group behind the standard of the Duchy of Lancaster:[16]

"Lord Mayor of London
Sir John Popham

Sir John Fortescue
Sir Robert Cecil, Principall Secretarie.

Near the end of the procession came

Earles Daughters
Baronesses
Maides of Honour of the Privie Chamber"

rather inappropriately followed by Ralegh, the Captain of the Guard, "with all the guard following, five and five in a ranke, holding their holberds downeward."[17]

Ralegh had been in the West on the day the Queen died, but posted straightaway to London. Popham and Cecil had corresponded about the possibility of violent events, and this concern was still evident three days after the death. A letter from Sir John seems to hint that Ralegh's movements needed watching: "Even now I have a letter from my son, who is at my house in the westmost part of Somerset. . . . The party that came now to me was at Sarum, where he heard of the proclamation of the King, which was very well liked of. He says that so it was also yesterday at noon at Andover, and no speech by all the way of any unquietness, but all things stood in very great quiet. But he tells me sundry horses are sent up out of the west parts, some to Sir Walter Ralegh, some to young Sir William Courteny,[18] and some to others; and what some foolish people might descant upon this, or such like, I cannot tell, but I assure myself the former bruit [rumor] delivered is but a vain bruit. Besides my own son, I have four sons-in-law in Somerset, and many other gentlemen of the best quality in those parts my very near kinsmen, and I should marvel if any such matter had been in those parts, and that they should give neither the State here, nor to me, any knowledge of it."[19]

By passing on such a rumor, Popham was cementing his alliance with Cecil against Ralegh. The new King disapproved of Sir Walter too, and James knew his own mind. He was approaching thirty-seven, had ruled Scotland for twenty years, and had a family. James had been turned against Ralegh by several considerations, including the charge of atheism, Ralegh's warlike approach to the Low Countries, the likelihood that his buccaneering would upset the peace process with Spain, and his tobacco habit. Furthermore, the King and Queen retained some affection for Essex, and Ralegh seemed very close to Essex's worst enemy, Lord Cobham. Ralegh was not likely to prosper under

James, and perhaps the very first request made to James when he first set foot in his new kingdom, at Berwick, was from the Bishop of Durham asking for the return of Durham House.[20]

Egerton, Popham, and Coke investigated the legal position and on 29 May 1603 signed a certificate thus: "According to his Majesty's command they have heard the counsel learned of Sir Walter Ralegh and Edward Darcy, touching such title as they pretended to the house called Duresme Place, and also what could be said to entitle his Majesty thereto. They find that neither Ralegh or Darcy has any right of interest in it, and so themselves acknowledged. On consideration of the title of the Bishop of Durham, they are of opinion that it belongs to him and not to his Majesty."[21]

Ralegh was unceremoniously required to leave Durham House at extremely short notice. His protest was received on 9 June; it is addressed to Egerton, Popham, and Coke: "This letter seemeth to mee very strange seinge I have had the possession of the howse almost xx yeare and have bestowed well nire 2000*li* upon the same out of myne own purse. I am of oppinion that if the Kings Majestye had recovered this howse or the like from the meanest gentelman and sarvant hee had in Inglande that His Majestye would have geven six moneaths tyme for the avoydance [= *vacating*] and I do not know butt that the poorest artificer in Londun hath a quarters warni[n]ge geven hyme by his land lord. . . . the cource taken with mee is bothe contrary to honor, to custome and to civillety, and therfore I pray your lordships to pardon mee till I have acquynted the Kings Majestye with this letter, and then if his Majestye shall thinck it reasonabell I will ob[e]ly it."[22]

Very soon it was no longer a matter of houses, but of life and death. In July 1603 the Bye or Surprise Plot was discovered. Two priests planned to capture the King and hold him until he promised to relax anti-Catholic legislation. Wherever he was, Popham conscientiously gathered information on suspects, and passed it immediately to Cecil, writing two detailed letters on 19 July from Richmond Green in spite of being "very weary of my travel."[23] According to one of Popham's agents, the Catholics alleged that the plot was in fact devised by Cecil and others of the Council, "and intended to be put upon young Catholics by the means of Watson and Clarke, the two priests."[24] In the course of investigating such rumors, suspicion fell on one of Watson's chief assistants, George Brooke, a disaffected Cambridge prebend whose brother was the foolish eighth Lord Cobham.

Cobham seems to have occupied a curious position of undeserved influence at Court, and one of the main purposes of the Essex rebellion had been to remove him from it. Ralegh had long been intimate with Cobham, and so was given the task of finding information against him. Vague evidence suggested Cobham had been in negotiations with Count Aremberg, the Spanish Minister in the Low Countries, to seize the King and place Arbella Stuart on the throne. This became known as the Main Plot. Cobham was arrested, and the evidence appeared to the government to implicate Ralegh. Cobham said Ralegh had instigated the communication with Aremberg, and both had been promised pensions by Spain. Brooke and Cobham, even though he was Cecil's brother-in-law, were put in the Tower. So, once again, was Ralegh.

While they languished there, plague was infecting London, so it was thought fit for the King and Queen to ride into the country on a Progress. The royal party stayed for a few nights at nineteen homes, including Lord Pembroke's at Wilton. After four nights at Tottenham Park in Savernake Forest, home of Edward Seymour, Earl of Hertford,[25] at last the monarch came to Littlecote House. Sir John Popham and Lady Amy entertained the King and Queen on 5 and 6 September 1603.[26] Unfortunately the visit is not documented, but we can guess that when the King was not pursuing his passion for hunting, his Majesty and the Lord Chief Justice discussed Ralegh and the trial to come, as well as some more distant prospects: fen drainage, perhaps, or the colonization of Virginia.

Because the plague continued in London, Ralegh's trial was to take place at Wolvesey Castle, palace of the former Bishops of Winchester.[27] He was taken from the Tower on 10 November, and the next day wrote from Bagshot in Surrey, asking Cobham to exculpate him:

"I beseche your lordship as you would have God showld comforte you so deale with me in this matter. You knowe in your soule that you never acquainted me with your Spanish imaginations. . . . I never suspected you afterwards.You knowe that you offered me the monie *bona fide* for the peace. I trust in God that you never spake these words of the Kynge, and if you be clere of it your peers will never condeme you for your Spanishe intent, seinge as you have chainged your thoughts and discovered it [made it known] to the Kynge first. Your brother is no lawefull wittnes against you, havinge sought to injure you as he hath heretofore. Good my lord, according to the truth wright accordingly and that effectually. And directe it to my Lord Cheefe Justice [Popham] and the rest of the Commission."[28]

Cobham's reply, sent not to Popham but to Sir Walter himself, made a dramatic public appearance very soon.

The trial of Ralegh is notorious as one of the most unsavory episodes in English legal history; and the men who presided over it were the two Lord Chief Justices, Sir John Popham and Sir Edmund Anderson. There were nine other commissioners and a jury consisting of four knights, four esquires, and four gentlemen, all of whose names are recorded. The indictment stated that Ralegh had conspired "to deprive the King of his Government; to raise up Sedition within the realm; to alter religion, to bring in the Roman Superstition and to procure foreign enemies to invade the kingdom."[29] More particularly, Ralegh had met with Cobham at Durham House, where he had "had conference with him, how to advance Arabella Stuart to the crown and royal throne of this kingdom";[30] and that they had agreed that Cobham should treat with Count Aremberg, ambassador from the Archduke of Austria, "to obtain of him 600,000 crowns, to bring to pass their intended treason." Ralegh pleaded Not Guilty, and requested to be allowed "to answer the points particularly as they are delivered, by reason of the weakness of my memory and sickness." Popham replied: "After the king's learned council have delivered all the Evidence, sir Walter, you may answer particularly to what you will."

Popham's role was to clarify points of law and to give the judgment. He also found it necessary to act as a calming force on the proceedings, a difficult matter when Sir Edward Coke was in full swing. One would wish him to have done more in this respect. The prosecution was begun by Serjeant Hele, who referred to Ralegh as "a man of great wit, military, and a sword-man." He was quickly followed by Coke, the Attorney-General, "a dapper little savage"[31] whose disgracefully vindictive treatment of Ralegh is most discomforting to read.[32]

After a tedious general introduction and detailed treatment of the Bye Plot, Coke suddenly switched to personal insult:

"*Attorney:* . . . . I will prove you the notoriest Traitor that ever came to
    the bar. After you have taken away the King, you would alter Religion . . . . thou art a Monster; thou hast an English face, but a Spanish heart."

Ralegh, he said, had been prepared to accept money "for the peace"; but "you are not a fit man to take so much Money for procuring a lawful Peace, for peace procured with money is dishonourable." Coke spoke at length about Cobham's involvement; Ralegh declared, "I do not hear yet, that you have spoken one word against me; here is no Treason of mine done. If my lord Cobham be a Traitor, what is that to me?"

Att. All that he did was by thy instigation, thou Viper; for I *thou* thee, thou Traitor.[33]
Raleigh. It becometh not a man of quality and virtue, to call me so; But I take comfort in it, it is all you can do.
Att. Have I angered you?
Raleigh. I am in no case to be angry.
CJ Popham. Sir Walter Raleigh, Mr Attorney speaketh out of the zeal of his duty, for the service of the king, and you for your life; be valiant on both sides."

Popham's opinion on the law was required on the two related issues that now dominated the trial. Firstly, Ralegh stated that "You try me by the Spanish Inquisition, if you proceed only by the Circumstances, without two witnesses." Secondly, Ralegh asked that Cobham be sent for to affirm his accusation that Ralegh had masterminded a request for money from the Archduke Albert of Austria, who was in league with Spain. The lords said that was not necessary. Ralegh insisted that he should be brought face to face with Cobham: "I beseech you, my lords, let Cobham be sent for, charge him on his soul, on his allegiance to the king; if he affirm it, I am guilty." Ralegh maintained that a mere accusation could not be evidence, but the judges held that it was. Ralegh argued that the King was sworn at his coronation to observe in all judgments equity, not the rigor of the law.

LCJ. That is not the rigour of the law, but the justice of the law; else when a man hath made a plain Accusation, by practice he might be brought to retract it again.
Raleigh. Oh my lord, you may use equity.
LCJ. That is from the king; you are to have justice from us."

Ralegh had quoted several statutes and scriptural incidents in support of his claim that witnesses were essential. Popham ignored the biblical references, and told him that two of his legal instances were out of date. As Justice Gawdy put it, "The Statute you speak of concerning two Witnesses in case of Treason, is found to be inconvenient, therefore by another law it was taken away."

"*Raleigh.* The common Trial of England is by Jury and Witnesses.

LCJ. No, by Examination: if three conspire a Treason, and they all confess it; here is never a Witness, yet they are condemned.

Justice Warburton. I marvel, sir Walter, that you being of such experience and wit, should stand on this point; for so many horse-stealers may escape, if they may not be condemned without witnesses. If one should rush into the king's Privy-Chamber, whilst he is alone, and kill the king (which God forbid) and this man be met coming with his sword drawn all bloody; shall not he be condemned to death? My lord Cobham hath, perhaps, been laboured withal; and to save you, his old friend, it may be that he will deny all that which he hath said.

Raleigh. I know not how you conceive the law.

LCJ. Nay, we do not conceive the law, but we know the law.

Raleigh. The Wisdom of the law of God is absolute and perfect. . . . But now by the Wisdom of the State, the Wisdom of the Law is uncertain. . . . Indeed, where the Accuser is not to be had conveniently, I agree with you; but here my Accuser may; he is alive, and in the house. Susanna had been condemned, if Daniel had not cried out, 'Will you condemn an innocent Israelite, without examination or knowledge of the truth?' Remember, it is absolutely the Commandment of God: If a false witness rise up, you shall cause him to be brought before the Judges; if he be found false, he shall have the punishment which the accused should have had. It is very sure, for my lord to accuse me is my certain danger, and it may be a means to excuse himself.

LCJ. There must not such a gap be opened for the destruction of the king, as would be if we should grant this. You plead hard for yourself, but the laws plead as hard for the king. I did never hear that course to be taken in a case of Treason, as to write one to another, or speak one to another, during the time of their imprisonment. There hath been intelligence between you; and what under-hand practices there may be, I know not. If the circumstances agree not with the Evidence, we will not condemn you.

Raleigh. The king desired nothing but the knowledge of the truth, and would have no advantage taken by severity of the law. If ever we had a gracious king, now we have; I hope, as he is, such are his ministers. If there be but a trial of five marks at Common Law, a witness must be deposed. Good my lords, let my Accuser come face to face, and be deposed.

LCJ. You have no law for it: God forbid any man should accuse himself upon his oath!

Attorney. The law presumes, a man will not accuse himself to accuse another. You are an odious man: for Cobham thinks his cause the worse that you are in it."

When the Bye plot was dragged up again Ralegh was incensed: "I was never any Plotter with them against my country, I was never false to the crown of England. I have spent 4000 pounds of my own against the Spanish Faction, for the good of my country. Do you bring the words of these hellish spiders, Clark, Watson, and others, against me?" Coke instantly seized on Ralegh's metaphor: "Thou hast a Spanish heart, and art thyself a Spider of Hell; for thou confessest the king to be a most sweet and gracious prince, and yet hast conspired against him."

Ralegh's reply emphasized his own long anti-Spanish sentiments: "I have spent 40,000 crowns against the Spaniard. I had not purchased 40 pound a year. If I had died in Guiana, I had not left 300 marks to my wife and son. I that have always condemned the Spanish Faction, methinks it is a strange thing that now I should affect it!" Before long Coke threatened Ralegh: "Go to, I will lay thee upon thy back, for the confidentest Traitor that ever came at a bar. Why should you take 8,000 crowns for a peace?"

Lord Cecil intervened: "Be not so impatient, Mr Attorney, give him leave to speak."

"*Att.* If I may not be patiently heard, you will encourage Traitors, and discourage us. I am the king's sworn servant, and must speak: If he be guilty, he is a Traitor; if not, deliver him." At this point, "Mr. Attorney sat down in a chafe, and would speak no more, until the Commissioners urged and intreated him."

When Coke returned to the fray, he restated all the evidence for the direction of the jury, and "at the repeating of some things, Sir Walter Ralegh interrupted him, and said, he did him wrong.

"*Att.* Thou art the most vile and execrable Traitor that ever lived.
Raleigh. You speak indiscreetly, barbarously and uncivilly.
Att. I want word sufficient to express thy viperous Treasons.
Raleigh. I think you want word indeed, for you have spoken one thing half a dozen times.
Att. Thou art an odious fellow, thy name is hateful to all the realm of England for thy pride.
Raleigh. It will go near to prove a measuring cast [a throw in which the result is so close as to need measurement] between you and me, Mr. Attorney.
Att. Well, I will now make it appear to the world, that there never lived a viler viper upon the face of the earth than thou."

At this point Coke drew a letter from his pocket. It was a confession of Cobham, including in it a reference to a letter Ralegh had pinned to an apple and thrown into Cobham's window. In it Ralegh had asked Cobham to clear him of any involvement, and advised Cobham not to listen to priests, for Essex had done so and they had encouraged him to confess his guilt. Ralegh admitted he had "bid a poor fellow throw in the Letter at his window, written to this purpose; 'You know you have undone me, now write three lines to justify me.'"

"*LCJ*. But what say you now of the Letter, and the Pension of 1500l. per annum?
Raleigh. I say, that Cobham is a base, dishonourable, poor soul.
Att. Is he base? I return it to thy throat on his behalf: but for thee he had been a good subject.
LCJ. I perceive you are not so clear a man, as you have protested all this while; for you should have discovered these matters to the king."

Now it was Ralegh's turn. He "pulled a Letter out of his pocket, which the lord Cobham had written to him, and desired my lord Cecil to read it, because he only knew his hand; the effect of it was as follows: 'Seeing myself so near my end, for the discharge of my own conscience, and freeing myself from your blood, which else will cry vengeance against me; I protest upon my salvation I never practised with Spain by your procurement; God so comfort me in this my affliction, as you are a true subject, for anything that I know. I will say as Daniel, *Purus sum a sanguine hujus* [I am innocent of this blood]. So God have mercy upon my soul, as I know no Treason by you.'"[34]

Here, as the Report says, was much ado. Coke of course maintained that the letter had been written "by promise of mercy, or hope of favour." Popham "willed that the Jury might herein be satisfied," so the Earl of Devonshire confirmed that it had been written voluntarily, "and not extracted from the Lord Cobham upon any hopes of promise or Pardon." This was the last evidence.

The jury retired. They returned after fifteen minutes, the verdict, Guilty. Ralegh was asked by the Clerk of the Crown what he could say for himself why Judgment and Execution of Death should not pass against him.

"*Raleigh*. My lords, the Jury have found me Guilty. They must do as they are directed. I can say nothing why Judgment should not proceed. You see whereof Cobham hath accused me: you remember his Protestations, that I was never Guilty. I desire the king should know of the wrongs done unto me since I came hither.
LCJ. You have had no wrong, Sir Walter.
Raleigh. Yes, of Mr. Attorney. I desire my lords to remember three things to the king. 1. I was accused to be a practiser with Spain: I

never knew that my lord Cobham meant to go thither; I will ask no
mercy at the king's hands, if he will affirm it. 2. I never knew of the
practice with Arabella. 3. I never knew of my lord Cobham's practice with Aremberg, nor of the surprizing Treason.

LCJ. In my conscience, I am persuaded that Cobham hath accused you
truly. You cannot deny, but that you were dealt with to have a Pension to be a spy for Spain; therefore you are not so true to the king
as you have protested yourself to be.

Raleigh. I submit myself to the king's mercy; I know his mercy is greater
than my offence. I recommend my wife, and son of tender years, un-
brought up, to his compassion."

Now Popham had to give judgment. It was the climactic moment in the association of the two men, and it brought forth from
the Lord Chief Justice, speaking to Sir Walter Ralegh, his most
moving pronouncement: "I thought I should never have seen this
day, to have stood in this place to give Sentence of Death against
you; because I thought it impossible that one of so great parts
should have fallen so grievously. God hath bestowed on you many
benefits. You had been a man fit and able to have served the king
in good place. You had brought yourself into a good state of living; if you had entered into a good consideration of your estate,
and not suffered your own wit to have intrapped yourself, you
might have lived in good comfort. It is best for man not to seek to
climb too high, lest he fall: nor yet to creep too low, lest he be trod-
den on. It was the Poesy of the wisest and greatest Counsellor of
our time in England,[35] *In medio spatio mediocria firma locantur*
[The stability of moderation is found in the middle ground]. You
might have lived well with 3000*l* a year, for so I have heard your
Revenues to be. I know nothing might move you to be discontented: but if you had been down, you know fortune's wheel, when
it is turned about, riseth again. I never heard that the king took
away anything from you, but the Captainship of the Guard,
which he did with very good reason, to have one of his own knowledge, whom he might trust, in that place. You have been taken
for a wise man, and so have shewed wit enough this day. Again,
for Monopolies for Wine &c. if the king had said, It is a matter
that offends my people, should I burden them for your private
good? I think you could not well take it hardly, that his subjects
were eased, though by your private hindrance. Two vices have
lodges chiefly in you; one is an eager ambition, the other corrupt
covetousness. Ambition, in desiring to be advanced to equal grace
and favour, as you have been before time; that grace you had
then, you got not in a day or a year. For your covetousness, I am

sorry to hear that a gentleman of your wealth should become a base Spy for the enemy, which is the vilest of all other; wherein on my conscience Cobham hath said true: by it you would have increased your living 1500*l* a year. This covetousness is like a canker, that eats the iron place where it lives. Your case being thus, let it not grieve you, if I speak a little out of zeal, and love to your good. You have been taxed by the world, with the Defence of the most heathenish and blasphemous Opinions, which I list not to repeat, because Christian ears cannot endure to hear them, nor the authors and maintainers of them be suffered to live in any Christian Commonwealth."

Popham urged Ralegh to repent while he could. According to one account of the trial, his actual words were: "You shall do well, before you go out of the world, to give satisfaction therein, and not to die with these imputations on you. Let not any devil Hariot or any such doctor persuade you to think there is no eternity in Heaven; for if you think thus, you shall find eternity in Hell-fire."[36]

Popham's reference to Hariot gives his biographer a pang of heartache. It is distressing to find that the subject of one's work could get it so wrong. Way back in 1580, Ralegh had persuaded Thomas Hariot, aged twenty and just graduated from St Mary's Hall, Oxford, to join him as his mathematical tutor. Hariot sailed on the first Roanoke Voyage in 1585, spending a year there and writing a fine account of Virginia. He became a key member of the group that revolved round Ralegh at Durham House, and was reputed to be the greatest astronomer and mathematician of his time.[37]

In Howell's version, Popham continued: "In the first accusation of my lord Cobham, I observed his manner of speaking; I protest before the living God, I am persuaded he spoke nothing but the truth. You wrote, that he should not in any case confess anything to a Preacher, telling him an example of my lord of Essex, that noble earl that is gone; who, if he had not been carried away with others, had lived in honour to this day among us; he confessed his offences, and obtained mercy of the Lord; for I am verily persuaded in my heart, he died a worthy servant of God. Your conceit of not confessing any thing, is very inhuman and wicked. In this world is the time of confessing, that we may be absolved at the Day of Judgment. You have shewed a fearful sign of denying God, in advising a man not to confess the truth."

At this point Popham spoke in a fashion that seems to suggest that the years were impairing his clarity of mind, for he intro-

Coat of Arms of Sir John Popham. This photograph of the stained-glass window in the Middle Temple Hall is reproduced by kind permission of the Masters of the Bench of the Middle Temple. Photo: Chris Christodoulou.

Popham's Eau, near Wisbech, Cambridgeshire.

Effigies of Sir John Popham and Lady Amy.

duced casually, almost as an afterthought, a key point that had been much argued about in the trial itself. "It now comes in my mind," he said, "why you may not have your Accuser come face to face: for such an one is easily brought to retract, when he seeth there is no hope of his own life. It is dangerous that any Traitors should have access to, or conference with one another; when they see themselves they must die, they will think it best to have their fellow live, that he may commit the like Treason again, and so in some sort seek revenge."

It was a rare lapse, and Popham recovered his self-possession and his humanity as he came to the end: "Now it resteth to pronounce the Judgment, which I wish you had not been this day to have received of me: for if the fear of God in you had been answerable to your other great parts, you might have lived to have been a singular good subject. I never saw the like Trial, and hope I shall never see the like again." Popham pronounced the usual sentence—hanging, drawing, and quartering. Ralegh begged the lords to allow him an honorable, not ignominious death, and was returned to Winchester Castle. Coke had left the court before the end of the proceedings, and is said to have been astounded when told the verdict.

Popham's and Coke's performances at Winchester did not enhance their reputations. The two lawyers are mentioned together by Sir John Roe in a poem written soon after Ralegh's trial:

> "Trust and believe your friend:
> And so me; And when I true friendship end,
> With guilty conscience let me be worse stonge,
> Then with *Pophams* sentence theeves, or *Cookes* tongue
> Traitors are."[38]

Evidently Cecil too felt the trial had been unjust, and his influence was behind Ralegh's reprieve. In mid-December 1603 Sir Walter began his long sojourn in the Tower,[39] where he was given two rooms on the second floor of the Bloody Tower.[40] Thanks to Cecil he was able to live quite comfortably for much of his nearly thirteen years of imprisonment, during which he conducted scientific experiments, gained a reputation as a medicine man, and wrote his *History of the World.* Joseph Hall, the almost first Headmaster of Blundell's School, wrote later that "The court had his youthful and freer times, the Tower his later age: the Tower reformed the court in him, and produced those worthy monuments of art and industry, which we should have in vain expected from his freedom and jollity."

Ralegh was very anxious to make sure that his wife had a secure hold on the Sherborne estate—perhaps too much so. Cecil had promised that it would remain hers, and Letters Patent in 1604 put it into the hands of trustees for her. Unfortunately, however, Ralegh himself discovered a mistake in the original conveyance of 1592—a clerk had left out the vital words "shall and will from henceforth stand and be thereof seized." Ralegh was determined to make his wife's hold on Sherborne completely safe. He needed lawyers to advise on the matter and, surprisingly in view of his experience of them, chose Popham and Coke. While they were deliberating in the summer of 1605, Lady Ralegh petitioned the King, who granted her the estate. However, the lawyers declared that the omission of the essential words made the original conveyance invalid. Consequently the 1604 Letters Patent gave Lady Ralegh no protection.[41] The way was clear for the Raleghs to be dispossessed, in spite of the wishes at the time of both James and Cecil.[42]

The unhappy association between Ralegh and Popham is brought forcibly to mind by the juxtaposition of their coats of arms in the Middle Temple Hall. Ralegh's stained glass window was in 1602 on the wall opposite Sir John's, and some way away from it. After Ralegh's disgrace, the original glass was removed. When a modern reproduction, based on an early drawing, was restored to the hall in the nineteenth century, it was placed, inappropriately, side by side with Sir John's.

A pithy summing-up of the two distinguished Elizabethans was provided by Katharine Gawen, a papist gentlewoman, the wife of Thomas Gawen, gent., of Hurcott, indicted for uttering in English these false and scandalous words: "We had a late Queene, and she was a blodye Queene, and was wholy ruled by my Lord Cheife Justice, that bludsucker, and Sir Walter Raleighe, and nowe we have a Kinge whoe ys of our religion, and will restore us to our rightes, and those two bludsuckers are putt downe."[43]

She was wrong. Far from being put down, Popham not only remained a much-valued Justice and Privy Councillor, but at the age of seventy-four he undertook new major enterprises in East Anglia and Virginia.

16

Drainer of the Fens

KING JAMES NEEDED MONEY TO SUPPORT HIS INDULGENT LIFE-
style. For some years there had been throughout western Europe
interest in improving the many fens and marshes in its low-lying landscapes.[1] The Crown owned huge tracts of unexploited
land in East Anglia, and James's attention must have been
drawn to the rich potential for development in the Fenland there.

The Fens were at that time thirteen hundred square miles of
flat, low-lying, sodden country, largely unusable for agriculture
and liable to frequent horrific flooding. At high tides, water in the
rivers could not run out, and the low ground was soon awash. In
1570 there had been a "terrible tempest" and great floods, when
"a ship was driven upon an house" and corn and cattle and salt-
pans were flooded "to the utter undoing of manie a man."[2] In order to control flooding and make cultivation possible, the land
had to be drained.

Some areas had for centuries been used for common grazing.
Usually owned by the lord of the manor, they were essential to
the village folk and subject to customary rights of use. It was such
pastures that offered the greatest scope for improvement, for if
the land was not constantly flooded, it could be seeded and crops
grown. The land would have to be enclosed, but such agriculture
could be highly profitable, and the prospect for a landowner was
attractive. Enclosing a piece of common ground could often be
done by agreement with the tenants; the landlord would take
part for his own in exchange for giving up his right to use any the
remainder.[3] All attempts at draining during Elizabeth's reign
had been small and piecemeal, the object being to create small
enclosures dry enough to be worked. There had been no grand
schemes.

Even on a small scale, draining would not necessarily benefit
everybody. The losers, as so often, were the local people who could
make only a poor living from reeds, fowling, and fishing. Their
customary grazing land was essential to them, yet they were like-

ly to lose a third of it to the drainer and perhaps as much again to the landowner.[4] The part left to them, since it was common ground, could only be used in the old way; they could not share in the profits made by tillage of the drained fen. However, the landowner and drainer could use their land in whatever way promised the greatest profit; for them the fens were another imagined El Dorado.[5] It is not surprising to find that many landowners were vigorous supporters of draining. They had power too, dominating the Courts of Sewers, the local controlling bodies whose duty was to see that existing works, such as banks, drains, and sluices, were kept in repair.

Consequently, when draining was proposed there was often strenuous opposition. It was into this tricky situation that Sir John Popham was drawn. He had himself been born on the edge of a fenland area, the Somerset wetlands, where his father was Commissioner for Sewers. As a child he had absorbed the peculiar atmosphere of this remarkable tract of country. Then when he was thirty-one he had bought with his friends the manor of Upwell, near Wisbech in Cambridgeshire, lying in the very heart of the Fenland, and troubled by flooding and decaying drains.

It must have been Popham's local connection that led to his sitting in the Parliament of 1576 on a committee on land reclamation. For the next twenty-five years the matter was discussed, technical advances patented, and small-scale efforts at draining made. A valuable impetus was given by the offer of Humphrey Bradley in 1593 to gather private finance to carry out a major scheme if neither Burghley nor the Queen would.[6] Bradley claimed to be able to name potential backers, and one cannot help wondering whether Popham was one. Although the proposal was not accepted, a project did go ahead in 1597 by "certaine merchantes of London" to drain the land around Upwell, Outwell and Denver.[7] Unfortunately no documents have survived to tell us more, but this was Popham's area of interest, and he had good connections with London merchants. It is very likely that he took an active part in encouraging the proposal. The drain they dug was known as Londoners' Lode; it appears on maps of the time, and though no longer operational, can still be traced.

The bitter antipathy resulting from even such modest draining attempts as this soon led to the Privy Council's involvement; as the century drew to a close "seditious and scandalous speeches" were being made in the fens and "lewd words" bandied about,[8] though whether it was action or lack of it that was the problem is hard to tell. A policy for the whole region was needed, but not until 1600 was an Act finally passed "for the recovering of many hundred thousand Acres of marshes and other Grounds subject commonly to surrounding, within the Isle of Ely, and in the Counties of Cambridge, Huntingdon, Northampton, Lincoln, Norfolk, Suffolk, Sussex, Essex, Kent, and the County Palatine of Durham"—all the fenny areas in the whole country.[9]

In this year Sir John Popham became Justice of the Peace of the quorum for the Isle of Ely and Cambridgeshire, Bedfordshire, and Huntingdonshire, in addition to Norfolk and Suffolk, where he had acted since 1593.[10] He was at Wisbech on 27 June 1600, writing to Cecil that "Having some occasion to pass this way at this time" he had "thought good to advertise you of some such things as happened to my understanding by the way." He enclosed comments on the favorable impact of the new legislation concerning corn, and on the burning down of North Walsham in Norfolk, as well as notes on three examinations of discontented men, prisoners at Wisbech. One of them, Nicholas Knyght, was alleged to have said that he was above the Queen, "for she carried the sword in her left hand but he in his right hand, and she ruled in temporal causes but he in spiritual. When asked how he dared say such things, he said he cared not, for he had been before Popham and the proudest knave of them all."[11]

The conflicts over draining were more understandable. In a letter of 15 November 1600 to the Chief Justices and others the Privy Council wrote that "there ys a great controversie and dyfference in opynions" concerning "the openynge of a drayne called Clowes Crosse, which by one parte ys pretended will bringe great prejudice to the Isle of Ely and county of Cambridge, and by the other not onlie the contrary is affirmed but great commodity is supposed to growe to the other counties in draynynge vc [500] thowsand acres of grownde." Popham and his colleagues are requested as "persons of aucthorytie and judgment," and "havinge no particuler interest in the cause" to deal with these difficult people and resolve it for the public benefit.[12] It is surprising that Popham was not considered to have a private interest in this issue, as he could hardly have concealed his own landholding in the area.

The Act of 1600 did not produce immediate results, interest in fen drainage lapsing during the last years of Elizabeth's reign. James, however, needed money, and the Fens looked promising.[13] No doubt he was also anxious to improve the lot of his subjects; indeed James was the first monarch to take a responsible view of the plight of the inhabitants of the Fens.[14] With the fa-

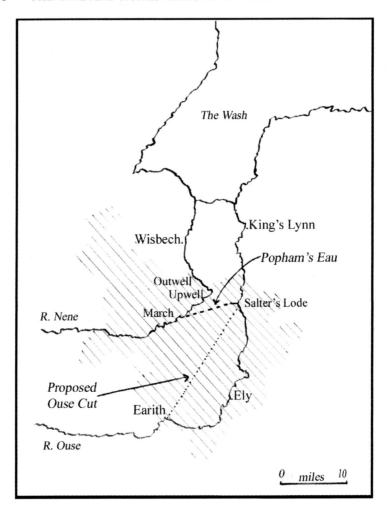

The Wash

King's Lynn

Wisbech.

Popham's Eau

Outwell
Upwell

R. Nene

March

Salter's Lode

Proposed
Ouse Cut

Earith

Ely

R. Ouse

0   miles   10

The Fens.

miliar mixture of motives—public service and private gain—
James looked for someone with the knowledge of the area, administrative skills and authority to push forward plans for reclamation. He found a national figure with local knowledge—Sir
John Popham.

The main focus of concern at this time was the very wet area
south of Wisbech, bounded by the rivers Nene and Ouse, both
running north to the Wash. The area in between, amounting to
307,242 acres,[15] had never been drained, but it was thought that
this could be done by giving the sluggish Ouse a bypass, a wide

drain being cut straight from Earith to Salter's Lode. Remarkably, it was considered quite feasible in engineering terms to carry out such difficult projects—indeed, what was proposed in East Anglia was thought easier than work which had already been done in Holland.[16]

Now, with Popham at the helm, action was characteristically rapid. It took two directions, the first being practical. On 11 July 1604 the King directed letters to the Commissioners of Sewers for the Isle of Ely, asking them to certify the names of those who would be willing to give up part of their surrounded lands to such as would drain them. New surveys were made by Mr Richard Atkyns of Outwell, "a person whose observations on these fenny grounds were very notable,"[17] and a better map drawn by William Hayward. The second direction was legal. It seems to have been felt that a new Act of Parliament was essential, even though the Act of 1600 authorized the draining of the fens in general. It may have been that the contrary interests were so strong that only an Act applying specifically to the disputed area could provide enough weight to override the opposition.

The Commissioners' prompt reply of 19 July to the King's request took the form of a very forceful petition to Popham on behalf of the people of the whole Isle. Two Bills, they said, had been preferred to Parliament, "for the recoverie of many hundred thousand acres by persons unknowne unto us pretending an universall and generall benefitt but intending indeed their owne private and particular profitt." They asked Popham, "by whose authoritie we hope all these oppressions may be suppressed and in whose sinceritie and justice the rest of all our hopes doth wholly rely" to stick to the improvement of existing drains, so that they retained "the use and libertie of our commons in the same manner as we and our forefathers have ever done heretofore."[18] Popham had evidently been given a hard time on a visit to the Fenland: "I did not think myself well dealt with at Wisbech at our last being there," he complained to Sir Thomas Lambert; "I hoped for better respects considering how I am put into that cause by his Majesty and my lords of the Councell."[19] It is easy to sympathize with the position of the Commissioners of Sewers. They wished the draining to be carried out, but not over their heads by strangers and profiteers.

In the twelve months after July 1604 both practical and legal initiatives were followed up most energetically, but it appears that the practical came first. Much discussion had gone on over what work should be done; it was all highly debatable, based largely on guesswork and constrained by the various local interests. By 24 June 1605 a new idea had been introduced: "Mr Hunt (who was the artist for the draining) told the Lords of the Council that he desired that a new river, 80 x 8 feet be made from March to Well River."[20] This is a most significant point in relation to Sir John Popham's role in the project, and it is particularly striking how keen the King was to set it in motion. He himself wrote from Greenwich to the Commissioners commending their efforts and "inciting them to fall in hand speedily with the work, and the rather, because that was a dry summer, and so the more proper for it; intimating also, that for the better expediting thereof, he had imployed his Chief Justice (Popham) to take pains therein."[21]

Popham certainly was taking pains. By 13 July 1605 he had managed not only to introduce yet another new Act of Parliament for consideration by the Commons, but also to present himself as the principal undertaker of the draining scheme. The proposal was entitled "An Act for the Draining of certain fenns and Low-grounds within the Isle of Ely, and Counties adjoining, subject to Hurt by Surrounding,"[22] and ran thus: "Whereas it is affirmed by skilful and expert Men . . . That the Fenns and Low-grounds, lying and being within the Isle of Ely . . . may be drained, if sufficient Authority be given: And whereas Sir John Popham, and others, have undertaken to do their best Endeavours . . . Be it therefore enacted . . . That the said Sir John Popham . . . shall have Power . . . to make Works for that purpose."

The plan was still to enlarge and improve the Ouse, and to construct two new cuts—presumably two narrower channels were more practicable than one very wide one—from Earith to Salters Lode. The Undertakers were to be entitled "for ever in Severalty" to 112,000 acres. After the draining, which was to be finished in three years, a body to be called the Governors of the Fens was to supervise the area. The list of thirty men of course included several well known to Popham: Sir Anthony Mildmay, founder of Emmanuel College, Cambridge; Sir Oliver Cromwell, uncle of the future Lord Protector; Sir Edward Coke; Sir Robert Wingfield; Sir Robert Cotton the bibliophile; and Sir Miles Sandys, who had acted for Popham over the acquisition of Littlecote. London merchants were Roger Offeild and John Eldred, who was Master of the Clothworkers' Company as well as "a well-known traveller."[23] Popham was to become not simply the supervisor of the scheme on behalf of the King, but the chief undertaker. As before in Ireland, he proposed to take on both the organization of the project and a huge and lasting financial responsibility.[24]

In spite of Popham's influence, the Act was rejected by the Commons, who were concerned for the plight of the poor fenmen.[25] Strangely, this does not seem to have made any difference. It may be that the Commissioners of Sewers were still working within the terms of a curious decree of 1598 by the Court of Star Chamber that in order to hasten the draining of the fens, they could make their own laws even though the then intended Act (of 1600) had not yet been established by Parliament.[26] For on the very same day on which the Act was rejected in London, the Commissioners of Sewers for the Isle of Ely, meeting at Wisbech, addressed to Popham, who was there in person,[27] an order along lines very similar to those of the defeated Act. Some of the details may be different, as we can read in an intriguing document now in Cambridge University Library,[28] but the main intention was the same. The Commissioners "ordered and decreed" that Popham, Sir Thomas Fleming,[29] Sir William Romney,[30] and John Eldred, citizen and clothmaker of London, "shall within the space of 7 yeares next coming at their own proper coste and charges draine all the fenns and surrounded groundes between the old course of the River of Ouse as it now runneth from Earithbridge to Salter's Load." A second provision, which did not appear in the Act, was Mr Hunt's latest suggestion that a passage should be made from the Nene eastward to the Ouse. In return the Undertakers would be entitled to 130,000 acres "to be taken out of the worst part of every particular fenn."[31]

Even though they had approved this undertaking, the Commissioners of Sewers for the Isle of Ely remained extremely anxious about what further legislation might entail for them. They recognized that the Lord Chief Justice offered them more security than anyone else, and immediately after the Wisbech meeting on 13 July wrote to Popham, explaining that they had heard about "a Bill lately preferred to the High Court of Parliament concerning the drayning of our Countrie the Isle of Ely with the confines of many other countries adjioyning; and have likewise credibly heard of the honorable respect your L. hath had for the setting down of such covenants and conditions in the same as may be least hurtfull or prejudiciall to the bodie of our poore Island, whereof your L. by a clause in the said Bill preventing the adjustment and future improvement of our commons by the Lords of Manors hath given us an evident remonstrance [demonstration]. We therefore the Inhabitants of the said Isle most humbly beseeche your L. that you would be pleased still to continue your honourable and gratious favour towards us as in that point principally (which of all others we have most cause to feare). So likewise in all other thinges which may concern the good estate and welfare of our countrie. And as your L hath hitherto hereby given us a tast of your provident and most religious care over us with an assured confidence of the continuance of the same. So we shall more and more thereby acknowledge our selves bound continually to pray for the encrease of your honorable estate here, and all happines in the life to come."[32]

Popham's "religious care" for the area led him to disregard the huge prime task of two new cuts for the Ouse.[33] The smaller project, the drain from the Nene to the Well, which linked with the Ouse, was the one that gained priority. It may be that this was the sensible product of Hunt's knowledge and experience, or that Popham was respecting local opinion, or that the Bill's cool reception made a cautious start advisable. One cannot help wondering, however, whether Popham's ownership of property very close by influenced the decision.

Whatever the reasons, detailed planning now went ahead. So "the Lord Popham, & c. ordain'd a new River to be made eighty Feet wide, and eight Feet deep., from March River to the Ham, cross Marmond, &c., through Neete-more, to fall into Well-creek, near London-lode; and from thence to Salter's-lode, Well-creek was to be dyked sixty Feet wide, and the Bottom sunk four Feet deep under Low-water Mark, viz. as deep as Ouse; that thereby the Fenns might be drain'd, and the extream Floods receiv'd."[34] On 23 July the King wrote to the Commissioners to commend their endeavor, and encouraged them to suppress all false rumors and clamp down on "mutinous speeches";[35] no trifling opposition was going to hamper this scheme. Less than four weeks after the July Act had been rejected, "Sir John Popham, fell in hand with the Work." On 7 August 1605 the new river was begun, "in the presence of Mr Hunt (the engineer) who cast the spit the wrong way."[36] It is unlikely that Popham was there to witness this inauspicious start. We know that a disturbance had occurred in Wells, Somerset, on 3 August, an "outrage in aid of Popish recusants" and he had gone to deal with it.[37]

Work started slowly, and the project continued to raise much heat among both landowners and local men. In September one Monford, a Norfolk man, went to the Archbishop of Canterbury to inform him that "The people of Norfolk and such as adjoined to the seas, which are now ordered to be drained, are all of them desperately bent, and cast out very broad speeches against the intendment, and all whom they hear to be undertaken in that affair. Some of them went into the most parts of England exclaiming amongst the baser sort against the work, as tending to the utter undoing of them, their wives and children, and affirming that this course of taking away their commons without their consent was but a beginning to deprive all the poor of the realm of theirs; that these beginnings must be withstood [lest] the inhabitants in the parts near the se[a] lose their lives, men, women and child[ren if] they suffer them to be drained; that if [the Chief] Justice come into those parts any more abou[t that] business, he shall be met with."[38]

In March 1606 the King received an anonymous letter. "It is geanrralie saide," the writer complained, "that the covetous bluddie Popham" by his offer to drain the fens would "take many poore mens commons from them for his owene profit. . . . He is cursed of all the pore of that parte of Englande and perforce the[y] will kill him or suchas shal be employed therein." The writer blames "this Popham and your greate lordes" for exploiting "the glashousses" and holds them responsible for the extortionate behavior of landlords, who "do aske so greate fynes and rentes for there landes as tenn tymes dubell, which is most lamentable and this is mentayned by the lord popham and other lordes and justices for there great profit, not respecting the good of the comonwelthe."[39]

By contrast a leading landowner at Outwell, Sir John Peyton,[40] who evidently saw himself as a pioneer of fen draining, had a different complaint. He wrote to Cecil expressing concern that the work was not progressing smoothly: "I beseech you to take into your protection such causes as concern my poor estate, amongst which there is now one in question touching the recovery of the fen about the Isle of Ely, that much imports me, and in which I have spent 30 years' industry, and made the first overture of the feasibility of that work, as by the fruits and effects thereof appeared unto my Lord Chief Justice upon his late view made in those parts for that purpose . . . . My son shall inform your lordship of the particulars."[41]

The son, Sir John Peyton the younger,[42] wrote that "Such as have been employed and are about the work have not as yet perfected the least part of their project . . . . The unwillingness of the people to the bettering of their estates, and their wilfulness not to conceive their own good have been the chief cause of the easy [slow] proceedings of the undertakers; which obstacle, though to the great loss of the country, will with these great wets without question be removed, and the county be the easier drawn to part from a convenient portion of the fens for the certaining of the rest, now they shall perceive their whole estates subject to be overthrown by one month's continual wet .... My father is like to part from a great deal and as much as any man there, that has an hereditary estate, and neither himself nor I shall be anyway unwilling to yield to such a proportion as shall be thought fit for the effecting of so general a good."[43]

In spite of all the difficulties, "the Work was prosecuted so well, that upon the 21st of December following [1606] the Waters were let through to ease the Isle, and help Well River."[44] It was a major achievement for which Popham is deservedly remembered.

The waterway had passed through much trouble, and was to encounter more on its journey to the present time. Soon after its opening, the channel was in difficulty, and it was "stopp'd up, in regard of the Insufficiency of the Banks."[45] The country "lay in its former Condition; and my lord Popham dying, his whole Project was rejected; and so nothing was done."[46] In 1609 "it was again pursued to be perfected, pretending the benefit of the whole countrey thereby, but intending a private end." Underlying problems remained; for instance, no compensation had been given to landowners whose grounds had been affected by the making of the new cut. So one of them, "Sinolphus Bell, Esq; having much Ground adjoining yearly drowned by this new River (called Popham-lode) obtain'd . . . a Law to keep the upper Doors thereof shut, until the Country would satisfy the parties injured . . . . And the Doors at the upper end were accordingly kept shut, so that no Waters could pass through this new River."[47]

After many years of disuse, Popham's waterway was resuscitated in 1650. The result may still be seen, a fine seven-mile stretch of drain performing its intended function and used also by small pleasure craft. It is known as Popham's Eau, a straight cut from the Nene, four miles east of March, into Well Creek, at Nordelph, just west of Salter's Lode. The word "eau" is not in this instance the French for water, but a corruption of ea, the Saxon for river. Several place names in the Fens end in ea—pronounced "ee"—and in earlier books Popham's Eau is referred to as Popham's Ea: "Fen-men still speak of Bourn Ee, Risegate Ee, Popham's Ee."[48] His waterway is another lasting monument to the unusual energies of this remarkable man.

17

Judge of Plotters

Popham's watery problems in the fens must have been almost a holiday for him. The main business of his life continued to be resisting the never-ending threat of plots against the sovereign.

James's accession was a crucial time for Catholics, as the King had two sons and a daughter who could succeed him. If he and they proved unrelentingly Protestant, there was no possibility of toleration in the foreseeable future. Although there had been rumors that the new King was well-disposed toward Catholics, the activists among them were set on resolving the matter immediately. James himself had been a marked man before he even left Scotland; Lewis Pykeringe, a passionately puritan member of his entourage, later wrote proudly that "Waiting on the King out of Edinburgh, the King imparted to him a treasonable plot of the Jesuits of which he had been informed by the Lord Chief Justice. One Jarrett, with some resolute men, should present the King a petition that Jesuits might remain in the kingdom: which, if it were refused (as his Majesty vowed with great protestations he should never grant), they were to offer violence to his person, though they sacrificed their lives in his blood."[1] The implication is that Popham had been communicating with James before Elizabeth's death about the dangers facing the new King in England.

Rumors of plots against his life were not what James wanted to hear. He was clear in his own mind that Catholics, or indeed puritans, who would conduct their devotions privately, were acceptable; activists were not. Unfortunately the militant minority were extremely determined, so that in the first years of James's reign there were many plots to remove him from the throne. Among the first were the Bye and the Main Plots, which aggravated the King's sense of vulnerability. It is hardly surprising that in January 1604 the King pronounced "emphatically and virulently" against the papists.[2] A proclamation was issued that all Jesuits and seminary priests were to leave the country before the opening of Parliament on 19 February, and Popham gave order to purge the Inns of Court of all popishly affected; those who refused to communicate once a month were to be expelled.[3] The King publicly declared his "utter detestation" of Catholicism, which he thought "superstitious"[4]—in spite of the views of his wife, Anne of Denmark. There was evidently to be no toleration whatever. It was at "about this time," April 1604, Popham wrote later, that the Gunpowder Plot was "set on foot as the only means to relieve that [Catholic] party."[5]

How much did he and Cecil know at the time about what was afoot? When we read the documents now, the names of the conspirators and their associates leap out at us, whereas to Popham and Cecil, one might think, they would have been just another bunch of probable troublemakers, to be watched like all the rest with utmost vigilance. Incidentally, more obvious disturbance at this time was created by Londoners who fomented trouble against the Scots now flocking to the city. The King himself wrote to Popham commanding him to apprehend certain loose people of the "damned crew of swaggerers" and bind them over to keep the peace.[6]

However, an intriguing document written after the event makes it clear that Popham not only knew what was going on but communicated it regularly to the King: "If it please your Matie can yow remember that the Lo: Cheife Justice Popham, and Sr Thomas Chaloner Kt. had a hand in the discovery of the practices of the Jesuites in the powder-plott, and did remember the same from tyme to tyme to your Matie, for two years space almost, before the said treason burst foorth. . . . the man that informed Sir Tho. Chaloner and the Lo: Popham of the said Jesuiticall practices, their meetings and trayterous designes, in that matter, whereof from tyme to tyme they informed your Matie, was one Wright, who hath your Maties hand for his so doing, and never received any reward for his paines."[7]

The background to this request for recompense is fascinating. Popham's key link, Sir Thomas Chaloner, was a governor of James's promising elder son, Prince Henry.[8] Chaloner had been contacted by Henry Wright, a part-time alchemist who acted as a government spy.[9] The "discoverer," or informant, was one Joseph Davies, who boasted that he could give the names of sixty plotters. He promised to discover thirteen or fourteen from his list, but was waiting two days "till Tesmond and Kemp come to town." Father Oswald Tesimond, known also as Anthony Greenway, was a Jesuit from the north and evidently worth waiting for.

However, Popham was feeling frustrated by inaction: "There were before so many hopes given, whereof nothing fell out too opportune, as I was desperate. But this morning [28 May 1604] I put it to the uttermost issue."[10] Evidently he organized a raid—and as far as Thomas Allison was concerned, it was a disaster. This man, who had for five years been one of the Chief Justice's spies,[11] now wrote furiously to Chaloner complaining of Popham's hasty conduct: "The course held to me (it seems by the Lord Chief Justice) has been so violent that in the late service about taking of Davies (had not Mr Wright carried all things with discretion) I had been discovered, discredited, and never been able to have done the King or State any further service." He had plans to provide further information on Catholics who had taken an "oath for secrecy," but would be glad "if I may have you and Mr Wright only to be dealers herein . . . otherwise I must be forced to give over doing any good in this kind for ever. As to the having the aid of a privy councillor for warrants upon occasion, I pray you make choice of such a one as will be moderate, and let me have my own course and time; for my Lord Chief Justice little knew what was a doing when he would have Davies taken so suddenly, who was a great means unto me to come to the knowledge of many matters."[12]

Popham's blood was up, as we see in the case of Thomas Pownde, who appeared once again in court in November 1604. A Lancashire man, Pownde had spent thirty years in jails for standing up against the State's intolerance.[13] During the hearing "the Lord Chief Justice amplified against the impudent lying of Catholics (as he invectively breathed out against them), saying it was no marvel that beyond the seas pamphlets were printed of inhumane proceeding against Catholics, and nominating the baiting of priests in bears' skins with dogs." But evidently Mr Pownde thought this was no lie: he "answered it was most true, and nominated Mr Browne, a priest who was so baited with dogs."[14] When it came to considering an appropriate punishment for Pownde, Secretary Herberdt suggested, in addition to the hefty fine of £1000 and imprisonment for life, that he be "nailed to the pillory, and at Westminster to have one ear cut off, and the other to be cut off at Lancaster." However, the Lord Chief Justice differed from Secretary Herberdt, "viz., That if Mr Pownde did not before the beginning of the next term confess and discover who were the relators of those reports to him that then his ears should be cut off, else not."[15] The sentence was later reduced to standing in the pillory in each place for one day, his ears nailed but not cut off.[16] How characteristic of Popham to make use of every possible source of information; he had a very thorough approach to his work.

By January 1605 the whole atmosphere at Court seems to have been impregnated with conspiracy. The King himself commanded that Popham should determine how to proceed with a man called Butler, one of several who had been "meddling in witchcraft and sorcery," and "first accused for prophecies of troubles to happen this year within this realm."[17] In April, Popham forwarded to Cecil a note which a servant had found "fixed to the wall of an entry here in Serjeants' Inn, which is a common passage. Yesterday afternoon there was brought from the Middle Temple another letter directed to his Majesty, and dropped down the night before in that Temple Hall, containing a libel of admonition unto his Majesty touching Spain, the religion, and other affairs at home, subscribed in the name of one Greene, which Mr. Attorney and myself labour to discover."[18]

Everyone seemed willing to report suspicious activities and hints of recusancy. On 15 August 1605, for instance, the sorcerer Butler reappeared, this time on shipboard. Popham took a declaration from George Escot, master of the *Speedwell* of Bridgwater which was being freighted at Cardiff ready for Portugal. One of the merchants on board, named David Butler, "being requested to come to prayer, which they commonly used twice a day, refused to come, whereupon [Escot], suspecting him not to be well affected, after they arrived at Mongey in Galitia (being set there by a contrary wind), made search in his chest, and there amongst other things found a letter now delivered to Sir John Popham. He returned with the said ship and landed at Minehead and came to Bridgwater, and not knowing Sir John Popham to be in the country made the letter known to the portreeve of Minehead, who being made privy with Butler's then being in the town, thought it fit to forbear to apprehend him or to do anything till Sir John Popham might be informed thereof."[19]

The letter was to Father Cresswell, Superior of the English priests in Spain, and came from a priest called James Morrys, in Monmouthshire. Popham sent the incriminating writing on to Cecil: "By the letter you may see what affection they bear both to his Majesty and his most renowned offspring. If he be not taken already, I doubt not but you will have a care to lay for him. . . . The means how this seaman got this letter was this. He, seeing the affection of this Butler and the boy that went over with him, took occasion to send them on land, and that while searched his coffer, and finding therein this letter, took it, and gave a blank paper the like fold and direction, which he left in the coffer, and with which blank Butler sent away the boy unto Cresswell."[20] One wonders whether the seaman had seen *Hamlet,* probably first performed in 1600.[21]

On 27 August the King, Queen, and Prince Henry went to Oxford for a three-day visit. Popham was at Littlecote, unwell: "I had resolved to have been now at Oxford to have done my most bounden duty to his Majesty, and to have waited on you with these things myself, but upon Saturday last, having occasion to ride some 5 miles to meet with some justices of this county about the affairs of the county, I fell into a fit of my old grief, of which I cannot yet be cleared, and therefore must humbly crave pardon for my absence."[22]

Popham wrote twice to Oxford, and Cecil was eventually obliged to reply: "The first preface which I shall use shall be to excuse myself for making no answer to your first messenger at Oxford; we courtiers being then so far in love with disputations as we could not attend any other business. I am sorry you have so ill a companion as the stone, though I doubt not but you will be soon eased thereof, which I wish, and as much good else as your heart can desire . . . . you may do well, seeing David Butler is apprehended, and the suspicion truly gathered by you that he is rather a factor for priests than for wares, to cause him to be sent up unto you to be strictly examined about him by you. . . .

"Our news are here not great, only those after which I know you hearken most are such as you would desire; for his Majesty with all his continues in perfect health . . . . I did not forget [to] recommend your duty and your excuse to his Majesty, both which he took in very good part, and willed me to say that he were weary of you, yet he would wish you to live as long as himself, assuring for conclusion that you are not meanly seated in his Majesty's gracious favour; to which if I can make the least addition, you shall be sure of my best offices."[23]

Popham replied: "I acknowledge myself most bounden to his Majesty for his gracious favour towards me, being an aged, decaying body, unable to perform that service unto him as in duty I ought, and in heart I most desire. Next I may not be unthankful unto yourself, to whom I find I am so much beholden, though absent; which I wish it lay in me in any measure to acquit. What you write touching Butler, God willing I will see effected."[24]

In spite of plague in London and two eclipses, of the moon on 19 September and the sun on 2 October, the autumn of 1605 appeared outwardly calm.[25] Cecil consulted Popham on various matters of trade, and Popham replied at length two days later, although the questions put to him were "of greater difficulty than I would anyway of myself have entered into." Nevertheless, he wrote, "in that you require it, as so short a time and as the state of my body (which lately was such as I thought I should never see London again) will permit, I will acquaint you with some points I have heretofore conceived concerning these matters." Popham went on to argue against company monopolies in foreign trade, for they sought only their own profit rather than the good of the commonwealth.[26] It is all unsurprising, ordinary stuff.

Then on 26 October William Parker, Lord Monteagle, received from his servant a letter he had been given by a stranger. It warned Monteagle to "have a care of your preservation" and to avoid going to Parliament, for "I say they shall receive a terrible blow this Parliament; and yet they shall not see who hurts them." Monteagle passed the letter to Cecil who, although he did not immediately inform the King, then hunting in Hertfordshire, did tell the Privy Council that an attempt on the House of Lords was in train. Popham and his colleagues had perhaps ten days in which to make inquiries. When the King eventually saw the letter, he insisted that a careful search of Parliament be made on the day before Parliament was due to open. A "very tall and desperate fellow" guarding thirty-six barrels of gunpowder was apprehended in the early hours of 5 November.[27]

John Johnson, for that was what he called himself, was taken to the King's chamber and immediately questioned, but to no effect. Clearly an expert team was needed: the task of finding out the truth was given to Popham and Coke. On the document that reports his first recorded examination, "taken this Tuesday the fifth of November 1605 before the Chief Justice of England and Sir Edward Coke Knight her Majesty's Attorney General," the name "Jhon Jhonson" appears at the bottom of each page.[28] He confessed "that about Christmas last he brought in the night times Gunpowder to the celler under the upper house of Parliament some by water and some by land, some whereof was putt in hoggesheads, some in Barrells, and some in ffirkins." The last had been brought in about a month ago, he said, and explained how he had meant to fire the powder with a match and touchwood, but when they came to apprehend him he had thrown these out of the window toward the waterside. Johnson would not have saved the Queen and her children; he did not know what would happen after the death of the King, but "the people of themselves would have drawne to a head." No Catholics had been warned, though afterward they would have been told the plot had been done "for restitution of religion." He had promised that he would not reveal the plot, but had not taken the sacrament on it. When he was asked to whom he made this promise, "he answereth that he cannot resolve to accuse any."

No doubt the authorities knew that Johnson was an alias, but he was sticking to it. His "master" Thomas Percy was no mystery. An energetic, rough man and a Catholic, he was a poor relation of the great "Wizard Earl" Henry Percy, ninth Earl of Northumberland.[29] Thomas Percy was known to have had for several months the lease of a storehouse below the House of Lords and the tiny dwelling attached to it.[30] He was obviously crucial to the whole undertaking. Where had he run to? On the same famous day Popham wrote from Serjeants' Inn to Cecil enclosing "a note I now receaved from Sir Harry Montague the Recorder by which it may be gathered that Percy is shifted away this morning and I doubt [fear] towards Gravesend."[31] Percy's house was searched; his wife said she had not seen him since midsummer. Several servants were questioned, including the porter who had carried three thousand billets [pieces of firewood] to the vaults under Parliament House.[32]

At this stage the only men known for sure to be part of the plot, Johnson and Percy, were both laymen. Others of a similar type who were suspected, and of whom Popham was instantly able to add particulars in a three-page letter to Cecil,[33] were Christopher Wright, a brother-in-law of Thomas Percy, and Ambrose Rokewood, a wealthy young man from Suffolk. His wife, the beautiful Elizabeth Tyrrwhitt, was cousin of tall and red-bearded Robert Keyes, "a trusty and honest man."[34] Tom Wintour, from Huddington Hall near Worcester, was a lawyer by training. Thus many of the suspects were related; all were young, well educated, comfortably off, and lay people.

But another angle was opening up. A letter had been found on Johnson from Mrs Elizabeth Vaux, a well-known recusant from Harrowden Hall, near Wellingborough in Northamptonshire. Following information from a disgruntled member of her family, Popham issued a warrant for her arrest. It was clear, he said, that she "expected something was about to take place."[35] She had written at Easter-time to a friend with Catholic sympathies, advising her to pray that "that may come to pass that we purpose, which if it do, we shall see Tottenham turned French"—the expression of the time for a miraculous event. Eliza Vaux had long been a devoted harborer of priests, and Popham told Cecil that two in particular made her house their chief resort.[36] One of them was Father Henry Garnet. At thirty-one he had returned to England in 1586 with Robert Southwell on the second Jesuit mission. Whereas Southwell had been captured and hanged in 1595, Garnet had survived for nearly twenty years, moving quietly around the country conducting secret Masses in the great Catholic houses. He was now Superior of the Jesuits in England. The other was John Gerard, Eliza Vaux's confessor, a dashing, manly priest with a taste for fine clothes. In 1595 Gerard had made a famous escape from the Tower by rope, politely leaving a letter of explanation for the Lieutenant.

It was known by 6 November that several of the conspirators had fled to Worcestershire, but Popham reported to Cecil that Percy was supposed to be in London. The Thames was to be guarded. He enclosed a list of suspected persons—the latest additions were Robert Catesby, John Wright, and John Grant.[37] Popham added notes of where they were likely to be found.[37] Robert Catesby, an attractive Warwickshire man, had been active in the Essex rebellion and heavily fined. His cousin Francis Tresham was one of those who had guarded Popham at Essex House. John Grant was a recusant and married to Tom Wintour's sister Dorothy. Jack Wright was brother of Kit, and like him had been educated at St Peter's, York, which though nominally a Protestant school seems to have encouraged Catholic leanings.

All these people had to be investigated: conspirators and their families, priests and their protectors, servants of all kinds. The day after the Plot's discovery, for instance, Popham examined John Cradock, a cutler and a Catholic who worked near Temple Bar. Cradock said that he had been employed by Ambrose Rokewood to put a Spanish sword blade into a particularly fine hilt—it was engraved in low relief with the story of Christ's Passion. Such images were an obvious statement of faith, and Rokewood went to great expense to hint at his allegiance, for the decoration of the sword cost £19 15s., an enormous sum.[38] The gathering of such spoken evidences, the sifting of possessions and papers, was a long and relentless business. The work kept Popham and his colleagues fully extended for five months.

On 7 November, probably following torture, Johnson was examined at the Tower before the commissioners, including Popham. "He confesses that his Christian name is Guye and his surname Fawkes and was borne in the citye of York." The conspiracy had begun eighteen months before, and the plot had been revealed to him by an Englishman in the Low Countries. It was confined to five persons at first, then two were added and afterward five more; all swore secrecy, so Fawkes refused to name them. The plotters intended to place the nine-year-old Princess Elizabeth on the throne, and marry her to an English Catholic.[39]

It was the examination on 8 November that produced what was wanted: confirmation of the names of the conspirators. Fawkes had been told about the plot by Thomas Wintour; they had imparted it to Catesby, Percy, and John Wright, "and taking a vow, among ourselves, for secrecy, Catesby propounded to have it performed by gunpowder, and by making a mine under the Upper House of Parliament, which place we made choice of the rather, because religion has been unjustly suppressed there, it was fittest that justice and punishment should be executed there." Popham's information was accurate: Fawkes named all the men he had listed, as well as Sir Everard Digby and many others. On 9 November Fawkes made a declaration to Robert Cecil, acknowledged the next day before the commissioners, including Popham. The signature is supposed to have been extorted by the rack and Fawkes to have fainted before completing it. The plot had been communicated to Hugh Owen, a veteran continental agent, and Gerard, the Jesuit, had given them the sacrament, to confirm their oath of secrecy.[40] That was that for Guy Fawkes, though the government continued to press for further information, Popham, Coke, and Waad examining him, for instance, on 9 January.[41]

On 9 November it was learned too that the main group of conspirators, including Catesby and Percy, had been shot and killed at Holbeach House, near Stourbridge, Worcestershire, following an explosion while they were trying to dry gunpowder in front of a fire. Several others, including Rokewood, had been taken prisoner. The justices in the midland counties nearest were busy men now, exploring every nook and cranny and sending their findings to Cecil.

The most distinguished suspect in London was the Earl of Northumberland, whose family connection with Thomas Percy, as well, perhaps, as his interest in new scientific ideas, put him in danger. After a preliminary hearing, Popham drafted some questions to be put to the Earl concerning his promising to join the Catholics, his intercourse with Percy, and his communications with Sir Walter Ralegh.[42] Northumberland's replies asserted that in the late Queen's time, the King allowed him to give hope to the English Catholics, which he did, but went no further;

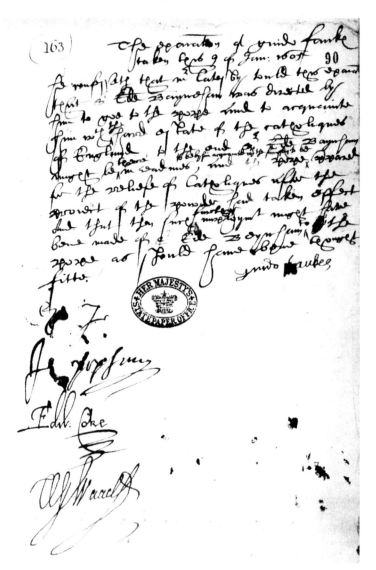

Notes of an examination of Guy Fawkes, showing his signature and those of Popham, Coke and Waad. Photo: The National Archives.

his association with Percy was only on business matters.[43] Now Northumberland's circle of intellectual friends included Ralegh, but Sir Walter denied any connection with the plot. The hint that Popham heard on 23 November that his "muskets, harquebuses and pistols were being made ready with speed" by a Sherborne locksmith sounds like a scurrilous rumor.[44] Another member of the circle was Thomas Hariot, whose lodging and study at the Earl's house, Syon, was searched.[45] Nothing was found, but Hariot was imprisoned briefly for having the King's horoscope cast; presumably this might have predicted the date on which James's death would be expected.[46] Northumberland was very heavily fined and sent to the Tower for life, though he was released in 1621.

The strain of Popham's work began to tell. On 2 December he wrote to Cecil: "Excuse me of my absence yesterday, which grew by means of an extreme rheum fallen into my shoulder and arm; but I am somewhat better now, and go with Mr Attorney to the Tower."[47] He had a busy day of examinations ahead, including those of Digby and Rokewood, but was suffering from writer's cramp as a result of making notes of his examinations in longhand.[48] He was laboring in a popular cause. An informant called Thomas Elliott sent via Cecil a petition to the King, which is marked "For my LCJ." The writer expresses his joy at the escape of the King from the "devilish, arrogant, perverse, and damned traitors, seminary priests, Jesuits and Papists." He recommends that they should be "quick lapped up alive in lead, with their arms spread abroad, and set upon the highest pinnacle in every city and port town in England, and let them there starve to death" to put the people in mind of this horrible treason. Also that near every church should be built a pair of gallows or gibbet, and all Papists and willful recusants hanged there. "Too much pity overthrows town and city, which pity good Queen Elizabeth ever used; and he fears the King will do so too."[49]

There had been plots against the monarch continuously for twenty-five years, but the Powder Treason was the one whose outrageous daring, right at the center of government, immediately seized the minds of everyone. It was the "September 11" of that era, with one crucial difference—it was foiled. Two days after Parliament reassembled on 21 January, Sir Edward Montague, Member for Northamptonshire, introduced a Bill for a public thanksgiving to be said annually on 5 November. Thereafter on that day the judges would process to Westminster Abbey to hear a Gunpowder Sermon, and a prayer would be said to the Lord to "scatter our enemies that delight in blood." Bonfire night became official.[50]

On 27 January the Gunpowder Plotters were brought for trial at Westminster Hall. Sir John Popham presided. Having met the eight survivors more privately, he would have observed with particular interest their demeanor in public. He would have known that the King, the Queen, and eleven-year-old Prince Henry, all potential victims of the explosion, were watching from places where they could not themselves be seen. Some of the men hung down their heads, others contrived "a stern look"; they must have irritated most of the audience by saying the Rosary, and the king particularly by "taking tobacco, as if hanging were no trouble to them."[51] The list of those charged began, interestingly, with three men who had not been captured: Garnet, Tesimond, and Gerard. As is clear from Coke's speech for the prosecution, the government wished to use the trial to demonstrate that from the very start this had been a Jesuit plot. Guy Fawkes, Gentleman, and his friends had been merely the tools of the priests. All except Digby pleaded Not Guilty, but of course there was no doubt about the outcome.

Coke spoke in a manner "somewhat more copious" than usual, and it was indeed a marvelous opportunity for him to enjoy himself. The conspirators had felt that the laws in force against Catholics were unjust, and should be revenged. "If any ask," said the Attorney-General, "who should execute this justice, it was Justice Fawkes . . . by what law they meant to proceed, it was Gunpowder Law, fit for Justices of hell." The plotters had started digging under the Houses of Parliament at an auspicious time: "it was in the entring of the Sunne into the Tropique of Capricorne, when they began their Myne, noting that by Myning they should descend, and by hanging ascend."[52] At the end, Popham described the laws made by Elizabeth against "recusants, priests and receivers of priests," explaining "the several occasions, progresses and reasons of the same; and having plainly demonstrated and proved that they were all necessary, mild, equal, moderate, and to be justified to all the world, pronounced judgement." The Plotters were executed in two batches a fortnight later.

Sir William Waad, Lieutenant of the Tower, had been the conspirators' jailer. Three years after the event he erected in the Council Chamber in the Queen's Building of the Tower a memorial in honor of those who had worked to convict the Plotters. The Latin text is wonderfully hyperbolic, but Sir John Popham's coat of arms is justly placed there, and he is described as "Juris & Justiciae Consultissimus" [most skilled in Law and Justice].[53]

On the very day of the trial of the conspirators, the government won a crucial trophy. From his hiding place at Hindlip in Worcestershire, hungry and cold, emerged at last the much-wanted priest Henry Garnet. He had been described in a warrant for his arrest as "of middling stature, full-faced, fat of body, of complexion fair, his forehead high on either side, with a little thin hair coming down upon the middle of the fore part of his head . . . his beard on his cheeks cut close, and his gait upright and comely for a feeble man."[54] His first examination was held in Star Chamber on 13 February 1606; Garnet cannot have been surprised, but he must have been sorry to see Popham entrusted with the process.

The first session was courteous and exploratory and did not mention the Plot at all. From Garnet, as the English authority on Catholic thinking, the government wanted confirmation that Jesuit doctrines were in themselves a danger to the state. There were known to be two fundamental points that were likely to make them so: the first was that a priest was not permitted by the religious authorities to reveal knowledge given to him under the seal of confession, although his duty to the state might require it. The second was the practice of equivocation, or avoiding outright lies by giving only part of the truth. On this Garnet was considered an authority; he had himself written a treatise on equivocation after the trial of Robert Southwell in 1595, where it had first become an issue of public interest.[55] In his speech at the trial of the Plotters, Coke had illustrated the technique: "A man is asked upon Oath this question, Did you see such a one today? he may by this doctrine answere: No, though he did see him, viz. reserving this secret meaning, not with purpose to tell my Lord Chiefe Justice. Or, I see him not *visione beatifica* [in a blessed vision], or, not in Venice, &c. likewise to answere thus, I was in the companie, reserving and intending secretly as added, this word NOT: as Strange the Jesuite did to my L Chief Justice and my selfe."[56]

Garnet was taken to the Tower, where because of his position and his remarkable personal qualities he was treated with unusual respect except by the Lieutenant, Sir William Waad, passionately anti-Catholic and his official guard. He was questioned there by Popham, Cecil, and Waad several times and in a pleasant manner, though of course the authorities were looking out for any admissions that could be used against Garnet later. At one point Waad forecast that the Jesuit Order would be dissolved by the Pope, and, as a first step, the priests would be sent out of England. Garnet answered with dignity: "I said that if it pleased the King to grant free liberty to other Papists, I would presently send away all Jesuits." Popham interrupted: surely this was more than Garnet had authority to do. "I would try," replied Garnet.[57]

Nothing emerged from these gentlemanly inquiries that enabled the Lords of the Council to connect Garnet with the Plot, so the task of establishing his involvement was handed over to the hard men, Popham and Coke. Gerard's narrative, written after the events—he managed to avoid capture and escaped to the continent—is of course fervently pro-Catholic and provides a chilling insight into the effects of religious intolerance. He relates that the two lawyers were "so forward, or rather desirous, to undertake the business that (as it is said) they offered, if they might have their full scope to deal with him as they thought good, they would undertake to prove him guilty in the Plot of Powder." Gerard begged forgiveness for them. "I pray God that the saying of the prophet David be not proved against them, *Veloces pedes eorum ad effundendum sanguinem,* [Their feet are swift to shed blood. Psalm 13:3] when they shall be cited to a higher tribunal, where neither the one [Coke] shall plead nor the other [Popham] be judge, but both be judged *secundum mensuram qua mensi fuerint.* [According to the measure they themselves have meted out to others. Matthew 7:2]"[58]

Garnet was examined several more times. According to Gerard, Popham and Coke managed to get nothing incriminating out of him, and so resorted to the first of several stratagems.

They gave out that he had confessed everything. That being the case, he could be sentenced without trial by Act of Parliament. The source is again Gerard, who tells us that Coke demanded from Parliament that Garnet and seven other Jesuits should be condemned by the High Court of Parliament. However, the House requested proofs of their guilt. Coke promised to give them the next day, but totally failed to convince the House, so the motion died, and was never revived.[59]

More determined than ever to achieve their goal, Gerard suggests, Coke and Popham tried a second stratagem. Garnet was a naturally trusting man, so when his gaoler offered sympathy and help, Garnet took up the offer. Garnet particularly wished to write to his friends. Carey, the gaoler, carried the letters straight to Cecil, who made copies and examined them minutely. Amazingly, Garnet himself added messages to his letters in orange juice, which remains invisible until heated. Several of the letters still exist, and are now in The National Archives.[60]

The third stratagem was that Carey placed Garnet, as a special favor, in a room in the Tower that had a hole in it so that he could talk to the prisoner in the next cell, Edward Oldcorne, known as Father Hall, with whom Garnet had spent his last ten days in hiding. Now government spies were able to listen in on their conversations. They are supposed to have overheard Garnet admit to Oldcorne that there was one man living who could incriminate him in the Plot.[61]

Finally, Garnet was tortured. The result was a key admission in a long letter of 9 March to the Council. Hitherto he had been bound by the seal of the confessional, and could reveal nothing he had been told there; now, to save himself from torture, he might, as Catesby had given him liberty to do so. He had known about the Plot from Catesby in general, and from Tesimond in particular.[62] This was the crucial admission, confirming that the unwillingness of priests to use their knowledge even for the safety of the state made them a constant threat. Garnet also revealed, however, that he was horrified by the proposal; he had tried his utmost to get the Pope to forbid such plots.

At last, after twenty-three recorded examinations, the councillors had Garnet's confession in their hands, but they were still not satisfied.[63] Garnet himself wrote later that "after I had acknowledged all that was true, my Lord Chief Justice said that they must have more of me than so; for I must forsooth confess that I was the very original of all, and the plotter: and besides I must confess such noblemen, as Catesby and the rest did build on, both in this action and also in the intended invasion from Spain; and for these two points I was to go to torture the second time [it was Good Friday]. But I pleaded that I was hardly dealt with, having told all I could, and bade them set down what they would have me confess, and so far as it concerned only my own credit I would acknowledge it without torture; whether torture were appointed as a punishment or a trial; what if I confessed nothing in my next torture, must I be tortured again? and that this was against the course of common laws. But they said No, not in cases of treason. For what! saith my Lord Chief Justice, this that you have confessed is nothing. Will you make your fault but a peccadillio? I entreated that in respect of my conference with the 3 deans all the forenoon (for I should have been racked that forenoon) and in respect of my long examination that afternoon, I being wearied, the torture might be deferred until another time, and desired Mr Lieutenant to be a mediator. They all said they were sorry, but it was so commanded. Well then, quoth I, this is the day in which my Saviour died for me! I am contented, and will appeal to a higher Judge. So I went to my chamber, but afterward Mr Lieutenant told me he had obtained a delay till the next coming of the Commissioners, though the Council's commandment was most peremptory; and my Lord of Salisbury told me that more than I had told should be brought out of my fingers' end."[64]

Garnet continued to be interrogated and to be required to give answers to interrogatories, being questioned by the King himself on theological points. Then on 15 March Popham drafted a lengthy list of proofs against him which was subsequently read and annotated by Cecil, and probably the basis of the prosecution at his trial. Garnet had been "a dealer" in the earliest negotiations in the Queen's time; he had become "the principal man" on whom Catesby relied, for who other than Garnet had assured him of the lawfulness of the plot? Garnet had recommended Fawkes for service in the conspiracy; he had known about the Plot about Whitsuntide 1605, "and yet never acquainted the State with it whereby it might be prevented." Neither had he made any effort to restrain the involvement of other Jesuits in the Plot.[65]

On 28 March 1606, in a time of plague, Garnet was arraigned at the Guildhall. The King was present but unseen, as were several ladies. Waad was still official custodian of the prisoner, and was understandably concerned that there was no seat for him in the chamber.[66] Popham, practical as ever, suggested that there should be a place railed in for him close to Garnet where he could maintain his formal guardianship.[67] During the trial, Popham's role was to listen, which must have needed considerable powers of concentration, for the proceedings lasted from 8 in the morning until 7 at night. The Serjeant read the indictment, and Garnet pleaded "Not Guilty." Then it was over to Coke, who again made the most of his opportunity. Garnet, he said, was "by country an Englishman, by birth a gentleman, by education a scholar, afterward a corrector of the common law print, with Mr Tottle the printer, and now is to be corrected by the law." He had "many excellent gifts and endowments of nature; by birth a gentleman, by education a scholar, by art learned, and a good linguist." But he was also by profession a Jesuit, and a Superior, "as indeed he is superior to all his predecessors in devilish Treason, a doctor of Jesuits that is a doctor of five Ds, as Dissimulation, Deposing of Princes, Disposing of Kingdoms, Daunting and deterring of subjects, and Destruction."[68]

After detailing Garnet's knowledge of the plans, and exposing the contradictions of his position in being unable to reveal what he had heard in confession, Coke emphasized the virtue of the royal family, which would have been destroyed. The prisoner was then allowed to reply, and questioned by the lords.

"*LCJ.* Garnet, you are Superior of the Jesuits, and if you forbid, must not the rest obey? Was not Greenwell with you half an hour at Sir Everard Digby's house when you heard of the discovery of your treason? And did you not there confer and debate the matter together? Did you not send him to Hall, to Mr Abington's house, to stir him up to go to the rebels, and encourage them? yet you seek to colour all this; but that's but a mere shift in you. And notwithstanding all this, you said no man living, but one, did know that you were privy to it; then, belike, some that are dead did know it. Catesby was never from you (as the gentlewoman that kept your house with you confessed), and by many apparent proofs and evident presumptions you were in every particular of this action, and directed and commanded the actors; nay, I think verily you were the chief that moved it.

"Garnet said, No, my Lord, I did not.

"Then it was extremely well urged by my Lord Chief Justice how he writ his letters for Winter, Wright, Fawkes, Baynam and Catesby, principal actors in this matchless treason." Besides, said Popham, Garnet had kept the two Bulls [the Pope's exhortations, one to clergy and the other to the laity, not to allow any monarch after James's death who would not promote Catholicism] to prejudice the King, and to do other mischief in the realm, "which, when he saw the King peacably to come in, then being out of hope to do any good, he burned them. . . . Then the Lord Chief Justice, making a pithy preamble of all the apparent proofs and presumptions of his guiltiness, gave judgment that he should be drawn, hanged and quartered."[69]

Henry Garnet was returned to the Tower to await his execution. While there he was made to answer yet more questionnaires about equivocation and civil laws, presumably so that the government could make use of them later. He tried further to clarify his position, and continued to write to his friends. There was a delay of several weeks before the sentence was carried out, perhaps because neither King nor Council really felt that Garnet's involvement in the Plot had been established. Garnet was executed on 3 May 1606 in St Paul's Churchyard,[70] without the usual enthusiastic response from the onlookers.[71]

After the execution Garnet's head and quarters were placed in a basket of straw. One piece of straw, a Catholic named John Wilkinson reported, was "thrown towards me." He delivered it to "Mrs N., a matron of singular Catholic piety," who showed it to a nobleman of her acquaintance. Both he and others were convinced that they saw a man's face in the straw.[72] The straw became a focus of popular fascination, a sign from heaven of Garnet's innocence, a national phenomenon, and a miracle known throughout the Christian world. Joseph Hall, the man who so narrowly escaped becoming the first headmaster of Peter Blundell's school, alluding to "the noise which Garnet's straw had made," wrote in a contemporary letter: "I had thought that our age had too many grey hairs, and with time, experience, and with experience, craft, not to have descried a juggler: but now I see by its simplicity it declines to its second childhood. I only wonder how Fawkes and Catesby escaped the honour of saints and privilege of miracles."[73]

18

Acting Lord Chancellor

It is hardly surprising that on 15 July 1606 a grant was made to Robert Earl of Salisbury and Sir John Popham of "the 15th of every cwt. of fine copper" from the mines of the counties of York, Lancaster, Westmoreland, Cumberland, Cornwall, Devon, Gloucester, Worcester, and the Principality of Wales.[1] The two men were deservedly rewarded, for they had been responsible for the successful prosecution of the Gunpowder Plotters. That the grant should be an income from copper mining seems appropriate too, for Popham had for years been the principal authority in the kingdom on matters of trade, commerce, and the coinage.

The nation's wealth depended on vigorous trade. Throughout his service under Elizabeth, Popham had been referred to whenever there was a question about weights and measures, rates of exchange, opening trade with Muscovy, Turkey, or the Levant, and monopolies.[2] In these matters as in everything else, he was always thorough and conscientious, even if he felt that he had no natural instinct for the subject. In 1598, for instance, Popham had evidently been asked by the Queen to advise on a matter concerning the tin trade, and had been unable to provide what was wanted quickly. The Queen seems to have rebuked him soundly, for on 9 August, in the middle of the vacation, he wrote a long letter of abject apology: *I do most humbly biseke your Majesty to beare with and pardon such errors and oversights as in the depth of your Judgement may easily be found to have passed therein.* He advises in detail on the management of the trade for the Crown's benefit, and on the transporting of gold coinage out of the realm, a subject on which he has written a *Brieff discorse to be delivered unto your majesty as oportunitye may serve / wherein, as I most trewly acknowledge that I have laid open to your Majesty's view the weakness of my understanding in matters of that nature yet hadd I rather subject the same to your Majesty's most gracious sensure and favourable construction who hath heretofore borne with my many imperfeccions in not performyng what your majesty hath comanded, then have my disobedience justly sensured against me / and ever so I do most humbly biseke hym never to cease to protect and preserve yow, who hitherunto hath never left to defend yow.'*[3]

A later example of Popham's thoroughness was his testing in his rooms of a miracle dye. Lord Berwick, Lord Treasurer of Scotland, had requested his opinion about a suit exhibited to King James for a privilege concerning dyeing. Popham replied that he had known of this suit eighteen months before the Queen's death.

> "To avoid all falsity as much as I could, I caused these trials to be made in my own chamber by a very perfect man whom I knew to be very skilful, one whom I durst trust and not then known to the parties that followed the suit. And when it was thus dyed I caused that party to try the colours so dyed with many very hard trials, whereby I found it endured all wearing trials . . . . Since which upon your former letters I have caused trials to be made of divers colours of the best sort, as French russets, violets, tawnys and such like, to be dyed in my chamber in my own sight; and that done, myself caused them to be tried with scalding wine, vinegar, water and salt, and other matter very apt to stain anything sufficient for any wearing trials, and yet it stained not at all. The trials gave me good satisfaction for the validity of that stuff.
>
> "Therefore my opinion is thus. If they still make the stuff as perfect and will sell it so cheap as they pretend, it will make fair and good wearing colours near as cheap as the falsest now too commonly used to be,—many of which colours will not endure one day's raining on it. If it continue in proof as heretofore has been made, it cannot but be greatly beneficial both to his Majesty and the merchandising of our cloths."[4]

James was at first more extravagant than his income could support, so it became important for the Council to be able to find ways to fill up the royal purse. The nearest approach to a workable scheme was the plan drawn up by Popham and Coke together for the abolition of feudal tenures, which they expected to increase James's revenues by £100,000 p.a.[5] Though this proposal continued to be debated, it was not put into practice. At the same time the Commons were anxious to abolish wardship, a very delicate matter that would affect the Crown's revenue. Sir Francis Popham sat on the committee of the Commons that in March 1604 requested a joint conference with the Lords on the subject, and Sir John was one of those who delivered the Lords' response.[6] A result of the discussions was Cecil's scheme whereby landowners could sell the wardship of their heirs while they were still alive. This explains an otherwise extraordinary Popham maneuver: it appears that Sir Francis had made Sir John and Lady Amy wards of his heir, and in December 1604 the grandparents sold this wardship for £500, thus realizing a very valuable asset.[7] Presumably the point of the new legislation was that the King could also sell his wardships, giving him a substantial additional income.

However, most of the King's money came from trade, which was still largely controlled by monopolies granted to individuals and companies who were prepared to pay for them to the Crown. Although monopolies were supposed to have been suspended on James's accession, in fact they still operated, and Popham was much occupied by the problems they created.

In February 1605, for instance, he and Coke "found a means to relieve the poor beer brewers of the Cinque Ports" against the excessive imposition resulting from a license given to Lord Aubigny.[8] Popham and others were required in 1605 to "take measures against such disobedient persons as resist the right of search and seizure of divers woods deceivable in the art or mistery of dyeing," granted by letters patent to Sir Arthur Aston, knt., John Auchmoutie, and others.[9] In the same year the makers of playing cards complained to Cecil that they had been "oppressed for 26 years with cruel monopolies, and above all by Sir Edward Darcie. They might buy no paper but from him and on his conditions: he constrained them to make but half the wonted number, that he might sell them at what price he listed . . . they must enter into bonds to sell to none but him: and he would cast them into prison at home, or cause them to be pressed into Ireland or the Low Countries . . . . hearing he seeks to get another patent, they have besought the King to make them a corporation: who referred their suit to the Lord Chancellor and the Lord Chief Justice."[10] Before long they are writing again to Cecil, thanking him for his past favors to them. "They understand that their case is to be heard by the Chief Justices, and pray that this may be done with expedition since the Judges are about to go on circuit."[11]

In June 1605 Popham and others wrote to the Council concerning "the farm of the alnage and measurage [alnage was a fee paid for measurement and inspection of cloth] that is sought to be granted by his Majesty of sundry kinds, as well of new made drapery as of other stuffs made within this realm . . . . We are resolved that all new made drapery made wholly of wool, as frizaddoes, bayes, northern dozens, northern cottons, cloth rash and other like drapery of what name so ever made as drapery for the use of man's body are to yield subsidy and alnage .... But as touching fustians, canvas, sackcloth and such like made of other stuff than wool or but mixed with wool, we are of opinion that no charge can be imposed for the search or measuring thereof .... As touching the narrow new stuff made in Norwich and other places with worsted yarn, we are of opinion that it is not grantable nor fit to be granted, for we cannot find that there was ever any alnage upon Norwich worsteds."[12] This most important decision was the making of the Norwich wool industry, for it gave the Norfolk manufacturers a significant advantage over those elsewhere.

Popham was not concerned only with the big players in the financial world—King, government, and merchants. He had in mind the welfare of the small men too. In September 1605, for instance, he replied to Cecil about a proposal to restrict trade with France and Spain to the large merchant companies based in London. "This I hold as a principle," he wrote, "that it is not convenient that merchants have such power passed over unto them that they may govern the estate of things both at home and abroad as they list." The consequences of such a new scheme are dangerous: "I fear me it will overthrow all the towns, shipping and mariners of the West parts, because the young merchants of those parts begin with very small stocks, and cannot deal here upon such credit as young merchants may do in London, and their stocks and credits have increased by their often returns. .... Now if they be barred of their often returns, they can hardly raise benefit sufficient to support their estates, much less to increase it, and then must both their shipping and mariners decay in those parts." Popham goes on to remind the Secretary of the merchants' basic motivation, "their own present good, without respect unto the State." The proposal would affect the State, "all men that live on their revenue or husbandry, and a multitude of artizans so deeply as will appear when it shall come in dispute."[13]

Popham's central role in the government think tank is illustrated by a letter from Cecil to Coke in October 1605. Cecil referred to the patent "for setting the trade of Levant at liberty" which involved making merchants joining the scheme pay £25. "This course was first thought upon by my Lord Chief Justice and yourself, but then because the first sum was 50*l* and should not have served for freedom to themselves and their posterity, they staggered at it, shooting still to overthrow the imposition, where contrariwise every man is now so greedy to come in, as we believe you will be troubled while you are drawing the patent with daily taking in those who will importune you." Interestingly, Cecil adds that "because it is a matter wherein I and the Lord Chamberlain have particular interest, I do besides my public duty desire you to take some more care of it in my respect."[14]

Clearly at this period Robert Cecil was anxious to profit wherever he could, the use of public office to provide private income being perfectly normal. It had been one of the first acts of the King's Lord Treasurer, Thomas Sackville, Earl of Dorset (nicknamed "Lord Fill-Sack")[15] to farm out the administration of customs to private individuals. They would pay the Crown for the privilege, which would give King James a steady income, and they would be able to make a good profit for themselves. A group with which Cecil was himself associated had won the contract. They did not profit from it for long. In February 1607 John Chamberlain wrote in his diary: "The King is at Oking [Woking]; the Quene is saide to be with child: the earle of Northampton [Henry Howard, first earl] further in grace than ever, or then any man; whereby yt is thought he hath overthrowne the earle of Salisburies patentees of the customes, and a new patent is making for Sir John Swinerton and his associats, who they say offers an hundred thowsand pound for a fine, and 4000 more yearly rent then is now payed. The former patent is not yet two yeares old, and yet the cheife justices have found meanes to picke a hole in yt, and though there were none, yet have they an old maxime in theyre barbarous law-phrase *nullum tempus occurrit regi* [no time disadvantages the king]."[16]

Another method by which the King could gain more income was by the taxation of goods, known as imposition, and an important judgment resulted from James's levying in 1605 of a duty on currants. The Levant Company had formerly held the monopoly, but when this lapsed the rate of duty could be set by the Crown. James fixed payment at 5s 6d on every hundredweight imported, but a London merchant called John Bate refused to pay. The Court of Exchequer held against him, arguing that the king was entitled to levy such a tax, and this judgment was approved by Popham and Coke.[17] The King could impose any new custom on a foreign commodity, "especially, as the Chief Justice says, when it is a luxury."[18] This seemed to open the way for the King to raise more revenues, which was necessary, but on the other hand it seemed to entitle him to make impositions wherever he wished, which was hardly in keeping with the temper of the Commons.[19] The judgment enabled Cecil to levy impositions on fourteen hundred articles, increasing hugely the income of the Crown.

The King's revenues and expenses provide Popham with all sorts of curious interest. A copper mine has recently been discovered in the mountains of Lancashire, called Furnes Fels, at Coniston; it being such a remote place, the brother-in-law of the director finds he has to live at too close quarters with the workmen, so he requires "an increase of years" relating to his accommodation.[20] There is a dispute concerning the maintenance of "13 petticanons or ministers skilfull in song, and 13 clerks, singers also, and 13 choresters, being singing children" of the King's Chapel of St George's, Windsor.[21] Sir William Waad, Keeper of the Tower, complains to Cecil that he has "received from divers merchants of London strange opposition for that little quantity of wine which had been paid . . . at the least 300 years to his Majesty's Royal Castle: wherein I have had very honourable assistance of my Lord Chief Justice and Mr Attorney General, whose chance it was to be here when my man that takes that duty was well beaten. This day one Busford, a merchant of London, has not only denied me that duty but has evil entreated my servant, and taken from him his bottles with very outrageous words; amongst others, he wished the pox on all offices and officers."[22]

A disease with the same name featured in an unusual case Popham judged in 1602 involving the College of Physicians of London. At that time medical practice was strictly controlled by the College, so that surgeons, whose knowledge was merely technical, were not allowed to prescribe medication. Roger Jenkins or Jinkins had been imprisoned for disobeying this prohibition, and resolved to fight the College over the matter. At the hearing, which was held in Popham's own house, Jenkins claimed that his practice had been proper because he was a surgeon, and in surgery the use of internal medicines was often necessary. Popham held for the College; in such an emergency, he said, a physician should be called in. No surgeon might practice physic, "no, not for any disease, though it be the great Pox [syphilis]."[23] Popham added that prescriptions written by physicians were often used fraudulently by quacks. To prevent such misuse, he advised that "all physicians in the future should write on their prescriptions the name of their patient and the date." It is a fine example of his practical mind at work in a pioneering cause.

The College were so pleased with the discomforting of Jenkins that they wrote to Popham a most fulsome "letter of thankesgeeving." They were already most infinitely bound to him for his most honorable favors in the past, yet "suche is your Lords great care, and contynuall good inclynation, to the maintenaunce of lerninge, good Orders and vertue: that not only wee, and our Societie that now is, are now againe more deepely obliged to your honour but also all our Posterytie in time to come, shall have just cause to pray for your Lords long lief and Prosperytie: whose unspottable Integrytie, hath been so well knowen to all England these many yeares . . . while the Memory of the Societie and College of Physitions of London shall remaine, so long shall your Lords honorable and most woorthie name be celebrated and recorded: among all such as ether love, or Professe the tytle of learninge."[24]

Incidentally, the College had for years been resisting the attempts by Simon Forman, the notorious astrologer, to get himself recognized as a medical practitioner. Forman had many noble patients, and in 1603 he asked Frances Howard, Lady Hertford, a regular client, to write in his behalf "to my Lord Chief Justice and to Sir Francis Popham, his son, that his lordship should not take part with the Doctors against me. He answered that he knew me not nor had granted any warrant against me, but only set his hand to a general warrant of the Doctors, and henceforth he would be better advised."[25]

More earthily, on 1 July 1606 Popham was a signatory to the Ordinances of the Gardeners' Company. This magnificent document, the finest we have that carries Popham's autograph, was also signed by Thomas Egerton, now Lord Ellesmere, and Thomas Sackville, Earl of Dorset. Housed in the Guildhall Library, London, the document is very well-preserved; the opening lines are beautifully illuminated and the seals intact.[26]

On 30 March 1607 Sir John Popham was appointed to supply the place of the Lord Chancellor in the Upper House. Thomas Egerton was indisposed, so Popham found himself enjoying another most distinguished role at the very center of government. A contemporary illustration of James in Parliament shows the sovereign seated with the Lord Chancellor on his right hand, ready to advise the King on the business of the day. Indeed, the Chancellor functioned as "the mouth, the eare, the eye and the very heart of the Prince," as Egerton himself wrote.[27] We have a complete list of the order of business during Popham's brief spell as acting Lord Chancellor.[28]

The sheer variety of topics the Lords considered is remarkable.

The first day was occupied with the second reading of an Act for the Repeal of the Act of 14 Eliz. concerning the length of Kersies, and the second reading of an Act for the relief of John Roger, gentleman, against Robert Tailor, Paule Tailor, and William Tailor.[29] On 1 April the Lords considered a Bill "Annexing Lands and Jewels and Ornaments to the Crown for ever," perhaps concerned with the property of traitors, and another "for the Attainder of divers Offenders in the late most barbarous, monstrous, detestable, and damnable Treasons." They then discussed a Bill for clearing the Passage by water to and beyond the city of Oxford. The Archbishop of Canterbury spoke on an order of the King about complaints made against ecclesiastical courts: the punishment of excommunication was unfit to be used except in great matters. Committees were organised on the Bill for carrying of Timber to Barnstable, and "for Free Trade with Spain, France, Portugall etc."

Two days later business resumed. The Lord Chief Justice made an excuse for the absence of the Lord Bishop of London, "for Want of health." The question as to whether the King had a right to purveyance had for many years been controversial, and a new Bill was under discussion. The King could not afford to give up his cheap food supplies without substantial compensation, but the Commons were unwilling to let him keep the privilege since he did not seem to be entitled to it. In due course the judges were asked to give their opinion. Nicholas Fuller, a puritan leader, was present when they gave their reply, and subsequently reported to the Commons how "I lately heard the chief not in place only but in judgement [Popham] say that the statutes for purveyors do not bind the King." All the King's prerogatives, Popham stated, were "allowed on behalf of the law for the public."[30] It was a judgment "in all men's opinions of dangerous consequence, that the prerogative was not subject to law, but that it was transcendent above the reach of Parliament."[31] It sounded as though James would definitely go on receiving his provisions at below market price. However, this judgment did not settle the matter, and purveyance remained a source of contention throughout James's reign.

Several Bills were brought up from the House of Commons: for the providing of a Learned and Godly Ministry; to enable suspended and deprived Ministers to sue and prosecute their appeals; concerning bringing in of wines in seasonable time; to restrain the Transportation of colored cloths undrest. An Act concerning the government of Wales was referred to committee, and Popham was one of those named to attend the Lords, to meet on 7 April at 2 PM at the Council Chamber at Court. Incidentally, it was for his conduct in such "Committees out of the House" that Popham was remembered when in 1621 the House of Lords set down Orders to regulate such committees. It was noted that "The Lord Cheife Justice Popham did often attend Committees, and though he were Cheife Justice, privie Councellor, and infirme, yet would hee very hardly ever bee persuaded to sitt down, saying it was his duty to stand, and attend, and desired the lords to keepe those formes which were their due."[32] Popham's example lasted until the Orders were revised in 1715.

On 5 April the Lords discussed an Act for the abating and to restrain the new Erection of Wears, Stanks, Kiddles, and other Obstructions, in great and navigable Rivers. The Act concerning Purveyors was referred to committees, the Lord Chief Justice and others being appointed to attend "at the Painted Chamber [the Star Chamber], near the Parliament Presence," on Tuesday, 8 April. There was a complaint by the Earl of Shrewsbury that Captain Roger Billings, servant to the Earl of Pembroke, had been arrested at the suit of Lewis Evans, a tailor, "contrary to the honour and privilege of this Court"; order was made for both men to appear before the Lords to answer for their breach of privilege. After this great matter, minor administrative points were dealt with concerning merely the Government of Wales, Free Liberty of Trade, and Matters Ecclesiastical. Egerton seems to have been back in his place on 7 April.

On 16 April 1607 the Council sitting at Whitehall were still concerned about the Crown's income, and felt that Popham was taking too much time about settling a disputed matter relating to the lease of the farm of customs on tobacco: "We have been very glad to find that your lordship has taken so much care as you have done about the book for the customs, considering how just a thing it is that his Majesty may be without danger to lose by any indirect means those profits which justly appertain unto him. Our purpose is now only to acquaint you that the delay of the dispatch gives great interruption of many payments, which breeds disorder and clamour; considering how the same are destined to the satisfaction of many particulars. Therefore, finding that all things are accorded, except in one particular, concerning the allowance to be made for the custom upon tobacco, wherein the farmers think they ought in equity to be otherwise dealt with than your lordship offers (upon which you refuse to set your hand to the book, which will beget a farther delay) although we doubt not but you see cause for that you do, yet because they are desirous to be heard, we must needs require you . . . to give them such a dispatch for the book upon this our letter as the same may be ingrossed."[33]

Popham returned the lease the same day. It would have been quite reasonable for him to be slowing up, for he was by now probably seventy-six years old. The tobacco trade must have interested him considerably, for it had originated in Virginia. Smoking had been popularized by Ralegh, and although the weed was hated by the King it was likely to provide him with a significant source of income. Trade with Virginia had been for several years a deep interest of Popham's and even as he worked on the customs book for the King he was bringing to a climax his own last remarkable enterprise—the planting of a colony on the East coast of America.

19

Virginia Planter

ON 31 MAY 1607 AN EXPEDITION SET OUT FROM PLYMOUTH BOUND for America. The promoter was Sir John Popham, and the leader was his nephew, Captain George Popham.

For Sir John, it was the culmination of years of activity and experience in related matters. His interest in trade may well have originated in his childhood near the port of Bridgwater. Since about 1520 ships from the West Country had frequently visited the coast of North America, known as Norumbega, for it was highly productive of hides and fish. Bristol, with which Popham was associated early in his career, had a strong connection with Newfoundland. A permanent settlement on the coast would be a valuable trading center, soon repaying investors in the project. There was the lure, too, of the discovery of a Northwest passage, the much sought-after route to the Orient supposed to run through what is now northern Canada.

Mining had long exercised Popham's mind. He would have been told by George of the supposed marvelous riches of southern America. Norumbega was rumored to have silver mines, and by 1600 seems to have become the northern equivalent of El Dorado. Gold, silver, and "pyllors of cristoll" were supposed to exist somewhere between Nova Scotia and Florida: mapmakers located it in what is now called Maine.[1] To find mines was certainly a principal objective of the Popham expedition.

Popham had read and thought about the exciting words of Ralegh's Patent of 1584, which had granted him liberty and license "to have hold occupie and enjoye" lands, countries and territories not already inhabited by Christian people.[2] To the acquisitive mind the idea of planting was irresistible. Ralegh's colonies at Roanoke had failed, and neither Popham nor Ralegh had planted successfully in Ireland, but here was another opportunity to show that it could be done. A plantation would establish a Protestant enclave to counteract any possible Catholic settlements. Several initiatives of this kind had been mooted during the early years of James's reign, one group proposing to ask the King to license three hundred Catholic households to go to Virginia.[3] No doubt such a suggestion would have stimulated Popham to a Protestant response.

There was a hint of patriotic endeavor in the idea. The French, now free of war with Spain, returned with the encouragement of their king, Henri IV, to their colonial ambitions. They were already active on the North American coast, so that a new phase of international rivalry for America had begun.[4] Although Englishmen had explored in the area, there were in 1605 no settled English colonies on the American coast. Furthermore, no one now had a monopoly on the exploration of Virginia, for Ralegh's patent had lapsed after his disgrace and the King had not reassigned it. Popham's sturdy sense of service to his sovereign and country, as well as his commercial instinct, must have encouraged him to proceed with an English settlement.

Finally, a colony would provide an alternative outlet for those who wished to work as well as those who ought to, and perhaps also a place to which criminals could be transported. There is no doubt that Popham had had this possibility in mind for some time. It was not a new idea, for the Vagrancy Act of 1597 had made gypsies liable to transportation, as was the practice in France and Spain.[5] Popham himself had probably been behind the Statute of 1598 which allowed that "wandering souldiers and Mariners, which will not settle themselves to work" should be banished "to such parts beyond the seas, as shall by six or more of the Privy Council for that purpose be assigned."[6] For so many who made their livelihood from military service a state of peace was a calamity, as they were cast upon their own resources for a living. Many knew no other trade than pillage, so kept up their old ways by becoming robbers and pirates, making travel in England dangerous by land or sea.

To deal with this problem a notable Order of 16 September 1603 was drawn up by Popham and Coke just after the King had stayed at Littlecote: "Forasmuch as it hath appeared unto us as well by our owne viewes in our travailes in this present Progresse of his Majestie as also by good and credible informacion from diverse and sondrie parts of the realme that rogues growe againe to increase and bee incorrigible and dangerouse, not onely to his Majesty's loving subjects abroad, but also to his Majestie and his most honourable Howsehold and attendants in and about his Court, which growing partly through the remissnes of some Justices of the Peace and other officers of the countrie, and partly for that there hath bin no suite made for assigning some place beyond the seas to which such incorrigible or dangerouse rogues might be banished according to the statute in that behalf made; wee therefore of his Majesty's Privie Councell . . . heereby assigne and thincke it fitt and expedient that the places and parts beyond the seas to which any such incorrigible or dangerouse rogues shalbee banished and convayed accordinge to the said statute shalbee theise countries and places following, viz., the New Fownde Land, the East or West Indies, France, Germanie, Spaine, and the Low Countries or any of them."[7]

The idea of American colonization was by no means new, but at this time it became particularly attractive, for reports from recent voyages had made the country sound most appealing. The voyage of Bartholomew Gosnold in 1602, which gave names to Cape Cod and Martha's Vineyard, had shown that New England was delightful as well as healthy, at least in summer.[8] The expedition of Martin Pring in 1603 confirmed a positive view of the area. It was Pring who first penetrated into and appreciated the amenities of Massachusetts Bay and the natives there. Apparently the people liked Elizabethan music: "We had a youth in our company that could play upon a gittern, in whose homely music they took great delight and would give him many things, as tobacco, tobacco-pipes, snakes' skins of six foot long which they use for girdles, fawns' skins and such-like. And danced twenty in a ring, and the gittern in the midst of them, using many savage gestures, singing Jo, Ja, Jo, Ja, Ja, Jo: him that first brake the ring the rest would knock and cry out upon." The English reported well of the Indian cultivation they saw, the gardens in which were sown "tobacco, pompions, cucumbers and such-like; and some of the people had maize or Indian wheat among them." They noted the timber and fur-bearing capacities of the country; as for trees there was plenty of sassafras, "a plant of sovereign virtue for the French pox," and so much valued by Elizabethan sailors.[9]

With such prospects it is not surprising that everyone was talking Virginia, and that playwrights satirized the fashion. A play by Ben Jonson, George Chapman, and John Marston called *Eastward Ho!* went through four editions in 1605. A venture is proposed to Virginia:

"*Scapethrift.* But is there such treasure there, Captain, as I have heard?

> *Seagull.* I tell thee, gold is more plentiful there than copper is
> with us; and for as much red copper as I can bring, I'll
> have thrice the weight in gold. Why, man, all their
> dripping-pans and their chamber-pots are pure gold;
> and all the chains with which they chain up their
> streets are massy gold; all the prisoners they take are
> fettered in gold; and for rubies and diamonds, they
> go forth on holidays and gather 'em by the seashore
> to hang on their children's coats, and stick in their
> caps, as commonly as our children wear saffron-gilt
> brooches, and groats with holes in 'em."[10]

And now, just when all these encouraging influences were in
the air, Popham and Sir Ferdinando Gorges received an amazing
gift: five genuine native Americans.

They were not the first "salvages" to visit our shores. Mariners
of Bristol had brought three natives of the New-found-land to England in 1501; they went to London, received royal hospitality,
and after two years were indistinguishable from Englishmen.[11]
In 1584 two Virginians, Manteo and Wanchese, had stayed sev-
en months in England, keeping company with Ralegh and Hariot at Durham House. Ralegh also brought natives back from
Guiana, and they remained in his service when he was imprisoned in the Tower. One was called Harry the Indian,[12] another
Leonard Regapo.[13] At Ralegh's home church at East Budleigh in
Devon two of the remarkable carved bench ends show faces with
definite Indian features and head dresses. It is likely that they
were carved from life.[14]

Popham's Indians had been captured in a disgraceful action by
George Waymouth, a native of Cockington, Devon, who had been
employed by the Catholic Lord Arundel of Wardour "for the discovery of the North-west passage" although prospecting, or finding a site for a Catholic community, may have been the true object of the voyage. Waymouth's expedition arrived in early 1605
at what is now known as Allen Island, to the east of Pemaquid
Point, where the sailors erected a cross.[15] They made contact
with the Indians, "all very civill and merrie . . . a people of exceeding good invention, quicke understanding and readie capac-
itie."[16] By June, however, the Englishmen began to find the Indians treacherous; it was necessary for the captain to charm
them with a demonstration of the effects of the "Loadstone" on
sword and knife; and, as eyewitness James Rosier put it, "This
we did to cause them to imagine some great powere in us; and for

that to love and feare us." The Indians came to supper, and behaved very politely, "neither laughing nor talking all the time, and at supper fed not like men of rude education, neither would they eat or drinke more than seemed to content nature." Their most noticeable habit was that of "drinking" tobacco, which sometimes they were seen to do out of the short claw of a lobster.[17]

The English resolved to take some Indians immediately. One, "yoong, of a ready capacity," and two others they wooed onto the ship. Two more they were unable to entice, so they "suddenly laid hands upon them on their own ground." It needed five or six men to take them, "for they were so strong and so naked as our best hold was by their long haire on their heads." Getting the natives was "a matter of great importance for the full accomplement of our voyage," but the English were "very loath to have done them any hurt." The *Archangel* party returned to Dartmouth with five "Salvages" as well as "2 Canoas with all their Bowes and Arrowes."[18]

In spite of their traumatic experience the Indians are described as not discontented at all, but merry and kind. Their names were Nahanada, a Sagamo or Commander, Amoret, Skicowaros and Maneddo, Gentlemen, and Saffacomoit, a servant. On their arrival at Dartmouth on 14 July 1605[19] the Indians seem to have been handed over to Sir Ferdinando Gorges, now reinstated as governor of the fortifications at Plymouth. Why Gorges felt entitled to make use of the Indians on their arrival we do not know, for the expedition was not his to command. In his own account, written much later, Gorges said that he "seized upon" them, and observed that they were crucially important: "This accident must be acknowledged the meanes under God of putting on foote, and giving life to all our Plantations."[20]

Gorges kept three of the Indians himself, but two, probably Amoret and Saffacomoit, he sent to Sir John Popham.[21] What they thought of him, or he of them, is unfortunately not recorded. Gorges, however, wrote in *Of the Use I made of the Natives:* "After I had those people sometimes in my Custody, I observed in them an inclination to follow the example of the better sort; And in all their carriages manifest shewes of great civility farre from the rudenesse of our common people; And the longer I conversed with them, the better hope they gave me of those parts where they did inhabit, as proper for our uses, especially when I found what goodly Rivers, stately Islands, and safe harbours those parts abounded with. . . . and having kept them full three yeares,

I made them able to set me downe what great Rivers ran up into the Land, what Men of note were seated on them, what powere they were of, how allyed, what enemies they had, and the like of which in his proper place."[22]

We have met Sir Ferdinando Gorges in his capacity as vacillating conspirator, and as the man who released Popham from imprisonment at Essex House. In return, Popham had supervised Gorges's release from the Tower on 27 November 1601.[23] On the accession of James, Gorges had been restored to military duty. He was something of an intellectual, corresponding with the mathematician Thomas Hariot on problems of fortification and navigation. Another friend was the Earl of Southampton, who had probably encouraged Gorges's fascination with the possibilities of colonization, though ten years at Plymouth fort, as well as many family connections with explorers of America, would have been enough to arouse it anyway.[24]

When Gorges learned from Waymouth's sailors of the potential of the Norumbega coast, he determined on action. He was an ambitious man, "very avaricious, and very despotic," impatient under disappointment, and "never considered a man of integrity."[25] Lacking financial resources himself, for he was a second son, he needed a backer. Remarkably in view of their experiences of each other, he turned to Sir John Popham.

What could Popham offer? Exploration had hitherto been carried out by private enterprise financed by two separate groups of merchants, those of London and of the West Country. With all these men Popham had excellent contacts. He had experience of major undertakings in Ireland and in the Fens as well as very good reasons for interest in the project, considerable wealth of his own, the ear of the Council and, most importantly, influence with the King. He knew from the Irish attempt that such a colonizing attempt could not be carried out piecemeal. A large organization, bringing together the various interested parties, had to be established. The initiative to proceed with a concerted approach to settlement in America came from Sir John Popham.

He would have felt a kind of kinship with Gorges, also a man of Somerset family and former admirer of Essex. Popham knew that Gorges had never been fully committed to the Essex rebellion. In his old age, he needed someone energetic to carry out his dreams, and probably the men shared a conception of the kind of organization required. Popham must have been very responsive to Gorges even though at this time he was still much engaged with the aftermath of the Gunpowder Plot. Before March 1606 the Court servant Sir Walter Cope wrote to Cecil: "My Lord Chief Justice, foreseeing in the experience of his place the infinite numbers of cashiered captains and soldiers, of poor artizans that would and cannot work, and of idle vagrants that may and will not work, whose increase threatens the State, is affectionately bent to the plantation of Virginia, in which he has already taken great pains, and means to disburse 500*l* per ann for 5 years, if the action prosper. He desires for his better expedition two lines from you in particular, or from the Lords in general, by virtue whereof he may call the undertakers, gentlemen merchants, etc., unto him, and by their advices set down the best manner of project; which being agreed upon, shall be speedily returned to your lordships, because the best season for the journey approaches."[26]

Popham and Gorges "busied themselves" about the matter, though it is not known exactly how the negotiations were managed. The Lord Chief Justice held early meetings in connection with the foundation of the Company at the Middle Temple, but no records remain of their contents. Popham himself, Gorges and Cecil were the key figures without whom nothing would have happened. Many other men must have contributed their energy, financial expertise, and knowledge of exploration; Sir Thomas Smith, the Governor of the East India Company, encouraged city merchants to invest in the scheme. Captain Waymouth, Sir Walter Cope, Edward Hayes and Richard Hakluyt are among those who may well have advised and negotiated, but all this seems to have been done informally by word of mouth.[27] Within a few weeks the essentials of the scheme had been agreed.

It was Popham who won the King's approval,[28] and on 10 April 1606 the Charter was issued. It was a major contribution to the successful colonization of America. Sir John Popham deserves to be celebrated for the vision and practical expertise he gave to establishing the Virginia Company, which achieved not only the colonizing attempt that carries his name, but also the more well-known and enduring settlement at Jamestown.

"James, by the grace of God etc. Whereas our loving and well-disposed subjects, Sir Thomas Gates and Sir George Somers, Knightes; Richard Hackluit, Clarke, Prebendarie of Westminster; and Edwarde Maria Winghfeilde, Thomas Hannam and Raleighe Gilberde, Esquiers; William Parker and George Popham, Gentlemen; and divers others of our loving subjects, have been humble sutors unto us that wee woulde vouchsafe unto them our licence to make habitacion, plantacion, and to deduce a Colonie of sondrie of our people into that parte of America com-

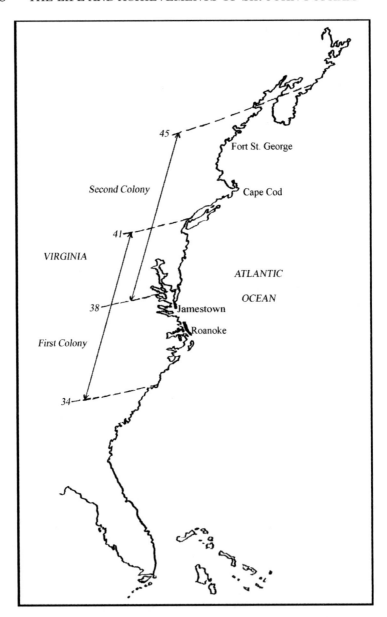

Virginia, showing the limits of colonization authorized by the Charter of 1606.

monly called Virginia . . . And to that ende, and for the more speedy accomplishemente of theire saide intended plantacion and habitacion there, are desirous to devide themselves into two severall colonies and companies, the one consisting of certaine Knightes, gentlemen, merchauntes and other adventurers of our cittie of London, and elsewhere, which are and from time to time shalbe joined unto them which doe desire to begin theire plantacions . . . in some fitt and conveniente place between fower and thirtie and one and fortie degrees of the said latitude . . . and the other consisting of sondrie Knightes, gentlemen, merchauntes, and other adventurers of our citties of Bristoll and Exeter, and of our towne of Plymouthe, and of other places which doe joine themselves unto that colonie which doe desire to beginn their plantacions and habitacions in some fitt and convenient place between eighte and thirtie degrees and five and fortie degrees of the saide latitude all alongst the saide coaste of Virginia and America as that coaste lyeth."[29]

Thus the southern company could settle the coast of what is now South Carolina, North Carolina, Virginia, and Delaware. The northern company's area extended from Connecticut and Massachusetts to New Hampshire and Maine, and included part of Nova Scotia. Curiously, there was a substantial overlapping area in the middle from thirty-eight to forty-one degrees, consisting of modern New Jersey and New York; this could be claimed by the first company strong enough to settle it. The name "Virginia" continued to be used for the whole eastern seaboard until 1616, when the northern section, once Norumbega, was renamed "New England."[30]

The Charter continues: "Wee, greatly commending and graciously accepting of theire desires to the furtherance of soe noble a worke which may, by the providence of Almightie God, hereafter tende to the glorie of His Divine Majestie in propagating of Christian religion to suche people as yet live in darkenesse and miserable ignorance of the true knoweledge and worshippe of God and may in tyme bring the infidels and salvages living in those parts to humane civilitie and to a setled and quiet governmente, doe by theise our lettres patents graciously accepte of and agree to theire humble and well intended desires." The London group was to be called the First Colony, while "Thomas Hannam and Raleighe Gilberde, William Parker and George Popham, and all others of the towne of Plymouthe in the countie of Devon, or elsewhere, which are or shalbe joined unto them of that Colonie, shalbe called the Seconde colonie."[31]

The patent also set out that there should be for each colony a thirteen-man Council, with a royal seal; the Plymouth group's would have the King's arms engraved on one side, and on the other his portrait, with the legend *Sigillum Regis Magne Britannie, Francie et Hibernie* [The seal of the King of Great Britain, France and Ireland] on one side and on the other *Pro Consilio secunde Colonie Virginie* [For the Council of the Second Colony of Virginia]. In addition, there would be "a Council established here in England, which shall in like manner consist of thirteen persons . . . which shall be called our Council of Virginia." The companies were given mining rights for gold, silver, and copper. They had power to coin their own money, to take over adventurers without restrictions imposed by the Crown, and to transport goods out of the country free of duties. The two companies had equal rights, but were not to place colonies within a hundred miles of each other.

The official approval was in place. Sir John Popham was strongly represented, with his nephew George and Thomas Hanham, his grandson, included among the grantees. When the Council of Virginia itself was established on 21 November 1606 the list included Popham's son, Sir Francis, and Thomas Warre, his thirty-one-year-old grandson, as well as several old cronies: Sir Ferdinando Gorges and Sir Henry Montague, Recorder of London; Sir William Romney and John Eldred, both of whom he had worked with in the Fens; and Sir William Waad, his colleague during the Gunpowder Plot inquiries.[32]

The next requirements were money and a cooperative spirit. Neither was easy to find. It was here that all Popham's persuasive skills were required, for not everyone approached thought Virginia was a good investment. Although the London merchants wanted a steady source of southern products such as sugar, wines, and citrus, the West Country ports were really more interested in developing the trade in fish, oil, and hides. Consequently when Popham and Gorges approached the Bristol City Council, they got little response. Only thirteen merchants promised contributions, the Mayor and sheriff twenty marks each and others amounts ranging from £12 10s. to 50s.[33] Nearly a year after the Charter, Popham was still making fund-raising his personal concern, but not even his power and influence could persuade Exeter City Council. On 27 March 1607 it was minuted: "And they agree where my Lord Cheef Justice hathe by his Lettres mocioned to the Cittie to have an Adventure from them to terra Virginia to be borne. That an answer shalbe made therunto that the merchantes of this Cittie have bene Charged in former tymes with such Adventures very much to ther Losse & hinderans That they are not mynded to adventure to the seme."[34]

Another problem was the rivalry between Plymouth and Bristol. The town of Plymouth informed Popham that it was willing to be the seat of the West of England branch of the Virginia Company, but insisted that none of the settlers' vessels should sail from Bristol.[35] Captain Henry Challons was appointed to explain to Popham the town's reasons. The composition of the council was controversial too. Walter Mathews, deputy mayor of Plymouth, and his fellow officers complained to Cecil that whereas "The Lord Chief Justice has recommended to us an enterprise for establishment of a Plantation in the parts of America; whereunto we were drawn to assent upon hope to obtain such free and reasonable conditions as had in former times been granted by the late Queen to certain gentlemen," it now appeared that they would be under the direction of a mixed bag of persons, "the greatest part strangers to us and to our proceedings . . . . We beg for your protection and help; and express our thanks to the Lord Chief Justice for his good affection towards us in this behalf."[36]

Gorges at Plymouth also protested to Cecil: "Through the motion of some persons well affected of these parts, in this idle time to bring to pass something worthy his Majesty's acceptance, it has pleased my Lord Chief Justice, out of an honourable disposition to advance their proceedings, to be a means for the obtaining of his Highness's good liking, as by his letters patents appear, to several parties granted." The Westcountrymen did not want the venture to be controlled by unqualified Londoners they did not know: "Their desire is principally to be assigned to Salisbury and the Lord Chief Justice, with such other worthy persons as Salisbury thinks fit to take to them. . . . That being granted, doubtless many worthy and brave spirits will easily be drawn to engage themselves in this design."[37]

In spite of the problems, Popham's influence prevailed, for the Plymouth Company sent out two expeditions before the London group had assembled one. The first was intended to carry out more exploration of the Northern coast, Captain Henry Challons sailing on 12 August 1606 with twenty-nine Englishmen[38] and two of the natives brought back by Waymouth: Maneddo, gentleman, who had stayed with Gorges, and Saffacomoit, servant, who had probably been with Popham. The object was to select a site for the colony and establish a base in preparation for the arrival of a larger group of settlers the following year.

Challons never reached his destination. Despite orders to the contrary, he sailed the southern route via the Canaries and Caribbean and was captured off Florida by the Spaniards. It was a great disappointment and a very real setback. Popham learned of the fate of his ship from Nevill Davis, a merchant in Seville where the prisoners were held. Davis wrote to the Lord Chief Justice: "Occasion being offered I am emboldened to send these few lines to signify the misery of divers poor men here prisoners that were taken in a small ship of Plymouth called the Richard, whereof was captain Henry Challines, and as it appears [they] were set forth by Sir Ferdinando Gorges and other gentlemen. They report your Honour to be one of the chiefest adventurers in this their pretended voyage, being for a new discovery in the norwest parts. . . . They were surprised by seven merchant ships which came from St. Domingo. . . . Here are 18 of them and two 'salvages' of the country they went into."[39]

It must be admitted that when Popham sent this letter on to Cecil he was not full of urgency for the men's recovery, being more concerned about the trading problems Davis had also told him about: "I received this morning from a merchant that is and has been a 'lydger' [lodger] in Seville ever since the peace concluded, these enclosed, by which you may perceive the state of things there, and how needful it seems to be to seek in time a better vent for our commodities than our former places of trade afford us. . . . I understand it will be in vain to seek for the delivery of such as be in captivity, unless it be by order from the King himself. How far forth you shall think fit that his Majesty's Ambassador be written to in that behalf I leave to your consideration. If the natives might be had again, in my opinion it would serve to good purpose."[40]

By the time Challons himself wrote to Popham, in June 1607, the situation was desperate: "We increase diseases and debts. Sixpence in England is not a penny here. Robert Cooke is already dead; the boatswain a prisoner, stabbed in the belly, in judgment not like to recover. The Indians are taken from us and made slaves; our ship is sunk in the river, not like to be recovered. We endure all indignities possible, as to hear her [sic] Majesty, and especially certain of your Honours of the Privy Council most untruly and vilely reproached. We beseech you to conceive hereof and relieve us before it be too late."[41] By then, however, Popham was no longer able to assist.

Fortunately there had been a back-up expedition. Immediately on Challons's departure, presumably in late August or September 1606 "it pleased the Noble Lord Chiefe Justice, Sir John Popham knight, to send out another ship, wherein Captain Thomas Haman [Hanam] went Commander, & Martin Prinne of Bristow Master, with all necessarie supplies, for the seconding of captayne Challons and his people."[42] Although Hanham, Popham's grandson, was nominally in command as his representative, probably the real leader was Martin Pring, a very experienced Bristol sailor.[43] The expedition was accompanied by the Indian Nahanada.

We know that Thomas Hanham wrote a journal, for Samuel Purchas referred to it when compiling the second edition of his *Pilgrimage* (1614): "Captain Thomas Hanham sayled to the River of Sagadahoc 1606. He relateth of their beasts, doggs like wolves, of colours blacke, white, red, and grisled: red deere, and a beest bigger, called the Mus, & c. of their fowles, fishes, trees: of some Oare proved to be silver."[44] And then comes Purchas's dreadful confession: "Reader, I had by me the Voyage of Captaine Thomas Hanham (written by himselfe) unto Sagadahoc . . . but our voluminousnesse makes me afraid of offending nicer and queasier stomackes: for which cause I have omitted them, even after I had with great labour fitted them to the Presse: as I have also done . . . the Voyage of Master Edward Harlie (one of the first Planters with Captain Popham) . . . with divers Letters from Captain Popham and others."[45]

It is acutely frustrating to know that such records once existed. The explorers arrived at the place appointed, but not finding Captain Challons there, "after they had made some Discovery, and found the Coasts, Havens, and Harbors answerable to our desires, they returned." On hearing their encouraging account, Gorges wrote later, "the Lord Chiefe Justice, and wee all waxed so confident of the businesse, that the yeere following everei man of any worth, formerly interessed in it, was willing to joyne in the charge for sending over a competent number of people to lay the ground of an hopefull plantation."[46]

Sir John had not been put off by the Challons misfortune—"all this hard handsell and Spanish Mischief"[47]—and he accepted Hanham and Pring's advice about the location of the colony. Now he and Gorges, full of determination, "set up our resolutions to follow it with effect."[48] The task before them was to attract colonists, find ships, and gather supplies for a permanent settlement on the coast. The job took them about six months in the winter and spring of 1606–7.

Concerns about the constitution of the Royal Council for Virginia led to its expansion. On 9 March 1607 more names were added, fifteen men to the executive of the London Company and ten to that of Plymouth.[49] The lists again included Popham's colleagues and family: in the first, Sir Thomas Chaloner (Gunpowder Plot) and Sir Oliver Cromwell (the Fens), and in the second Sir John Malet and Edward Rogers (sons-in-law) and Sir Bartholomew Michell (nephew).[50]

As usual, however, the real work was done by those closest to home. Sir Francis Popham was now thirty-six, a member of the Royal Council for Virginia and treasurer of the Company.[51] Popham sent him to Plymouth to see to the nuts and bolts of the expedition. He was entertained there by Sir Ferdinando Gorges, who promised to invest £30 in money or materials. It was easy to spend that kind of sum: the two men went shopping together to Jennings's store, where they bought "Iron pottes boxes Chafyng disshes lockes" costing £36 19s 11d.[52] Clearly finance was a major problem, though it was evidently hoped that investment would produce a profit as soon as the first cargoes returned from America. If all went well, a different form of organization would become necessary, but for the present it was a private venture. No corporation had been established and Sir John himself was the chief promoter of the expedition.[53] The settlement made in 1607 has ever since, and very properly, been called "The Popham Colony."

The activities attracted the attention of the Spanish Ambassador in London. On 16 March 1607 Don Pedro de Zuniga wrote in cipher to the King of Spain: "Sire . . . They brought 14 or 15 months ago about ten natives, that they might learn English, and they have kept some of them here [in London] and others in the country, teaching and training them to say how good that country is for people to go there and inhabit it. The chief leader in this business is the Justicario [Chief Justice], who is a very great Puritan and exceedingly desirous, whatever sedition may be spoken of, to say that he does it in order to drive out from here thieves and traitors to be drowned in the sea."[54] What was the point of Popham's diplomatic riposte? It seems to mean that whenever Popham was told by the Spanish Ambassador that the colonization enterprise was seditious (i.e., in violation of the treaties), he quickly replied that he undertook it only in order to drive thieves out of England to be drowned in the sea.[55]

Meanwhile on 19 December 1606 the London division of the Virginia Company had sent out their first party to settle in the southern area at Chesapeake Bay. The First Colonial Expedition, under the overall command of Captain Christopher Newport, consisted of three vessels with 105 adventurers. They founded Jamestown on 24 May 1607.

The northern group's Second Colonial Expedition at last set off on 31 May 1607. Two ships sailed from Plymouth to colonize the west side of the mouth of the Kennebec River, in what is now Maine. George Popham was the expedition's leader.

It is not entirely clear how George was related to Sir John; he has been variously considered his brother, nephew and cousin. A letter he wrote on the day he set off, and the Will he made at the same time, tell us two things: he was undoubtedly Her Majesty's Customer of the Port of Bridgwater, and Edward Popham, who went with him on the voyage, was his nephew.[56] One must be careful here: the word "nephew" was often used at this time in a less exact sense than is current now. There are two records of the Pophams employing it to mean "grandchild" and it sometimes simply meant "descendant." However, there is a possible true nephew in Edward, twenty-five-year-old son of Alexander Popham of Huntworth, though it seems unlikely that an eldest son, a married man and just appointed a Justice of the Peace, should embark on such an undertaking.[57] Nevertheless in 1640 this Edward caused to be made a magnificent family pedigree roll, in which he refers unmistakably to the Virginia experience of the George who was his uncle. This roll provides the best evidence that George Popham was truly Sir John's nephew.

This is the man we have presented so far. He may have been a captain in Ireland and undertaker there; he had had plenty of seafaring experience, including crossing the Atlantic, and he understood from what he had seen in Guiana the difficulties to be faced in dealing with a hostile native population. He cannot have been much more than forty-eight years old.

This is what makes us wonder whether we have got the right George. According to Sir Ferdinando Gorges, the leader of the expedition was "ould" and had long been infirm.[58] Furthermore, he turned out to be unable to deal with dangerous and difficult men. Fearful of conflict, George Popham of Virginia was a gentle, diplomatic soul. One cannot easily imagine him boarding a Spanish ship in anger; this George was no Pirate King.

We know that this George was certainly Customs Officer at Bridgwater, however. Now the records of men paying duties at the port tells us that a George Popham, a humble merchant, had from 1573 for at least twenty years carried on a trade shipping domestic merchandise at the Somerset port. He must have been an older man. The accounts of William Everys, Water Bailiff of Bridgwater, tell us when George was charged duties for landing and loading of goods: on 22 November 1594 he had to pay 8d "for the cranidge of 3 gryningstones and 2 houg sydes," on 20 March 1595 2d "for the heavinge of 2 packes wth the crane," on 10 April 9d "for the caridge of 4 wayes and ½ of colle" and on 19 April 9d "for the caridge of 3½ of coll" and 2d for "a tonne of salt."[59] It was in exactly these months that the other, younger George was on the Guiana expedition with Robert Dudley, so two George Pophams certainly existed at that time. It seems likely that a man who had traded so long at Bridgwater should eventually become its customs officer, especially if he had family connections. This George would have been a steady, reliable man. He could have been the one with experience of Ireland, though he had not made a mark as a captain. In these ways he seems more like the leader we come to know through the written accounts of the expedition.[60]

Thus, although we must accept it, the best documentary evidence is not entirely satisfying. Whatever the precise relationship, George's appointment is hard to explain. It is true that Sir John was "the head and front of the enterprise ... It was Sir John's colony,"[61] but nevertheless the Presidency was a most important role. No one would be surprised that Sir John chose a member of the family for his last great project, but it is very extraordinary indeed that he selected to lead his enterprise an old, infirm man whose character did not entirely suit him for the task.

Whoever he was, and whatever the reasoning behind his position, on 30 May 1607 Captain Popham was about to set sail. He penned a note to Robert Cecil: he had written recently to him "concerning a command I had from my Lord Chief Justice to appoint myself unto the discovery and population of the Western Colony in Virginia. I wish my desire might go accompanied with any of the least acceptable service therein, yet durste I promise by due endeavours to give my best addition unto the same." As he was to be away for some time—he evidently expected to return—he was anxious to have a deputy appointed to carry out his duties as "collector of customs within the port of Bridgwater" and offered "due commendation of this bearer, Mr Rowland Jones."[62]

George Popham took command of the *Gift of God*, which was described as a "flyboat" and had been provided by the Pophams.[63] As well as owning the ship, Sir John appointed the master, John Havercombe, and himself paid the quartermaster, Timothy Savage, his first month's wages—23s. He also employed John Fletcher as a "comon man" for 20s. a month.[64] The *Mary and John,* a "good ship" of about two hundred tons, had been chartered for the voyage by the Plymouth Company and was in the hands of Raleigh Gilbert, a man of twenty-five, sixth son of the famous explorer Sir Humphrey Gilbert and related to both Ralegh and Gorges. The purposes of the two Virginia Company expeditions seem to have been different. At Jamestown the intention was genuinely to settle; cultivation of cash crops was to be the basis of the colony's economy. In the north, however, the aim was to establish more of a permanent trading post for fish and hides, to prospect for minerals, to search for a northwest passage, and to counteract the increasing French influence in the area.[65] Only men were sent, so there could have been no expectation that they would stay for a long period; further consignments of colonists would replace those who returned. It was a reasonable aim.

A detailed account of the first months was kept by Robert Davies, Captain of the *Mary and John.*[66] According to Davies the two ships "Departed from the Lyzard the firste daye of June Ano Domini 1607 being Mundaye about 6 of the Cloke in the afternoon" and thence headed toward the Azores. They arrived together on 26 June and proceeded separately to Virginia, the *Mary and John* having been waylaid briefly by two Dutch ships on 29 June. George Popham inexplicably did not go to the aid of the larger ship: he "never woold Com roome unto us notwithstandynge we makinge all the Seignes that possybell we myght."[67] This incident may well have contributed to later tensions among the settlers. On 5 July the *Gift of God* met the *Penelope,* homeward bound from the West Indies, and persuaded a cooper called Lancelot Booker to join them, for 34s a month.[68] The *Mary and John* made landfall on 31 July, and the *Gift of God* met the rest of the party on 7 August 1607, eight miles to the east of Pemaquid.[69] It was an impressive piece of navigation.

Skicowaros was reunited with Nahanada, who had been returned to Pemaquid a year earlier by the Hanham-Pring expedition. How delighted, and surprised, the two Indians must have been to meet again in their home land. It was obviously hoped that the anglicized Indians would help the settlers to establish friendly working relations, and to some extent they probably did; but of course the men had originally been taken by force, so distrust was built into the relationship from the start.

More than a hundred colonists were on board the two ships, and in the morning on Sunday, 9 August, they landed on what they called St George's Island, now Allen Island, where Waymouth's cross stood, and there they heard "a Sermon delyverd unto us by our preacher giving God thanks for our happy meting and Saffe aryvall into the Contry."[70]

The ships then sailed for the mainland, toward the river Sagadehoc, now named the Kennebec River in the State of Maine, which they entered on 16 August. Looking out for a suitable site for the colony, the Englishmen explored upstream the next day. After preliminary skirmishes with the Indians, on Tuesday, 18 August the place of settlement was fixed: "we all went on shore and thear mad choies of a place for our plantation whch ys at the very mouth or entry of the Ryver of Sagadehocke on the West Syd of the Ryver beinge almost an Iland of a good bygness." They certainly chose a marvelous place. Sabino head is a sheltered spot with a wonderful view of estuary, curving beach, and islands. "Wensday beinge the 19th Auguste we all went to the shore whear we mad choise for our plantation and thear we had a Sermon delyvered unto us by our preacher and after the Sermon our pattent was red wth the orders and Lawes thearin prescrybed and then we retorned abord our ships again."[71]

Who were the men who stood on Sabino Head on that summer day in 1607? There were nine Council Members:

Capt. George Popham, President
Capt. Raleigh Gilbert, Admiral
Capt. Edward Harlow, Master of Ordnance
Capt. Robert Davies, Serjeant-Major, Captain of *Mary and John*
Capt. Ellis Best, Marshall
Capt. James Davies, Captain of the Fort
Capt. John Elliott, Captain of the *Gift of God*
Mr. Robert Seaman, Secretary
Mr. Gome Carew, Chief Searcher (for mines).[72]

Gentlemen who were not members of the Council included John Havercombe, Master of the *Gift of God*; Richard Seymour, Chaplain and a cousin of Ralegh and of Gorges; and Edward Popham. Lower than the gentlemen in the social scale but nevertheless "Notables" were Master Turner, Physician; John Hunt, Draftsman; and Christopher Fortescue, Ship Master. "Other Persons" included Master Patterson; Master Digby, Shipwright, and several officers of the *Gift of God*: Peter Grisling, Master's Mate; John Diamond, Quartermaster; Timothy Savage, Quartermaster; and Lancelot Booker, Cooper. We know the names of two of the sailors, John Fletcher and John Goyett. Finally there were about one hundred members of the commonalty who included soldiers, craftsmen including smiths and carpenters, farmers, and traders. Whether there were in addition any former inmates of the jails of England—"the scum of people and wicked condemned men"[73]—is not known.

After the formalities, the fort had to be laid out and the work begun: "Thursday being the 20th of Auguste all our Companyes landed and thear began to fortefye. our presedent, Capt. popham Sett the fyrst spytt of ground unto ytt and after hem all the rest followed and laboured hard in the trenches about ytt." In the days following "all hands Laboured hard about the fort Som in the trentch Som for fagetts & our ship Carpenters about the buildinge of a small penis or shallop."[74] A second account by William Strachey speaks of "the President overseeing and applying every one to his worke."[75] The fort was named St George.

The early days of the colony involved delicate negotiations with the local people: "Saturday being the 5th of September there came into the entrance of the river of Sagadehoc nine canoes in the which was Dehanada [Nahanada] and Skidwarres [Skicowaros] with many others in the whole near forty persons men women and children. They came and parled with us and we again used them in all friendly manner we could and gave them victuals for to eat." Skidwarres and one more native stayed with the English until night, when Captain Gilbert returned them to their people on the further side of the river, "and there remained amongst them all the night and early in the morning the Salvages departed in their canoes for the ryver of Pemaquid promising Capt. Gilbert to accompany them in their canoes to the river of Penobskott where the bashabe [big chief] remayneth."[76]

The colonists did a little trading, much work on the fort, and exciting exploration led by Gilbert, going up to the headwaters of what is now called the Kennebec River. They found "aboundaunce of Spruse Trees such as are able to maast the greatest shipp his Maiestie hath," and many other trees including pine, oak, and walnut. They also noted plenty of grapes and hops, as well as some pods "in which they supposed, the Cotton wooll to grow: and also upon the Banckes many shells of pearle."[77] It sounds idyllic, but the Englishmen were deep in foreign territory. A striking incident at this place illustrates how unpredictable was the relationship with the local inhabitants.

One morning there arrived a canoe carrying four natives and their Sagamo (leader) who said he was Sabenoa, Lord of the River of Sachadehoc. The Englishmen gave him gifts and took him into their boat, though he insisted on having "one of our men to be put into his Canoa, as a Pawne of his saffety." Immediately they had taken a man, the Indians paddled away at full speed up the river, landed, and made for their village "neere a league in on the Land from the River-syde." Gilbert and nine men followed the Sagamo to the Indian village, where they found "nere 50. able men very strong and tall, such as their like had not seene, all new paynted and armed with their bowes and arrowes." Peace was established, the hostage given back, and willingness to trade in exchange for beads, knives, and copper apparently agreed.[78]

Gilbert and his followers returned to their shallop, and within half an hour three canoes arrived, with sixteen savages bringing some tobacco and a few skins to trade. The Captain saw that these were of no value, and made an undiplomatic gesture of rejection, commanding all his men to go aboard. As he moved to put out from the shore, "the Salvadges perceaving so much, subtilly devised how they might put out the fier in the shallop, by which meanes, they saw they should be free from the daunger of our men's Pieces [guns]." One of the savages jumped into the Shallop and grabbed the Firebrand "which one of our Company held in his hand, thereby to light the Matches, as if he would light a Pipe of Tobacco." The Indian threw the brand into the water and leaped out of the boat. Capt. Gilbert immediately commanded his men to take up their muskets, and one man "with his Targett [shield] on his arme, to steppe on the shoare for more fier." However, the natives resisted and would not allow him to take any; some others held fast the boat rope so that the shallop could not put off. So Capt. Gilbert "caused the Musquettiers to present their Pieces, the which the Salvadges seeing presently lett goe the boat roap and betook them to their Bowes and Arrowes and ran into the bushes, nocking their Arrowes but did not shoot neither did ours at them." Both sides had exhibited considerable restraint. The shallop moved off to the farther side of the river, and soon one of the canoes came to them and "would have excused the fault of the others. Capt Gilbert made shew as if he were still freindes and entertayned them kyndly and so left them."

At the Englishmen's fort, by contrast, the atmosphere was more tranquil. On 4 October 1607 "ther came 2 Canoas to the Fort, in which were Nahanada and his wife and Skidwares and the Basshabaes brother, and one more called Amenquin, a Sagamo, all whome the President feasted and entertayned with all kyndnes both that day and the next, which being Sonday the President carryed them with him to the place of publique prayers, which they were at both morning and evening, attending yt with great Reverence and sylence."[79]

In a third brief account of the colony, by Samuel Purchas,[80] we learn that the Indians "seemed affected with our mens devotions, and would say, King James is a good King, his God a good God, and Tanto nought. So they call an evill spirit which haunts them every Moone, and makes them worship him for feare. Hee commanded them not to dwell neere, or come among the English, threatning to kill some and inflict sicknesse on others, beginning with two of their Sagamos children, saying he had powere, and would do the like to the English the next Moone, to wit in December." The English were in a frightening physical situation too, for they heard of cannibals nearby with teeth three inches long, but fortunately "they saw them not." George Popham must have felt that in counteracting Tanto he was carrying out a worthwhile task. He seems to have been able to calm the troubled Indians and maintain a comfortable relationship with them.

Two days after the feasting and prayers "the salvadges departed all except Amenquin the Sagamo who would needes stay amongest our people a longer tyme: upon the departure of the others the President gave unto every one of them Copper, beades, or knives, which contented them not a little, as also delivered a Present unto the Basshaba's brother to be presentes unto the Basshaba, and another for his wife, giving him to understand, that he would come unto his Court in the River of Penobscot and see him very shortly bringing manie such like of his country commodities with him." According to Purchas, "one of the savages, called Amenquin, for a straw hat and knife given him, stript himselfe of his cloathing of Bevers skinnes, worth in England 50 shillings, or three pound to present them to the President, leaving only a flap to cover his privities."[81]

The impression we are given is that George Popham was a kindly, peaceable man. The French Jesuit Père Biard, who visited Fort St George later, said he was "A very honorable man, and conducted himself very kindly towards the natives."[82] But he was not able to maintain harmony among his own men. Unfortunately the daily record of the colony's activities stops on 6 October, so we do not know the details. One of the ships had to go home to report on progress and gather supplies. Capt. Robert Davies was dispatched in the *Mary and John,* sailing on 14 October 1607 and taking his diary with him.

The colonists must have worked fantastically hard that autumn. "After Capt. Davies' departure they fully fynisshed the

Fort, Trencht and fortefyed yt, with 12. pieces of Ordinaunce and built 50. howses therein: besyde a Church and a store-howse and the Carpenters framed a pretty Pynnace of about some 30. tonne. which they called the Virginia, the chief Shipwright being one Digbye of London."[83] A pinnace was a small, fast, maneuverable craft, probably a three-master, which could be rowed and was suited to scouting or as a landing craft.[84]

The *Mary and John* carried letters from George to Sir John Popham "importuning a supplie for the most necessariest wantes to the subsisting of a Colony to be sent unto them betymes the next yeare."[85] It also carried a marvelous illustration of Fort St. George, a detailed plan drawn by John Hunt on 8 October 1607, less than a week before the ship sailed.[86] The *Mary and John* got home to England on 1 December 1607, and the crew then learned that the Lord Chief Justice had died less than two weeks after the expedition's departure from England.

This unhappy event, coming before the colonists had even struck land, must have been a particularly severe blow to Sir Ferdinando Gorges. Sir John had died in June; Gorges took over the reins and by now had for six months been the chief motivator of the undertaking, Sir Francis playing a less significant part. On hearing what the sailors from the *Mary and John* reported, Gorges was at first saddened. He wrote to Cecil: "This present day, heere is arrived on of our shipps out of the Partes of Virginia, with greate newes of a fertill Contry, gallant Rivers, stately Harbors, and a people tractable, (so discreete Course bee taken with them,) but no returne, to satisfy the expectation of the Adventureres, the which may bee an occasion, to blemish the reputation of the designe, although in reason it could not be otherwayes, both because of the shortnes of theyr aboad there (which was but two monethes) as also, theyr want of meanes to follow theyr directions, theyr number being so small, and theyr business so great, beside in very truthe, the defect and wante of understandinge of som of those imployed, to performe what they were directed unto, from whense, there did not only proceede confusion, but thorough pride and arrogansay, faction, and privat resolution, as more at large your Lordshipp shall perceave, by my next."[87]

However, with manly fortitude he continued: "For my owne opinion, I am confident, there will be divers reasons to perswade a constant resolution, to persue this place." He reminded Cecil of the natural riches, the fish, trees, the "grapes very fayre and excellent good, whereof they have already make [sic] wine, much like to the Claret wine that comes out of France," furs—"if they can keep the Frenchmen from the trade"—and rumored alum mines.

Two days later the unpleasant details came out: "It seemes to bee moste certayne, that ther is no enterprise, (how well so ever intended,) but has his particular impedimentes meeting with many oppositions, and infinite Crosses, as in this small attempt, begun by my Lord Cheefe Justice out of a noble zeale to his prince and Contry, (amongst many others,) it is experienced for firste as hee was honorable himselfe, so hee thought all others weare, beleeving what they toulde him, and trustinge to what they promised, by which meanes, his Lordshipp was not a litle deceaved of what hee expected, for neither were his provisions answerable to his Charge bestowed, nor the persons imployed such as they ought; in as much as the wantes of the on[e] was cause of inabilety, to performe what was hoped; & the Childish, factious, ignorant, timerous, and ambitiouse persons (for of that nature I founde the commposition to bee) hath bread an unstable resolution, and a generall confusion, in all theyr affayres.

"For firste the President himself is an honest man, but old and of an unwildy body, and timerously fearfull to offende, or contest with others that will or do oppose him, but otherwayes a discreete carefull man. Captayne Gilberte is described to mee from thense to be desirous of supremasy and rule, a loose life, prompte to sensuality, litle zeale in Religion, humerouse, head stronge, and of small judgment and experiense, other wayes valiant inough, but hee houldes that the kinge could not give away that, by Pattent, to others, which his Father had an Act of Parliament for, and that hee will not bee put out of it in haste; with many such like idle speeches, which (allthough hee bee powrlesse to performe oughte) weare not unfit to bee taken notice of . . . besides hee hath sent (as I am farther informed) into England for divers of his freindes, to come to him, for the strengthening of his party on all occasions (as hee termes it) . . . which I thought it my duety to advertise your Lordshipp in time, that som course may bee taken to prevent mischiffe."[88]

The request for supplies obviously had to be attended to immediately, and Gorges told Cecil on 20 March that he had sent two ships out from Topsham,[89] though in the event no vessel left on a successful voyage before at least August 1608. Meanwhile, at the colony the food situation was so acute that George Popham was forced to send back a second batch of colonists, in fact all but forty-five of the company. The second ship, the *Gift of God* with fifty men and boys on board, left Sagadehoc on 14 December. They did not have enough food for the journey, and had to call in at the Azores to sell masts and cannon in order to buy provisions to see them home. The ship reached Plymouth on 7 February 1608, bringing with it an account of the situation that contrasts dramatically with what was already known of the reality. The President's famous letter, in Latin, was addressed to the King:

"George Popham, President of the Second Virginia Colony, does humble obeisance at the feet of his most illustrious Sovereign. If your Divine Majesty's indulgence may be pleased to accept a few words from a most diligent and devoted, howbeit unworthy, servant, I consider that they will far from detract from your Highness's fame, since they seem to be conducive to the glory of God, to the scale of your Eminence and to the advantage of the British people.

"I have therefore deemed it perfectly proper to inform your Majesty that nobody in the world is more admired by the people of Virginia and Moasso [Mawooshen, an Indian name for the area] than the Lord James, Emperor of the Britons, because of his wonderful sense of justice and his scarcely credible constancy which bring great happiness to the natives of your provinces. For they say moreover that no God is truly worthy of worship except the Lord King James's, and that they would willingly give military service under his authority and command. Tahinda, one of the natives who has been to Britain, has broadcast your praise and your fine qualities to them here.

"What good I might do, and how much, in undertaking this enterprise and in consolidating their feelings, is for those to judge who have given it informed consideration at home; for I recognise that all personal endeavours are as nothing when compared with my obligations towards the King. I am firmly convinced that the glory of God is beginning to shine out freely in this region, that your Majesty's empire is being enlarged and that the common welfare of the British (settlers) has been increased in a short time. As regards commercial resources, all the native inhabitants repeatedly assert that there are nutmegs, mace and cinnamon in these parts; furthermore there is bitumen, Brazil wood, cochineal and ambergris, along with many other important and valuable things, and all very plentiful at that.

"Moreover they impress upon me that, in the opposite or western part of this province no more than seven days journey from our Fort St George at Sagadahoc, there is some Sea which is extensive, wide and deep; but they have no idea how far it extends. This can be none other than the Southern Ocean, stretching towards the land of China which doubtless cannot be far away from this region.

"Therefore, if it may please you to take divine notice of the subject of my testimony, I have no doubt that Your Highness will accomplish a task which is most acceptable to God, which brings honor to Your

Majesty and which is of great advantage to your kingdom; and this with fervent entreaties I earnestly implore you to do. I pray also to God, the Good and the Great, that he will long preserve the glorious Majesty of my Sovereign Lord James.

"At Fort St. George, Sagadahoc, Virginia; 13th December, 1607. Your Majesty's devoted servant in all things,

George Popham"[90]

In spite of this delightful optimism, the returned sailors could not bring any joyful news. Gorges reported: "Our second shipp is returned out of the partes of Virginia, but with advertisement of nothinge more, then wee receaved at the first, only the extremity of the winter hath ben great, and hath sorely pinched our People, notwithstanding (thankes bee unto God) they have had theyr healthes exceedingly well, although theyr Cloathes were but thinne and theyr Dyets poore, for they have not had on[e] sicke from the time they came thither, to the instant of theyr comminge away. Ye President, and his People, feedes us still with hopes of wonders that wilbee had from thence in time, but I feere mee, ther must go other manner of spiritts, to settle those busines, before it wilbe brought to passe, for I find the continuance of theyr idle proceedinges, to have mutch prejudicialld the publique good, devidinge themselves into factions, each disgracing the other, even to the Savages, the on[e] emulatinge the others reputations amongst those brutish people."[91]

It was a small community left at Fort St George. The colonists had provided crews for two ships, and were left with only their one homemade pinnace. In addition, they had a tremendous challenge to face, "the extraordinary frost" that was felt in most parts of Europe; "yt was here likewise as vehement, by which noe boat could stir upon any busines."[92] Gorges later wrote that "they were strangely perplexed with the great and unseasonable cold they suffered with that extremity as the like hath not been heard of since, and it seems, was universall, it being the same yeare, that our Thames were so lockt up that they built their boates upon it, and sould provisions of severall sorts to those that delighted in the Novelties of the times."[93] It must have been a terrible experience, and it told on the elderly President. By the time his Latin letter to the King had reached England, George Popham, the colonists' "noble President" was dead.[94] The Indians later told Père Biard that being afraid of the English settlers, they had used magic arts to kill the Captain.[95] His "last words" on 5 February 1608, are given by Abbott, although they must be a complete invention: "I die content, My name will be always associated with the first planting of the English race in the New World. My remains will not be neglected away from the home of my fathers and my kindred."[96] If George Popham conceived anything like this, it was wishful thinking, for his grave is entirely lost.

After the President's death, Raleigh Gilbert took over command. Relationships with the Indians soon deteriorated. According to Biard the English under him "changed the fashion. They drove away the savages without any consideration; beat, bruised, and tore them with dogs without restraint." The Indians sought revenge. One day when the English went fishing, the natives pretended friendship, went aboard the English boats, and "at a given signal, each one chooses his man and kills him with knife strokes."[97] Eleven Englishmen died.

It is not difficult to believe the story that things came to a horrifying climax, though no account was printed until 1795, by which time it was probably much embellished. A group of Indians had come to the fort to trade. They were peacefully strolling around the enclosure when some of the settlers thought they would have some fun. Loading a cannon with powder, they asked the Indians to pull the huge heavy gun across the fort. While they were laboring at this strange task, one of the Englishmen put a light to the powder. The blast killed or wounded several Indians, the rest fleeing in terror and outrage. Soon the tribes gathered for revenge. They attacked the fort, and drove the settlers out. But at the moment of triumph the Indians found the colony's gunpowder store. They accidentally put a flame to it, with catastrophic results. Such Indians as survived ran back to the woods, never to return. The explosion seemed to them to be the work of a god too angry and powerful to fight against. The settlers returned to Fort St George, but their storehouse was on fire and their gunpowder gone. They had no food or the means of hunting it, and hostile Indians surrounded them.[98]

It is hardly surprising that the moment the Englishmen had the chance to get out, they took it. Strachey's account, however, is rather different. In October 1608 "when Captain Davies arrived . . . (sett out from Topsam, the porte towne of Exeter, with a shipp laden full of victualls, armes, instruments and tooles &c) albeyt he found Mr George Popham, the President, and some other dead yet he found all things in good forwardnes and many kinds of furrs obteyned from the Indians by way of trade; and the new pynnace all finished.

"But by reason that Capt. Gilbert received letters that his brother was newly dead[99] and a faire portion of land fallen unto his share, which required his repaier home, and no mynes discovered being the mayne intended benefit expected to uphold the charge of this plantation, and the feare that all other wynters would prove like the first, the company by no means would stay any longer in the country especyally Capt. Gilbert being to leave them and Mr. Popham dead; wherefor they ymbarqued in the new arrived shipp and in the new pynnace, the *Virginia,* and sett saile for England. And this was the end of that Northern colony uppon the river Sachadehoc."[100]

Gorges later added another reason: "the miseries they had past, were nothing to that they suffered by the disasterous news they received of the death of the Lord cheif justice, that suddainely followed the death of their President, but the latter was not so strange, in that he was well stricken in years before he went, and had long been an infirme man. Howsoever heartned by hopes, willing he was to dye in acting something that might be serviceable to God, and honourable to his country, but that of the death of the cheife justice was such a corrasive to all, as struck them with despaire of future remedy."[101] Zuniga, in a report on 30 July 1607 about the colony, wrote that Sir John had died, 'who was the man, who most desired it, and was best able to aid it."[102]

Gorges was left to cope on his own. He did not manage to win support from the King, who preferred to spend money on favorites, and was more interested in theology than colonization.[103] As he could not raise further finance, the return of the settlers must have been something of a relief. After many years of effort to achieve settlement, Gorges became in 1639 lord of the Province of Maine, and is celebrated as its founder, although he never visited the New World.[104]

Sir John's death left Lady Amy and Sir Francis in control of the Popham interests in the Plymouth Company. They soon took the captain of *The Gift of God,* John Havercombe, to the High Court of Admiralty for calling in at the Azores and selling off the ship's equipment in exchange for food. The sale had clearly been authorized, and Havercombe was eventually acquitted. Sir Francis did send some further fishing and trading expeditions to the Maine coast, but lacking Sir John's inspiration, the Plymouth Company's activity fizzled out, too little money and time being invested in it.[105]

Sir John's energies had brought about the charter of the Virginia Company as a whole, so the early experiences of the London branch also require a brief reference here. They afford a striking parallel to those of the Plymouth group. One of the men specified in the Charter of 1606 was Edward Maria Wingfield, whom we met briefly at Kimbolton. He was the only one of those named in the Charter to sail with the First Colonial Expedition, leading the party that founded Jamestown just a few months before George Popham set off to Sagadehoc. On 13 May 1607 Wingfield was elected President,[106] but he too seems to have been totally unqualified for leadership. Although "a valiant Gentleman," according to another settler,[107] he was evidently undiplomatic, pompous, and petulant. Soon falling out with his starving, mutinous colleagues, Wingfield was deposed on 10 September 1607, his replies to the charges against him being preserved in a draft entitled "A Discourse of Virginia."[108] In April 1608 Wingfield returned to England, where he lived in Huntingdonshire at Stoneley, part of the Kimbolton Castle estate.

In 1609 the London Company of the Council of Virginia invited the northern group to join them in furthering the Jamestown colony. The early history of settlement in North America focuses on Jamestown and on Plymouth, Massachusetts, where the Pilgrim Fathers landed in 1620, thirteen years after the Popham Colony began.[109] However, the settlement at what is now Popham Beach in Maine has aroused much interest recently, for the Hunt plan of Fort St George is the only such record of an initial English settlement in America.[110] It is believed to be an elaboration, or picture of what was intended, for when the plan was completed the colony had only existed for five weeks. However, Hunt was a very accurate draftsman, and his plan is now being used as the basis for archeological exploration of the largely undisturbed site.[111]

The remains of specific buildings of the settlement have been identified. The storehouse has been found, with European artifacts such as glass beads, iron hardware, lead munitions, and ceramics, as well as a most evocative caulking iron, used for shipbuilding.[112] The building was a post and beam structure with a thatched roof, wattle and daub walls and an earthen floor. The Admiral's house, the biggest dwelling at about twelve by thirty feet and the settlers' meeting place, was found to have a chimney at one end exactly as the Hunt plan showed. Fragments of liquor bottles and etched wine glass were found there, suggesting that Raleigh Gilbert lived in some style.[113] The pottery discovered, which included North Devon, Delft, and Bellarmine ceramics,

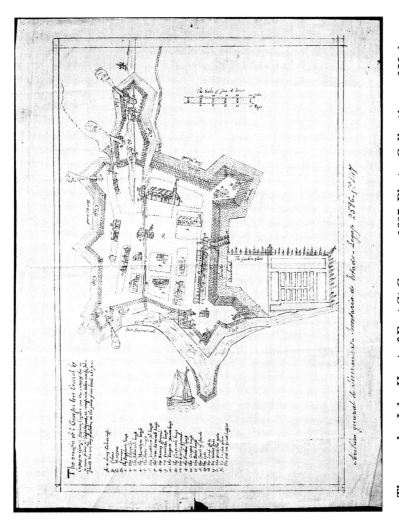

The map by John Hunt of Fort St George, 1607. Photo: Collections of Maine Historical Society, no. 7542.

was finer and more ornamental than that found in the store-house. Armor and lead munitions appropriate to his military role in the colony, glass buttons and jet beads suitable for a gentle-man's dress, all indicate that Raleigh Gilbert maintained his so-cial position.

Hunt's plan also included a sketch of the pinnace *Virginia,* and at last the colony's amazing achievement in building a ship has been recognized. She was a most significant craft. After return-ing the Popham colonists, the *Virginia* recrossed the Atlantic with Jamestown colonists in 1609, and served the settlers throughout their terrible winter of 1609–10. When Sir Thomas Gates decided to abandon the colony, the *Virginia* was ordered to leave first. Thus it may well have been this pinnace which met the incoming new Governor de la Warr, and was sent back with the news of his arrival. By "a tide or two" the Jamestown colony was saved.[114]

The *Virginia* deserves to be celebrated. Using Hunt's drawing and other sketches of ships of the time, a private group has re-cently been established to research, build, and operate a recon-struction of the craft. She will be seen as a symbol of Maine's ship-building tradition, and will help celebrate the four-hun-dredth anniversary in 2007 of the first English settlement in the New World. The new *Virginia* will be used for educational pur-poses, to increase public awareness of Maine's place in early Eu-ropean exploration, and to keep alive the name of Popham in the annals of American history.

20

Ghost

O~N~ 10 ~JUNE~ 1607, ~WHILE THE COURT OF STAR CHAMBER WAS SIT~ting, "News was broughte that Sr John Popham, the Lo. Cheife Justice of Englaund, was deade, some sayde of an ulcer in his bladder, others that he had taken pilles & the phisique never wroughte upon him, others that he dyed of griefe for sharpe wordes from the Kinge's Majestie."[1] According to Roger Wilbraham's marvellous story, Popham had been in good health, but "taking the pills of the empiric Raleigh in the very same hour, just after he had signed several warrants, died suddenly."[2] During his years in the Tower Ralegh had acquired a considerable reputation as a concocter of medications, and his "balsam of Guiana" had often been used by the Queen.[3] It was supposed to revive anyone, although very sadly it had not succeeded with Prince Henry. What an exquisite irony it is that Ralegh should provide pills for the man who had condemned him to death. As has been remarked before, if Popham did take them, they certainly finished him off.[4]

William Hawarde reflected that Popham was "a moste worthye man, & the state & Common wealthe receved the greateste losse of him that ever felle since Queene Elizabethe's deathe; he was a Father of the Common wealthe, a maine piller of the gospelle and true religion, a severe & an uprighte Justicer, & the onelye supporter of the Common Lawes of Englaunde: an infinyte losse the lawe & professors thereof have of him, the government & governors will have a greate misse of him, the lewder & looser sorte of people will rejoyce, the godlye and vertuous doe lament and mourne, & not wthoute juste cause."[5]

Sir John's last case, in the Court of Wards, brought him together, most fittingly, with his two closest colleagues and friends. He and Sir Edward Coke sat as judges assistant to the Master, Sir Robert Cecil. Reporting this case, Coke spoke of Popham as "a most Reverend Judge, and a person of great learning and integrity." He paid tribute to the Lord Chief Justice as a man "of a ready apprehension, profound judgment, most excellent understanding, and knowledge of the true reasons of the Law, admirable experience and knowledge of all business which concerned the Commonwealth; accompanied with a rare memory, with perpetual industry and labour for the maintenance of the tranquillity and public good of the realm, and in all things with great constancy, integrity and patience."[6] Egerton called him "a man of great wisdom and of singular learning and judgement in the Law."[7]

Later commentators thought Popham's achievement was that as a result of firm sentencing, England enjoyed private peace and home security. Thomas Fuller wrote in 1662 that "his Justice was exemplary on Theeves and Robbers." Former soldiers, now idle, "infected the Highways with their Felonies, some presuming on their multitudes, as the Robbers on the Northern Rode, whose Knot (otherwise not to be untyed), Sir John cut asunder with the Sword of Justice." Popham had convinced King James that leniency was not a sound policy, and "In a word, the deserved death of some scores, preserved the lives and livelyhoods of more thousands: Travellers owing their safety to this Judges severity many years after his death."[8] Sir Francis Bacon in 1615 called Popham "a great judge in his time",[9] and Coke's loyalty also endured; twenty-six years later, in 1633, he urged judges when dealing at assizes with capital offenders to "follow the example of reverend Judge Popham."[10]

His efforts in the settlement of Virginia were appreciated by those who took part in Popham's project. Nevill Davis, the merchant at Seville who was still trying to get Captain Henry Challons and his crew released, wrote to Cecil in August: "Mr Osley from the Court wrote me of the death of my Lord Chief Justice, being very sorry his Majesty has lost so worthy a councillor. Captain Challines with his poor company laments his loss; for he laboured greatly for their enlargement."[11] Captain John Smith also expressed his admiration later, when in his *Generall Historie of Virginia* (1624) he referred to the western colony, on the Sagadehoc, planted by "that honourable Patron of vertue" Sir John Popham.[12] And in 1665 it was recognized, by David Lloyd, that it was this remarkable man who "first sett-afoote the Plantations,—e.g. Virginia."[13]

The most touching tribute, however, comes from the man who must have known Popham best, his clerk. Poor James Clarke found himself under attack by Sir John's grandson Richard Warre, who seems to have been a bully.[14] Warre abused Clarke, casting aspersions on his breeding and justiceship. At an appearance in court, Clarke responded to the attack: he quietly answered that "he that breede mee did alsoe breed you", meaning Sir John Popham. In the course of his defense Clarke spoke of the "love and devotion" which he bore to Richard's "good and honorable graundfather" and referred to himself as one whom "his said grandfather did so much love and affect."[15]

In October William Udall, an agent of Popham's, wrote to Cecil from his lodging at Clerkenwell: "I was suitor to you that since God had taken so worthy a councillor as the late Lord Chief Justice, you would direct me to some man of worth by whom I might effect service for the King and country." Still prosecuting the search for Catholic priests and seditious printing presses, he commented: "These times will want the late Lord Chief Justice. If you direct me to any men of sort, I will perform, not as those who go abroad with warrants from the High Commission and make all England, Protestants and others, exclaim against their extortions; but in such silent sort as I did with the late Lord Chief Justice . . . He being dead I have lost all my recompense, and have no help but from you. He had many things in his custody, taken by my means, the note of which I here enclose. They are in his servant Pemmarton's custody. Give direction that they be delivered as you appoint, and that such be delivered to me as shall be thought convenient. Mr Levinus [Monck] your secretary has seen the work of Alabaster, held incomparable. They are not fitting to be kept but at your command."[16] The work of alabaster would have been a religious figurine, no doubt formerly carried by a priest.[17] A month later Udall wrote again to Cecil on the same subject: "I have within these three years discovered and caused to be taken five presses for printing, without any recompense. The late Lord Chief Justice ever promised, but death prevented his performance."[18]

Not everyone was so complimentary. In June 1608 there was put about a jest concerning Sir Edward Stanhope, Doctor of the Civil Law and Chancellor of the Diocese of London, who had died worth £40,000 but had a reputation as a miser. "News in Court out of Hell" went the joke, "that rich Doctor Stanhope put a case to the Devil. He said it concerned Common Law, and he would be advised by Sir John Popham, who said it was an Exchequer case, and he would put it to Dorset, L. Treasurer."[19] Death did not prevent Sir John Popham continuing to entertain popular imagination, and the manner in which he met his end is the subject of several stories well known in his Somerset homeland.

To the south of Wellington is a fine ridge of hillside, and Popham used to ride and hunt over it toward his manors of Hemyock and Churchstanton.[20] One day he was just below the summit, about half a mile west of where now stands the monument commemorating the Duke of Wellington's victory at Waterloo. There is a valley there known as Wilscombe Bottom, and at the head of it is a "zoggy" deep place. Sir John is said to have been out hunting one day; as he rode along the wood path, his horse stumbled at the edge of the precipice, and threw him into the pool, whence he never rose.[21] The pool is said to be bottomless, and therefore an entrance directly to Hell. It is known to this day as Popham's Pit.

> "There Sir John would have been doomed to stay for ever, but that for the goodness of his wife his spirit was granted this respite: it should emerge from the Pit the following New Year's Eve, at midnight, and advance a cock's stride toward the tomb of his spouse in Wellington Church. This rate of progress he was to keep up yearly on the same fateful night, until he had reached the church door, when at last he should have rest, and attain the same state of happiness that she had won. Her saintly life and her loving prayers should then have achieved for him what nothing else in earth or heaven would have done."[22]

After Popham's death an oak tree grew up at Wilscombe Bottom that was thought to contain his spirit, and the place grew so dangerous in the common estimation that the people of Wellington made a determined attempt to lay the ghost. "They sent for a conjurer to advise them and he said that the oak must be uprooted. So the people got teams of horses and put chains of cold iron round the oak, covered their ears in case it might scream when it was uprooted, and began to haul. The conjuror must have been a doubtful character, for the chains snapped at first pull, and the teams and drivers ran home as fast as they could go. The chains were mended with the help of three blacksmiths for luck, but no one would risk the danger again till an old ploughman, who was very much respected for the sanctity of his life, went to one of the farmers and said that if he could have the help of ten oxen he would pull up the tree. He said he had seen the oxen kneeling on Christmas Eve, and he was sure no harm would come to them. They let him take the oxen, but they kept well away. He took a Bible in his pocket, and singing psalms so loudly that they could be heard from [Wilscombe] to Wellington, he wound the chains round the oak. Then he called to the oxen and the tree came out as easily as a carrot. It screamed loud enough as it came, but it did the ploughman no harm, nor the cattle, and the Wellington people covered their ears. The ghost escaped from the tree somehow, though, before it was burned, and took refuge in Wilscum [Wilscombe] Copse, but it had been so daunted that it did not trouble anyone for a hundred years."[23]

In 1909 Mr F. Milton, a noted local naturalist, wrote to *The Wellington Weekly News:* "my father used to say, 50 years ago, that some men were at work cutting down trees in a wood near the Monument one day, and when they began cutting at one of them it cried most piteously and cried so much that they were obliged to let it be. The inference was that Popham's ghost, on its way to Wellington, had just reached that tree. After the ghost had taken one or two more annual cock-strides they were able to cut down the tree without any more trouble."[24]

It was reported that the Hanging Judge himself, with his head awry from his broken neck, was seen by a cowman in his own farmyard.[25] And "Old Mr Farrant, who lived at Park Farm many years ago, told me that for a long time he had been troubled with noises in the house, in the passage, and behind the boards, scratching and groans and sighing. 'Twas old Sir John there.' Of course, this was very disturbing, so the services of a 'white witch' were sought, and 'he mumbled a lot of stuff what nobody could make any rightship of, and weeshed (wished) him back to the Pit again.'"[26]

The tomb of Sir John and Lady Amy, who died five years after her husband in 1612, is a prominent feature at the east end of the north aisle in Wellington Church. It was moved to its present position in 1938, when no bones were found.[27] The tomb had been moved before, in 1848, but whether his remains were there then is not recorded.[28] The inscription reads: "Sir John Popham Knighte and Lord Chief Justice of England and of the Honourable Privie Councell of Queene Elizabeth and after to King James, aged 76, died 10th day of June 1607 and is here interred."

The tomb comprises a massive rectangular base on the table of which lie life-size effigies of Sir John and his wife. His face is taken from a death mask, and he wears his judge's robe, cap, and chain; she is in Elizabethan gown, ruff, and headdress. The two figures are surmounted by a canopy raised on eight Corinthian pillars, with an obelisk at each corner symbolizing eternity. On the sides are shields of arms (Sir John claimed twenty-two quarterings, signifying the noble alliances of his ancestors) and on the underside a motif of Tudor roses. Around the base are beautifully carved wooden figures. They probably represent, at the west end, Sir John's parents,[29] and at the east end his only son Sir Francis and his wife Anne Dudley; on the south side appear, kneeling on cushions in a row, the six daughters of Sir John, wearing deep ruffs, faced by three maids with serving ruffs of simpler form; and on the north side the five sons of Sir Francis face their eight sisters, who wear lace collars. The tomb is alabaster, and the details are picked out in color; it is thought to be the work of Cornelius Cure and his son William, master masons to King James I from whom they held a joint patent. They were refugees from Holland who had settled in Southwark; their other work includes the tomb in Westminster Abbey of Mary Queen of Scots.[30]

According to Lord Campbell, Sir John left behind him the greatest estate that had ever been amassed by a lawyer.[31] His first wish was to establish a home for the poor. To make such a bequest was conventional rather than notably charitable, but as we know Popham had thought of such a foundation before and now showed that every detail had been considered.

The Will had been made on 21 September 1604, almost three years before Popham's death. After the usual pious preliminaries, Popham wrote: "And whereas I have of longe tyme had a purpose to erecte an Hospitall for the mayntenance and keeping of Twelve poore and ympotent or aged people beinge suche as have bene of Honest fame and of good reporte especiallie trewe workinge or labouringe people whereof Sixe to be Menn and the most discreet of the Menn to be the President of the Menn And Sixe other to be women and the moste modest & discreetest of the women to be the Matrone of the Women. And the same President and Matron to be allwaies appointed by suche of my name as shall enjoye my Mansion Howse in Wellington aforesaide. And for the education of twoe poore Men children ffatherlesse and Motherlesse not being base borne untill suche tyme as they shalbe nyne yeares oulde or bounde to be apprentice. And if the same shall not be erected and founded by me in my lief tyme Then my Will is that my well beloved wief my sonne and heire Sr ffrauncys Popham Knighte and James Clarke of the Middle Temple London Esquier or the survivors or survivor of them shall buylde the same Hospitall wth a Gardeine or little plott adjoyninge thereunto betwene that Howse and the Highe waye in that place wthin the Burroughe of Wellington aforesaid wch I have thereunto assigned wth two severall and divided competent Rowmes for the same poore people And a Howse of Correction or Workinge howse in the Middest of yt accordinge to the plott wch

I have made and wch Mr Prowse of Wellington aforesaid now hathe in his custodye."[32] After making provision for land to support the hospital, Popham establishes that there shall be six Governors, to be chosen out of the families of Popham, Rogers, Mallet, Warre, Halswell of Halswaye and Symes of Pawsford.[33]

The children were to be educated in the hospital by the matron: those committed to the House of Correction were under the government of the President and Matron, who were each to receive eighteen pence per week. The poor inmates were to be given twelve pence weekly, the children eight pence until they were nine years old "or placed wth some Master or Mistres as apprentices for Tenn Yeares at the leaste in Husbandrie." Apprenticeship began early. In addition all the inmates were to receive "a Gowne of ffrize," a cloth with a woolly surface, of value according to their position—up to nine shillings for the President and Matron, six for the rest. The poor were to have a pair of shoes and a shirt or smock, but the total cost of apparel for the President and matron was not to exceed 13s 4d per year, and that of the poor not more than 9s. Popham was always careful with money, and this meticulous but niggardly provision seems characteristic of Protestant charity.

Another fascinating detail: "And I doe advise that one peece of Timber shalbe sett up over againste the said Hospitall in or neere the ffoote pathe of the Highe waie there wth an yron Box uppon it to be closse locked with a Notche in the toppe to putt into the same Box the Charitie of suche people as doe passe by either on horse back or foote which everie nighte shalbe taken owte by the President and Matron eache of which shall have a keye thereof . . . and to be punctually toulde and putt into some stronge Chest to be provided for that purpose."

To cover his debts and legacies Popham specified that his Overseers should sell "my Howse and Landes thereunto belonging at or neare the Charter Howse in or neare London and my Mannor of Lower Court in Twynnynge in the Countie of Glouc[34] and all my Landes Tenements and Hereditamente in Twynnynge and Styple Ashton in the Counties of Glouc and Wiltes." He also wished his "Stocke in the Countie of Lincoln aswell of cattell and corne as any other thinge wth my Stocke at Petwicke all debts due to me and all my Wool not solde at my deathe togethr wth all my redye money and debts owinge me at my deathe wch will appeare in a litle Note booke wch I have allwaies wth me shall goe to the payment of my debts and Legacyes."[35]

He gives to Amye his wife the parsonages of Wellington and

Buckland for eight years "yf shee soe long live and the yeares soe longe endure." His granddaughters are to receive a thousand pounds on their approved marriages—generous bequests indeed. His servant Myles Gyles gets £40, Mary Sidenham his wife's late gentlewoman 40s yearly. Sara Popham, one of the daughters of Ferdinando, Sir John's deceased nephew, £40. Why she should be singled out we do not know. Marmaduke Noble his cook gets £10 yearly for life out of Popham's manor of Shabcombe[36] in Devon "if I do not otherwise advaunce him in my lief and that he doe soe longe Well and trewlie serve my said sonne Sr ffrancis Popham in his howse and do serve noe other." All his other servants get a year's wages. "And thoughe I have bene at greate charges in the education of John Mason yett in respect he hathe longe served me I doe freelie forgive and discharge unto him the valewe of his marriage due unto me and all my charges bestowed on him."[37]

The Middle Temple gets £40 "in satisfaccon of all Reckoninge to that Howse wch notwithstanding the Under Treasurers accompte made I have ever doubted neare soe much did remayne to that Howse and Tenn poundes more to be bestowed in some plate fitte to be ymployed in the howse." His grandchild Amye Mallett receives £100 provided she is still unmarried at the time of Sir John's death; Sir Edward Coke, Attorney General "one Bason and Ewer of silver double guilte newe of the price of ffourtie poundes. And my Will is that my wief shal have and enioye the Mansion Howse that I have lately buylded in Wellington wth the Stable and all the lands that I have in my owne handes beinge adioyninge to the same." She also gets £400 a year for life out of his property in Wiltshire and Berkshire.

Each of his five daughters receives "one Bason and Ewer of silver double guilte of the valewe of £30 6s 8d to be newly made wth my Armes to be sett in them for a remembrance of me"—not much, one may think. A similar gift is made to John Horner, son of Popham's deceased daughter Jane, and George Rogers, godson, is also remembered. A ring of gold is given to his sons-in-law and "cousin" Edward Popham of Huntworth[38] and James Clarke Esq and Sir Randall Brereton, knight, William Pole and Bartholomew Michell Esquires;[39] the rings are to be worth £5 and in them is to be engraved *Timete Dominum et amate invicem* [Fear the Lord and love each other]. James Clarke "my trustie frend" is given £20 "to have a care and regarde allwayes to theis causes and my Children."

Popham also gives "for a Stocke in Wellington to keepe the Poore at worke Twentye poundes," and ten pounds for a similar stock at Taunton, Bridgwater and North Petherton in Somerset and Ramsbury in Wiltshire. The parish stock was a fund to provide a flock of sheep or herd of cattle, the profits from which were directed to the relief of the poor. Lastly his grandchild Amy Pyne, who is separated from her husband, receives £13 6s 8d yearly. Popham appoints as Overseers of his will his sons-in-law and Edward Popham. The will was proved on 17 June 1608 by Sir John's executors, his wife and son.

Sir John's wish to provide for the poor of Wellington was realized, the Hospital of Sir John Popham, Knight, being built in Mantle Street. It stood a short distance from his own first dwelling in the town, and for over three hundred years provided accommodation for the needy. A rebuilding on a slightly different alignment took place in 1833,[40] but by 1936 it was felt that a more modern facility was required. Three entirely new blocks were built in Victoria Street, and these handsome buildings, providing self-contained flats for six men and six women, are used for the same purpose to this day. Sir John's coat of arms is placed over the entrance to the central block. The original almshouses were sold, and ironically now house the Catholic Church of St John Fisher. It is probably just as well that one man's power and influence do not last too long.

Popham's will also provided support for two apprentices in Wellington. That endowment, known as Sir John Popham's Education Foundation, is today worth about £10,000. The income it generates is used to help local young people take part in various activities, recently, for instance, a Rugby Club juniors tour to Ireland.

Almost half a century after Popham's death, some of his legal work was put into print. A compilation entitled *Resolutions and Judgements upon cases and matters agitated in all courts at Westminster, in the latter end of the reign of Queen Elizabeth,* was made by John Goldesborough of the Middle Temple and published in 1651, with four subsequent printings.[41] Five years later a volume written by Popham himself at last came to the press. *Reports and Cases adjudged in the time of Queen Elizabeth,* originally in French but done into English, was printed in London in 1656,[42] with another printing, a little less decorative, in 1682.[43]

Six contemporary portraits are known. One at Harvard Law School shows Popham without the chain of office of Lord Chief Justice, but nevertheless is dated 1602.[44] The portrait at Kimbolton is magnificent, if severe; the National Portrait Gallery has a fine watercolor copy of this by George Perfect Harding

(d. 1853).[45] Two good portraits painted on wood are in private hands, and Blundell's School has an undistinguished picture, acquired between 1790 and 1803.[46] Popham may be seen at his best in the splendid portrait that still hangs in the Great Hall at Littlecote. In scarlet robes, wearing his judge's collar, holding gloves and stick, the Lord Chief Justice is the embodiment of solidity and success.

Shakespeare observes in *Julius Caesar* that

> "The evil that men do lives after them,
> The good is oft interred with their bones."[47]

Sir John Popham haunts us as highwayman, murderer, and hanging judge. This book has sought to dig up and bring to light his worthy achievements, so that we may remember him too as conscientious lawyer, devoted servant of Queen Elizabeth, a cornerstone of the government of England and a man of visionary enterprise. His personality is certainly still to be felt in the buildings he made and at the places that carry his name: the Hospital at Wellington; Blundell's School in Tiverton; Popham's Eau, near Wisbech; Littlecote, near Hungerford; and in partnership with his nephew, Popham Beach in Maine.

Appendix 1: The Family of Sir John Popham

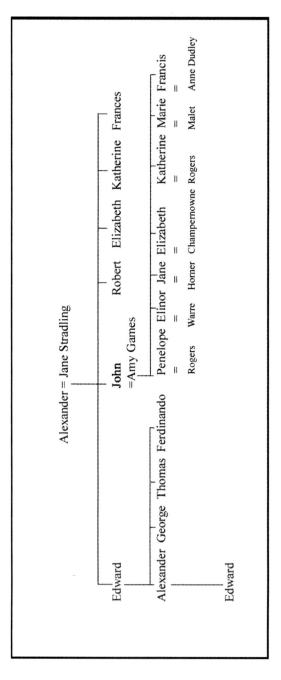

The Family of Sir John Popham.

Appendix 2: Offices Held
by Sir John Popham,
with Date of Appointment

1568	Autumn Reader, Middle Temple
?1570	Member of Parliament for Lyme, Dorset
1571	Recorder of Bristol, Recorder of Bridgwater
1571	Member of Parliament for Bristol
1573	Lent Reader, Middle Temple
1573	Justice of the Peace of the quorum, Somerset
1578	Assize judge, Oxford circuit
1578	Serjeant-at-Law
1579	Solicitor-General
1581	Assize judge, Northern circuit
1581	Attorney-General
1581	Treasurer, Middle Temple
1581	Speaker of House of Commons
1581	Second Justice at Lancaster
1592	Assize judge, Norfolk circuit
1593	Justice of the Peace of the quorum for Norfolk and Suffolk
1592	Lord Chief Justice of England
1599	Privy Councillor
1600	Justice of the Peace of the quorum for Bedfordshire, Cambridge and the Isle of Ely, and Huntingdonshire
1601	Commissioner of the Duchy of Lancaster
1602	High Steward of Dunwich
1607	Steward of the Court of the Marshalsey
1607	(acting) Lord Chancellor

Notes

ABBREVIATIONS

AC	Bristol and Avon County Archives
APC	Acts of the Privy Council of England, New Series. Dasent, J. R., ed. London: HMSO, 1890–1934
BC	Balliol College Library
BL	British Library
BOD	Bodleian Library
CCP	Calendar of Carew Papers
CColP	Calendar of Colonial Papers
CPL	College of Physicians of London
CPR	Calendar of Patent Rolls, Edward VI, Elizabeth I. Vol. 1, 1939; Vol. 5, 1966
CSPD	Calendar of State Papers, Domestic Series
CSPIrel	Calendar of State Papers, Ireland
CUL	Cambridge University Library
DNB	*Dictionary of National Biography*
DRO	Devon Record Office
GL	Guildhall Library
GPB	Gunpowder Plot Book
HH	Hatfield House Library
HL	Huntington Library
HLRO	House of Lords Record Office
HMC	Historical Manuscripts Commission
HMCS	Calendar of the Manuscripts of the . . . Marquis of Salisbury. London: HMSO, 1883–1976
JHL	Journals of the House of Lords
LP	Lambeth Palace Library
MT	Middle Temple Archives
NRA	National Register of Archives
NPG	National Portrait Gallery
NY	New York Public Library
OED	*Oxford English Dictionary*
SA and NH	Somerset Archaeological and Natural History Society
SC	Somerset County Archives
TNA	The National Archives (U.K.), formerly the Public Record Office
VCH	Victoria County History

CHAPTER 1. GYPSY

1. George is given as a brother by F. W. Popham, p. 51, but the kinship has been much debated. See chapter 9, pp. 105–6, chapter 19, pp. 245–46, Notes, p. 280 n. 12.

2. The earliest recorded ancestor, Agnes de Popham, was so named because of her family interest in the Hampshire Manor of Popham, already well-established in 1189. F. W. Popham, p. 4.

3. He was twice appointed Escheator for Somerset and Dorset, which made him responsible for collecting revenues falling due to the Crown where a tenant had died without heirs. Maxwell Lyte, 1928, p. 226.

4. F. W. Popham, p. 22 ff. The area is now called the Somerset Levels.

5. The home now of the United World College of the Atlantic.

6. The Monument Inscription states that John died in 1607 aged seventy-six, but F. W. Popham gives 1531 as the date of birth of his elder brother Edward.

7. Court House survived in its Tudor form until destroyed by fire in 1825. Sketches suggest that the house had five gabled sections, and was three-storyed with mullioned windows. The site of Court House is now occupied by Huntworth House, where some fragments of the original building are still to be seen. Huntworth is a small cluster of houses now separated from Bridgwater by the M5.

8. Hill, p. 31.

9. Campbell, p. 210.

CHAPTER 2. HIGHWAYMAN

1. John Jones, *Balliol College,* pp. 53–54.

2. Ibid., p. 53.

3. F. W. Popham, p. 40.

4. Hopwood, vol. 1, p. 82.

5. Campbell, p. 210.

6. Wood, vol. 1, p. 292.

7. Fuller, p. 25.

8. MT Minute Book, printed in Hopwood, vol. 1, p. 107.

9. Andrew Clark, vol. 2, p. 158.

10. Campbell, p. 210.

11. Bindoff, p. 134.

12. His brother-in-law William Pole of Shute, near Lyme, was influential in the area.

13. Campbell, p. 211.

14. Andrew Clark, vol. 2, p. 158.

15. AC/S1/5. Messuage: a dwelling house. Advowson: the right to appoint a clergyman to a living.

16. Bantock, p. 18.

17. The judges in the Court of the Exchequer were called Barons.

18. The National Archives (formerly Public Record Office) [hereafter TNA]: STAC 8/163/26. Clarke later married Jane Broughton of Sandford; they had four sons and two daughters. Squibb, p. 86.

19. Hopwood, vol. 1, p. 164.

20. Sparry was father of Francis, one of the men left in Guiana by Ralegh in

1595. This Hartopp evidently died young, for his heir, who was Popham's god-son, became a ward of Her Majesty. Popham had taken on some responsibility for supervising his finances, but by 1596 was finding the duties "too trouble-some" and requested to be relieved of them. CSPD Addenda, Elizabeth, vol. 33, 61, p. 376.

21. Hopwood, vol. 1, p. 165.

22. Mockler, p. xiii.

23. Ibid., p. xiv.

24. There were three other courts of justice: Parliament, the Star Chamber, and Requests. In addition there were three courts of revenue: the Exchequer, Wards and Liveries, and the Duchy of Lancaster.

25. Mockler, p. 9.

26. Caraman, 1964, p. 8.

27. Andrew Clark, vol. 2, p. 159.

28. Caraman, 1964, p. 9.

29. They were discovered by Mrs Ann Thomas in the library at Littlecote in Wiltshire; eight are now in the Bodleian Library at Oxford and one in private hands.

30. BOD Bookstack Vet.A1c.35 (1).

31. AC/C10.

32. Vanes, p. 8.

33. In Tudor times "subsidy" usually meant a levy of 4s in the pound on lands and 2s 8d in the pound on moveables.

34. Hasler, vol. 2, p. 163; Sacks, pp. 197–98.

35. Neale, pp. 184–85.

36. Hartley, p. 194.

37. Vanes, p. 9.

38. Guy, p. 32.

39. Neale, p. 190.

40. Ibid., pp. 218–19.

41. Hasler, vol. 3, p. 234.

42. Hartley, p. 202.

43. Neale, p. 219.

44. Ibid.

45. *DNB*.

46. A desperate attempt by a group of powerful Catholic earls to restore the fortunes of Mary Queen of Scots, who would be married to the Duke of Norfolk, England's premier peer.

47. Hartley, p. 212.

48. Sacks, p. 200.

49. Haigh, p. 90. Attendance was usually not more than 150 of the 400 mem-bers, most talking done by a hard-core group of regulars among whom the offi-cial element—office holders and men of business—predominated. Popham is one of the eleven regulars Haigh names.

50. Neale, p. 242.

51. Ibid., p. 285.

52. Black, p. 195.

53. Black, p. 196.

54. CPR, vol. 5, 3235, p. 458.

55. Burke, vol. 1, p. 888.

56. *DNB*.

57. CPR, vol. 5, 3194, p. 454.

58. *DNB*. His death in 1577 was unexpected: he had presided at the trial in 1577 of "a scurvy foul-mouthed bookseller" at which over three hundred people were taken ill from "the stench of the prisoners," and died in a few days.

CHAPTER 3. HOMEBUILDER

1. Watkin, p. 37.

2. Allen and Bush, p. 17.

3. Thorne, 1950, p. 28.

4. For the dating of the births of John and Edward, see F. W. Popham, p. 40.

5. Dunning, p. 40.

6. Michell, pp. 82–83.

7. F. W. Popham, pp. 48–49. One of her grandchildren founded Taunton, Mass.

8. Hanham was a Master of the Bench when Drake was welcomed to the Middle Temple Hall in August 1586.

9. VCH Bedfordshire, vol. 3, p. 410.

10. Humphreys, 1889, pp. 59–62.

11. Gibson, p. 181.

12. "Family of Horner, Co. Somerset." *Miscellanea Geneaologica et Heraldica,* NS. 4 (1884): 160.

13. Watkin, p. 37.

14. Fuller, p. 367.

15. Ibid., p. 193. Fortescue's disposal of land in Wellington may have been a result of his coming into property in Buckinghamshire.

16. The total tally of John Popham's grandchildren seems to have been forty-seven, though early death reduced this number considerably.

17. Sir Edward Phelips's career, as well as his house, was strikingly similar to Popham's. He made a fortune as a lawyer, became Speaker of the Commons and led the Prosecution at the Gunpowder Plot trial. He was later Chancellor to Prince Henry's household.

18. Barnes, p. 20.

19. Seaby, p. 153.

20. Osborne, p. 17.

21. Elworthy, p. 60.

22. Watkin, p. 61.

23. Chas. H. Fox, in a letter to *The Wellington Weekly News,* 19 July 1899.

CHAPTER 4. THE QUEEN'S SERVANT

1. McGrath, 1985, p. 6.

2. Sacks, p. 187.

3. F. F. Fox, p. 113.

4. Thomas Churchyard in Nichols, vol. 1, pp. 393–407.

5. McGrath, 1985, pp. 6–12.

6. F. F. Fox, p. 115.

7. Grinsell, p. 32.

8. Hartley, p. 454.

9. For instance, those of Sir George Croke or Sir Edward Coke. Popham's own book of Reports covers cases between 1592 and 1598 in which he took part. See Holdsworth, vol. 5, p. 361, and chapter 20, p. 269.

10. Hall, p. 142.

11. Hall, p. 143.

12. Oman, p. 78.

13. BL Add 33271 f 18b.

14. Oman, pp. 78–80.

15. Campbell, p. 212. Another view given by Foss, vol. 5, p. 180 is that the note in the *Chronicle of Creations of the Order of Serjeants at Law,* January 1578, "non dederunt aurum" [they did not give gold], suggests that as the appointment of Popham and Rhodes was an addition to the main call of serjeants, they were not required to give a separate feast. Baker, p. 173.

16. He was appointed to the Northern circuit in 1581 and to the Norfolk circuit in 1592. See Cockburn, p. 19 and pp. 265–68. See also chapter 16, p. 195.

17. HMC 12, Wells, vol. 2, p. 301.

18. Campbell, p. 212.

19. Hasler, vol. 3, p. 235; Campbell, p. 212.

20. CPR, vol. 9, 94, p. 20.

21. Bantock, pp. 25–26.

22. AC/C20.

23. D'Ewes, pp. 280–81. All further quotations in this chapter relating to the Parliament of 1581 are from d'Ewes, pp. 280–310 unless otherwise stated.

24. Elton, 1982, p. 295.

25. Graves, p. 148.

26. McGrath, 1967, p. 207.

27. Neale, p. 380.

28. Hartley, p. 528.

29. Neale, p. 412.

30. Private bills could be brought by individuals or corporations.

31. A mystical puritan sect, originating in Holland.

32. Kelsey, p. 216.

33. Ibid., pp. 232–33.

34. Williamson, p. 240.

35. Hopwood, vol. 1, p. 257.

36. TNA: STAC 8/163/26.

37. Hall, p. 144.

38. Neale, p. 413.

39. Hasler, p. 235.

40. Neale, p. 399.

41. Plurality: the holding of two or more benefices concurrently by one person. Dispensation: the granting of license to omit what is enjoined by ecclesiastical law. *OED.*

42. Hartley, pp. 522–23. Tenths and fifteenths were temporary aids, issuing out of a tax on personal property, formerly really a tenth and fifteenth part of the moveables belonging to a subject. *OED.*

43. Ibid., p. 547.

44. John M. Robertson, p. 869.

CHAPTER 5. ATTORNEY-GENERAL

1. D'Ewes, p. 310.

2. Black, p. 178.

3. Roy, p. 21, says that Popham "may be counted among the ranks of the more militantly Protestant, those God-fearing, xenophobic, and industrious men sometimes described by their critics as Puritans—although of course they would not have recognised themselves by this term."

4. APC, vol. 13, p. 249.

5. It was usual for Crown's counsel to number 3. Bellamy, p. 146.

6. Waugh, p. 190.

7. Robert Parsons, another Somerset and Balliol man, escaped to Rouen and became organizer of the Jesuit mission to England.

8. CSPD, vol. 150, 61, p. 30.

9. APC, vol. 13, p. 290.

10. APC, vol. 13, p. 298. The second Earl had actually died in October 1581, when the third Earl was not quite eight years old.

11. Rachel Lloyd, pp. 221–24.

12. This may have been John's nephew, son of his brother Edward, or a cousin, one of the sons of Marmaduke (d. 1624). The family of John's uncle George Popham of Wedmore also had Georges in every generation. F. W. Popham, p. 122.

13. APC, vol. 13, p. 96.

14. Her grandfather, James IV, had married Margaret, daughter of Henry VII.

15. *DNB*.

16. CSPD, vol. 165, 10, p. 144.

17. Howell, cols. 1115–16.

18. Ibid., col. 1128.

19. Lady Arbella or Arabella Stuart was James's father's brother's daughter, English-born, and a Protestant.

20. Guy, p. 332.

21. Camden, vol. 3, p. 135.

22. Ibid., p. 134.

23. Howell, cols. 1150–51.

24. APC, vol. 14, p. 224.

25. HMC, vol. 24, 12th Report, app., pt. 4, Rutland, vol. 1, p. 233.

26. Strype, vol. 3, p. 362.

27. Nichols, vol. 2, p. 496.

28. The death of Bromley in 1587 necessitated the appointment of a new Chancellor. W. T. Jones, pp. 41–42 believes that although Popham was the obvious candidate from among the ranks of the law, he may have shown no desire for the position, being more interested now in criminal than civil law. The Queen may have thought that after his mighty efforts as prosecutor in the trials surrounding Mary, he should remain as Attorney-General.

29. Dasent, p. 139 says that the original document authorizing the payment was sold at auction in London in 1910.

30. Howell, cols. 1229–30.

31. This and the following examples in this paragraph are to be found in APC, vols. 13–15, except where stated.

32. BL Lansdowne lxi f 78.

33. Alum, a whitish mineral salt, a double sulfate of aluminium and potassium, was used in dyeing and medicine.

34. DRO, Exeter City Archives, Exeter "Ancient Letters," L. 92. HMC 73, City of Exeter, p. 63.

35. TNA: SP 12/159/13. CSPD, vol.159, 13, p. 100.

36. CSPD, vol. 158, 66, 67, p. 96.

37. Connor, p. 242.

38. CSPD, vol. 157, 73, p. 87.

39. CSPIrel, vol. 105, 15, p. 473.

40. TNA: PRO 30/34/1.

41. Raleigh, bk 1, ch 8, sect 15, sub-sect 5, pp. 175–76.

42. Green, 1888, p. 62–63. "Petronel" is derived from "petrinal," a dialect form of "poitrine," chest.

43. CSPD, vol. 202, 66, p. 420.

44. Green, 1888, p. 58.

45. TNA: SP 12/213, 2. In October payment was authorized by the Privy Council to John Masson, Popham's servant, "for bringinge letters in post for her Majesties affaires from his master's house in Wallington in the countie of Somerset to the Court at St. James." APC, vol. 15, pp. 322–23.

Chapter 6. Undertaker in Ireland

1. Quinn, 1966, p. 106.

2. See chapter 19, pp. 245–46.

3. TNA: SP 12/140/24.

4. Ellis, p. 326 says that in October 1585, there were 574,645 acres of land, worth just over IR£9887, available for settlement.

5. Maxwell, pp. 243–44, quotes J. Lodge, *Desiderata curiosa Hibernica,* Dublin, 1772.

6. MacCarthy-Morrogh, p. 50.

7. Williams, Penry, p. 298.

8. CCP, 601, p. 419.

9. MacCarthy-Morrogh, p. 48.

10. Black, p. 475.

11. TNA: SP 63/124/80, CSPIrel, vol. 124, 80, p. 77.

12. Popham was often referred to as Sir, although he was not in fact knighted for another six years.

13. CSPIrel, vol. 139, p. 103. A note by Burghley on this document refers to "Denzil Hollis's master, that is Sir John Popham, and his two sons, John and George" as well as his two sons-in-law. It must be a mistake for "cousins." Sir John Stowell of Cothelstone was active in Somerset against the Armada. Clifton lived at Barrington, St Barbe at Ashington, and Coles at Pitminster, where there is an effigy in the church. Edward Rogers and Richard Champernowne were Popham's sons-in-law; Carew was Sir Walter Ralegh's brother. Chydley may well have been the person Popham described in a letter of 25 November 1590 as "my cosyn," and for whom he sought help from Sir Julius Caesar. BL Add 12506 f 283.

14. MacCarthy-Morrogh, p. 42.

15. Collier, p. 118.

16. Spedding, vol. 4, p. 117.

17. CSPIrel, vol.124, 87, pp. 84–89. A shortened version is in Maxwell, pp. 242–43.

18. Quinn, 1966, p. 112.

19. CSPIrel, vol. 124, 81, pp. 77–78.

20. Ibid., vol. 128, 83, pp. 278–79. Popham later referred to Norreys as "a wise gentleman, but a very worldly man." CSPIrel, vol. 165, 13, p. 530.

21. CCP 636, 23, p. 453.

22. CSPIrel. vol. 132, 39, pp. 449–50.

23. A Hugh Worth is described on 29 March 1600 as "a man of the Lord Chief Justice." HMCS, vol. 10, p. 85.

24. CCP, 636, pp. 446–55.

25. CSPIrel, vol. 125, 31, p. 113.

26. Ellis, pp. 326–27.

27. CSPD, vol. 200, 15, p. 403.

28. CSPIrel, vol.142, 10, pp. 130–31.

29. Ibid., vol. 132, pp. 449–50.

30. MacCarthy-Morrogh suggests that Sir Francis might have regretted the decision to withdraw, as the Mallow seignory of 6,000 acres was valued in the 1630s at £15,000 to £18,000. CSPIrel, vol. 132, 39, pp. 449–50.

31. Quinn, 1966, p. 115.

32. CCP 646, p. 458.

33. Ibid.

34. CSPIrel, vol. 136, 11, pp. 6–8.

35. MacCarthy-Morrogh, p. 98.

36. CSPIrel, vol. 136, 34, pp. 31–32.

37. CSPIrel, vol. 136, 21b, pp. 14–26.

38. Ibid., vol. 137, 20, pp. 59–61.

39. CSPIrel, vol. 136, 34, pp. 31–32.

40. Bagwell, p. 189.

41. CSPIrel, vol. 142, 10, pp. 130–31.

42. CSPIrel, vol. 137, 2, p. 51.

43. Ibid., vol. 137, 31, p. 62.

44. John Popham continued for many years to advise on Irish affairs. In April 1599, for instance, Wilbraham noted his effective influence in persuading the Queen to act against the rebel leader Florence McCarthy. Scott, p. 24.

45. Quinn, 1966 p. 135. HMCS, vol. 12, p. 3.

46. Quinn, p. 111.

Chapter 7. Lord of Littlecote

1. Andrew Clark, pp. 158–59. Littlecote is still in Wiltshire, although the postal address is now Berkshire.

2. *Littlecote, a History,* pp. 18–19. The valley had evidently attracted the Romans, who built a number of villas in the area; one discovered in Littlecote Park contains the mosaic floor of a temple dedicated to Orpheus.

3. Hall, p. 145: "His matters had come before every permanent Court in the kingdom—in the Chancery, the King's Bench, the Exchequer, the Common Pleas, the Courts of Wards and Liveries, Requests, and Star-chamber, the Spiritual Courts, and were even the subject of grave discussion in the Council Chamber" and before the Queen.

4. Hall, p. 188. Sir Edward Darrell, Vice-Chamberlain to Henry VIII's first wife, Katherine of Aragon, had been doubly related to them.

5. Hall, p. 144.

6. Hall, p. 244.

7. Ibid., pp. 240–41.

8. TNA: SP 46/44/9. The lawyer who took down the deposition was Darrell's cousin Antony Bridges. A transcription is printed in Hall, pp. 248–50.

9. Long, 1858, p. 212. The four articles by Long provide the first skeptical review of the story.

10. Hall, p. 145.

11. Ibid., p. 9.

12. In 1565, for instance, he had been ordered by William Cecil not to cut wood at Chilton Foliat. TNA: SP 46/44/9.

13. Hall, p. 269.

14. Hall, pp. 270–71.

15. Ibid., pp. 271–72.

16. When Popham was appointed Speaker in 1581, it was Bromley who warned him that the House should not meddle in the Queen's affairs. Bromley was involved in the trials of Northumberland and Babington. He presided at the trial of Mary Queen of Scots, but the strain of taking responsibility for her death overtaxed him and he died on 2 April 1587.

17. TNA: SP 46/44/86.

18. Hall, p. 13.

19. Hall, p. 97.

20. Hall, pp. 99–101, 206.

21. *Littlecote, a History,* p. 9.

22. Whitlock, p. 100.

23. "Rokeby" XXVII in J. Logie Robertson, p. 362. Long, 1860, pp. 213–14 notes that a story similar to the Littlecote legend was reported in 1616 from Flanders by Dudley Carleton.

24. See also Whitlock, p. 100.

25. Wiltshire, p. 118.

26. F. W. Popham, p. 45.

27. Hall, p. 195. Toft: a homestead.

28. Quotations in this paragraph are from *Littlecote, a History,* unless otherwise stated.

29. Sotheby's Catalogue, *Littlecote,* 1985.

30. Andrew Clark, p. 160.

31. Williamson, p. 227.

Chapter 8. Lord Chief Justice

1. Sewell, p. 21.

2. F. W. Popham, p. 46. Sutton's Will of 1611, printed by Herne, pp. 200–228, is of great interest in that it provides an insight into the financial transactions relating to Francis Popham's marriage.

3. APC, vol. 18, p. 411.

4. *DNB.*

5. CSPD, vol. 223, 77, p. 590.

6. As Burghley told Whitgift in 1584. Black, p. 199.

7. Black, p. 204; Harrison, 1928, p. 27.

8. *DNB.*

9. APC, vol. 21, pp. 325–26.

10. Stow, f 762.

11. Harington, 1653, p. 13.

12. Elliot Rose, pp. 64–65.

13. APC, vol. 19, pp. 320–21.

14. Ibid., p. 282.

15. APC, vol. 21, p. 275.

16. APC, vol. 20, p. 80.

17. Ibid., pp. 114–15.

18. Harington, 1804, vol. 1, pp. 171–72. In 1584 Harington married Mary, daughter of George Rogers of Cannington. In the same year her brother Edward Rogers married Popham's daughter Katherine. Healey, opp. p. 292.

19. Harrison, 1928, pp. 6–7.

20. APC, vol. 18, p. 324.

21. APC, vol. 19, pp. 111–12.

22. Ibid., vol. 20, p. 13.

23. Ibid., p. 176.

24. Ibid., p. 167.

25. Mockler, p. xv.

26. Osterley in Middlesex was the home of Lady Gresham, widow of Sir Thomas, founder of the Royal Exchange. The Queen visited there on 7–9 April 1592.

27. TNA: SP12/242/14.

28. Robbins, p. 223.

29. The Letters Patent appointing him are in the British Library, BL Add 5485.

30. Bruce, pp. 116–17. 5 February 1603: "Mr Asheford told me these verses under written are upon a picture of the nowe Lord Keeper, Sir Thomas Egerton, in the Lord Chief Justice Popham's lodging."

31. Caraman, 1964, p. 157.

32. Collier, p. 167. HL EL 2099.

33. Thornton, p. 4. Wood, p. 229.

34. Black, p. 185.

35. See Caraman, 1995, pp. 97–107, for a vivid account of Southwell's trial. See also chapter 17, p. 215.

36. MacCaffrey, p. 39.

37. Wardle, p. 136.

38. Sir John Popham, p. 84. Anyone who could read (originally a Clerk) was normally allowed exemption from secular punishment in all cases of felony or treason not touching the Queen's person.

39. Cecil, p. 85.

40. LP MSS 701 f85.

41. Chambers, vol. 4, p. 108.

42. BL Lansd 77.50. Sutton also wanted to found a school, and in 1611 bought the site of the former monastery of monks of La Grande Chartreuse. Thus began Charterhouse School, for forty poor scholars.

43. Presumably the reference in HMC 62 Lothian p. 79, dated only 11 April, is to the same institution. It was agreed at Ilminster that a House of Correction for rogues should be built at Wellington by the Lord Chief Justice "at his owne

charge." The hospital eventually built after Popham's death contained a House of Correction.

CHAPTER 9. GEORGE'S GUIANA

1. His elder brother was born in 1557.

2. APC, vol. 10, p. 439. Roger Sydenham had been a captain in Ireland, was married in 1575 and became Ranger of the Forest of Exmoor in 1592. Liberties: proper areas of authority.

3. CSPIrel, vol 105, 15, p. 473. See chapter 5, p. 66. Ferdinando, the fifth son, was admitted to the Middle Temple in 1585. F. W. Popham, p. 23 gives his year of birth as 1561.

4. Cummins, p. 224.

5. Of Italian ancestry, Caesar was a very different character from his namesake. Famous for his charity, he was poorly rewarded by Elizabeth but became Chancellor of the Exchequer under James, who knighted him in 1603.

6. BL Add 12505 f 298. Richard was father of Popham's son-in-law Roger Warre.

7. K. R. Andrews, p. 261. Thomas Sutton also owned a privateer; his, of course, captured a Spanish vessel worth £20,000. Sewell, p. 20.

8. Friel, p. 32.

9. K. R. Andrews, p. 32.

10. BL Lansdowne 1592.

11. Charles Nicholl, pp. 29–30.

12. Harlow, pp. 82–83.

13. Seville, Archivo General de Indias (Estante i, Cajon i, Legajo I/26, Numero 33). A transcript is in the British Library, BL Add MSS 36316 f30.

14. Waldman, p. 99. Ralegh was ready to sail by September 1594 but did not get away until 6 February 1595.

15. Robert Dudley maintained, unsuccessfully, that his mother, Lady Douglas Sheffield, had been formally betrothed to Leicester.

16. Cavendish had been on the first Roanoke expedition. The unique globe by Molyneux, the first made in England, records the voyages of Drake and Cavendish. It is now in the Library of the Middle Temple.

17. Arthur Gould Lee, p. 59.

18. This was a result of the marriage of Francis Popham to Ann Dudley. The marriage of Elizabeth Popham to Richard Champernowne had created a similar link between Pophams and Raleghs.

19. G. F. Warner, p. 74 fn. Ralegh describes the golden man ritual and then writes: "the same is also confirmed by a letter written into Spaine which was intercepted, which Master Robert Dudley told me he had seen."

20. Three accounts of the voyage are printed by G. F. Warner.

21. G. F. Warner, p. 70.

22. Robert Dudley's claim for recognition of his legitimacy eventually came to court, and judgment was given against him in 1605 in Star Chamber (G. F. Warner, pp. xlvi–xlvii). His witnesses had been suspect; further discussion involved a motion concerning them at which Sir John Popham spoke (p. xlvii fn). Having lost his case, Dudley left England for Italy, carrying away with him a young maid-of-honor and noted beauty, Elizabeth Southwell, disguised as a page. After they had both declared themselves Catholics, he formally married

her, although his second wife, Alice Leigh, who had borne him seven daughters, was still living. He lived in exile in Italy for thirty years, his legitimacy being recognized in 1644 by Charles II, and died in 1649. Arthur Gould Lee, pp. 117, 246.

23. TNA: SP 12/246/4.

24. In his text Ralegh only mentions Dudley once and ignores his voyage altogether. Ralegh did his best to stop Dudley organizing another expedition to Guiana. See G. F. Warner, p. 75.

25. Latham and Youings, pp. 126–27.

Chapter 10. Privy Councillor

1. The Oxfordshire rising of 1596 led to three leaders—a fuller, a bricklayer, and a miller—being tried before a special commission headed by Popham. Two were found guilty of high treason and executed. Sharp, p. 44.

2. Edward Hext to Burghley, printed in Pound, pp. 94–97.

3. Then as now, guns were thought to contribute to crime. In 1600 Popham gave the Lords a summary of the statutes "that prohibit the use of guns in some kind," delivering also "a form of a preamble to the proclamation, relying principally upon the murders, robberies and other insolencies committed by use of them contrary to law." HMCS, vol. 10, p. 417.

4. Prothero, p. 101. Sturdy beggars were those capable of work.

5. APC, vol. 26, pp. 169–70.

6. Ibid., p. 325.

7. Hill, p. 124.

8. Judges, pp. 265–91.

9. Judges, p. 507. Hutton nevertheless died a felon's death at York for a robbery in 1598.

10. Ibid.

11. Rowse, 1962, p. 197.

12. Guy, p. 350.

13. Donne wrote an an epigram, "A Burnt Ship," about the affair: Grierson, p. 67. Egerton's son Thomas was with him, and on returning to civilian life Donne became through his influence Secretary to the Lord Keeper, his job being to investigate alleged malpractices in the law: Carey, p. 69. In this connection Donne must have known Popham.

14. By the end of the voyage there were sixty-six Cadiz knights. Kenny, p. 194.

15. HL HA 10347.

16. Cross, 1969, p. 196.

17. Powell, p. 162.

18. Evidently this was a widespread nuisance. Popham presided at Taunton on 15 July 1595 when John Chappell and others, keepers of a tippling house at Hinton St George, were told that "no person shall entertain within their tippling houses any persons living within 1000 yards, except at market times." Shorrocks, p. 167.

19. Latimer, 1908, pp. 109–11.

20. HMCS, vol. 5, p. 386.

21. Ibid., p. 155.

22. Ibid., pp. 436–37.

23. HL EL 6225.

24. HMCS, vol. 9, p. 73. Hanham was still abroad on 3 December 1600, when he sent his grandfather "directions for remittances." HMCS, vol. 10, p. 403.

25. Hopwood, vol. 1, p. 372.

26. In his draft will, made before 1592, Hastings wished Popham and Edward St Barbe to have rings worth £3 6s 8d with the inscription *vere amat qui semper amat* [He loves truly who loves for ever]. Cross, 1969, p. 118.

27. Cross, 1966, p. 143.

28. HL HA 10348.

29. Harrison, 1931, pp. 192–93, 241–42, 267–68; 1933, pp. 17–18. This Darrell does not seem to have been related to William "Wild" Darrell of Littlecote.

30. APC, vol. 26, pp. 317–18.

31. Ibid., vol. 27, p. 448.

32. Ibid., vol. 28, p. 399–400.

33. Ibid., p. 507.

34. APC, vol. 26, p. 382.

35. Ibid., p. 548.

36. APC, vol. 30, p. 253; HMCS, vol. 12, p. 220.

37. Jegon, Master of Corpus Christi College 1590–1603, was Vice-Chancellor 1596–99 and 1600–1601. He became an unpopular Bishop of Norwich, with a reputation for miserliness. *DNB*.

38. Cooper, vol. 2, pp. 576–77.

39. CUL MS Mm 1. 35, p. 364.

40. Ibid., 1. 38, p. 4.

41. Scott, p. 20. See also Cockburn, p. 116. Wilbraham had been Solicitor-General in Ireland, where he was hated for his excessive fees and exactions. He now practiced at the English bar. Scott, p. ix.

42. APC, vol. 29, p. 296.

43. CSPD, vol. 274, pp. 384–85.

44. Hill (?1570–1610), fellow of St John's College, Oxford, "lived most of his time in the Romish persuasion." *DNB*. He supported the view that matter was composed of atoms.

45. Trevor-Roper, pp. 20–22. Pole and Basset had married daughters of Sir William Periam.

46. Courtenay was knighted by Essex in 1599, and died without issue in 1605.

47. APC, vol. 28, p. 375.

48. Wardle, pp. 155, 159. See also chapter 8, p. 103.

49. Keeton, p. 7.

50. Morris, p. 18.

51. Caraman, 1964, p. 252.

52. HMCS 6, p. 554.

53. HMCS 7, p. 88.

54. APC p. 206.

55. HMCS 9, p. 220.

56. HMCS 12, p. 39. In 1607 one George Willoughby complained to Cecil that Popham had done nothing in his suit for five years. HMCS 24, p. 122.

57. HMCS, vol. 9, p. 367.

58. Ibid., vol. 14, pp. 117–18. See also Notes, p. 290 n. 7.

59. McClure, vol. 1, p. 48.

60. Shorrocks, p. 170.

61. HMC, vol. 11, 10th. Report, pt. 2, Gawdy, p. 65.

62. HMCS, vol. 14, p. 291.

63. Caraman, 1964, pp. 276–77.

64. HH 59.85.

65. CSPD, vol. 268, 61, p. 97.

66. The list wrongly refers to Fortescue as Thomas. APC, vol. 29, p. 738.

67. Elton, 1982, p. 93 fn 20.

68. Camden, vol. 1, p. 75, quoted in Barnes, p. 20.

69. HMCS, vol. 9, p. 251.

70. Nichols, vol. 3, p. 454.

71. CSPD, vol. 273, 35, p. 351. On 2 February 1600 Popham received a libellous letter that he forwarded to Robert Cecil, observing "By the very phrase of the letter directed to me, I conceived it to be done as a wry screw to me." HMCS, vol. 10, p. 27.

CHAPTER 11. KIMBOLTON'S KILLER

1. Stratford, *If you came this way,* p. 17.

2. Dixon, p. 19, Rose, p. 823.

3. Waugh, p. 116. On 2 July 1600 Popham suggested to Sir Nathaniel Bacon that Norwich Castle be used for recusants. Bacon, p. 178.

4. Edward Maria Wingfield lived very near the Castle, at Stonely Priory. We shall meet him again in 1607, when he and George Popham were to have parallel experiences of colonization in Virginia.

5. Stratford, 2000, p. 14.

6. Wingfield, p. 127.

7. Stratford, 2000, pp. 9, 11.

8. In 1615 the Castle was owned by Sir Henry Montague, Recorder of London in 1603, Chief Justice of the King's Bench, trusted councillor of Charles I and in 1626 Earl of Manchester. It was he who in 1618 finally restated Popham's sentence of death on Sir Walter Ralegh.

9. VCH Huntingdon, vol. 3, p. 76.

CHAPTER 12. PRISONER OF ESSEX

1. Thus Sir Robert Cecil later summarized Essex's ambitions: CSPD, vol. 278, 54, p. 554.

2. *Henry V,* Chorus to act 5.

3. Chapter 10, p. 131.

4. Guy, p. 447.

5. CSPD, vol. 274, 58, p. 404.

6. Francis Fortescue in a letter to his father-in-law, John Manners. HMC 24, 12th Report, App., Pt. 4, Rutland, vol. 1, p. 361.

7. Lacey, p. 76.

8. CSPD, vol. 278, 84, pp. 577–78.

9. Johnson, p. 406.

10. Charles was son of the Earl of Northumberland, who died suspiciously in the Tower, and brother of the Wizard Earl, Henry Percy, ninth Earl of Northumberland.

11. Phillips (d. 1605) was a senior member of the company, perhaps a dancer and probably composer of "Phillips gigg of the slyppers" in May 1595. He seems

to have been business manager for the Lord Chamberlain's Men. Cerasano, p. 332. In his will of 4 May 1605 he bequeathed 30s in gold to Shakespeare and Condell. Heminges and Burbage were "overseers" of his will. Southworth, p. 242.

12. TNA: SP 12/278/85. Chambers, vol. 2, p. 205.

13. Gayley, p. 9.

14. TNA: SP 12/278/85. The money was paid to them by Sir Gelly Merrick. Howell, col. 1445.

15. Water [Walter] Gunter kept a tabling house near Temple Bar. HMCS, vol. 10, p. 27.

16. Blount later said that he had "loved Essex, as being bewitched with too good an opinion of him." Howell, col. 1447.

17. CSPD, vol. 278, 78, p. 575.

18. Akrigg, p. 128.

19. Johnson, p. 406.

20. Gorges had been advised by Blount "not to go naked to Sir Walter, not to go home to him, but to meet him upon the water, and to take some pistols with him." Howell, col. 1424.

21. Howell, col. 1426.

22. Essex had "assumed the militant protestant mantle of Leicester, Walsingham and the Sidneys." Guy, p. 440.

23. *DNB*.

24. Constable had been knighted by Essex in Ireland in 1599. After the rising the Queen directed Popham that Constable, who was never tried, should be bailed (like Gorges). Much later, Constable fought valiantly for the Parliamentarians, and was one of those who signed the warrant for the execution of Charles I. *DNB*.

25. CSPD, vol. 278, 72, p. 573. Salisbury is described by Camden as "an old Souldier of prompt boldnesse."

26. Ibid., vol. 278, 97, pp. 585–87.

27. Coke said later that this was merely "a buz, and so invented by them for a buz," and that on the contrary, they intended to kill Sir Walter. Howell, col. 1422. The long-standing conflict between Essex and Ralegh was intensified by Ralegh's inexplicable intimacy with Henry Brooke, Lord Cobham. A weak and undistinguished man, son of one of Elizabeth's favorite courtiers, he had married Robert Cecil's sister Elizabeth, and was very friendly with Cecil too. One of the objects of the Essex rising was to displace Cobham from his position at Court.

28. Howell, col. 1426.

29. Bacon says that Essex later "made defence of his action of imprisoning the privy councillors by pretence that he was inforced to it by his unruly company." How then, Bacon asked, could he maintain that the Queen's person would remain unharmed just because he said so? Howell, col. 1418 fn.

30. CSPD, vol. 278, 97, p. 587.

31. Howell, col. 1428.

32. CSPD, vol. 278, 56, p. 557.

33. Howell, col. 1428.

34. Ibid.

35. CSPD, vol. 278, 46, pp. 547–48.

36. Bacon, quoted by Howell, col. 1429.

37. CSPD, vol. 278, 54, p. 555. Francis Bacon had fun with this idea at the prosecution of Davies. The actions of the conspirators, he said, were deliberate: they

did not meet "by constellation." Though Davies was "a man skilful in strange arts," they were not spirits that were sent abroad, but letters. Howell, col. 1438.

38. Caraman, 1964, p. 277.

39. Howell, col. 1429. One of the guards was Francis Tresham, who cheekily told Egerton that "he had been stayed two years for a motion in the Chancery, and hoped his lordship was now at good leisure to hear him." At his trial Popham spoke strongly of Tresham's insolence, and he was lucky to escape with his life. Jardine, 1832, vol. 1, 326.

40. Camden, pp. 540–41.

41. Camden was an eyewitness of these events.

42. Thomas Smith or Smythe was to become Governor of the East India Company and a most influential adviser on foreign trade. See chapter 19, p. 237.

43. Camden, p. 549.

44. CSPD, vol. 278, 49, 50, p. 551.

45. HMCS, vol. 11, p. 53.

46. HMC 24, 12th Report, app., pt. 4; Rutland, vol. 1, p. 371.

47. Fuller, p. 25.

48. HMC, vol. 24, Rutland, vol. 1, p. 372.

49. Ibid., p. 373.

50. APC, vol. 31, p. 174.

51. Stebbing, p. 209.

52. Chambers, vol. 2, p. 206.

53. Guy, p. 451.

54. Foss, vol. 5, p. 182.

55. Howell, col. 1450.

56. *DNB*.

57. APC, vol. 32, p. 387.

58. Howell, col. 1426.

59. McClure, vol. 1, p. 129.

60. CSPD, vol. 281, 24, p. 72.

61. HMCS, vol. 11, pp. 353–54.

62. HMCS, vol. 11, p. 361.

63. McClure, vol. 1, p. 131.

64. Harrison, 1933, p. 292.

Chapter 13. Friend of Blundell

1. Prince, pp. 89–91.

2. APC, vol. 22, p. 89. Bonde had been Master of the Haberdashers' Company in 1587–88 and Lord Mayor of London.

3. Stow, p. 786.

4. Incledon, pp. 33–46.

5. In view of Popham's own central role in the formation of the Virginia Company (see chapter 19), it is intriguing that among the grantees of the Second Virginia Charter of 1609 were Captain John Blundell and Gorge Whitmoore, haberdasher.

6. Hoskins, p. 187.

7. Lady Ann Drury, daughter of Sir Nicholas Bacon. Her husband Sir Robert was a supporter of Essex, a soldier and another quarrelsome, ambitious man. The death of the Drurys' daughter Elizabeth in 1610 inspired Donne's *Anniversaries*.

8. John Jones, *Bishop Hall,* pp. 15–17. Hall became Bishop of Exeter and of Norwich, and wrote commendatory verses to the *Anniversaries.* Carey, pp. 101–4. Cholmley became Canon and Sub-Dean of Exeter Cathedral.

9. Snell, p. 88.

10. BC C.20.2. John Jones, *Balliol College,* p. 84.

11. They had been expressly forbidden by a Visitor's injunction in 1542.

12. Ibid., p. 80, p. 183.

13. Ibid., p. 85.

14. It appears from BC C.20.2 of 14 March 1602 that Popham was expecting the scholarships to be at both Emmanuel and Sidney, for the candidates for all three colleges are named. Perhaps it was Emmanuel's turning down the arrangement that caused Popham to think of establishing Fellowships at the two other colleges instead.

15. BC C.20.2. John Jones, *Balliol College,* p. 84.

16. Mahood, p. 58.

17. Dunsford, p. 342.

18. Cherry and Pevsner, p. 150.

19. Richmond, p. 17.

20. Cherry and Pevsner, ibid.

21. Richmond, p. 18.

Chapter 14. Cecil's Correspondent

1. HMCS, vol. 11, p. 243.

2. HMCS. vol. 11, pp. 297–98.

3. McClure, vol. 1, p. 126. Davies was readmitted to the Society in November 1601 after making an open apology to Martin. See also Arlidge, pp. 5, 77–80.

4. Williamson, p. 239; Arlidge, p. 5.

5. HMCS, vol. 12, p. 47.

6. Donald, p. 2 quotes Thomas Robinson, *Natural History,* 1709.

7. Donald, p. 366.

8. HMCS, vol. 12, p. 145.

9. and Lord Windsor. According to Donald, p. 3, copies of this report by George Bowes and Francis Nedham, a former agent of Walsingham, still exist.

10. Donald, p. 2, 42.

11. HMC 55, Var. Coll., vol. 7, Dunwich, p. 88.

12. Chant, pp. 14, 18.

13. HMCS, vol. 12, pp. 522–23.

14. Ibid., p. 2.

15. For a full account of the fascinating lives of Sherley, his father and two brothers see D. W. Davies.

16. Davies, p. 141.

17. CSPD, vol. 284, 78, p. 223.

18. HMCS, vol. 12, pp. 53–54.

19. CSPD, vol. 283, 6, p. 144.

20. Ibid., 86 II, p. 181.

21. Thomas Felton had been given a particular charge to discover the lands and goods of recusants.

22. Foley, p. 8. See also CSPD, vol. 274, p. 421.

23. Foley, p. 22.

24. CSPD, vol. 286, 14, p. 271.

25. Foley, p. 28.

26. Ibid., p. 30.

27. Foley, p. 427.

28. Ibid., p. 432.

29. CSPD, vol. 284, 72, p. 220.

30. HMCS, vol. 12, p. 314.

31. Elton, 1974, pp. 393–94.

32. HMCS, vol. 12, p. 314.

33. HMCS, vol. 12, pp. 314–15. Ellys's declaration, with details of the plot, is HMCS, vol. 12, pp. 366–67.

34. HMCS, vol. 12, pp. 332–33.

35. McClure, vol. 1, p. 160.

36. Nichols, 1823, vol. 3, pp. 593–94.

37. McClure, vol. 1, p. 172.

38. Chambers, vol. 3, pp. 500–501.

39. Foley, p. 38. The document referred to is CSPD James, vol. 7, 50, p. 99, and is endorsed by Cecil "A note of the Jesuits that lurk in England."

40. Foley, p. 49.

41. CSPD, vol. 285, 59, p. 263.

42. Foley, vol. 1, p. 52.

43. HMCS, vol. 12, pp. 499–500.

44. CSPD, vol. 287, 51, pp. 300–301.

45. Foley, vol. 1, p. 55.

46. CSPD, vol. 287, 12, pp. 284–85.

47. HMCS, vol. 12, p. 621.

48. Ibid., p. 199.

49. Ibid., pp. 652–53.

50. HMCS, vol. 15, p. 363.

51. HMCS, vol. 16, p. 165.

52. CSPD, vol. 287, 53, p. 302.

53. HMCS, vol 12, p. 671.

54. Ibid., p. 673.

Chapter 15. Ralegh's Opposite

1. Howell, vol. 2, col. 16.

2. Prest, p. 29.

3. Katherine Champernowne was sister to John, Richard's grandfather. Her children included the explorer Sir Humphrey Gilbert by her first marriage, and Ralegh by her second.

4. Fuller, p. 262.

5. Thompson, p. 28.

6. Ibid., p. 27.

7. NY Gilbert Holland Montague Collection 1307, reproduced in Latham and Youings, pp. 47–48.

8. Andrew Clark, vol. 2, p. 183.

9. TNA: PRO 30/34/1. This document, which has not hitherto been noted, is a copy of Sir Humphrey Gilbert's patent with amendments in Popham's hand. See chapter 5, pp. 66–67, and chapter 19, pp. 231, 232.

10. Rowse, 1959, p. 182.

11. APC, vol. 18, p. 387.

12. In 1593. APC, vol. 24, p. 119.

13. See chapter 9, pp. 106–7.

14. Thompson, p. 92.

15. Coote, p. 151.

16. In 1581 Popham had served as Second Justice at Lancaster. In 1601 he was appointed a Commissioner in the interim before Sir John Fortescue became Chancellor of the Duchy. Somerville, pp. 474, 396–97.

17. Nichols, vol. 3, pp. 624–26.

18. See chapter 10, p. 125.

19. HMCS, vol. 15, p. 11.

20. Stebbing, pp. 182–83.

21. HMCS, vol. 15, p. 111.

22. Latham and Youings, pp. 245–46.

23. HMCS, vol. 15, pp. 200–202.

24. Ibid., p. 216.

25. Edward Seymour, son of the Duke of Somerset, had suffered in prison for many years under Elizabeth for marrying Lady Catherine Grey, sister of Lady Jane. He was taken out of his country retirement to go on a diplomatic mission, negotiating peace with Spain. His son William later eloped with Lady Arbella Stuart.

26. Nichols, 1828, vol. 1, p. 256.

27. The ruins of Wolvesey Castle, in the center of Winchester, are open to the public.

28. Latham and Youings, p. 257–58.

29. The account of the trial quoted here and in the following pages is from Howell, vol. 2, cols. 1–35.

30. Arbella was herself present at the trial, and was able to speak to the court through Lord Admiral Nottingham: "The lady doth here protest upon her salvation, that she never dealt in any of these things; and so she willed me to tell the court." Howell, vol. 2, col. 23.

31. Thompson, p. 188.

32. Campbell says that while Attorney-General, Coke "perverted the criminal law to the oppression of many individuals; and the arrogance of his demeanour to all mankind is unparalleled" (p. 268). Coke was "hardened against all the dictates of justice, of pity, of remorse, and of decency" (p. 266). But as Chief Justice after Popham's death he became "entitled to the highest admiration," and was considered the most brilliant lawyer of that time. He was the only colleague to whom Popham left a gift in his Will.

33. Thee and thou, which were and still are used when referring to God, were also used to express disrespect. In *Twelfth Night* (1600–01) Shakespeare has Sir Toby advise Sir Andrew in his challenge to Cesario, "If thou thou'st him some thrice, it may not be amiss." See also Phillips, p. 76.

34. Presumably this was the reply to Ralegh's letter from Bagshot. See above, pp. 181–82.

35. Burghley.

36. BL Harleian 39/28 f 322. Howell simply says "Let not any devil persuade you."

37. Hariot remained a lifelong friend of Ralegh, visiting him frequently in the Tower. He saw the 1607 comet, afterward known as Halley's, from Ilfracombe, Devon, on 17 September, and noted sunspots. He gave algebra its modern form.

Hariot was a great advocate of smoking, which he had presumably acquired on his Virginia voyage, and one of its first European victims, for he died of a cancer of the mouth. Rukeyser, pp. 285–86.

38. Roe was born in 1581, attended Queen's College Oxford, was a soldier in Ireland and probably knighted by Essex. He served also in Holland and Russia, and died by 1608 of the plague. He was "an infinite spender," and Grierson suggests (p. lvi) that he and Jonson may have behaved so noisily at a performance of a masque that they were turned out by the Lord Chamberlain. This occasioned the poem, entitled *To Ben. Johnson, 6 Jan 1603*. It was formerly believed to be by Donne.

39. Ralegh was eventually released to make a further voyage to Guiana. He failed to find a gold mine and against the King's specific orders attacked a Spanish fort. On his return in 1618 Popham's death sentence was confirmed by the Lord Chief Justice, Sir Henry Montague, at that time owner of Kimbolton Castle.

40. Coote, p. 318.

41. Thompson, p. 228.

42. James soon needed an estate for his favorite Robert Carr, and Cecil suggested Sherborne. The king purchased the estate compulsorily in 1608, but Prince Henry, who was very close to Sir Walter, then demanded it for himself so that he could eventually return it to the Raleghs.

43. HMC 55, Var. Coll., vol. 1, Quarter Sessions in Wiltshire, p. 73. She appears again in 1605, HMC 55, vol. 1, pp. 77–78.

CHAPTER 16. DRAINER OF THE FENS

1. Albright, p. 51.
2. Darby, 1956, p. 13.
3. Albright, p. 51.
4. Ibid., p. 53.
5. Harris, p. 23.
6. Harris, p. 23. CSPD, vol. 244, 97, pp. 334–35.
7. Darby, 1956, p. 21.
8. Ibid.
9. 43 Eliz. Cap. 11, printed in Wells, vol. 2, pp. 34–38.
10. A. Hassell Smith, app. 1, p. 354. MacCulloch, app. 1, p. 396.
11. HMCS, vol. 10, pp. 201–2.
12. APC, vol. 30, p. 770.
13. Albright, p. 53, gives an example: the King owned the West Fen and "by an enclosure following the draining, conjured a revenue of £18 per annum into a return of some £600 a year."
14. Day, p. 51.
15. CUL MS EDR A8/1 f 100.
16. The use of experts from Holland is mentioned in a letter from Popham to Sir Thomas Lambert, evidently an Isle of Ely Commissioner of Sewers. CUL MS Dd v 3 ff 44–46.
17. Dugdale, p. 378.
18. Petition of 19 July 1604, CUL MS EDR A 8/1/f 88. Another petition of July 1605, ff 94–95 recommends local knowledge and small-scale draining.
19. CUL MS Dd v 3 ff 44–46.
20. Dugdale, p. 380.
21. Ibid.

22. Badeslade, p. 23.
23. Beaven, vol. 2, p. 176.
24. CUL MS EDR A8/1 ff. 96–101.
25. Darby 1983, p. 57, note 162.
26. CSPD, vol. 248, 102, p. 115.
27. Dugdale, p. 383.
28. CUL MS EDR A8/1 ff. 96–101.
29. Sir Thomas Fleming became Solicitor-General in 1595, had helped prosecute Essex's friends in 1601, was knighted 1603, and in 1604 appointed Chief Baron of the Exchequer. Later he helped try the Gunpowder Plot conspirators, and gave judgment in Bate's case. On Popham's death Fleming succeeded him as Lord Chief Justice of the King's Bench.
30. Sir William Romney or Rumney, a member of the Haberdashers' Company, had recently been Master of the Merchant Venturers and Deputy Governor of the East India Company.
31. CUL MS EDR A 8/1 f 100.
32. CUL MS EDR A 8/1 f 102. The letter follows the order of 13 July 1605.
33. The Old Bedford Level was eventually constructed between 1630 and 1638 by Vermuyden.
34. Badeslade, p. 24.
35. Dugdale, p. 384.
36. Ibid., p. 385.
37. HMCS, vol. 17, pp. 396–97.
38. HMCS, vol. 17, p. 435.
39. The glasshouses consumed wood, which became scarcer for the poor. TNA: SP14/19/47, CSPD James, vol. 19, p. 300.
40. Peyton (1544–1630), Governor of Jersey, had become by his marriage to Dorothy Beaupré (widow of Sir Robert Bell) a leading landowner at Outwell, the next village to Upwell. A soldier, he became recorder of Norfolk and Huntingdon and Lieutenant of the Tower, having charge of Ralegh in 1603. The prisoner's "strange and dejected mind" made him call for Peyton five or six times a day in his grief. In January 1604 Peyton is said to have been disgraced for entertaining intelligence between Cobham and Ralegh, "with whom his son was very intimate." *DNB.*
41. HMCS, vol. 17, p. 452.
42. Peyton (1579–1635) was at Queens' College, Cambridge, a man of literary tastes and friend of Sir Robert Cotton. He became Lieutenant of Jersey for his father in 1628.
43. HMCS, vol. 17, p. 452.
44. Badeslade, p. 24.
45. Ibid.
46. Badeslade, p. 25.
47. Ibid., pp. 24–25.
48. Miller and Skertchly, p. 12.

CHAPTER 17. JUDGE OF PLOTTERS

1. HMCS, vol. 17, pp. 620–21.
2. Fraser, p. 84.
3. HMCS, vol. 16, p. 35. Ironically, the Inns had a reputation for being ungovernable. See Elliot Rose, p. 65.

4. Fraser, p. 85.

5. HMCS, vol. 18, p. 75.

6. CSPD, vol. 7, 29, p. 95.

7. TNA: SP 14/216, pt. 2, 237.

8. Chaloner, b. 1561, naturalist, philosopher, and soldier, discovered alum in Yorkshire. He taught Robert Dudley (chapter 9) at Christ Church, Oxford, and was a great favorite of James I.

9. He later applied directly to Salisbury for a reward for his services. He wrote on 26 March 1606 saying that he had "discovered the mode of distilling the water of life, and of turning metals into gold. Begs that in compensation for his services in discovering villainous practices he may have a place that will bring him in money to supply his furnaces &c." CSPD, vol. 19, p. 305. See also HMCS, vol. 15, pp. 215, 393.

10. HMCS, vol. 16, p. 118.

11. Ibid., pp. 399–401.

12. Ibid., pp. 118–19.

13. Waugh, p. 117

14. HMC, vol. 55, vol. 3, p. 143.

15. Ibid., p. 141

16. Haynes, p. 42.

17. HMCS, vol. 17, p. 36.

18. Ibid., p. 162. Cecil had been appointed Viscount Cranborne in August 1604, and in May 1605 became Earl of Salisbury.

19. Ibid., p. 373.

20. HMCS, vol. 17, pp. 395–96.

21. Hamlet relates in act 5, scene 2 how he had used the same stratagem.

22. HMCS, vol. 17, p. 396. Popham had been ill in April and September 1604.

23. Ibid., pp. 408–9.

24. The letter is dated 6 August 1605, but this must be a mistake for 6 September. HMCS, vol. 17, p. 355. Popham was ill again on 11 September.

25. Fraser, p. 143.

26. HMCS, vol. 17, p. 418.

27. Fraser, p. 169.

28. TNA: SP 14/216, pt. 1, 6.

29. Northumberland (1564–1632) was interested in alchemy and astrology, and his performing experiments, thought to be magic, earned him this nickname.

30. Fraser, pp. 119–20.

31. TNA: SP 14/216, pt. 1, 9.

32. CSPD, vol. 16, 14, p. 240.

33. TNA: SP 14/216, pt. 1, 10. The letter was written on 5 November, and a note added on the following day.

34. Fraser, p. 108.

35. CSPD, vol. 16 [GPB 10], p. 240.

36. Ibid.

37. TNA: SP 14/216, pt. 1, 20.

38. TNA: SP 14/16/16.

39. Ibid.: SP 14/216/37.

40. CSPD, vol. 16 [GPB 54], p. 247. Owen was known as "The Welsh Intelligencer." Fraser, p. 72.

41. TNA: SP 14/216, pt. 2, 163.

42. CSPD, vol. 16, 100, p. 261.

43. Ibid., vol. 16 [GPB 113], p. 261.

44. HMCS, vol. 17, p. 505.

45. Ibid., vol. 17, p. 507.

46. TNA: SP 14/216, pt. 2, 122.

47. HMCS, vol. 17, p. 533.

48. An example can be seen in the record of the hearing of Richard Wenman on 3 December. TNA: SP 14/216, pt. 2, 141.

49. HMCS, vol. 17, p. 591.

50. Mockler, p. 19.

51. Fraser, p. 219.

52. *True and Perfect Relation,* p. 9.

53. Text and translation kindly provided by the Governor of the Tower of London, Major-General Geoffrey Field.

54. The words of the warrant for his arrest, quoted in Mockler, p. 15.

55. Sir Thomas Lake wryly observed in October 1606 that equivocation was "an older art than our Garnet's." HMCS, vol. 18, p. 331. See chapter 8, p 102.

56. Thomas Strange was examined on 6 December 1605. CSPD, vol. 17, 12, p. 267.

57. Caraman, 1964, p. 355.

58. Morris, p. 164.

59. Morris, pp. 164–65.

60. TNA: SP 14/216, pt. 2, 241–45.

61. Morris, p. 170. Garnet wrote in his Declaration of 9 March that "I had great reason to perswade myself, that no man living (one onely excepted) could touch me therein." Presumably the one person was Tesimond.

62. HMCS, vol. 18, p. 73. The letter is reprinted in *English Historical Review* 3 (July 1888): 510–19.

63. Caraman, 1964, p. 384.

64. HMCS, vol. 18, p. 107.

65. Ibid., p. 75.

66. TNA: SP 14/216, pt. 2, 216.

67. Caraman, p. 393.

68. *True and Perfect Relation.*

69. Ibid.

70. The Porter in *Macbeth,* act 2, scene 3, refers both to "a farmer that hang'd himself on the expectation of plenty" and "an equivocator, that could swear in both the scales against either scale, who committed treason enough for God's sake, yet could not equivocate to heaven."

71. Mockler, p. 20.

72. Jardine, 1857, pp. 268–70.

73. Ibid., p. 270.

Chapter 18. Acting Lord Chancellor

1. TNA: SP 14/141/19.

2. Stone, pp. 30–31, quotes Popham as illustrating a new trend among government officers, led by Burghley, to appreciate the value of statistics in understanding England's economic workings.

3. HL EL 2329.

4. HMCS, vol. 16, p. 215–17.

5. Dietz, p. 131.

6. HMCS, vol. 23, pp. 130–35.

7. CSPD, vol. 10, p. 179.

8. HMCS, vol. 17, p. 65.

9. Ibid., p. 174.

10. HMCS, vol. 17, p. 179.

11. Ibid., vol. 23, p. 209.

12. Ibid., vol. 17, p. 274.

13. Ibid., p. 419.

14. HMCS, vol. 17, pp. 467–68.

15. Coward, p. 139. Sackville was the distinguished joint author of *Gorboduc,* the first English tragedy, as well as being a most experienced statesman.

16. McClure, vol. 1, p. 243. James's favor to the Catholic Howard family was a threat to Cecil.

17. Coke was now Chief Justice of the Common Pleas.

18. Roger Wilbraham. Scott, p. 87.

19. Keir, pp. 181–82.

20. CSPD, Addenda, James I, vol. 37, pp. 457–58.

21. HMCS, vol. 24, p. 95.

22. HMCS, vol. 18, p. 120.

23. CPL Annals, vol. 2, pp. 141–43. Sir George Clark, pp. 155–56.

24. CPL Annals, p. 143.

25. Rowse, 1974, pp. 154–55.

26. GL MS 3400.

27. The original document appointing Popham, with half the seal remaining, is in the archives of the House of Lords, HLRO Parchment Collection, dated 30 March 1606.

28. The whole text is printed in JHL, vol. 2, pp. 404–8.

29. We think of a Bill becoming an Act, but at this time the words seem to have been interchangeable.

30. Scott, p. 83.

31. Lockyer, pp. 50–51, 168–73.

32. HMC 17, House of Lords, vol. 10, ns (1712–14), no 2924.

33. HMCS, vol. 19, p. 110. John Eldred, a tobacco merchant and presumably related to the Master of the Clothworkers' Company (chapter 16, p. 198), refused to pay the composition demanded by the farmers of tobacco duties and encouraged others not to pay. Tobacco merchants were as hostile to the new impositions as Levant merchants were to the new levy on currants. Dietz, p. 132.

CHAPTER 19. VIRGINIA PLANTER

1. C. E. Clark, p. 6.

2. See above, chapter 5, pp. 66–67.

3. HMCS, vol. 18, p. 173.

4. Rowse, 1959, p. 63.

5. Hill, p. 132.

6. 39 + 40 Eliz. Cap. IV, section 4, printed in Prothero, pp. 101–2.

7. APC, vol. 32, pp. 503–4.

8. Quinn, 1979, vol. 3, p. 357. Extracts from this book are reprinted by permission of the publisher, Palgrave Macmillan.

9. Rowse, 1959, pp. 94–95.

10. Edited by C. G. Petter, act 3, scene 3, pp. 60–61.

11. Sir Sidney Lee, p. 316.

12. Coote, p. 359.

13. Lee, p. 321.

14. Another theory is that the faces show a Green Man of the type common in medieval church carvings. See *All Saints, East Budleigh.*

15. Quinn and Quinn, p. 267, note 2.

16. Quinn, 1979, vol. 3, p. 370. *A True Relation,* by James Rosier, "a Gentleman employed in the voyage" was printed in London in 1605.

17. Ibid., pp. 371–72.

18. Ibid., p. 386.

19. Howe, p. 96.

20. Gorges, *Briefe Narration,* printed in Baxter, 1890, vol. 2, p. 8.

21. According to Burrage, vol. 1, p. 3.

22. Of Gorges's Indians, Nahanada was returned to his home country by Pring; Skicowaros accompanied the Popham expedition; and Maneddo went with Challons. Of Popham's, Saffacomoit went with Challons. What happened to Amoret is not known.

23. APC, vol. 32, p. 387. See chapter 12.

24. Preston, p. 139.

25. Sullivan, p. 73.

26. HMCS, vol. 18, p. 84. Cope was a politician and antiquarian who built the mansion in London now called Holland House. Hayes, who went on Sir Humphrey Gilbert's expedition of 1583, had written enthusiastically about Newfoundland and fishery prospects. Hakluyt was Prebendary of Westminster, a man with a passion for Geography whose writings on voyages of exploration had contributed to his preferment.

27. Quinn, 1974, p. 483. For Thomas Smith's involvement in the Essex rebellion, see chapter 12, p. 146.

28. C. M. Andrews, pp. 85, 89.

29. Quinn, 1979, vol. 3, p. 192. Gates, knighted at Cadiz, had afterward been at Gray's Inn. Somers had sailed twice to the Azores, had been a prominent buccaneer and was mayor of Lyme in Dorset. Wingfield we met briefly in Kimbolton (chapter 11); see p. 258. William Parker was another experienced sea captain, merchant, and mayor of Plymouth in 1601. Hanham had been at the Middle Temple and was Popham's grandson. For Hakluyt see above, n. 26; Popham, pp. 245–46; Gilbert, p. 247.

30. Quinn, 1979, vol. 3, p. xxi.

31. CColP, vol. 1. Printed in Quinn, 1979, vol. 5, pp. 191–96. The draftsman of the charter was Sir Edwin Sandys (1561–1629), admitted to the Middle Temple in 1590, a close associate of Popham and brother of Miles Sandys. It is not known why Popham and Gorges were not themselves named in the charter.

32. Quinn, ibid., pp. 199–200.

33. Latimer, 1900, p. 27.

34. Quinn, 1979, vol. 3, pp. 427–28.

35. Ibid., pp. 428–29.

36. HMCS, vol. 18, p. 133.

37. Ibid., pp. 133–34.

38. Quinn, 1979, vol. 3, p. 403.

39. HMCS vol. 19, p. 26.

40. Ibid., p. 47.

41. Ibid., pp. 155–56. Some of Challons's men broke bail and escaped, and others were suddenly released in 1608.

42. Gorges, *A Briefe Relation,* 1622, printed in Baxter, 1890, vol. 1, p. 205.

43. Macinnes, p. 71. Baxter, 1890, vol. 1, p. 205, fn 256, refers to his memorial in St Stephen's Church, Bristol. It includes the lines: "His painefull, skillfull traveles reach't as farre/ As from the Artick to th' Antarctick starre."

44. Baxter, 1890, vol. 1, p. 205.

45. Quinn, 1979, vol. 3, p. 424. Edward Harlow was Master of Ordnance in the Popham Colony.

46. Gorges, *A Briefe Relation,* 1658; Baxter, 1890, vol. 1, p. 205.

47. Strachey, p. 159.

48. Gorges, *Brief Narration;* Baxter, 1890, vol. 2, p. 11.

49. Quinn, 1979, vol. 5, pp. 198–99.

50. Mitchell or Michell was the son of Popham's sister Elizabeth.

51. Quinn and Quinn, pp. 332, 377, 391, 464.

52. Ibid., p. 377. Who bought what, and for whom, later became problematical.

53. Preston, p. 145.

54. Brown, vol. 1, p. 46.

55. This helpful explanation is given by Brown, p. 46, n. 2.

56. Popham left "twenty pounds to my Nephew Edward Popham with me in voyage five pounds to Thomas Oxnam my servant all the rest unto the above Lettice Maior whom I make my sole executrix." In a further note he adds "The halfe line blotted was mine own doing," which perhaps indicates something of his character. TNA: PROB 11/112/58.

57. According to F. W. Popham, p. 29.

58. Gorges was himself forty when he wrote this. He repeated it in later accounts, written in 1620 and about 1641, when he was well over seventy himself and certainly knew what it was to be old.

59. SC D/B/bw 1480 f4, f8.

60. F. W. Popham states that George was Sir John's brother, but no source is given. If we ignore Edward's contribution and take a loose interpretation of "nephew," we can make George a cousin of Sir John and a man of a similar age. But he cannot have been both Bridgwater merchant and voyager to Guiana.

61. Poole, Ballard, and Kidder, p. 26.

62. HMCS, vol. 19, pp. 141–42. Rowland Jones was appointed.

63. From the Dutch *vlieboot,* a broad-beamed craft of shallow draught with a square, built-up stern: a medium-sized cargo carrier. Friel, p. 34.

64. Quinn, 1979, vol. 3, pp. 451–52.

65. Brown, p. 80; Quinn and Quinn, p. 333.

66. *The Relation of a Voyage unto New-England.* The manuscript—a copy made after 1647 by William Griffith—is in Lambeth Palace Library, MS 806.2. Raleigh Gilbert also kept a journal, according to Purchas, but it has not survived. "Roome" was a common naval term, perhaps here meaning "near." Quinn and Quinn, p. 397.

67. Quinn, 1979, vol. 3, pp. 429–30.

68. Ibid., p. 447.

69. Bradford, 2000, p. 4.

70. Quinn, 1979, vol. 3, pp. 432–33.

71. Ibid., p. 434.

72. Brain, p. 4. The basis of this list is John Smith, 1624, book 6, p. 203.

73. D. Lloyd, p. 760.

74. Thayer, p. 67.

75. Strachey, p. 167. His compendium of 1612, *The Historie of Travell into Virginia Britania,* draws heavily on Davies, but includes some additional material. William Strachey was wrecked in the Bermudas in 1609 with Sir Thomas Gates, and wrote the famous account of the ordeal that became a source of Shakespeare's *The Tempest.*

76. Quinn, 1979, vol. 3, p. 435.

77. Strachey, p. 171. The pods of the milkweed have cotton-wool like seeds. Quinn and Quinn, 1983, p. 412, fn 7.

78. Ibid., pp. 170–71.

79. Ibid., p. 172.

80. Compiled for the second edition (1614) of his *Pilgrimage.* Purchas used sources that are now not available. Quinn, 1979, vol. 3, pp. 426–27, and see p. 243.

81. Quinn, 1979, vol. 3, p. 427.

82. Baxter, 1907, p. 4.

83. Strachey, pp. 172–73.

84. Friel, p. 32.

85. Strachey, p. 172.

86. F. W. Popham, p. 27.

87. HMCS, vol. 19, pp. 353–54.

88. Quinn, 1979, vol. 3, pp. 438–39. When Sir Humphrey Gilbert's patent was reassigned to Ralegh in 1584, it was John Popham who checked and revised the draft. See chapter 5, pp. 66–67.

89. HMCS, vol. 20, p. 109.

90. TNA: CO 1/1/16. Quinn and Quinn, pp. 452–55. Reprinted by permission of the publisher.

91. Quinn, 1979, vol. 3, pp. 440–41.

92. Ibid., p. 437.

93. Baxter, 1890, vol. 2, p. 16.

94. Smith, 1624, bk. 6, p. 203.

95. Baxter, 1889, p. 276.

96. Abbott, p. 65.

97. Baxter, 1899, p. 277.

98. Abbott, pp. 65–68. The story was first printed in Sullivan, 1795. The archeological evidence is that Raleigh Gilbert's house was burned before the colony ended, but the storehouse only afterward. Brain, p. 27.

99. Sir John Gilbert died 8 July 1608. Raleigh Gilbert married in 1615 and lived at Compton Castle, Marledon, Devon until his death in 1634. Bradford, 2000, p. 7.

100. Quinn, 1979, vol. 3, p. 426 says that the decision to abandon the settlement was made on 30 September 1608. Only "some old walles" remained when the site was visited by Samuel Maverick in 1624.

101. Gorges, *Brief Narration,* in Baxter, 1890, vol. 2, p. 16.

102. Brown, p. 104.

103. Rowse, 1959, p. 100.

104. Gorges died in 1647 at Ashton Court, Bristol, residence of his fourth wife, the widow of John Popham's friend Sir Hugh Smyth, the notorious Justice of the Peace.

105. Quinn, 1979, vol. 3, p. 426.

106. This has led the Wingfield family to claim that Edward Maria was the first President of the United States. Stratford, 2000, p. 15.

107. Barbour, p. 95.

108. Quinn, 1979, vol. 5, pp. 276–85.

109. The historical claims of the Popham Colony were debated in furious style in the *Boston Daily Advertiser* in 1866, reprinted in Poole, Ballard, and Kidder.

110. Somehow it was copied by the Spanish spymaster Zuniga, and a copy was filed away in the Archivo General de Simancas, not being rediscovered until 1888.

111. Brain, pp. 14–30.

112. Brain, p. 24.

113. Ibid., p. 27.

114. Bradford, 2002, pp. 4–6.

Chapter 20. Ghost

1. Hawarde, pp. 322–23.

2. Scott, pp. 98–99.

3. On one occasion he had supplied some to the French Ambassador's wife, who had spoken to him at the Tower, "the pale being down." HMCS, vol. 17, p. 480.

4. Lefranc, p. 680.

5. Hawarde, ibid.

6. George Wilson, vol. 3, pt. 6, p. 75.

7. Howell, vol. 2, col. 669.

8. Fuller, p. 25.

9. Howell, vol. 2, col. 1029.

10. CSPD Charles I, vol. 255, 44, p. 352.

11. HMCS, vol. 19, p. 216.

12. John Smith, book 6, p. 203.

13. D. Lloyd, p. 760.

14. Warre is mentioned on 5 May 1607 as deputy to his grandfather as Steward of the Court of the Marshalsey. Willson, p. 291.

15. TNA: STAC 8/163/26.

16. HMCS, vol. 19, p. 281.

17. Turner, pp. 517–20.

18. HMCS, vol. 19, p. 336. William Udall was constantly asking Popham and Cecil for payment for his services. See HMCS, vol. 15, p. 217, for instance.

19. Harrison, 1958, p. 93. Thomas Sackville, Lord Dorset, had a similarly grasping reputation.

20. Mathews, p. 76. Hemyock Castle was originally a Norman fortified manor house. The castle remained in Popham hands and was garrisoned by them in the Civil War for Parliament. On the Restoration, the manor became a farm and the castle was used as a stone quarry for other buildings. Parts remain, and the castle may still be visited on public holidays.

21. Mathews, p. 76.

22. Mathews, p. 77.

23. Tongue, p. 55. Reproduced with the permission of the publisher. According to this author, horses, like cats and dogs, are supposed to see ghosts; where horses fail to deal with supernatural troubles, oxen must be used. The stories were collected between 1906 and 1952.

24. Mathews, p. 78.

25. Tongue, p. 103.

26. Mathews, p. 78.

27. Thorne, 1955, p. 6.

28. Isaac, pp. 13–14.

29. Isaac, p. 14.

30. See Thorne, 1950, pp. 28–30.

31. Campbell, p. 229.

32. Humphreys, pt. 1, pp. 77–81. George Prowse, later of Kingston, near Yeovil. Squibb, p. 165.

33. The Syms family were relatives through the Horners. Halsway Manor, near Crowcombe, was a Stradling property.

34. In 1601 Popham wrote a letter from "my house at Aldersgate," which may well be the property referred to here. The land at Twynnyng in Gloucestershire can be identified: two fields named Popham on the tithe map of 1841 are now part of a market garden.

35. No records seem to remain of Popham's connection with Lincolnshire. Petwick is a farm in Oxfordshire, between Wantage and Stanford-in-the-Vale.

36. The manor of Sobbcomb, or Shapcomb, is in the hundred of Axminster in the deanery of Dunkeswell, five miles from Honiton.

37. John Mason or Masson had carried Popham's messages in 1588. See chapter 5, p. xx.

38. The great-nephew who had been on the Popham Colony expedition.

39. Brereton is mentioned by d'Ewes in 1581 in connection with the case of Arthur Hall. Michell was Popham's nephew and an adventurer in the Virginia voyage: Quinn, 1979, vol. 3, p. 453.

40. The plans are TNA: MPA 1/88.

41. BL 6120. b. 10.

42. BL 31512. b. 24.

43. BL 5805 f. 14.

44. But see Strong, vol. 1, p. 254. The portrait was acquired in 1931.

45. NPG 2405. Another portrait, NPG 478, probably does not portray Sir John; Strong, pp. 253–54. Strong also mentions three other pictures: another version of NPG 478, formerly at Serjeants' Inn; a seventeenth-century copy of the pre-1592 portrait; and a poor copy, on canvas, of the head and shoulders.

46. Fisher, pp. 33–35.

47. *Julius Caesar* (1599), act 3, scene 2, 81–82.

Bibliography

Abbott, John S. C. *The History of Maine.* Boston: D. B. Russell, 1875.

Akrigg, G. P. V. *Shakespeare and the Earl of Southampton.* London: Hamish Hamilton, 1968.

Albright, Margaret. "Entrepreneurs of Fen Draining in England." *Explorations in Entrepreneurial History.* Vol. 18 (1955), 51–64.

Allen, Gillian, and Robin Bush. *The Book of Wellington.* Buckingham, 1981.

All Saints, East Budleigh. 2d ed. East Budleigh, 1991.

Andrews, C. M. *The Colonial Period of American History.* New Haven: Yale University Press, 1964.

Andrews, K. R. *Elizabethan Privateering Voyages to the West Indies 1588–1595.* Cambridge: Cambridge University Press, 1964.

Arlidge, Anthony. *Shakespeare and the Prince of Love.* London: Giles de la Mare, 2000.

Bacon, Sir N. *The Official Papers.* Camden Society, 3^d Series, 26. London: Camden Society, 1915.

Badeslade, T. "The History of the Ancient and present State of Draining." *History of Ancient and Present State of Navigation.* London: L. Davis and C. Reymers, 1766.

Bagwell, R. *Ireland under the Tudors.* London: Longmans, 1885–90.

Baker, J. H. *The Order of Serjeants at Law.* London: Selden Society, 1984.

Banks, F. L. *Blundell's Worthies.* London: Chatto & Windus, 1904.

Bantock, A. *The Earlier Smyths of Ashton Court.* Bristol: Malago Society, 1982.

Barbour, P. L. *The Jamestown Voyages.* Cambridge: Cambridge University Press, 1969.

Barnes, Thomas Garden. *Somerset 1625–40.* London: Oxford University Press, 1961.

Baxter, James Phinney. *The Beginnings of Maine.* Portland, Maine, 1889.

———. *Sir Ferdinando Gorges and his Province of Maine.* Boston, Mass., 1890.

———. *The Chief Actors in the Sagadehoc Drama.* Portland, Maine, 1907.

Beaven, Alfred B. *The Aldermen of the City of London.* London, 1908.

Bellamy, John. *The Tudor Law of Treason.* London: Routledge & Kegan Paul, 1979.

Bindoff, S. T. *The House of Commons 1509–1558.* London: Secker & Warburg, 1982.

Black, J. B. *The Reign of Elizabeth.* 2d ed. Oxford: Clarendon Press, 1959.

Bradford, J. W. *Raleigh Gilbert.* Excerpt from a manuscript in progress: *The Popham Colony in Context.* 2000.

———. *A Study and Review of the Pinnace* Virginia's *Concept Design.* Maine's First Ship, 2002.

Brain, Jeffrey P. *The Popham Colony.* Salem, Mass.: Peabody Essex Museum, 2001.

Brown, A. *Genesis of the United States.* London: William Heinemann, 1890.

Bruce, John. *Diary of John Manningham.* London: Camden Society, 1868.

Burke, John. *Jowitt's Dictionary of English Law.* London: Sweet & Maxwell, 1977.

Burrage, Henry S. *Gorges and the Grant of the Province of Maine.* Portland, Maine, 1923.

Camden, William. *Annales.* 3d ed. 1635.

Campbell, John Lord. *Lives of the Chief Justices of England.* London: John Murray, 1849.

Caraman, P. *Henry Garnet.* London: Longmans, 1964.

————. *A Study in Friendship.* Saint Louis, Mo.: Institute of Jesuit Sources, 1995.

Carey, John. *John Donne Life, Mind and Art.* London: Faber, 1981.

Cecil, Algernon. *A Life of Robert Cecil.* London: John Murray, 1915.

Ceresano, S. P. "The Chamberlain's-King's Men." In *Companion to Shakespeare,* edited by D. S. Kastan. Oxford: Blackwell, 1999.

Chambers, E. K. *The Elizabethan Stage.* Oxford: Clarendon Press, 1923.

Chant, Katharine. *The History of Dunwich.* Suffolk: Dunwich Museum, 1974.

Cherry, Bridget, and Nikolaus Pevsner. *The Buildings of England, Devon.* 2d ed. London: Penguin, 1989.

Clark, Andrew, ed. *Brief Lives.* Oxford: Clarendon Press, 1898.

Clark, Sir George. *The Royal College of Physicians.* Vol. 1. Oxford: Clarendon Press, 1964.

Clark, C. E. *Maine.* New York: American Association for State and Local History, 1977.

Cockburn, J. S. *A History of English Assizes.* Cambridge: Cambridge University Press, 1972.

Collier, J. Payne, ed. *The Egerton Papers.* London: Camden Society, 1840.

Connor, R. D. *The Weights and Measures of England.* London: HMSO, 1987.

Cooper, C. H. *Annals of the University of Cambridge.* Vol. 2. Cambridge: Warwick & Co., 1843.

Coote, S. *A Play of Passion.* London: Macmillan, 1993.

Coward, B. *The Stuart Age.* 2d ed. London: Longman, 1994.

Cross, Claire. *Letters of Sir Francis Hastings.* Somerset Record Society, vol. 69. Frome: Somerset Record Society, 1969.

————. *The Puritan Earl.* London: Macmillan, 1966.

Cummins, John. *Francis Drake.* London: Weidenfeld & Nicolson, 1995.

Darby, H. C. *The Draining of the Fens.* 2d ed. Cambridge: Cambridge University Press, 1956.

————. *The Changing Fenland.* Cambridge: Cambridge University Press, 1983.

Dasent, A. I. *Speakers of the House of Commons.* London: John Lane, 1911.

Davies, D. W. *Elizabethans Errant.* Ithaca N.Y.: Cornell University Press, 1967.

Day, J. W. *History of the Fens.* London: George G. Harrap & Co., 1954.

Dietz, F. C. *English Public Finance 1558–1641.* New York: Century, 1932.

Dixon, W. Hepworth. "Kimbolton Castle." *Athenaeum,* no. 1732 (5 January 1861).

Donald, M. B. *Elizabethan Copper.* London: Pergamon, 1955.

Dugdale, Sir William. *The History of Imbanking and Draining of Divers Fens and Marshes.* London, 1772.

Dunning, Bob. *Bridgwater.* Exeter, 1992.

Dunsford, Martin. *Historical Memoirs of the Town and Parish of Tiverton.* Exeter, 1790.

Ellis, Steven G. *Ireland in the Age of the Tudors.* London: Longman, 1998.

Elton, G. R. *England under the Tudors.* London: Methuen, 1974.

———. *The Tudor Constitution.* 2d ed. Cambridge: Cambridge University Press, 1982.

Elworthy, F. T. *Some Notes on the History of Wellington.* Taunton, 1892.

d'Ewes, Sir Simonds. *The Journals of all the Parliaments during the Reign of Queen Elizabeth.* London, 1682.

Fisher, Arthur. "Sir John Popham's Portrait." *Devon Notes and Queries* 3 (1905): 33–35.

Foley, Henry. *Records of the English Province of the Society of Jesus.* Vol. 1. London, 1877.

Foss, E. *The Judges of England.* London, 1870.

Fox, F. F., ed. *Adams's Chronicle of Bristol.* Bristol: J. W. Arrowsmith, 1910.

Fraser, Antonia. *The Gunpowder Plot.* London: Weidenfeld & Nicolson, 1996.

Friel, I. "The Three-Masted Ship and Atlantic Voyages." In *Raleigh in Exeter,* edited by Joyce Youings. Exeter: University of Exeter, 1985.

Fuller, Thomas. *The History of the Worthies of England.* London: J. G., W. L., and W. G., 1662.

Gayley, C. M. *Shakespeare and the Founders of Liberty in America.* New York: Macmillan, 1917.

Gibson, William. "A Continuous Patrimony." *Proceedings of the SA and NH* 132 (1988): 181–85.

Graves, Michael A. R. *The Tudor Parliaments.* London: Longman, 1985.

Green, Emanuel. *Preparations in Somerset against the Spanish Armada.* London: Harrison and Sons, 1888.

———. "On the Levies in Somerset for Service in Ireland." *Proceedings of the SA and NH.* Vol. 27, pt. 2: 25–42. Taunton: J. F. Hammond, 1882.

Grierson, Sir Herbert. *The Poems of John Donne.* Oxford: Oxford University Press, 1933.

Grinsell, L. V. *History and Coinage of the Bristol Mint.* Bristol: City of Bristol Museum & Art Gallery, 1986.

Guy, John. *Tudor England.* Oxford: Oxford University Press, 1988.

Haigh, Christopher, ed. *The Reign of Elizabeth I.* Basingstoke: Macmillan, 1984.

Hall, Hubert. *Society in the Elizabethan Age.* London: Swan Sonnenschein, 1888.

Harlow, V. T. *The Discoverie of Guiana by Sir Walter Raleigh.* London: Argonaut Press, 1928.

Harington, Sir John. *A Breife View of the State of the Church of England.* London: For J. Kirton, 1653.

———. *Nugae Antiquae.* Edited by Thomas Park. London: Verner & Hood, 1804.

Harris, L. E. *Vermuyden and the Fens.* London: Cleaver-Hume Press, 1953.

Harrison, G. B. *An Elizabethan Journal.* London: Constable & Co., 1928.

———. *A Second Elizabethan Journal.* London: Constable & Co., 1931.

———. *A Last Elizabethan Journal.* London: Routledge & Kegan Paul, 1933.

———. *A Second Jacobean Journal.* London: Routledge & Kegan Paul, 1958.

Hartley, T. E., ed. *Proceedings in the Parliaments of Elizabeth I.* Leicester: Leicester University Press, 1981.

Hasler, P. W. *The House of Commons 1558–1603.* London: HMSO, 1981.

Hawarde, William. *Les Reportes del Cases in Camera Stellata.* Edited by W. P. Baildon. London, 1894.

Haynes, Alan. *The Gunpowder Plot.* Stroud: Sutton, 1994.

Healey, C. E. H. Chadwyck. *The History of West Somerset.* London: H. Sotheran & Co., 1901.

Herne, Samuel. *Domus Carthusiana.* London: T. R. for R. Marriott and H. Brome, 1677.

Hill, Christopher. *Liberty Against the Law.* London: Allen Lane, 1996.

Holdsworth, Sir William. *A History of English Law.* London: Methuen, 1903–72.

Hopwood, Charles Henry, ed. *Middle Temple Records.* London: Butterworth, 1904.

Hoskins, W. G. "The Elizabethan Merchants of Exeter." *Elizabethan Government and Society.* Edited by S. T. Bindoff, J. Hurstfield, C. H. Williams. London: Athlone Press, 1961.

Howe, Henry F. *Prologue to New England.* New York: Farrar & Rinehart, 1943.

Howell, T. B. *State Trials.* Vols. 1, 2. London: Longmans & Co., 1816.

Humphreys, A. L. *The Materials for the History of the Town of Wellington.* London: Henry Gray, 1889.

———. *The History of Wellington.* Part 1. London, 1908.

Hurstfield, Joel. *The Queen's Wards.* London: Longmans, Green & Co., 1958.

Incledon, Benjamin. *Donations of Peter Blundell.* Exeter, 1804.

Isaac, L. F. *The Parish Church of St John the Baptist, Wellington.* Wellington Museum Society, 1994.

Jardine, D. *Criminal Trials.* Vol. 1. London: Knight, 1832.

———. *A Narrative of the Gunpowder Plot.* London, 1857.

Johnson, Paul. *Elizabeth I.* London: Weidenfeld & Nicolson, 1974.

Jones, John. *Bishop Hall.* London: L. B. Seeley & Son, 1826.

Jones, John. *Balliol College: A History.* 2d ed. Oxford: Oxford University Press, 1997.

Jones, W. T. *The Elizabethan Court of Chancery.* Oxford: Clarendon Press, 1967.

Judges, A. V., ed. *The Elizabethan Underworld.* London. G. Routledge & Sons, 1930.

Keeton, George W. *Shakespeare's Legal and Political Background.* London: Sir Isaac Pitman & Sons, 1967.

Keir, D. Lindsay. *The Constitutional History of Modern Britain.* 8th ed. London: Adam & Charles Black, 1966.

Kelsey, Harry. *Sir Francis Drake.* New Haven: Yale University Press, 1998.

Kenny, Robert W. *Elizabeth's Admiral.* Baltimore: Johns Hopkins Press, 1970.

Kimbolton Castle, A Brief Guide. Kimbolton School.

Lacey, Robert. *Robert, Earl of Essex.* London, Weidenfeld & Nicolson, 1971.

Latham, Agnes, and Joyce Youings. *The Letters of Sir Walter Raleigh.* Exeter: Exeter University Press, 1999.

Latimer, John. *The Annals of Bristol in the Seventeenth Century.* Bristol: W. George's Sons, 1900.

———. *Sixteenth-Century Bristol.* Bristol: J. W. Arrowsmith, 1908.

Lee, Arthur Gould. *The Son of Leicester.* London: Victor Gollancz, 1964.

Lee, Sir Sidney. "The Call of the West, III: The American Indian in Elizabethan England." *Scribners Magazine* 42 (1907).

Lefranc, Pierre. *Sir Walter Raleigh, Écrivain.* Paris: Les Presses de L'Université Laval, 1968.

Littlecote, a History. Warner Holidays Ltd., 1997.

Lloyd, D. *The Statesmen and Favourites of England since the Reformation.* London, 1665.

Lloyd, Rachel. *Dorset Elizabethans.* London: John Murray, 1967.

Lockyer, Roger. *The Early Stuarts.* 2d ed. London: Longman, 1999.

Long, C. E., "Wild Darrell of Littlecote." *Wiltshire Archaelogical and Natural History Magazine* 4 (1858), 6 (1860); "The Littlecote Legend," 7 (1862).

Lyte, Sir H. C. Maxwell. "List of Escheators for the Counties of Somerset and Dorset." In *Collectanea ii,* edited by T. F. Palmer, London, 1928.

MacCaffrey, W. T. *Exeter 1540–1640.* 2d ed. Cambridge, Mass.: Harvard University Press, 1975.

MacCarthy-Morrogh, M. *The Munster Plantation.* Oxford: Clarendon Press, 1986.

MacCulloch, Diarmaid. *Suffolk and the Tudors.* Oxford: Clarendon Press, 1986.

McClure, Norman Egbert, ed. *The Letters of John Chamberlain.* Philadephia: American Philosophical Society, 1939.

McGrath, Patrick. *Papists and Puritans Under Elizabeth I.* London: Blandford Press, 1967.

———, ed. *A Bristol Miscellany.* Bristol: Bristol Record Society, 1985.

Macinnes, C. M. *A Gateway of Empire.* Newton Abbott: David & Charles (Holdings), 1968.

Mahood A. S. "Some Notes on Blundell's School." *Report and Transactions of the Devonshire Association* 84 (1952): 52–80.

Manning, J. A. *Lives of the Speakers.* London: E. Churton, 1850.

Mathews, F. W. "Tales of the Blackdown Borderland." *Somerset Folk Series* 13 (1923).

Maxwell, Constantia. *Irish History from Contemporary Sources.* London: G. Allen & Unwin, 1923.

Michell, George B. "Michell of Cannington." *Proceedings of the SA and NH* 73 (1927).

Miller, S. H., and S. B. J. Skertchly. *The Fenland Past and Present.* Wisbech, 1878.

Mockler, Anthony. *Lions under the Throne.* London: Muller, 1983.

Morris, John, ed. *The Conditions of the Catholics under James I: Father Gerard's Narrative of the Gunpowder Plot.* London, 1872.

Neale, J. E. *Elizabeth and her Parliaments 1559–1581.* London: Jonathan Cape, 1953.

Nichols, John. *The Progresses and Public Processions of Queen Elizabeth.* London, 1823.

———. *The Progresses of King James the First.* London: J. B. Nichols, 1828.

Nicholl, Charles. *The Creature in the Map.* London: Vintage, 1996.

Oman, Charles. *British Rings.* London: Batsford, 1974.

Osborne, Bertram. *Justices of the Peace 1361–1848.* Shaftesbury: Sedgehill Press, 1960.

Petter, C. G., ed. *Eastward Ho!* London: A. & C. Black, 1994.

Phillips, O. Hood. *Shakespeare and the Lawyers,* 1972.

Poole, W. F., E. Ballard, and F. Kidder. *The Popham Colony.* Boston, Mass., 1866.

Popham, Frederick W. *A West Country Family: the Pophams from 1150.* Sevenoaks, Kent, 1976.

Popham, Sir John. *Reports and Cases.* London, 1656, 1682.

Pound, J. F. *Poverty and Vagrancy in Tudor England.* London: Longman, 1971.

Powell, Rev. Arthur Herbert. *The Ancient Borough of Bridgwater.* Bridgwater: Page & Son, 1907.

Prest, Wilfrid, "Legal Education at the Inns of Court." *Past and Present* 38 (1967): 20–39.

Preston, R. A. *Gorges of Plymouth Fort.* Toronto: University of Toronto Press, 1953.

Prince, John. *Worthies of Devon.* Exeter: C. Yeo and P. Bishop's, 1701.

Prothero, G. W. *Select Statutes and other Constitutional Documents.* 4th ed. Oxford: Clarendon Press, 1913.

Quinn, David Beers. *The Elizabethans and the Irish.* Ithaca, N.Y.: Cornell University Press, 1966.

———. *England and the Discovery of America, 1481–1620.* London: Allan & Unwin, 1974.

———. *New American World.* Vols. 3, 5. London: Macmillan, 1979.

Quinn, David B., and Alison M. Quinn. *The English New England Voyages 1602–1608.* London: The Hakluyt Society, 1983.

Raleigh, Sir Walter. *The History of the World.* London: Printed for Walter Burre, 1614.

Richmond, Lucy. "From the Archive: Blundell's School, Tiverton, Devon." *SPAB [The Society for the Protection of Ancient Buildings] News* 10, no. 4 (1989).

Robbins, Michael. *New Survey of England—Middlesex.* London: Collins, 1953.

Robertson, J. Logie, ed. *The Poetical Works of Sir W. Scott*. London: H. Frowde, 1894.

Robertson, John M. *The Philosophical Works of Francis Bacon*. London: G. Routledge & Sons, 1905.

Rose, Edward. "Kimbolton Castle." *Illustrated London News* 94 (29 June 1889).

Rose, Elliot. *Cases of Conscience*. London: Cambridge University Press, 1975.

Rowse, A. L. *The Elizabethans and America*. London: Macmillan, 1959.

———. *Ralegh and the Throckmortons*. London: Macmillan, 1962.

———. *Simon Forman*. London: Weidenfeld & Nicolson, 1974.

Roy, Ian. "An English Country House at War: Littlecote and the Pophams." *War, Strategy and International Politics,* edited by L. Freedman, P. Hayes, and R. O'Neill. London: Oxford University Press, 1992.

Rukeyser, Muriel. *The Traces of Thomas Hariot*. London: Victor Gollancz, 1970.

Sacks, D. H. *The Widening Gate*. Berkeley: University of California Press, 1991.

Scott, H. C., ed. *The Journal of Sir Roger Wilbraham*. London: Royal Historical Society, 1902.

Seaby, W. A. "Wellington House." *Somerset Arch. Soc. Proceedings* 97 (1952): 152–59.

Sewell, M. *Charter-House*. London: M. Sewell, 1849.

Sharp, Buchanan. *In Contempt of all Authority*. Berkeley: University of California Press, 1980.

Shorrocks, Derek, ed. *Bishop Still's Visitation 1594 and The "Smale booke" of the Clerk of the Peace for Somerset 1593–5*. Taunton, 1998.

Smith, A. Hassell. *County and Court*. Oxford: Clarendon Press, 1974.

Smith, John. *The Generall Historie of Virginia*. London: For M. Sparkes, 1624.

Snell, F. J. *Chronicles of Twyford*. Tiverton: Gregory & Co., 1892.

Somerville, Sir Robert. *History of the Duchy of Lancaster*. London, 1953–.

Sotheby's Catalogue, *Littlecote,* 1985.

Southworth, John. *Shakespeare the Player*. Stroud: Sutton, 2000.

Spedding, James. *The Letters and the Life of Francis Bacon*. Vol. 2. London: Longman, 1862.

Squibb, G. D. *The Visitation of Somerset and the City of Bristol 1672*. London: Harleian Society, 1992.

Stratford, J. *From Churchyard to Castle*. Kimbolton School, 2000.

———, ed. *If you came this way*. Kimbolton School.

Stone, Lawrence. "Elizabethan Overseas Trade." *Economic History Review,* 2d Series, 2, no. 1 (1949): 30–58.

Stebbing, W. *Sir Walter Ralegh*. Oxford: Clarendon Press, 1891.

Strachey, William. *The Historie of Travell into Virginia Britania*. Edited by Louis B. Wright and Virginia Freund. London: The Hakluyt Society, 1953.

Strong, Roy. *Tudor and Jacobean Portraits*. London, 1969.

Stow, John. *Annales*. T. Dawson for T. Adams, 1615.

Strype, John. *Annals of the . . . Church of England*. Oxford, 1824.

Sullivan, James. *The History of the District of Maine*. Boston, 1795.

Thayer, Henry O. *The Sagadahoc Colony*. Portland, Maine, 1892.

Thompson, Edward. *Sir Walter Ralegh*. London: Macmillan, 1935.

Thorne, R. L. *The History and Antiquities of the Town of Wellington*. Wellington: R. L. Thorne, 1950.

———. *A Short History of Wellington Parish Church*. Wellington, 1955.

Thornton, J. W. *Colonial Schemes of Popham and Gorges*. Boston, Mass., 1863.

Tongue, R. L. Edited by K. M. Briggs. *Somerset Folklore*. London, 1965.

Trevor-Roper, Hugh. "Nicholas Hill, the English Atomist." *Catholics, Anglicans and Puritans: Seventeenth Century Essays*. London: Secker & Warburg, 1987.

A True and Perfect Relation of the whole proceedings against the late most barbarous Traitors, Garnet a Jesuite, and his Confederates, 1606.

Turner, Jane, ed. *The Dictionary of Art*. New York: Grove, 1996.

Vanes, J. *Bristol at the Time of the Spanish Armada*. Bristol, 1988.

Waldman, Milton. *Sir Walter Raleigh*. London: Collins, 1950.

Wardle, F. D., ed. *The Accounts of the Chamberlain of the City of Bath, 1568–1602*. Somerset Record Society, 38. Frome, 1923.

Warner, G. F., ed. *The Voyage of Robert Dudley to the West Indies*. London: Hakluyt Society, 1899.

Watkin, Bruce. *Medieval Wellington*. Wellington, 2000.

Waugh, Evelyn. *Edmund Campion*. London: Longmans, 1961.

Wells, Samuel. *History of the Drainage of the great Level of the Fens called Bedford Level*, 1830.

Whitlock, Ralph. *The Folklore of Wiltshire*. London: Batsford, 1976.

Williams, Penry. *The Later Tudors*. Oxford: Clarendon Press, 1995.

Williamson, J. B. *History of the Temple*. 2d ed. London, Murray, 1925.

Willson, David Harris. *The Parliamentary Diary of Robert Bowyer 1606–7*. Minneapolis, 1931.

Wilson, George, ed. *The Reports of Sir Edward Coke, Knt.* London: Rivington and Sons, 1777.

Wiltshire, Kathleen. *More Ghosts and Legends of the Wiltshire Countryside*. Melksham: Colin Venton, 1984.

Wingfield, Jocelyn R. *Virginia's True Founder.* Athens, Georgia: Wingfield Family Society, 1993.

Wood, Anthony à. *Athenae Oxonienses*. London: for Tho. Bennet, 1691.

Index

Page numbers in italics refer to illustrations.

abuses: financial, 30; in the church, 52, 53–54
Adams, William: *Chronicle of Bristol,* 41
Allison, Thomas, 205
Alsatia, 22
alum, 65, 253, 281 n. 33, 296 n. 8
Anderson, Sir Edmund, 62, 100, 103, 168, 171, 182; reports Armada, 68–70; in Ireland with JP, 78–80
Anne, Queen (wife of James I), 181, 204, 207, 208, 214, 261
Appellants, 169
Aragon, Katherine of, 136, 283 n. 4 (chap. 7)
Archangel (ship), 235
Archduke of Austria, 182, 183
Aremberg, Count, 181, 182
Armada, Spanish, 67, *69,* 79, 89, 94; arrival of, 68–70; destruction of, 80–81
Arundel, Philip Howard, 1st Earl of, 93, 101
Arundel of Wardour, Lord, 234
Atkyns, Richard, 197
Aubigny, Lord, 223
Aubrey, John, 19, 24–25, 27, 91, 176; *Brief Lives,* 22; on Darrell legend, 83, 87, 90

Babington, Anthony, 62–63
Bacon, Sir Francis, 54, 75, 262
Bacon, Sir Nicholas, 29, 33, 43
Bancroft, Richard, 94, 228
Barneby (priest), 165
Barnes, Mother, 85–87, 283 n. 8
Barrow, Henry, 101
Basset, Sir Robert, 125, 287 n. 45
Bath, 103, 125–26, 166
Baynham, Sir Edmund, 219

Bear (ship), 110
Bell, Sir Robert, 29–30, 32–33, 50, 278 n. 58, 295 n. 40
benefit of clergy, 284 n. 38
Berrio, Antonio de, 107–8, 112
Berry, John, 157
Berwick, Lord, 222
Biard, Père, 251, 255, 256
Biron, Charles, 151
Blackall, Christopher, 127
Black Dog of Newgate, The (Hutton), 116–18, *117*
Blount, Charles. *See* Mountjoy
Blount, Sir Christopher, 142, 143, 289 n. 16
Blundell, Peter, 152–55, 158
Blundell's School, 133, 153–58, 191, 220, 270
Bonde, Sir George, 152, 290 n. 2
Bonneville, Antony, 165
Borough, William, 68
Bradley, Humphrey, 194
Brereton, Sir Randall, 268, 303 n. 39
Bridges, Antony, 283 n. 8
Bridgwater, 17–18, 34, 50, 106, 121, 206; George Popham and, 245–46; JP and, 17, 18, 24, 119, 231, 269
Brief apology concerning the possession of William Somers, A (Darrell, John), 122
Briefe View of the State of the Church of England, A (Harington), 96
Brief Lives (Aubrey), 22
Bristol, 41, 106, 119, 166, 300 n. 43; coins issued by, 41–42; election of 1571, 28–29; and Newfoundland, 241; visit of Queen to, 40–41; restriction of trade in, 28–29, 31; and Virginia, 239, 240, 241
Bromley, Sir Thomas, 54, 64, 87, 89, 280 n. 28, 283 n. 16
Brooke, George, 180, 181
Browne, Robert, 101

Browne, Sir Valentine, 75, 78
Buckhurst. *See* Dorset, Thomas Sackville
Burghley, Thomas Cecil, Lord, 147
Burghley, William Cecil, Lord, 45, 129, 162, 176, 194, 281 n.13; invites JP to be Lord Chief Justice, 99; and Mary Queen of Scots, 63, 64; and Munster plantation, 73–76, 81, 281 n.13; and the Queen, 56, 62, 104
Burke, Lord, 98
Butler, David, 206–7
Butler, Samuel, 156

Cadiz, 118, 119, 135
Caesar, Sir Julius, 281 n.13, 285 n.5
Calvinists, 31
Cambridge, 138; dispute over enclosure, 123–24; Emmanuel College, 121, 155, 157, 198, 291 n.14; Queen's College, 295 n.42; Sidney Sussex College, 157, 158; Trinity College, 95; University Library, 199
Camden, William, 147, 148, 290 n.41
Campbell, Lord, 22, 24, 266, 293 n.32; *Lives of the Lord Chief Justices,* 12, 19
Campion, Edmund, 57, 58
Carey (Garnet's gaoler), 216
Carleton, Dudley, 128, 129
Carleton, George, 49, 52
Cartwright, Thomas, 32, 95
Cary (Carey), Sir George, 130, 177
Catesby, Robert, 143, 210, 211, 217, 219, 220
Catholics, Catholicism, 37, 43, 143, 145, 263; at Balliol, 21; at Court, 169–70; and Garnet's Straw, 219; at Inns of Court, 204; legislation against, 50, 55–56, 102; Mary Queen of Scots a focus for, 31; not eligible as undertakers in Ireland, 75, 135; persecution of, 170, 205; proposed settlements in America, 231–32; reasons for planning Gunpowder Plot, 203–4, 214; split within, 169; at St Peter's, York, 210; support of Fitzgeralds for, 72; a threat to the realm, 55, 170

Cavendish, Thomas, 109, 285 n.16
Cecil, Robert, 1st Earl of Salisbury, 106, 112, 163–65, 201, 223, 296 n.18; demands Champernowne's singer, 120; character, 159, 163, 225; and Cobham, 289 n.27; and Essex, 138; and Gunpowder Plot, 204, 206–18, 221; and Ireland, 82; and JP, 129, 159–62, 163, 207, 121, 128; letters from JP, 130, 150, 159–62, 167, 206–7; letters to JP, 150, 171–72, 207; and *Madre de Dios,* 178; offices held, 45, 124, 130, 261; portrait, *160;* Queen's respect for, 159; and Ralegh, 112, 178, 185, 191, 192; and trade, 224, 225–26; and Virginia, 237, 241, 242, 252–53, 262
Cecil, William. *See* Burghley, William Cecil
Chaderton, Dr, 155–56
Challons, Henry, 241–43, 262, 300 n.41
Chaloner, Sir Thomas, 109, 204–5, 244, 296 n.8
Chamberlain, John, 128, 161, 168, 169, 225
Champernowne, Richard, 37, 75, 51–52, 106–7, 174; and castrato slander, 119–20
Chancery Lane, 37, 106
Chapman, George: *Eastward Ho!,* 233–34
Charterhouse, 267, 284 n.42
Cholmley, Hugh, 156, 291 n.8
Chronicle of Bristol (Adams), 41
Chydley ("cosyn" of JP), 75, 281 n.13
Clark, Sir William, 168
Clarke, James, 26, 51, 155, 266, 268, 276 n.18; attacked by Richard Warre, 262–63
Clarke, William, (priest), 165, 180, 185
Clench, John, 171
Clifton, Sir John, 75, 281 n.13
cloth trade, 18, 50, 175, 228; JP and, 152–53, 222; at Norwich, 65, 223–24
Cobham, Henry Brooke, 8th Lord, 143, 179, 180–88, 289 n.27

coinage, 41–42, 221

Coke, Sir Edward, 100, 102, 165, 180, 198, 226; appreciation of JP, 261–62; autograph, *212;* bequest by JP to, 268; compliments councillors held by Essex, 149; and Crown finances, 222–26; his performance assessed, 52, 182, 293n.32; Queen visits, 150–51; prosecutes Garnet, 216–7, 218; prosecutes Gunpowder Plotters, 208, 214; prosecutes Lopez, 103; prosecutes Ralegh, 182–86, 191; Reports, 279n.9; and trade, 224, 225

Coles, John, 75, 281n.13

Constable, Sir William, 143, 289n.24

Cope, Anthony, 52

Cope, Sir Walter, 237, 299n.26

copper, 162, 226

Coppinger, Ambrose, 168

Cotton, Sir Robert, 198

Courtenay, Sir William, 125, 179, 287n.46

courts: Admiralty, 68, 106, 257, 277n.24, 282n.3; Chancery, 27; Common Pleas, 26, 44, 62; King's (Queen's) Bench, 26; Parliament, 216; Quarter Sessions, 28; Wards and Liveries, 45, 261. *See also* Star Chamber

Cradock, John, 210

Cresswell, Joseph, 206–7

Cromwell, Sir Oliver, 198, 244

Cuffe, Hugh, 81

Cure, Cornelius and William, 266

Darcy, Sir Edward, 180, 223

Darrell, John: *A Brief apology concerning the possession of William Somers,* 122

Darrell, William: affair with Lady Hungerford, 84–85; character of, 84, 87, 282n.3, 283n.12; alleged child-murder by, 83, 85–87, 135; correspondence with JP in Axford case, 87–88; employed by Walsingham, 89; extension of Littlecote, 91; and JP, 84–85, 87, 90, 283n.4 (chap. 7); legends relating to death, 89–90; makes Littlecote

over to JP, 89; reference to in *Rokeby,* 90

Davies, Sir John, (lawyer and poet), 161, 291n.3

Davies, Sir John, (supporter of Essex), 144–46, 289n.37

Davies, Joseph (informant), 204–5

Davies, Robert, 247, 248, 251, 256

Davis, Nevill, 242, 262

Davison, William, 64–65

Dee, Dr John, 176

de la Warr, Thomas West, 3rd Baron, 260

Digby, Master, 248, 252

Digby, Sir Everard, 211, 213, 214, 219

Donne, John, 118, 286n.13, 290n.7, 291n.8

Dorset, Thomas Sackville, 1st Earl of and 1st Baron Buckhurst, 130, 164, 225, 227, 263, 298n.15, 302n.19

Douai, 56

Drake, Sir Francis, 37, 50, 68, 120, 285n.16

Drury, Lady Ann, 156, 290n.7

Drury, Sir Robert, 128, 290n.7

Dudley, Anne (daughter-in-law of JP), 38, 93, 266

Dudley, Elizabeth, 93

Dudley, John, 93, 162

Dudley, Katherine, 121

Dudley, Robert. *See* Leicester, Robert Dudley

Dudley, Sir Robert (explorer), 118, 178, 285n.15, 285n.22; and Guiana expedition, 109–12, *111*

Dunwich, Suffolk, 162

Durham House, 175, 178, 180, 182, 188

dyeing, 222, 223

Eastward Ho! (Jonson, Chapman and Marston), 233–34

Ecclesiastical Commission, 94–95, 122

Egerton, Sir Thomas: Attorney-General, 100, 104, 122, 127–28, 164; and Durham House 180, 164; and Essex, 139, 142–64; and Gardeners' Company, 227; on JP, 262;

Lord Chancellor, 227, 229; Lord Keeper of the Great Seal, 130; portrait of at JP's chambers, 100, 284 n.30; entertains Queen, 168; Solicitor-General, 56, 61, 75, 95

El Dorado, 105, 107–8, 110, 112, 194, 231

Eldred, John, 198, 199, 240, 298 n.33

Elliot, Captain, 129

Elliott, Thomas, (informant), 213

Elizabeth, Princess, 211

Elizabeth I, Queen of England, 24, 37, 66, 67–68, 89, 93; visits Bristol, 40–41; and Catholics, 55, 72; and Cecil, 138; and commerce, 128; death, 172–73; dislike of *Richard II,* 141; and Essex, 118, 131, 138–39; 141–42, 148; excommunication of, 30; and fen drainage, 194; visits Friars, 104; funeral procession, 37, 178–79; and Ireland, 78; and JP, 40, 44, 47, 54, 129, 130; rebukes JP, 48–49, 221–22; libels against, 50, 60, 131; proposed visits to Littlecote, 92, 149, 166–68, 150; and Lopez, 103; and Mary Queen of Scots, 31, 61, 64, 65; and matters of justice, 128; and money, 30, 74, 106, 119; and Parliament, 29, 31, 42, 48–50, 54; and priests, 165, 213; and Ralegh, 63, 108, 174–76, 178; and religion, 32, 52, 57, 58–59, 96; and the succession, 29, 61–62

enclosure, 122–24, 193

England, Enterprise of, 60

equivocation, 102, 215, 219, 297 n.55, 297 n.70

Essex, Frances, Countess of, 145–46

Essex House, 142–49, 236

Essex, Robert Devereux, 2nd Earl of, 97, 103, 124, *139,* 163, 289 n.22; affection of James I for, 179; at Cadiz, 118; compared with Cecil, 138; character of, 138–39; enemies of, 176; execution, 148; and Gorges, 141–42, 146–47, 149, 236; and Ireland, 125, 131, 135; rebellion, 138–49, 181, 185–86, 188, 289 n.29; returns to England 131,

138–140; rivalry with Ralegh, 138, 178; Shakespeare's view of, 138

Exeter, Devon, 65–66, 102–3, 125, 240–41, 256

Falcon (ship), 174

Fawkes, Guy, 208–11, 214, 218, 219, 220; autograph, *212*

Felton, 165, 291 n.21

Fen drainage, *190,* 193–202, *196,* 295 n.33, 294 n.13, 294 n.16; anxiety of Commissioners concerning, 197, 199–200; controversy over, 194–95, 197, 202; JP undertaker for, 200–202; Londoners' Lode, 194; Popham's Eau, 200–202

Fenner, Sir Edward, 171

Fens, 18, 193

Fetyplace, George, 32

First Part of the Life and Reign of Henry IV, The (Hayward), 140

Fitgerald of Desmond, Gerald, 14th Earl of Desmond, 73, 177

Fitzgerald of Desmond, James Fitz-Maurice, 72

Fitzwilliam, Sir William, 79

Fleming, Sir Thomas, 199, 295 n.29

Flowerdewe, Edward, 32

Ford, Thomas, 51

Forman, Simon, 227

Fortescue, Sir John, 37, 100, 128, 130, 293 n.16; and the Queen, 37, 104, 166; and Wellington, 37, 278 n.15

Fort St. George, 249, 251–52, 254–55, 256, 258, *259*

Friars (Friern), 100, 104

Frobisher, Martin, 41

Fuller, Nicholas, 228

Fuller, Thomas, 12, 19, 22, 148, 262

Games, Amy. *See* Popham, Lady Amy

Gardeners' Company, 227

Garnet, Henry, 27, 127, 165; contrast with JP, 27; emerges from hiding, 214–15; and equivocation, 215; examined by JP and Coke, 216–17, 297 n.16; execution, 219; Garnet's straw, 219–20; hears rumor of JP's death, 101; opinion of JP, 127,

129, 146; suspect in Gunpowder
  Plot, 210, 214; trial, 218–19
Gates, Sir Thomas, 237, 299n.29
Gawdy, Sir Bassingbourn, 129
Gawdy, Sir Francis, 171, 183
Gawen, Katherine, 192
Generall Historie of Virginia (Smith),
  262
Gerard, John, 210, 211, 214, 216–17
Gift of God (ship), 246–48, 253–54,
  257
Gilbert, Raleigh, 237, 239, 301n.99;
  admiral of Popham Colony,
  247–50, 253; in command, 256–57,
  258, 260
Gilbert, Sir Humphrey, 37, 71, 82,
  174, 247; his patent for Virginia,
  67, 292n.3, 292n.9, 301n.88
Gilbert, Sir John, 150, 301n.99
Globe, (theater), 126, 141–42
Golden Hind (ship), 37
Golden Lion (ship), 68
Goldesborough, John, 269
Gorges, Sir Ferdinando: 142,
  301n.104; character, 236; and
  Essex rebellion, 141, 146, 147,
  148–49, 289n.20; founder of
  Maine, 257; friend of Ralegh, 142;
  partner with JP in coloniza-
  tion,149, 236–37, 240–45, 247,
  299n.31; receives native Ameri-
  cans, 234–36; reinstated at Ply-
  mouth fort, 236; takes over
  promotion of Popham Colony,
  252–53, 255, 257
Gosnold, Bartholomew, 233
Grant, John, 210
Greenwich Palace, 100, 131, 198
Gregory XIII, Pope, 55, 60
Grenville, Sir Richard, 78, 93, 177
Gronno, Geoffrey, 164
Guiana, 107–8, *111;* Dudley's expedition to, 109–12; Ralegh's expeditions to, 108, 109, 112, 178,
  185, 294n.39. *See also* Popham,
  George
Guildhall, 103, 218; Library, 227
Gunpowder Plot (Powder Treason),
  204, 208–14, *212;* Garnet and,
  214–220
gypsies, 19, 22

Hacket, William, 95–96
Hakluyt, Richard, 237, 299nn.26 and
  29
Hale, Arthur, 164
Hall, Arthur, 50, 303n.39
Hall, Hubert, 43, 84, 282n.3; *Society
  in the Elizabethan Age,* 12, 52
Hall, Joseph, 155–56, 191, 220,
  291n.8
Hamond, William, 104
Hammond, John, 68
Hanaper, 32
Hanham, Anne or Amy (granddaugh-
  ter of JP), 35, 120
Hanham, John (grandson of JP), 121
Hanham, Thomas (son-in-law of JP),
  35, 44, 59, 77, 120–21, 278n.8
Hanham, Thomas (grandson of JP),
  35, 121, 287n.24; and Virginia,
  237, 239, 240, 243
Harding, George Perfect, 270
Harington, Sir John, 97, 284n.18; *A
  Briefe View of the State of the
  Church of England,* 96
Hariot, Thomas, 176, 188, 213, 236,
  293n.36, 293n.37
Harlow, Edward, 243, 248, 300n.45
Hartopp, Mr., 26, 276n.20
Harvard Law School, 269
Hastings, Sir Francis, 119, 121,
  287n.26
Hatton, Sir Christopher, 49, 60, 61,
  64, 76, 176
Havercombe, John, 246, 248, 257
Hawarde, William, 261
Hayes, Edward, 237, 299n.26
Hayward, John: *The First Part of the
  Life and Reign of Henry IV,* 140
Hele, Serjeant, 182
Henri IV, King of France, 232
Henry VIII, King of England, 17, 21,
  83, 136
Henry, Prince, 204, 207, 214, 261,
  294n.42
Herberdt, Sir John, 205
Herbert, Sir William, 81–82
Hertford, Edward Seymour, 1st Earl
  of, 166, 168, 181, 293n.25
Hertford, Frances Howard, Lady, 227
Hext, Edward, 114
Hill, Henry, 128

Hill, Nicholas, 125, 287 n.44
Hippesley, John, 43
History of the World (Ralegh), 191
Horner, John (grandson of JP), 121, 268
Horner, John (Little Jack), 35, 44, 68
Horner, Thomas (son-in-law of JP), 35, 126
Hospital of Sir John Popham, Knight. *See* Popham Hospital
Howard of Effingham, Charles Howard, 2nd Baron (also 1st Earl of Nottingham), 68, 118, 130, 165
Hungerford, Lady Anne, 84–85
Hungerford, Sir Walter, 84–85
Hunt, John (draftsman), 248, 258, *259,* 260
Hunt, Mr (draining engineer), 198, 199, 200
Huntingdon, Henry Hastings, 3rd Earl of, 121
Huntworth, Somerset, 17, 18, 24, 25, 276 n.7
Hutton, Luke: *The Black Dog of Newgate,* 116–18, *117*

imposition, 225–26, 298 n.33
Inner Temple, 65, 97
Instrument of Association, 67–68
Ireland, *72;* base for Catholic campaign, 59; cost of the wars in, 165, 167; new currency for, 163; defeat of Tyrone, 135; English soldiers in, 72–73; Essex in, 131, 138; JP visits, 69–70, 79; Ralegh in, 73, 75–79, 177; settlement of Munster, 71–82, 236; Spanish ships wrecked in, 80–81

James I, King of England, 178, 203, 204; accession, 293; admired by native Americans, 251; attitude to Ralegh, 179; enthusiasm for fen drainage, 193, 195–96, 197, 198; dislike of tobacco, 230, 179; and Essex, 179; and Garnet, 218; George Popham's letter to, 254–55; at Gunpowder Plot trial, 214; JP communicates with concerning plots, 203–4; visits Littlecote, 181; against papists, 203–4;

in Parliament, 227; and purveyance, 228; and religious activists, 203; grants Sherborne to Lady Ralegh, 192; and Virginia Company, 237; weary of JP, 207
Jamestown, 237, 245, 247, 258, 260
Jegon, John, 123–24, 287 n.37
Jesuits, 55–57, 101, 125, 169–70, 280 n.7; dangerous doctrines of, 102, 215; Gunpowder Plot, 204, 214; and plots of, 203, 204. *See also* Garnet, Henry
Jones, John (priest), 127
Jones, Rowland, 246
Jonson, Ben, 93, 294 n.38; *Eastward Ho!,* 233–34
Justice of the Peace, 38–39, 114, 123, 177; JP as, 38, 119, 132

Kennebec, River, (Sagadehoc, River), 245, 248–50, 254, 257, 262
Keyes, Robert, 209
Kildare, Gerald Fitzgerald, 11th Earl of, 73
Kimbolton, Huntingdonshire (now Cambridgeshire), 136, 269; legends concerning JP, 132, 135–36; JP purchases windmill at, 136; portrait of JP at, 132, *134;* School, 135, 136; Wingfields of, 75, 258
Kingsmill, George, 171
Knevett, Sir Henry, 85
Knollys, Sir Francis, 46
Knollys, Sir William, 130, 142–43, 149

Lambert, Sir Thomas, 197, 294 n.16
Lancaster, Duchy of, 178, 293 n.16
land reclamation. *See* Fen drainage
legislation: concerning Bristol, 31; against Catholics, 50, 55–56, 102, 180; for cloth trade, 50, 152–53; discussed in JP's acting Chancellorship, 227–29; for enclosing the Fens, 195, 197, 198, 199; against gypsies, 19; discussed in Parliament of 1581, 50, 52–54; for the poor, 114; against priests, 56, 102, 169; against recusants, 56, 96, 102; concerning rites and ceremonies, 32; against rogues, 115;

for the subsidy, 30; against treason, 31; against vagrancy, 232–33
Leicester, Robert Dudley, Earl of, 56, 57, 93, 109
Levant, 221, 224–25
Levermore, John, 102–3
Levermore, Mrs, 65
"Limbo," 117–18, 166
Lincoln's Inn, 168
Line, Anne, 165–66
Littlecote, Wiltshire, 88, *133,* 282 n.1, 282 n.2; alleged child-murder at, 88, 135; JP's contribution to house, 91; legends relating to, 89–90, 132; proposed visits of Queen to, 149–50, 166; visit of King to, 181
Lives of the Lord Chief Justices (Campbell), 12, 19
Lloyd, David, 12, 19, 262
Lopez, Dr, 103–4
Lord Chamberlain's Players, 141–42, 148
Lundy Island, 125

Madre de Dios (ship), 106
Maine, 231, 239, 257, 258, 270. *See also* Popham Colony
Malet, Sir John (son-in-law of JP), 38, 244
Manners, John, 63
Manningham, John, 100
Marlowe, Christopher, 176
Marprelate Letters, 102
Marston, John: *Eastward Ho!* 233–34
Martin, Richard, 161
Mary and John (ship), 247–48, 251–52, 255
Mary, Queen of England, 24, 58, 135
Mary, Queen of Scots, 31, 32, 55, 61, 101, 103; and Babington Plot, 62; claim to throne, 60, 280 n.14; execution, 64, 65; and Throckmorton Plot, 60; tomb, 266; trial, 63–64
Mathews, Walter, 241
Medina Sidonia, Duke of, 81
Merchant Venturers, 28–29, 31, 152, 295 n.30
Merrick, Sir Gelly, 142
Michell, Sir Bartholomew (nephew of JP), 244, 268, 303 n.39

Michell, Sir Richard, (brother-in-law of JP), 25, 34
Middle Temple, 27, 93, 121, 206, 268, 285 n.16; coats of arms of JP and Ralegh at, 192, *189;* Commons committees at, 51; JP admitted to, 21–22; JP chambers at, 26, 51; JP Reader at, 26; JP Treasurer of, 51; Martin quarrel, 161; meetings concerning Virginia at, 237; Ralegh at, 174; *Twelfth Night* performed at, 161
Mildmay, Sir Anthony, 136, 198
Mildmay, Sir Walter, 155
Milwarde, Mr, 152
mines, mining, 162, 221, 226, 231, 240, 291 n.9 (chap. 14)
Miscellany (Tottel), 27
Mission, English, 57, 59
Monck, Levinus, 263
monopolies, 28–29, 31, 223–24, 232; opposition of JP to, 208
Montacute, 38
Montague, Sir Edward, 213
Montague, Sir Henry, 209, 240, 288 n.8 (chap. 11)
Monteagle, William Parker, 1st Baron, 142, 208
Morris, William, 158
Morrys, James, 206
Mountjoy, Charles Blount, 8th Baron 135, 166
Munden, John, 59
Munster Plantation, 71–82; Commission at Cork, 79–80; conduct of undertakers, 81–82; JP promotes, 73–75; JP an undertaker in, 75–78

National Archives, The, 57, 75
National Trust, The, 38
native Americans: first visitors to England, 234; captured by Waymouth expedition, 234–36; return voyages of, 241, 242, 243, 299 n.22; in Virginia, 233, 247–51, 255, 256; carvings depicting, 234, 299 n.14
New Inn, 26
Newport, Christopher, 245
New York Public Library, 176
Nonsuch Palace, 129
Norfolk, Duke of, 31

Norreys, Thomas, 76, 282n.20
North, Sir Roger, 130
Northampton, Marquess of, 126
Northern Rising, 30, 277n.46
Northumberland, Henry Percy, 8th
    Earl of, 60
Northumberland, Henry Percy, 9th
    Earl of, 125, 209, 211–13, 296n.29
Northwest passage, 231, 234, 242,
    254
Norumbega, 231, 236, 239
Norwich, 33, 65, 224
Nottingham, Charles Howard, 1st
    Earl of. *See* Howard of Effingham
Nugent, William, 73

oath *ex-officio,* 94–95
Offeild, Roger, 198
Of the Use I made of the Natives
    (Gorges), 235
Oldcorne, Edward, (Father Hall),
    216–17, 219
O'Neill, Hugh. *See* Tyrone
O'Neill, Shane, 71
Orchestra (Davies), 161
Orinoco, River, 107, 110–112, 178
Osterley, 99, 284n26
Owen, Hugh, 211, 296n40
Oxford, Edward de Vere, 17th Earl
    of, 128
Oxford, 145, 207, 228; Balliol Col-
    lege, 21, 157, 158; St John's Col-
    lege, 57, 96, 287n.44; other
    colleges mentioned: Oriel, 174; St
    Mary's Hall, 188; Corpus Christi,
    157; Christ Church, 109; Queen's,
    294n.38

Page, Francis, 165–66
Pale, The, 71
Parker, William, 237, 239, 299n.29
Parliament: committees of, 30–31, 42,
    51, 194, 229; JP a Member of, 24,
    29, 277n.49; JP as Speaker, 46–47,
    48, 52; session of 1571, 29–31; ses-
    sion of 1572, 31–32; session of
    1576, 42; session of 1581, 46–54;
    session of 1607, 227–29
Parsons, Robert, 57, 58, 165, 280n.7
Pembroke, Henry Herbert, 2nd Earl
    of, 66, 181, 229

Penelope (ship), 247
Penry, John, 102
Percy, Sir Charles, 141–42, 288n.10
Percy, Thomas, 209, 210, 211
Periam, Sir William, 102, 103, 171,
    177, 287n.45
petronel, 67, 281n.42
Peyton, Sir John (the elder), 201,
    295n.40
Peyton, Sir John (the younger),
    201–2, 295n.42
Phelips, Sir Edward, 38, 278n.17
Philip II, King of Spain, 31, 55, 60,
    107, 118
Phillipps, Augustine, 141–42, 288n.11
Physicians of London, College of,
    226–27
Pilgrimage, Purchas his (Purchas),
    243, 251
Pilgrim Fathers, 102, 258
piracy, 66, 70, 105. *See also* priva-
    teering
Pius V, Pope, 55
plague, 100, 181, 207, 218
plots: Ridolfi, 31; Throckmorton, 60;
    Babington, 62; Basset, 125; re-
    vealed by John Ellys, 167; Bye or
    Surprise, 180, 182, 184, 203;
    Main, 181, 203; of Jarrett, 203.
    See also Gunpowder Plot
Plowden, Edmund, 52
Plymouth (Devon), 109, 141, 235,
    254; branch of Virginia Company,
    239–40, 245, 247, 257; rivalry with
    Bristol, 241
Pole, William (nephew of JP), 34,
    125, 268, 287n.45
Pole, William, (brother-in-law of JP),
    34
poor, the, 65, 114, 266–67, 268–69; in
    the Fens, 193, 199, 201
Popham, Agnes de, 276n.2
Popham, Alexander (father of JP),
    17, 24, 194, 266, 276n.3, 276n.7
Popham, Alexander (nephew of JP),
    119, 245
Popham, Alexander (1669–1705), 136
Popham, Lady Amy (wife of JP), 21,
    24, 34, 223, 257, 264; and royal
    visits, 104, 150, 166, 181; in JP's
    will, 266, 267–68; effigy, *190*

Popham Beach, 258, 270

Popham Colony, 82; archaeological findings, 259–60; Capt. Davies returns, 251; death of President, 255; destruction of fort, 256, 301 n.98; effects of Gilbert's leadership, 256; expedition sets out, 247; Fort St George constructed, 249, 252; George Popham's kindliness toward natives, 250–51; *Gift of God* returns from, 253–54; historical claims of, 302 n.109; Hunt plan of Fort St George, 258, *259, 302* n.110; *Mary and John* returns from, 252; names of settlers, 248; pinnace *Virginia,* 249, 252, *259,* 260; relations with natives, 249–50; settlers return, 257, 301 n.100

Popham, Edward (brother of JP), 17, 24, 25, 34, 276 n.6

Popham, Edward (nephew of George Popham), 245, 268, 269

Popham, Elinor (daughter of JP), 25, 35, 268

Popham, Elizabeth (sister of JP), 17, 34

Popham, Elizabeth (daughter of JP), 25, 37, 120, 174, 268

Popham, Ferdinando (nephew of JP), 34, 66, 105, 268, 285 n.3

Popham, Frances, 17, 34

Popham, Sir Francis (son of JP), 25, 37, 93, 136, 162, 227; depicted on JP's monument, 266; feoffee of Blundell's School, 155; heir of JP, 266, 268, 282 n.30; knighted by Essex, 118; marriage, 93, 283 n.2; MP, 118; and Virginia Company, 240, 244, 252, 257, 300 n.52; and wardship, 222–23; writes to JP concerning Ralegh, 179

Popham, George (nephew of JP), 243, 300 n.56; Captain in Ireland, 59, 73; character, 250–51, 253, 254–55, 300 n.56, 300 n.58; death, 255–57; and Guiana, 107–13, 178; kinship with JP, 245–46, 276 n.1, 280 n.12, 281 n.13, 300 n.60; letter to King, 254–55; privateer, 34, 105–6; and Spanish letters, 107–9;

undertaker in Munster, 76, 78; and Virginia, 113, 231, 239–57

Popham Hospital (almshouse), Wellington, 39, 104, 266–67, 269, 270

Popham, Jane (daughter of JP), 25, 35, 93

Popham, Jane or Joan (mother of JP), 17, 266

Popham, Sir John (JP): birth 17, 276 n.6; and gypsies, 18–19, 115–16; at Oxford, 21; marriage, 21; at Middle Temple, 21–26, 51, 91, *189,* 279 n.15; highwayman, 22, 24; acquires property 25, 32–33, 37, 44–45; family man, 34, 35, 93, 120–21, 272, 278 n.16; and Wellington, 34–35, 38–39, 91; and Parliament, 24, 29–32, 42, 194, 229, 277 n.49; rapid promotion, 43–44; health, 45–46, 207, 213, 296 n.22, 296 n.24; Speaker of the Commons, 46–54; and Queen Elizabeth, 37, 40, 49, 104, 129, 130; prosecutes in treason trials, 56–63, 280 n.28; and prosecution of Mary Queen of Scots, 63–65; and trade and finance, 66, 97, 128, 162–63, 221–26; and Armada, 67–68, *69,* 80–81; and Ireland, 69–82, 163, 282 n.44; undertaker in Munster, 72–78, 282 n.30; and Littlecote, 83, 90–92, 149–150, 167–68, 181, 282 n.2; and William Darrell, 84–85, 87–90; Lord Chief Justice, 99–101, 114–19, 122–29; and religious dissent, 94–96, 101–2, 127, 165–66, 169–171; promotes privateer, 105–6; and Guiana, 108, 109, 113; Privy Councillor, 130, 131; and Kimbolton, 132–37; and Essex rebellion, 138–49; held hostage, 144–46; and Peter Blundell, 152–54; establishes Blundell's School, 154–58, 291 n.14; friend of Cecil, 159–63, 166–68, 171–73; and Ralegh, 66–67, 174–192, 293 n.27; at trial of Ralegh, 181–91; and Fen drainage, 194–202; and Catholic plots, 167,

169–70, 203, 204; and Gunpowder Plot, 204–19, 221; and Guy Fawkes, 208–11, *212;* and Henry Garnet, 27, 215–19; and King's income, 222–26; acting Lord Chancellor, 227–29, 298 n.27; and Virginia, 231–47, 252–53, 257; and Gorges, 234–37; and Virginia Charter, 237–40, 290 n.5, 299 n.31; sends Challons expedition, 241–43; prepares Virginia expedition, 243–47, 252; death, 101, 252, 257, 261–62; monument, 265–66; effigy, *190;* estate, 266; will, 45–46, 266–89; 302 n.20, 303 n.34, 303 n.35, 303 n.26; likenesses: *frontispiece, 134, 190,* 269–70, 303 n.45

— legacy to posterity, 262; Blundell's School, 157–58; Hospital at Wellington, 269; legends, 18–19, 34, 90, 115–16, 263–65, 302 n.23; Littlecote, 91; Popham Colony, 258, 260; Popham's Eau, 202; *Reports and Cases,* 103, 269, 279 n.9
Popham, Katherine (aunt of JP), 46
Popham, Katherine (daughter of JP), 25, 38, 268, 284 n.18
Popham, Katherine (sister of JP), 17, 34, 278 n.7
Popham, Marie (daughter of JP), 25, 38, 268
Popham, Penelope (daughter of JP), 25, 35, 59, 120, 268
Popham, Robert (brother of JP), 17, 34
Popham's Eau (Cambridgeshire/Norfolk), *190, 196,* 200–202, 270
Popham's Pit, 264–65
Pownde, Thomas, 205
pox, 226, 233
Pring, Martin, 233, 243, 300 n.43
prisons: Bridewell, 95; Clink, 165; Fleet, 99; Gatehouse, 165; King's (Queen's) Bench, 103, 164; Newgate, 98, 116–18
privateering, 105–6, 119, 174. *See also* piracy
Privy Council: functions of, 29, 30, 48, 130–31
prophesyings, 48

Puckering, Sir John, 100–101
Purchas, Samuel: *Purchas his Pilgrimage,* 243, 251
puritans, 46, 48, 102, 280 n.3
purveyance, 96, 228
Pykeringe, Lewis, 203
Pyne, Amy, 269

Ralegh, Carew, 75, 281 n.13
Ralegh, Sir Walter, 106, 118; at Cadiz, 118; and Cecil 178; friendship with Cobham, 289 n.27, 293 n.34, 295 n.40; commander of *Falcon,* 174; compared with JP, 174, 176–77; concocter of medicines, 261, 302 n.3; and Robert Dudley, 285 n.19, 286 n.24; loses Durham House, 180; education, 174; and Essex rebellion, 142, 143, 148, 185–86; rivalry with Essex, 138, 142, 178; granted Babington's property, 63; and Guiana, 108–10, 112, 178, 285 n.14; and Gunpowder Plot, 211–13; and Ireland, 59, 73, 75–79, 174–75; JP's view of, 178; later career, 294 n.39; and the Main Plot, 181; marriage, 177–78; offices held, 45, 177; parentage, 37, 292 n.3; portrait, *175;* privateer, 106; and the Queen, 174–76, 179; at the Tower, 191, 295 n.40; trial of, 181, 182–91; and Virginia, 67, 176–77, 231, 292 n.9
recusants, recusancy, 55–56, 102, 132, 206, 209, 288 n.3 (chap.11), 291 n.21; JP and, 96, 124, 165, 200
Reports and Cases (Popham, Sir John) 103, 269, 279 n.9
Resolutions and Judgements . . . (Goldesborough), 269
Revenge (ship), 93
Rhodes, Francis, 43
Rich, Penelope Lady, 146
Rich, Robert, 1st Earl of Warwick, 126
Richard (ship), 242
Richardson, William, 170
Ridolfi, Roberto, 31
Rivers, Anthony, 165, 169, 170–71
Roanoke, 176, 188, 231
Roche, Lord, 80
Roe, Sir John, 191, 294 n.38

Rogers, Edward (son-in-law of JP), 38, 75, 77, 244, 284 n.18
Rogers, George, 268
Rokeby (Scott), 90, 283 n.23
Rokewood, Ambrose, 209, 210, 213
Romney, Sir William, 199, 240, 295 n.30
Russell, Sir William, 168

Sackville, Sir Thomas. *See* Dorset
Sagadehoc, River. *See* Kennebec, River
Salisbury. *See* Cecil, Robert
Salisbury, Owen, 143, 145, 289 n.25
Sandys, Sir Edwin, 299 n.31
Sandys, Sir Miles, 198, 299 n.31
Sarum (Salisbury, Wiltshire), 66, 88, 179
Scott, Sir Walter: *Rokeby,* 90, 283n23
Sea, (estate in Somerset), 46
separatists. *See* puritans
Serjeant-at-Law, 43–44, 171, 279 n.15
Serjeants' Inn, 44, 100
Seymour, Richard, 248
Shakespeare, William, 126, 161, 288 n.11; plays of: *Hamlet,* 207, 296 n.21; *1 Henry IV,* 24, 126; *2 Henry IV,* 127; *Henry V,* 138; *Julius Caesar,* 270; *Macbeth,* 297 n.70; *Richard II,* 141–42; *The Tempest,* 301 n.75; *Twelfth Night,* 161, 293 n.33
Sherborne, 178, 161, 192, 213, 294 n.42
Sherley, Sir Anthony, 163–64
Shrewsbury, George Talbot, 6th Earl of, 61, 229
Sidney, Sir Henry, 71
Smith, John, 262
Smith, Sir Thomas, 146, 237, 290 n.42
Smyth, Hugh, 25, 28, 45, 301 n.104
Smyth, Matthew, 25, 45–46
Society in the Elizabethan Age (Hall), 12, 52
Somers, George, 237, 299 n.29
Southampton, Henry Wriothesley, 2nd Earl of, 58, 138, 236, 280n10; and Essex rebellion, 140, 141, 143, 148
Southwell, Elizabeth, 285 n.22

Southwell, Robert, 102, 210, 215
Sparry, Mr, 26, 276 n.20
Speedwell (ship), 206
Spenser, Edmund, 77, 176
Stanhope, Sir Edward, 263
Star Chamber, 61, 64, 94, 139, 199, 229
St. Barbe, (Sentbarb), Edward, 75, 281 n.13, 287 n.26
St Leger, Sir Warham, 79
Stow, John, 153
Stowell, Sir John, 75, 126, 281 n.13
St Peter's, York, 210
Strachey, William, 249, 256, 301 n.75
Stradling, Sir Edward, 17
Strange, Thomas, 215
Stuart, Lady Arbella, 61, 172, 181, 182, 280 n.19, 293 n.25, 293 n.30
subsidy, 28, 30, 54, 277 n.33, 279 n.42
Sutton, Sir Thomas, 93, 104, 283 n.2, 284 n.42, 285 n.7
Swan, (theater), 168
Sydenham, Roger, 105, 285 n.2

Tesimond, Oswald (Anthony Greenway or Greenwell) 204, 214, 217, 219
Throckmorton, Arthur, 118
Throckmorton, Elizabeth, (Lady Ralegh), 177–78, 192
Throckmorton, Francis, 60
tin, 128, 177, 221–22
Tiverton, Devon, 152–57, 270
tobacco, 179, 214, 229–30, 233, 293 n.37, 298 n.33
Topcliffe, Richard, 56, 102, 163
Totnes, Devon, 122
Tottel, Richard: *Miscellany,* 27–28, 218
Tower, The, 57, 59, 60, 94; controversy at, 98; Ralegh in 181, 191, 261; memorial to JP and colleagues at, 214; Gerard's escape from, 210
transportation, 115, 232–33
treason, 30, 31, 57, 58, 103, 183–84, 217; penalties for, 56
Tresham, Francis, 143, 210, 290 n.39
Tyrone, Hugh O'Neill, 2nd Earl of, 131, 135, 140, 172
Tyrrwhitt, Elizabeth, 209

Udall, John, 102
Udall, William, 263, 302 n. 18
Upwell, Norfolk, 32, 194, 295 n. 40
Uvedale, Henry, 34

Vanbrugh, Sir John, 136
Vaux, Elizabeth, 209–10
Vennar, Richard, 168
Vernon, Frances, 163
Virginia, 181, 188, *238;* attractions
    of for colonists, 233–34; Charter
    of Company, 237–39, 290 n. 5;
    Council of, 240, 243–44; founding
    of Jamestown, 244–45; JP's inter-
    est in, 231–32; London and Ply-
    mouth branches, 247, 258;
    London Company expedition,
    258; Plymouth Company expedi-
    tions of: Challons, 241–42,
    Popham, 243–44, 246, Pring, 243;
    Popham Colony, 246–60, *259,*
    262; Ralegh and, 66–67, 176, 188,
    231
Virginia (ship), 249, 252, 256–57,
    259, 260

Waad, Sir William, 211, 214, 226,
    240; autograph, *217;* and Garnet,
    215, 217, 218
Wadham, Nicholas, 44
Waldron, Humphrey, 22, 46
Waldron, John, 155
Walmsley, Sir Thomas, 171
Walsingham, Sir Francis: Secretary,
    56, 66, 68–70, 80; spying operation
    in Babington case, 62; and
    William Darrell, 87, 89
Warburton, Sir Peter, 184
wardship, 44–45, 222–23
Warner Holidays, 91
Warre, Richard (grandson of JP), 35,
    106, 121, 302 n. 14
Warre, Roger (son-in-law of JP), 35,
    44, 77, 78, 79
Warre, Thomas (grandson of JP), 35,
    121, 240
Watson, William, 165, 180, 185

Waymouth, George, 234, 236, 237,
    241, 248
Wellington, Somerset, 37–39, 93, 121,
    152, 153, 281 n. 45; Armada report-
    ed to, 68, *69,* 80; bequests by JP to
    town, 39, 268; Church, 35, 39, 265;
    Hospital (almshouse), 39, 104, 105,
    270, 284 n. 43; JP builds Mansion
    House at, 37, 38, 268; JP's family
    settles in, 26, 34, 35; legends at, 34,
    264–65; Popham's Pit, 264
Wellington Weekly News, *265*
Wentworth, Paul, 48
Wentworth, Peter, 42, 48, 52
Westminster Hall, 22, 26, 27, 147,
    157, 213
Whitehall, Palace, 131, 140, 142, 229
Whitgift, John, 94–95, 130, 150
Whitmore, Ann, 154
Wilbraham, Roger, 81, 124, 261,
    282 n. 44, 287 n. 41
Wingfield, Edward Maria, 135, 237,
    258, 288 n. 4 (chap. 11), 301 n. 106
Wingfield, Sir Edward, 135
Wingfield, Sir Richard, 135, 136
Wingfield, Sir Robert, 198
Wintour, Tom, 209, 211, 219
Wisbech, Cambridgeshire, 32,
    194–96, 199
Wood, Antony à, 12, 19, 22
Woodrington, Henry, 144–45
Worcester, Edward Somerset, 4th
    Earl of, 142–44, 148, 149
Worth, Hugh, 77, 282 n. 23
Wray, Sir Christopher, 29, 57, 99
Wright, Christopher (Kit), 209, 219
Wright, Henry, 204–5, 296 n. 9
Wright, John, 210, 211
Wyatt, Captain, 110
Wyndham, Francis, 32–33, 44
Wyngate, Robert, 35, 121

Yelverton, Sir Christopher, 171
Youghal, 79

Zuniga, Don Pedro de, 244, 257,
    302 n. 110